THE
BATTLE
AND THE
BREEZE

THE NAVAL REMINISCENCES OF
ADMIRAL OF THE FLEET
SIR EDWARD ASHMORE

EDITED BY ERIC GROVE

Royal Naval
MUSEUM
PUBLICATIONS

SUTTON PUBLISHING LIMITED

First published in 1997 by
Sutton Publishing Limited · Phoenix Mill
Thrupp · Stroud · Gloucestershire · GL5 2BU

in association with the Royal Naval Museum

British Library Cataloguing in Publication Data
A catalogue record for this book is available from the British Library

ISBN 0-7509-1252-9

 ALAN SUTTON™ and SUTTON™ are the
trade marks of Sutton Publishing Limited

Typeset in 10/12 pt Plantin Light
Typesetting and origination by
Sutton Publishing Limited.
Printed in Great Britain by
Butler & Tanner, Frome, Somerset.

CONTENTS

Ye Mariners of England
That guard our native seas
Whose flag has braved a thousand years
The battle and the breeze!

The spirits of your fathers
Shall start from every wave
For the deck it was their field of fame
And Ocean was their grave.

Britannia needs no bulwarks
No towers along the steep
Her march is o'er the mountain-waves
Her home is on the deep.

Thomas Campbell (1774–1844)

Editor's Introduction

Sir Edward Ashmore is one of the most significant naval officers of the post-war era. He played a key role in naval policy-making in the 1960s and 1970s, laying the foundations for the Fleet of today, not only in terms of its ships and aircraft, but also its communications and its structure. The Sea Harriers, Batch 2 Type 22 frigates, satellite terminals, and principal warfare officers of the current Royal Navy all result from decisions in which Ashmore played a major role.

After holding the main sea-going command east of Suez at the time of the withdrawal from Aden, he was the first C.-in-C. Fleet at Northwood, before becoming First Sea Lord under the Labour government of the mid-1970s. The illness of the incumbent Chief of Defence Staff meant that Ashmore was briefly appointed to his country's highest military position in 1977.

The memoirs of such a significant figure had to be worthy of publication. Reading them soon demonstrated that not only did they give many insights into life at the top of the service, but they also illuminated what made for a successful career as a naval officer. Sir Edward's perceptive remarks about himself and his contemporaries throughout his life tell the reader much about why he was able to do so well in an environment to which he was eminently suited.

Edward Ashmore had a varied career. His wartime experiences took him from the Arctic to the Pacific and earned him a DSC. The son of a Russian who had fled from the Revolution, he visited the Soviet Union just before the Second World War, and was assistant naval attaché there after it. He always took great interest in his surroundings, and one of the problems of editing the original manuscript was deleting the personal reflections on the people and places he encountered. It was crucial, however, to concentrate on the naval side of the story, emphasising those aspects of historical significance, while leaving just enough background for the reader to obtain some impression of the wider aspects of a very full life.

Those who wish to read the original manuscript in full will find it in Portsmouth at the Royal Naval Museum, whose encouragement and assistance is very gratefully acknowledged. Sir Edward's papers are eventually destined for the archive at Churchill College, Cambridge.

Foreword

The account that follows was written in the 1980s for my family. I kept no diaries other than my midshipman's journal, and it relies very much on my personal recollection. I have tried to keep it accurate and without hindsight, and hope it is not overcritical or ungenerous. It certainly does not deserve to be, since I have had so much kindness, understanding and support throughout my service life. I believe it will show two things most clearly. One is how much luck and timing had to do with a naval career, both during the war and later. The other, through the recurrence of familiar names, family friends, Father's friends, my friends, is how the Navy, even in its wartime expansion, was like a large family. Life has changed so much in the mid-twentieth century – manners and society, too – that I hope the story may be of interest.

The title derives from Thomas Campbell's tribute to the mariners of England. In my modern context the breeze relates to the fun and spirit of life afloat, the battle sometimes to affairs ashore.

I greatly appreciate Eric Grove's enthusiasm for making much of it available to a wider readership, and feel that he has left enough life and colour in his editing to result in a readable as well as orderly book.

CHAPTER ONE

Launched

1919–39

I was born at 3 Norwood Villas, Queenstown, County Cork, Ireland, at 7 p.m. on 11 December 1919. My father, a lieutenant in the Navy, was serving on the admiral's staff there during 'the troubles'. I am told that the servants were discovered that night in the kitchen, drinking my health and wishing me every success as a good Sinn Feiner.

I was blessed with two exceptional parents. Leslie, my father, a rather intense and scrupulously honourable man, was devoted to the Service and went far in it. His father, Arthur Haliburton, had been senior partner in the family firm, Ashmore & Sons of Mincing Lane, London, who were import/export merchants. Another partner was a 'wicked uncle' called Henry Beckwith Ashmore. The firm fell into financial difficulties, and Father returned one day for the holidays from his very expensive preparatory school, Sandroyd, to discover that their big house at Esher had been sold, his pony and trap had gone, and his unhappy parents were living on his mother's savings. There had been a court case, Henry had fled to Paris; Grandfather faced the music, was bankrupted, and was fortunate, I was told, to escape prison.

Thanks to an elderly lady and distant relation, Lizzie Stringer, who had taken a fancy to my father, his preparatory school fees were paid, and he continued through Sandroyd to enter the Royal Naval College, Osborne, at the age of 13½. Education at Osborne, and later at Dartmouth, was free, though whether this had much to do with Father entering the Navy or not I am uncertain. In any case, once he had joined, he took to the life like a duck to water.

He served in the West Indies and then, during the First World War, in submarines. In his book, *A Russian Scrapbook*, he describes his experiences with our submarine flotilla in the Baltic. Father never forgot the murders and other atrocities associated with the Russian Revolution in Petrograd and in the Baltic Fleet. They made a deep impression on his sensitive nature and for a long time he did not know what had happened to many of his Russian friends. When there was no longer any war for them to fight, the British submarine crews were ordered to destroy their boats and then made their way home via Archangel.

In 1919 father became resident British naval officer at Sevastopol during the Allied Intervention, his job consisting largely of running a network of intelligence agents. Later, as the White Armies in the south collapsed, he organised the evacuation of refugees from the Crimea in British ships. Earlier, in *Adamant,* a British submarine depot ship at Sevastopol, he had met a Russian officer on General Denikin's staff of about his own age who spoke excellent English and was the life and soul of any party. The officer's name was Cornelius Shutt, and he and Father lived in the Kist Hotel in Sevastopol, which overlooks the Fleet landing place. Corney (as young Shutt was known) took Father out to Balaclava to meet his father, mother and two sisters, Tamara and Kyra. Six weeks later, my father and Tamara were married in the Orthodox church in Balaclava. Corney and an officer in the Imperial Navy called Nicky Chirikov held the crowns over their heads. After delivering a letter from the King to the Dowager Empress, and three days' honeymoon in Yalta, Father and Mother moved together back to the Kist.

It was the end of February 1919 and things were going from bad to worse for the White Armies. Mother narrowly escaped death twice. The second occasion was as she was standing on the gunwale of a harbour craft alongside the ship on which she and her husband were to be evacuated. Someone pushed both her ankles off the boat. Father caught her and hauled her safely aboard the British ship. She never saw Russia again. Mother was then just 23. Thanks to an English governess, she spoke excellent English as well as fluent French. She was both indomitable and captivating. Her dreadful experiences left no scars upon her spirit, and she bore the loss of so much that she had loved in Russia with great fortitude. The young couple spent some time in Constantinople until they could board ship for England, where they arrived in the summer of 1919. In November Father was posted to Ireland, where things were pretty unpleasant, but Mother, despite being heavily pregnant, went too. I appeared the following month.

Father next had spells of naval duty in Gosport and at Devonport, and eventually the family settled in Saltash on 1 February 1921. A splendid brother, Peter, joined us three days later. By this time Father was thoroughly unhappy in a submarine service deeply divided between the supporters of Max Horton and those of Noel Laurence. (The dispute dated back to 1915, when Laurence broke an agreement not to conduct active operations until all boats for the Baltic Flotilla were safely clear of the Sound.) Despite doubts about the effect on his career, he left submarines and on rejoining general service was sent to *Ramillies* in Portsmouth in June 1922. We moved from Saltash to a small house in Emsworth to be near him.

His next appointment was to the Rhine Flotilla, a group of motor launches under the White Ensign, as part of the Allied occupation forces based at Cologne. It was a time of great privation and rampant inflation in Germany, and I remember seeing a man faint in the park (through lack of food, I was told). Garrison life rather suited my parents: Father was not away as much as when he was in the Fleet, and Mother, as always with her gift for friendship, found some very congenial families for us all to enjoy.

For Christmas 1925 Mother took us to Castle Hill, Bletchingly, the home of her English relations, the Brandts. Their lovely house became a second home for us and their kindnesses over the years were legion.

In January 1926 the Rhine Flotilla sailed for England. The Motor Launches came down the coast of France, and then had a fairly hairy passage across the Channel in the winter gales. (Father kept the bell of his own launch, and it hangs outside our front door today.) Very soon he was appointed First Lieutenant of *Warspite*, the flagship of Admiral Sir Roger Keyes in the Mediterranean, and off he had to go, leaving us behind. Eventually, enough money was saved up to enable us to follow by train. Father had found us a flat on the top of a new building at 75 Strada St. Anna, Floriana. Malta was lovely: the Fleet was often in port, and ships gave children's parties. But then Father was suddenly ordered home to be First Lieutenant at a new training establishment for boy seamen just being commissioned in Gosport, HMS *St Vincent*. We were left in Malta, and there was no money to pay for us to go home. Mother set her charm to work and after we had been waiting around for about four months, the Governor, General Duquesne, who had been Commander of the Army of Occupation in the Rhineland when we were in Cologne, personally decreed that Mrs Ashmore and her children were to be given a passage in a troopship, so we came home in *Neuralia*.

We came back to a rented house at No. 2 Village Road, Alverstoke, and 'The Oaks' was to be very much our home and base for some years. Peter and I walked to lessons at the Holt Corner School, just along the road. Father loved his job, and hit it off very well with his captain, Percy Noble (later to be a distinguished Admiral). We were taken to *St Vincent* to improve the swimming learnt in Malta in the establishment's swimming bath, and also to be taught to pull an oar. Father was then promoted to commander. It was the most splendid news for my parents: pay and prospects in the Navy depended entirely on selection for promotion. The number of passed-over lieutenant-commanders was legion. Father had never lost his anxiety at what might happen as a result of his leaving submarines, but his gift for dealing with people – with young people in particular – had shone through at *St Vincent*. Percy Noble had recommended him for early promotion, and was to keep his eye on him thereafter.

Commander Ashmore was appointed to command a sloop in the South Africa Squadron, HMS *Wallflower*. Our parents took a bold decision – we were to go too – and in great excitement we started to prepare for our journey. Father travelled ahead by Union Castle Line, but our passages had to be paid. The cheapest way to The Cape was by Natal Line, so we eventually embarked in SS *Umvoti* as three of roughly twelve passengers on board. During the voyage, Peter and I had the run of the ship, including the rigging, which we used to run up and down when we felt like it. We entered Table Bay after thirty-two days at sea, having, I suppose, averaged all of 8 knots. There was no house for us, so we stayed in the British Hotel in Simonstown until Mother could find one. We eventually moved into a wooden bungalow called 'Rochford' at Boulders Beach, near the Simonstown golf course. School loomed into an otherwise cloudless sky and we went as weekly boarders to the Western Province Preparatory School at Claremont. There was only a small contingent from Simonstown, English boys like ourselves, including two who became great friends later. The bulk of the boys at the school were Afrikaners, many of them from up-country. They certainly took the mickey out of us. The initiation of new boys by way of bullying was thoroughly unpleasant for the recipients but was mitigated for us by one senior boy whom I shall always remember for his intervention. His name was Nettleton, and he later received the VC in Bomber Command before meeting his death in the war.

Wallflower came and went from Simonstown on patrols up either coast, and I remember seeing her enter harbour under auxiliary sail. She eventually left for England to pay off and Father took her up to Aden, took over command of *Cyclamen*, another Flower Class sloop, and brought her down to the Cape.

Eventually, around Easter 1931, in great luxury, we travelled first class in SS *Guildford Castle* home to England. On arrival, we went back to 'The Oaks' in Alverstoke, and a school had to be found. This was very important: our parents had been very brave, according to the ideas of the day, in taking us out to South Africa at all. It was far more usual for children to be left at boarding school in England and they were worried lest the idiosyncracies of education at the Cape should disadvantage us at the Common Entrance Examinations to public school. That they were able to consider boarding school for us at all was entirely due to the generosity of 'Uncle' Augustus Brandt, who out of kinship and friendship for my grandfather, and now out of genuine affection for my mother and her family, paid for our education. I am sure Mother saw in it a tribute to the affection in which her father, whom they called 'Cousin Willy', was held.

A school was found at Yardley Court, Tonbridge, Kent, where two brothers called Bickmore ran a small day and boarding establishment. By comparison with the Western Province, life was sheer heaven: you knew exactly where you stood all the time and the joint headmasters were admirable. Although Father was by no means anxious for us to join his service, both Peter and I had already decided to join the Navy if we could and we worked hard to pass the entrance examination for Dartmouth. However, much depended on the interview and medical examination, which were all too soon upon me.

I do not remember much about the interview, although, of course, an admiral was present. I was not asked anything very difficult or specific – indeed, they gave me an opportunity to talk about our travels. But the medical examination was an ordeal. I had been carefully briefed by my parents to say that I was 'under treatment' if there was any doubt about anything. And doubt there was. I had to wear spectacles for reading, but being 'under treatment' by a very distinguished ophthalmic surgeon, Mr Stewart Duke Elder, satisfied the doctor. I went into the dentist after a boy called Rabbit, who failed to pass. The dental surgeon took one look at me and said, '*You* ought to have been called Rabbit, not the last chap.' However,

I said I was 'under treatment', again by a well-known dental surgeon at Portland Place, and this seemed to work the oracle. So, anticipating success, I was measured by the Gieves' representative at the Civil Service Examination centre in London, and eventually I heard that I had passed. I discovered later that it was quite a good pass (except for Latin, which was, entirely thanks to Yardley Court, a successful scrape – I have often said, and meant it, that one of my reasons for joining the Navy was to give up Latin).

I put on uniform for the first time in September 1933, at Bletchingly, was well photographed, sadly parted company with Peter for a while, and set off for the Royal Naval College at Dartmouth. I did not know what I was in for, but I knew I was joining a good show and was not particularly daunted. Yardley Court had been so much easier than the school in South Africa that I didn't feel too much apprehension about the Royal Naval College itself. In retrospect, this was probably the time at which childhood really ended and a new stage of life began. It is perhaps a good moment in writing this account to look back over the years then behind me and try to draw some kind of conclusions, without too much hindsight, about what I felt.

There was some confidence I think: I was not much good at games but not too bad at lessons. Over and above that, Father was a commander in the Navy, which was quite something, and we as a family had seen Germany, Malta and South Africa; we had had experiences which, before the days of air travel, were uncommon. I had some inkling of the quality of my marvellous mother, and then there were always the Brandts and Castle Hill, Bletchingly and the interesting and cosmopolitan society that one met there. I had cousins and relations all over Europe: some odd, some startling, some delightful. I had heard Russian, French and German spoken. Although I understood nothing of the first and little of the other two languages, I did feel part of a rather wider world than that known by most English boys of my age. However, I would have died rather than let on that I thought this. I had some strong impressions in my mind: the Mediterranean Fleet in the Grand Harbour, the winds and battlements of Malta and, of course, the goats; the awful settlement called 'Tin Town', where the blacks lived near Simonstown. I could still recall the Afrikaner accent, and the difference between the two preparatory schools had made a great impression.

I was driven up to Paddington to join the train to Kingswear and given half-a-crown for my lunch. Thirty-two of us joined by the same train on the same day, and we became the Greynvile Term when we reached the college. It was a long walk from the river up to D Block, where our dormitory was to be found, lugging far too heavy a suitcase. We were greeted by our term officer, Lieutenant A.G. Poe, Lieutenant Malim, our term engineer officer, and the Chief Petty Officer who was to be our Term Instructor, and then shown all round the college before the rest of the cadets came back from leave. We were also met – most importantly – by two senior cadets who were to be our term cadet captain and cadet captain for our first term. They were called Meyrick and Easton respectively, and very good they were too: helpful and fair and, if necessary, perhaps moderately sympathetic.

There was so much to do. We had to learn one another's names, be tested to see if we were fit to sing in the choir (which I wasn't), unpack and find out how to lay out kit in our sea chests (a matter of extreme accuracy and detail), learn the rudiments of the routine and the parade that took place every morning, and generally find our way around. Each term had a large room called a gunroom with oak tables and benches, and lockers against the walls in which we could stow our personal books and equipment. In the dormitory, each cadet had his own sea chest at the end of an iron bed. Attached to the dormitory was a wash place and a plunge filled with very cold water, through which we had to scramble each morning before washing. A cadet captain sent you round again if you did not look sufficiently wet. In the evenings, after games, the plunge was hot and we were allowed a good soak. We usually had one bath a week. No one was allowed to put his hands in his pockets, of course, and we had to double past the gunrooms of senior terms on our way to class or to the mess hall, where we were fed. This hall was hung with portraits of admirals of long ago, all looking rather better fed than we felt. Inscribed along the façade of the college was King Charles II's famous dictum, 'It is on the Navy under the good providence of God that our strength, prosperity and peace depend', and from the parade ground below the message was clear to see.

As well as the normal instruction, which was monitored for each of us by a master known as a tutor, we had classes in navigation and pilotage, ship construction and seamanship – this being the responsibility of senior ratings supervised by our term officer. A considerable slice of our syllabus was devoted to marine engineering. The engineering workshops were at Sandquay, where the work was largely practical. The first thing we had to do was to make a nut gauge without losing any of our fingers or thumbs, but we progressed to pattern-making, foundry work and a good deal of machining with lathes. In the various shops were boilers, reciprocating engines, diesel engines and even turbines, on which we were instructed. It was all enjoyable, including seamanship instruction, which covered buoyage, rigging (including rigging sheerlegs), how to work the main derrick which ships like *Rodney* and *Nelson* had, colours and meanings of flags, details of the sailors' kit and distinguishing badges, and a host of other subjects which come less readily to mind. For all these, the *Seamanship Manuals*, Volumes One and Two, were our Bible. There were models on which we could work anchors and cables but, long before using them, there was a great deal of knotting and splicing to be done in rope and wire.

Academic subjects were well taught, and history lessons covered a large slice of early naval history based on *Sea Kings of Britain*, which we much enjoyed. I remember Admiral Goodenough, who had done brilliantly in command of the light cruisers at Jutland, giving us a lively and quite incomprehensible account of the battle with all sorts of maps and slides to complicate it.

There were games and sports in plenty: rugger, soccer, hockey, tennis, and so forth. In the summer, we were given a choice of playing cricket, or sailing and boating on the river. As well as the service cutters, whalers and gigs used for practical seamanship, in which we used to go outside the harbour and sail in the open sea, there were a number of small craft and even a couple of old motorboats available for recreational expeditions. Needless to say, I chose the river. I was lucky to be small enough to be a coxswain in the regattas, thus, unlike those lads who pulled the oars, saving an endless amount of anointing various parts of one's anatomy with methylated spirit.

Except on Sundays (when chapel, which I enjoyed, was compulsory morning and evening), every cadet had to do what was called a 'log' daily. This was a stated amount of exercise: playing in an organised game was a full log, half-a-mile's run was a half log, and so on. Fencing was extra and had to be paid for, so I did not do it, but boxing was made compulsory by our term officer. Another imposition on us small boys was to do a 'dead man's dive' from the top diving board in the swimming pool, which seemed very high at the time. On Sundays, when there was no log to be done, we often used to make up a small team and go for a long walk to one of the well-known farmhouses in the area, have an enormous cream tea and somehow stagger back to the college in time for evening chapel. One could sometimes do this on Saturdays, I remember, after beagling. When it rained hard in the afternoon so that the grounds were unfit for play (which was usually not often enough for me), the commander decreed an 'optional landing'. When this was 'piped', we were relieved of exercise 'ashore' (as we called everywhere outside the college grounds), and could retire instead to the excellent library and read.

The five junior terms made up the Junior College, and the other six of the eleven terms at Dartmouth made up the Senior College. As each term passed, you became one term more senior than you were before; the cadet who had been cadet captain in the earlier term became the term cadet captain, and somebody else became cadet captain. We were very fortunate in the boys we had, and some of them have remained friends ever since. As time passed, the Greynviles began to provide cadet captains in our turn, and since there were only 31 of us by then, one having died, a fairly large number (of whom I was not one) had to undertake this duty. Each term was strictly segregated, and this meant that there was no bullying. When Peter joined a year after me in the Benbow Term, I had to request 'permission to see my brother'. This was readily given, but it was hard for both of us to find the time.

Every naval officer was supposed to be able to dance, so dance we did: the Senior College on what was called the quarterdeck, the juniors in D Block, every Saturday evening. Most terms produced bands, and on leaving the college, each gave a term-end dance to which sisters and other girls could be invited; otherwise, we had to dance with one another (not an inspiring experience).

Ceremony at the college was considerable. There was a parade every morning in almost any weather, and I have seldom known anything feel so cold as a rifle butt before 8 a.m. on a December morning. There was a full parade of cadets with the college band on Sundays, when divisions were inspected and then marched past the captain, or whoever happened to be visiting us. At the term end, prizes were given by a distinguished admiral or member of the Board of Admiralty, who would then address us. I best remember Admiral of the Fleet the Earl of Cork and Orrery telling us that what the Navy needed was 'not brains but bowels'. It was quite in keeping with what my father had led me to expect from the man who was known throughout the service as 'Ginger' Boyle.

In the summer of 1936, the German sail training ship *Gorch Fock* visited the Dart, and anchored for two days. This was the first time I saw the Swastika. The German cadets were older than us, marched well, and sang as they marched. They did their best, and their ship, which we were allowed over, was beautifully clean, but the impression, I am sorry to say, was not really very welcome to us. Our senior officers had been in the previous war with Germany, and the news from Germany in the papers and at Bletchingly was all disquieting.

Classwork was going well, and I enjoyed it, and with others of my term was brigaded with a few of the term above us in what was called an Alpha Class. This aimed to allow us more private study on a university pattern than direct teaching in the classroom and was undoubtedly beneficial. I had tried to learn a little Spanish earlier on, one hour a week, but had given that up and now had to concentrate on the core subjects. Regular tests indicated how one was progressing but extra seniority could be gained by passing out of the college well and this was a big carrot.

I think this rather calm account perhaps gives little impression of the almost ceaseless activity in which we were engaged. In the Senior College, for example, we were up at 6.30 a.m., plunged, dressed, squared-off, out of the dormitory in three-and-a-half minutes flat, and down to work before breakfast. Then there was the parade ground, from which we doubled away to our classes. I think we hardly ever walked. Discipline was maintained by the whole college hierarchy, from the captain down. Term officers could award extra work and drill, and the drill consisted of extremely unpleasant marching, running and hopping, usually with rifle and pack, to the point of exhaustion. Poe, who was formal and strict, was relieved as Greynvile Term Officer after a year or so by Lt. 'Dago' Kennedy, a relaxed Fleet Air Arm pilot whom we much liked. Cadet captains could give beatings, but only with the approval of the term officer, who might also wield the cane himself. Such 'unofficial cuts' ('official cuts' were a very rare formal punishment for particularly terrible misdemeanour), as they were known, were certainly not abused. More usually we were given what were called 'slack parties'. These were a way of pulling up and tautening the behaviour of anyone who was considered to be in any way sloppy or below par. Sometimes, usually two or three times a term, the whole term would be sharpened up in this way. We would be sitting in the gunroom after tea, or after having finished our prep, and the cadet captain would say, 'I am going to shake you up,' get his watch out on the table, and order, 'Into sea boots and oilskins; down here in three minutes, Go!' More of the same would follow until the great man was content. Sometimes he would not be satisfied until we had doubled down to Sandquay and back in our oilskins and sea boots, for example. This was often a summer activity, too. Some of us withstood this better than others (they were the ones who became cadet captains in their turn); myself, I simply endured it.

In the spring of 1937 I passed out second in my term, with a sufficient number of prizes to half fill a bookshelf, about as fit to join the cadet training cruiser as the system could make me. A year later, Peter passed out top of his term, which was marvellous. When Admiral Sir Frank Twiss, who was captured by the Japanese during the war when *Exeter*, in which he was gunnery officer, was sunk, and spent long years in Japanese prisoner-of-war camps was released, someone said to him, 'Frank, it must have been simply awful.' 'Oh well,' said Frank Twiss, 'it was not so bad really after Dartmouth.' I know exactly what he meant.

In September 1936 the family had moved to a flat in Coleherne Court in London, Father having been appointed as the commander in the Second Sea Lord's office. Here, he was responsible for the appointment of all the seaman officers in the Navy below the rank of captain. It was very hard work, but he enjoyed the job, and his excellent memory for faces and names stood him in good stead. He was always fair, and nearly always popular. He liked his immediate master, Captain Edward-Collins, who was Naval Assistant to the Second Sea Lord. Good-looking and always extremely well turned out, Father was making his mark on a wide cross-section of naval opinion.

On completion of Dartmouth training in those days, one did a spell in a cadet training cruiser. *Frobisher* was her name (shortly to be relieved by *Vindictive*), and the Greynviles joined her at Chatham for the summer cruise to the Baltic between March and July 1937. We were also joined on board by a public school entry, who had escaped the rigours of Dartmouth, but spent some six months' naval training in *Erebus* at Portsmouth. They were a year or more older than us, and attraction was neither instant nor mutual. However, we were soon set to work so hard that there was no time nor energy for ructions.

Frobisher was a lovely, graceful ship, and tolerably comfortable at sea. Our captain, E.J. Spooner, was a clever, quiet man (who was to die miserably and gallantly after Singapore fell). In *Frobisher*, we worked as seamen alongside the relatively few members of the crew. We were allotted responsibilities on the 'Watch and Quarter Bill' and assigned to divisions and parts of the ship. I was a fo'c'sle man, which was handy as there was much to learn about working the anchors and cables, and afforded a good view when manning the side on entering and leaving harbour. However, we were all given a good run at everything to be done in the ship. We did not stand regular watches and every day began at 6.30 a.m. with scrubbing and washing the upper deck, all of us barefooted and usually shivering. We had formal instruction, a good deal of practical navigation and learned to put the rudiments of seamanship gained at college into effect. Periodically, the wooden decks had to be holystoned – a dreadful job performed on hands and knees for hours to make a white teak deck whiter – and there was never a shortage of brass to be cleaned. We slept in hammocks in broadside messes, segregated from the crew. Each mess had its own eating space, with the food cooked for us after those of us detailed off as 'cooks of the mess' for the day had drawn the stores, prepared the vegetables, and so on. We learned how to lash up and stow a hammock, for unless this was done properly the hammocks couldn't possibly fit into the bin (called a hammock netting) provided for them. We were called away as seaboat's crew in open water and did a great deal of boatwork when in harbour. There were no winches, and cadets manned the falls to hoist or lower the boats, taking turns to be in charge. But it was indeed a cruise and there was much to enjoy as well as experiencing, in microcosm, the life of a pre-war sailor on the lower deck.

The first port of call was Copenhagen, after which we went to the German Naval College at Flensburg for a get-together with our German opposite numbers. There was much rather partisan discussion of the comparative merits of their training under sail and our type of training cruise. They were older than us and, we thought, rather condescending, though we had to give them full marks for their English. But the Nazi infection was rife: we heard the Horst Wessel song rather too much. (One remembered the Kiel Regatta in 1914, which was the last get-together of the two navies before the First World War.)

From Flensburg we went to Tallinn, the capital of Estonia, where Uncle Corney had worked for years after the Revolution and in whose flat several naval officers whom I was later to know had stayed while learning Russian. Reval (as Tallinn was called before the Revolution) was one of the ports from which Father's submarine squadron had operated during the war and he had had many friends there, now all gone, so the town was of special interest.

From Tallinn we went up the Gulf of Finland to a little place called Lappvik, some 50 miles east of Helsinki, for intensive boatwork. It was grand to be among the lovely islands and there was time for picnics, saunas and swimming. We had a short spell in Helsinki itself (nothing like so much fun as it had been with the family, on holiday the summer before), and then went south to Aarhus in Denmark.

Then it was back to Chatham to pay off, and by now I knew that my first appointment as a midshipman was to be *Rodney* – the Home Fleet flagship, wearing the flag of Admiral Sir Roger Backhouse – in September. As a result of the exams at Dartmouth and in *Frobisher*, I had acquired the maximum seniority available (five months), and this would be applied when I eventually, as I hoped, became a sub-lieutenant.

After a family holiday in Brittany, I was ready, with great trepidation, to join my first proper ship in the Fleet as an officer. I rather wished it could have been a smaller one. I joined *Rodney* at Devonport, and was allowed to do so in plain clothes. She had a large gunroom of some 30 midshipmen, including engineers and paymasters, and the six or so of those of us who joined as junior midshipmen were very small fry indeed. We were given 24 hours to 'sling our hammock' (which meant finding our way around), met the captain and commander, were told how to behave if the Commander-in-Chief ever came within sight of us, and were then turned over to the tender mercies of the snotties' nurse (a terrifying submarine officer doing his general service time, who rejoiced in the name of 'Hairy' Brown), the sub-lieutenant and the senior midshipmen. The ship seemed enormous after *Frobisher*, and became packed with senior officers (or so it seemed to me) when the Fleet staff came on board at Portsmouth, a couple of days after I joined. I already knew that I was only to be in *Rodney* for three months before receiving another appointment, and it was an experience I would not have missed.

As a midshipman of the watch, by day one of my unusual duties was to call everybody to attention on the quarterdeck when Roger Backhouse poked his head above the hatch furthest aft before 'Colours', while by night I used to accompany the master at arms on rounds of the mess decks. An interesting task was to accompany the sergeant of marines, whose duty it was to wind the chronometers on which we relied for an accurate longitude when navigating by the sun, moon or stars. There were three of these chronometers on gimbals in the bowels of the ship, as near as possible to the centre of gravity so as to suffer as little movement as possible. Their winding was meticulously recorded in the log. I also did magazine rounds, no mean feat in that great ship with its 16-in guns, separate ammunition and host of vertical and very long ladders. Alternatively, as midshipman of the watch at sea and not immune from carrying messages, I was cantering up and down the cascade of ladders in the enormous superstructure known as 'Queen Anne's Mansions'. My action station was rate officer in the 16-in turret manned by the Royal Marines. The noise of the detonation of the largest guns in the Fleet compared with the clanging energy of the machinery in the turret itself. 'Free the turret,' was the order, then 'Free the slide,' and all hell seemed to be let loose as the loading mechanism went into the loading and ramming cycle.

Soon after joining I was made midshipman of the launch, the large, open boat capable of laying out a battleship's anchor, but normally used for carrying libertymen to and from the shore. We could carry 130 in calm weather, rather fewer if the weather was foul. The crew consisted of myself, a leading seaman and two seamen, bowman and stern sheetsman, with a stoker to work the engine. I handled the boat, which was steered by tiller, and had to beware of being trapped between an uncontrollable tiller and a stern bollard when officer-in-charge. We would man her over the lower boom by Jacob's ladder and she surged violently in heavy weather, making the process frightening if not hazardous. But all this was as nothing compared to the experience of having to control the libertymen as they came to the boat after shore leave. There would be a patrol with a warrant officer or lieutenant in charge on the jetty, but the loading of the boat, conduct within it and safety were my responsibility.

Sailors of that time were a splendid, tough, cheerful lot, and *Rodney*'s were mostly from her home port, Devonport. By modern standards, they were not educated; their pleasures were simple and, like their language, crude. While anyone too drunk to stand or be half carried by his mates would be arrested by the patrol, anyone likely to be able to make his way up the accommodation ladder and confront the officer of the watch would be allowed to board the boat. Ensuring they got safely in and out without falling overboard was the business of myself and my crew, and I had to get them to keep quiet before bringing them alongside *Rodney* so as not to cause a disturbance. On the long passages from shore to where the battleship lay, singing and spinning yarns naturally went on. This then had to stop. Often, they didn't like it, so I would go round and round the *Rodney* until they did stop. Then, after the last trip of the night, I had to help the crew swill the vomit and so forth out of the boat so she would be scrubbed and smart at the beginning of another day. Considering everything, the men were really remarkably well behaved and probably more responsive to a 17-year-old midshipman than they might have been to a different type of officer.

A quite special relationship developed with my coxswain and crew. The boat was difficult to handle: she was single-screwed, and would kick hard to port when going astern. It was important to bear this in mind when coming alongside, and difficult if the tidal stream which you had to stem was going the wrong way along the jetty. However, she was a good, solid boat and almost impossible to damage – indeed, very often the jetty was at more risk. Running the launch was a 24 hours on, 24 hours off business, alternating with another midshipman and crew. At other times, I was writing up my journal or under instruction, and several times a week there was practical signalling, to work up our ability to read semaphore and flashing and to distinguish flag hoists.

I received my first salute on boarding *Rodney* in plain clothes. Hats were *de rigueur*, so that salutes could be returned or exchanged ashore. As much as anything, I think that salute really made me feel that I had joined the Fleet. A midshipman's pay was five shillings a day, compared with a shilling a week as a cadet at Dartmouth and a shilling a day in the training cruiser. Our expenses, apart from any money we felt we were able to spend ashore, consisted in paying a monthly mess bill and a laundry bill. This probably took something like two-thirds of your pay, and then, of course, if anything went wrong with your uniform, you had to sort that out. Father knew the form, and made me an allowance of £5 a month.

For our domestic arrangements we had a large gunroom, heavily dominated by senior midshipmen, some of whom had been in the ship for nearly two years and were preparing to take their certificates. We slung our hammocks in the after-cabin flat, where our chests were also stowed, making it very congested. Two or three of us shared a marine orderly, who cleaned our shoes and looked after our kit. The bathroom was a fairly large, tiled compartment, and the baths were of the portable tin variety, filled with salt water from the fire main, and then trundled across the tiles to a steam jet to make it as hot as you liked. Junior midshipmen had to fill the senior midshipmen's baths for them, and wait till they had finished before taking their own baths. Dinner in the gunroom was pretty formal for those not on duty, and the sub-lieutenant made certain that we understood the customs of the service. 'Breadcrumbs' meant cover your ears so that you don't hear what your betters are saying. 'A fork in the beam' meant clear the mess at once. Last man out was usually fined a round of port for the senior midshipmen, something your mess bill could ill afford.

For much of my time in her, *Rodney* was taking part in the Home Fleet's autumn cruise, which was for weapon training, based on Invergordon and the practice areas in the Moray Firth. My chief recollections are of endless gunnery practices and sizeable Fleet manoeuvres at sea. At one time we had the 2nd Cruiser Squadron, some destroyer flotillas, the carriers *Courageous* and *Furious*, and the R Class battleships, *Ramillies*, *Royal Oak*, *Revenge* and *Resolution* at sea in company, with the battlewagons usually astern of the Fleet flagship in line ahead. In one night encounter exercise, as we were returning to Portland from the north, the cruisers were on the 'A–K' Line, trying to spot periscopes as dawn broke, and the Fleet entered the submarine probability area. Little had changed in such matters since Jutland and the Grand Fleet, but for the weapon training we now had two radio-controlled targets. One was *Centurion*, an old battleship which was controlled by a specially fitted destroyer, *Shikari*. I was detailed off several times to go into the marking ship, a Fishery Protection Vessel, *Sheldrake*, in order to keep records of the 6 in and 16 in firings at *Centurion*. We had a rake on which we had to measure the angular displacement between the firing ship and the target ship, and had a grandstand view of the fall of shot. *Centurion* would be manoeuvred by radio from *Shikari*, and a white smoke signal would be released on the target to show when a good hit had been obtained. Black smoke from *Shikari*, as I remember, meant 'Hold everything!' There were also firings at battle practice targets towed by the net layer, *Guardian*, throw-off firings at cruisers and destroyers and sub-calibre firings at high-speed targets.

The other modern target was called the 'Queen Bee', a radio-controlled aircraft, of which several were carried both in *Rodney* and in cruisers. After a few practice shots at drogues towed by aircraft from *Courageous* or *Furious*, the 'Queen Bee' would be deployed and controlled so as to provide a reasonable profile for anti-aircraft fire from the heavy ships. Every 'Queen Bee' seemed to have a mind of its own. My job during these firings was to record the angle of sight of the target aircraft, and to do this I had to be on a sponson not far from the admiral's bridge. I distinctly remember the Commander-in-Chief, Admiral Sir Roger Backhouse, complaining bitterly to the Fleet Gunnery Officer in my hearing that he didn't know how the guns could be expected to hit the target unless it would steer a steady course. I know now what he meant, but it didn't give one a great deal of confidence at the time, and we midshipmen thought far more of our multiple pom-poms and the 0.5-in machine guns as a means of air defence. These were aimed by what was called 'eye shooting', rather like using a shotgun and aiming off, and my anti-aircraft action station was in charge of one of the pom-poms with the duty of target indication and selection. This allowed the trainer to concentrate on his aim and not be bothered about when to shift target and to which target to shift next. That was my responsibility, discharged by hitting his shoulder and pointing. *Centurion* was also used as a target for aircraft from *Courageous*, *Furious* and, occasionally, shore-based aircraft. From

Sheldrake I watched several high-level and dive-bombing attacks, and their failure ever to hit somewhat restored one's confidence. Life was full of novelty, and I was only occasionally seasick.

Midshipmen were obliged to keep journals with daily entries. These were inspected weekly by the snotties' nurse, so that one's literacy was supervised. We also had to do a 'journal sketch' once a week, usually a detailed drawing either illustrating an evolution or depicting part of the ship such as the pumping and flooding system, although maps were acceptable. I padded out my journal with remarks on current affairs (which are quite amusing to read today). Troubles in Palestine, the activities of Hitler and Mussolini, the Nyon patrol and the Sino-Japanese War all featured largely. I suspect it was the easy option, as the alternative would have been to pad things out with technical matters concerning the ship and her routine. We received marks for our journals at the final board, so we had to take them seriously.

It was mid-October when time came for the Fleet to move south to Rosyth, and Disney Vaughan-Hughes of my term and I were detailed off to take passage in *Whirlpool*, *Rodney*'s drifter (a trawler-sized vessel used for transporting large numbers of libertymen or quantities of stores between the ship and shore when anchored well out). There was an ex-lower-deck lieutenant called Collins in command, and a chief stoker as engineer officer. I suppose there were about four or five other crew. The most memorable thing about *Whirlpool* was her performance in the filthy weather in which we battled our way south. I have never been so seasick, and I remember well coming on the bridge to take over the middle watch and looking round for Vaughan-Hughes. He was lying in a heap in the after corner of the bridge, and near him was the deck log, in which he had entered 'Sea and Swell 99'. I know how he felt. Cold, drenched and only half alive, eventually we came alongside *Rodney* in the Firth of Forth in the early morning. I have never been so glad to see a battleship since.

A cause for great excitement and activity at Rosyth was the Commander-in-Chief's harbour inspection of his flagship, which took several days. He came to X Turret, my action station, and I was in place in what was called 'The Cabinet' as rate officer. The Fleet gunnery officer came up and asked me to call out a 'rate' as an example of what I would do. So I sang out 'Inclination 120 degrees right, own speed 15 knots, enemy speed 8 knots.' 'Well, Snotty,' said the Fleet gunnery officer, 'What sort of ship do you think you're firing at?' I was aghast, and had to say rather lamely, 'A submarine on the surface, Sir.' Perhaps he thought it was a rather suitable target for the Royal Marines' turret.

Another thing I shall never forget about our time at Rosyth concerns the launch. The ship was open to visitors, moored south of the Forth Bridge, and I was taking people from the dockyard down to her and back. With a full load embarked, I moved for about the third time in the afternoon down to the ship and arrived to be greeted by an infuriated officer of the day – 'Hairy' Brown no less. He refused to let me come alongside, but bellowed at me from the quarterdeck as I lay off. The trouble was that the ship was about to be closed to visitors, and the launch was needed to take the first libertymen ashore in half-an-hour's time. Despite my protests, I was ordered in no uncertain terms to land my poor cargo at South Queensferry, miles from where they had started (and where, presumably, they had to return). They very naturally didn't like it, and didn't like the way the Navy was treating them, in the person of yours truly. I took the boat alongside the jetty at South Queensferry, and most of them refused to disembark. To my horror, I then saw the Commander-in-Chief's green barge approaching astern of me, and coming to the same jetty showing the 'negative' disc (indicating he was on board in plain clothes). Some of my passengers said to me, 'What's that?' I said, 'That's the Commander-in-Chief.' 'Oh,' said they, 'We'll tell him how you're treating us,' and began to get out quickly. I thought my naval career had come to an untimely end. However, when the great man leapt ashore (he was very tall, Roger Backhouse, six foot something), dressed in tweeds with a walking stick, off for his constitutional, he swept up the jetty at a rate of knots. They all fell back in front of him, no one said a word, nor did he ask me what I was doing. I was then able to clear my boat quickly, and take her back to the ship to embark libertymen. I was, needless to say, torn off a tremendous strip for having left Rosyth Dockyard so late; I should either have left earlier with my boat half full or not taken anybody at all. (This, I am sorry to say, had not occurred to me at the time, nor the fact that the tidal stream would be running against me.)

In mid-November we went to Portsmouth, where the Commander-in-Chief said goodbye and transferred to *Nelson*, his usual flagship, which had just finished a refit. *Rodney* sailed to her home port, Devonport, to start giving Christmas leave. While we were there, I saw for the first time our newest cruiser, *Birmingham*, which was distinguished by a different and more graceful bow line from the rest of the Southampton Class. On 1 December, to my great excitement and pleasure, I received my appointment to join her on 1 January at Portsmouth, and was told that she was to sail towards the end of that month to join the China Fleet. So I left *Rodney* just after my 18th birthday, and went home to Bletchingly.

This was to be our family's last Christmas together for a very long while, far longer than any of us then realised. It was a very happy one. We had learnt then that Father had been appointed to command the heavy cruiser *Kent*, which was going as flagship to China in the spring of 1938, where the new Commander-in-Chief was to be Vice-Admiral Percy Noble, his old master and friend. Obviously, by hook or by crook, Mousse (as we now called our mother) would come out, and so, if possible, would Peter when he went to sea. I had already done some three or four months of my midshipman's time, so I only had 20 months more to do, but at least for some of it we might see each other.

December 1937 was an anxious period, particularly for those at Castle Hill who knew Germany well. I was rather more interested in the war zone to which I was being sent. I had read *Tshushima* and *Rasplata* while at Dartmouth, and was now engaged in reading a book called *Japan Must*

Fight Britain by a lieutenant-commander in the Imperial Japanese Navy called Toto Ishimaru. This, as it turned out, was to be horribly prophetic.

We midshipmen joined *Birmingham* on Sunday 2 January at Portsmouth. Two paymaster midshipmen were already installed, White and Collins, and there were eight others of us. Cleeve from my term was the only other Dartmouth entry, the other six were public school entries straight from *Vindictive*. I, for my sins, was senior midshipman in the gunroom, a job I would have run a mile from had it been possible. The 'pubs' were not only a good deal older than Cleeve and me, but also bigger, had never endured a slack party in their young lives, and were going to find it hard to knuckle down to the sub-lieutenant, let alone to a sprog 'senior' midshipman like me. However, the sub-lieutenant turned out to be Tim Meyrick, who had been the Greynviles' Term Cadet Captain when we joined Dartmouth, and if ever there was an 'officer and a gentleman', it was he. The gunroom was small, and the mess included an engineer sub-lieutenant and a paymaster sub-lieutenant; We also collected an RNVR sub-lieutenant, as well as various midshipmen 'additional for passage', which made it seem smaller still at the start of the commission. The ship was very busy getting ready for deployment, but Captain Brind made ample time to see us, and we were shown around our new home and assigned our various stations.

My special duty was to be commander's 'doggie', which was an interesting but rather too conspicuous job. It involved attending on the commander from before 'hands fall in' in the morning, when I had to shake him and report the weather (in sufficient accuracy at least for him to know whether it was seaboots or barefoot to scrub and wash the upper deck); attend on him for 'both watches of the hands' (when working parties were told off for the various jobs that had to be done in the ship that day); run messages for him to divisional officers, captains of top, and so on; be present at 'Colours', 'Defaulters' and 'Special Sea Dutymen' – indeed, to be on call whenever and wherever the commander wanted until dismissed to instruction or to some other duty, such as running a boat. It was the best possible way of getting to know the ship and the people in her, and also getting to know the Commander. He, like the Captain and the First Lieutenant and two other officers on board, was a gunnery officer, and his name was Denis Marescaux Lees. He was terrifying at first, a little man with a loud voice and what seemed to be a hot temper. I was always afraid his telescope would be flung at me, but in fact he had a great sense of humour, a kind heart, and was a very good executive officer indeed.

The first few days of *Birmingham*'s first commission were worrying because we had a fire in the hangar, about which, of course, there had to be a Board of Enquiry. This was followed by another case of suspected sabotage. I don't know to this day if it was, but one has to remember the circumstances at the time – some 600 men of all sorts, some of them mere boys of 16 who had only just joined the Navy, and others long married, were facing separation from their families for up to two years in an uncertain world situation. It would be surprising if there was not one desperate man among them.

Perhaps I should now add that the ship's company shook down very well and that it was an exceptionally happy commission throughout. The snotties' nurse was a lieutenant, Jasper Synnott, who was the navigator and, like many navigators, quiet, self-effacing and rather studious. Combining these two roles was a common arrangement, the idea being that the midshipmen were out of trouble at sea, when the navigator was very busy doing the navigating and that he could keep a good eye on them in harbour when he didn't have so much to do. He was a very nice man, as were all the officers, and the most important one, 'Daddy' Brind (as our captain was known), was exceptional.

At the end of January we were given a weekend's leave before the ship was due to sail for the Far East. I promptly went sick at home, and rejoined at midnight on the Sunday by car, with Mousse driving, to be sent straight to the sick officer's cabin. I remember looking out of the scuttle to see England disappear, and came to about three days later, just before arrival at Gibraltar, where we stopped only to fuel. Eventually, we paused for two days in Malta, leaving in style with guard and band paraded as we passed the Fleet. We were screened out by destroyers and 'attacked' by submarines, one of which claimed a hit. I then went to my action station down in the 6-in armament transmitting station (a sort of control room), where I had the rather important job of converting the orders of the spotting officer into spotting corrections, and giving them to the bandsman at the appropriate manual control on the fire control table. For example, the spotting officer would say, 'Up ladder, shoot,' and I would have to say, 'Up 400, shoot, up 400, shoot, up 400, shoot.' This was one of the less complicated of the conversions one had to do; any mistake was horribly conspicuous to everybody watching the fall of shot. (My first effort was only a sub-calibre shoot on passage to Suez, and therefore not so worrying.)

We entered the Suez Canal on St Valentine's Day, and passed another Portsmouth ship, a Red Sea sloop on her way home, moored alongside the canal to let us by. The ships' companies exchanged the usual insults. By the evening I was 'east of Suez, where the best is like the worst' for the first time in my life. On passage through the Red Sea, we shifted into 'half whites' (a long since abandoned rig of monkey jacket and drill trousers). The usual drills and exercises went on, interspersed with formal instruction in navigation, meteorology, ship construction, and so forth. At Aden I remember helping to hand round 'small eats' at Brind's cocktail party for the locals, and being struck by how everybody, in what appeared to me to be the most arid of places, thoroughly enjoyed being stationed there. The other excitement at Aden was that four of us midshipmen were detailed off to run the ship's two fast 35 ft motorboats. We spent a full day being instructed on how to handle them by the coxswains, the idea being that we should start running them properly as midshipman of the boat on arrival in Colombo. These motorboats were great fun, quite different from *Rodney*'s launch. You handled them from a forward cockpit, steering with a wheel, and controlling the two engines by throttles (the enjoyment only slightly spoilt by the engineer officer having put screws into the controls to stop us using full throttle).

Birmingham had an aircraft complement of three Walrus amphibians, one in each hangar, and one normally on the catapult. These were being flown more now that the weather was better and sea conditions more favourable, but they were difficult to handle and therefore rather accident-prone. Brind was anxious to make full use of them and well aware of their capabilities for reconnaissance, for wind-finding and for communication purposes. We had two Fleet Air Arm pilots and an observer, who were among the most popular officers in the ship as far as the midshipmen were concerned. Unfortunately, flight opportunities in the Walrus were few and far between for any except the air crew, although I was once catapulted off (a rather lingering experience). At the end of a flight when at sea, the ship would make a slick with her wake, the aircraft would touch down in that, then come alongside and be hoisted on board by the crane, using a wonderful gadget called the 'Thomas Grab' to connect with the strop on the aircraft's upper wing: bringing an aircraft safely inboard was a great deal more complicated and difficult than hoisting any boat.

I shall never forget my first sight of Ceylon when we arrived at Colombo. Japanese and French warships were in port, a British destroyer as well, and everywhere beyond you could see the shining city and the lush green of the palm trees – such a contrast with the aridity of Aden. The next day I was on duty running the second motorboat and had some difficulty, breaking the rail and stanchion of the port gangway. The commander stopped my leave. We had a delightful shipwright officer; I talked to him about the situation, and he made certain that repairs were made in record time. However, no sooner was I running my boat again without having been ashore, when very nearly the same thing happened. However, it couldn't have been quite as bad as I thought, because the commander relented and I did get ashore eventually.

So on we went towards Singapore, being 'attacked' by 12 aircraft from the carrier *Eagle* before entering the Malacca Strait. I was lucky enough to have the morning watch for the approach to Singapore harbour, and after sheet lightning and black clouds in the small hours, caught that lovely smell of the Spice Islands as the sun rose and the deep green of Sumatra's mountains to starboard and the beaches of the Malay Peninsula to port came into view. No sooner had we anchored than I was in the motorboat once more and running the captain ashore for his calls. We spent several days in and out of Singapore, working up our weapons in the Singapore practice areas and going eventually up the Johore Strait to the naval base. It was March, and extremely hot. Several hundred Hakka women with baskets were still excavating what was to be the graving dock in the new base.

Our noses were kept to the grindstone as usual, including sailors landing in gaiters and tropical rig as a formed company with a midshipman attached to each platoon commander, marching through the tropical heat around the base area. Security there was tight, with a general alertness towards potential Japanese spies. Indeed, after one run ashore, we were kept in the police station for what seemed like hours because one of us had an undeclared camera. I also remember incessant general drills, until the commander eventually expressed himself reasonably satisfied with everybody's performance. These drills involved a series of evolutions at speed, such as furling or spreading awnings, weighing by hand, sending away fire or boarding parties, getting out the collision mat to cover a notional hole in the ship's side, and also more lighthearted tasks, such as ordering the cooks to race round the ship in whalers or the midshipmen to race to the bridge with a plate of fried eggs and bacon. As Commander Lees's 'doggie', I was in the thick of it, and very glad when the pipe 'Drills completed, return all gear' was made.

We were in and out of Singapore until just after Easter, when we sailed for Hong Kong. It was very hot in harbour, and the midshipmen used to take hammocks and straw mattresses up on deck, lay them out and sleep under the quarterdeck awning. It is never long in Singapore before there is a heavy downpour and it was seldom that we had a full night's sleep. Even so, anything was better than the damp heat of the chest flat. The ship went into the floating dock for a spell, mainly for painting. There was a very bad storm at one stage, in which I happened to be the nearest midshipman available at the bottom of the dock and near the only boat that was undamaged, and so was able to take it away and rescue two of our midshipmen and the sailing dinghy that had capsized in the storm. It was quite a skylark, but all went well, though I don't think either Compton or Baillie-Grohman was particularly grateful. They were two of my most troublesome messmates, and a perfect pain in the neck to the senior midshipman because they refused to turn out at 6 a.m. to go up on deck and do PT with the delightful leading seaman gunnery instructor who took us, a man called Crockford. Of course, if any officer came along and found out that the midshipmen were incomplete, it was my fault, and I got the blame. Eventually, I could take it no longer and had to run Baillie-Grohman in to the Sub; B-G was promptly beaten. I solved one problem, turning out for PT, but now I had another one on my hands, and was considered as the lowest form of animal life in the gunroom for quite a while. It taught me something about the difficulties encountered by the leading hand of a sailors' broadside mess.

As we left for Hong Kong, we underwent the last of several 'attacks' that had been made on us during exercise periods and the work-up, this time by Vildebeest torpedo-bombers based at RAF Seletar. These attacks were very impressive; of course the aircraft were not under fire but almost invariably they could claim two or three hits with their torpedoes on our ship and they certainly earned our respect. One of the things 'Daddy' Brind made his midshipmen do (and as far as I was concerned, it was a welcome alternative to a journal sketch every week) was to write an essay or report on some subject. He used to read these late into the night in his cabin with great interest, marked them for us and sent for us to discuss them. We had to write our opinion of the naval base at Singapore, we had to write about what we saw as the Japanese threat and we had to write about torpedo attack on ships at sea from aircraft. My journal shows that I was more than once criticised for taking too depressing a view.

Hong Kong in April 1938 was beautiful to see and exciting to know, added to which we had twice as many Hong Kong dollars as Straits dollars to the pound so everything was half price compared with Singapore. At both ports a chit system operated, by which you signed for anything you ordered and your chits came home to roost with your mess bill at the end of the month. Father (remembering, I think, his trouble with his laundry bill) was extremely anxious that I shouldn't overdo it, but everything was so cheap that it really was no problem. There was an excellent junior officers' club, a great choice of cinemas on both sides of the harbour, with Kowloon-side served by wallah-wallahs as well as the Star Ferry, and golf at Fanling and Deepwater Bay – it really was splendid.

Vice-Admiral Percy Noble, C.-in-C. China Station, came on board, inspected divisions, and then addressed the officers and ship's company. He welcomed us to the station, told us how important we were going to be to him and generally made a very good impression. Our first base was Wei-Hai-Wei, which we reached after ploughing through a typhoon. The 10,000 ton ship stood it well. I remember chiefly the noise and then the astonishing, still centre, with shore-birds perching on us in the lull. We finally came to anchor on 8 May.

I thought Wei-Hai-Wei a lovely place. The little island, with various British naval installations off which we anchored, had a magnificent view of the mountains of Shantung round the edge of a great bay dotted with fishing junks and sampans. I had seen my first French and American warships at Hong Kong, but here we saw our first Japanese cruiser. The officer of the guard who came on board was certainly impressive with his Samurai sword, white gloves and smart boots. The weather was clear and bright, though getting warmer fast, and so much less humid than Hong Kong in April. There was plenty to do ashore, a good little nine-hole golf course, a 'neat, smart horse' for hire for a shilling an hour, tennis courts and a splendid officer's club, where you could find club sandwiches, every kind of omelette, or cheesey-hammy-eggy-topside if you felt inclined. I had to land with range parties for the musketry range on several occasions. This was hard work, but a nice change, good exercise and interesting. Regatta practice was also starting, and that was a very important affair. Another activity was going ashore with Lieutenant Fanshawe, our observer, to set up a bombing and marking range.

Our opposite number at Wei-Hai-Wei was an ancient Japanese cruiser, *Kuma*. She anchored not far from us and seemed to be marking us as their guardship. She had a rather decrepit-looking admiral on board, and there was no social interchange at all with the Japanese officers. Their Navy was, after all, engaged in a war with Chiang Kai-shek. The ship was notably scruffy and had clearly unrigged some of her wireless aerials before she entered harbour, but we were impressed by the way that officers and men together devoted considerable lengths of time to PT on the upper deck every morning and evening, and by the way their boats, though dirty and not particularly graceful, were handled. I suppose we regarded her with a mixture of disdain and apprehension. We certainly kept an eye on her and logged any change of routine.

In early June, the bulk of the British China Squadron arrived from Hong Kong. *Medway* (the submarine depot ship), some O Class submarines,

Cumberland, *Suffolk* and the 6th Destroyer Flotilla all entered harbour. *Birmingham* was despatched to Chefoo, the American base in the Yellow Sea, for the King's Birthday. We gave a children's party for the British and American communities, and dressed up as pirates, but I otherwise remember only a short walk ashore. We returned to Wei-Hai-Wei to find *Ashigara*, wearing the flag of the vice-admiral commanding the northern part of the Japanese Fleet, in harbour. She was a most impressive ship, and I took rather a good photograph which, enlarged, did me a good turn by standing in for a journal sketch.

Time at sea for exercises was now enlivened by having *Eagle* and her aircraft, destroyers and submarines in company, and for a short time I was detached to *Dainty*, under Commander Walton, whose First Lieutenant, Alan Noble, was the son of the Commander-in-Chief. This was tremendous fun and less uncomfortable than I had expected. All we midshipmen wanted to be in destroyers when we became sub-lieutenants, and it was good to have a little practical experience which bore out all our expectations – few officers, plenty of action and easier relationships than those in bigger ships.

A month had to be spent on an engineering course. We stood watches in engine and boiler rooms, went round with the Senior Engineer for lighting up, learned how to operate the throttles and how to turn on sprayers, were briefed on how to deal with emergencies such as fire or flooding down below, and generally acquired, on top of our previous rather theoretical knowledge, some practical grasp of what went on in the main machinery compartments of the ship.

Soon after, we midshipmen went to *Eagle* for our air course, in which, as well as 'instruction', we experienced a good deal of flying in Swordfish, sometimes wheeled and sometimes with floats fitted. There was no gunroom in *Eagle*, and we didn't live in great comfort, but we did have a fascinating time in a very different sort of ship from any previously experienced. We saw a great deal of the pilots and the other air crew, who were a mixed and happy team from both Navy and RAF. We were passengers in aircraft flying off the deck and landing into the arrester-wires with what seemed a sickening jerk.

The most vivid memory I have is being in the back seat of a Swordfish in an open cockpit at 12,000 ft on a lovely, sunny day and feeling an almost overwhelming desire to jump out. However, I held on to my seat instead, and the next thing we did was a dummy torpedo attack on my own ship, *Birmingham*, leaving Wei-Hai-Wei. Down we came, and as the pilot flattened out just above sea-level to launch his 'torpedo', I had no need to hold on to my seat at all, being firmly anchored to it. The course also included bombing runs and lectures about the Fleet Air Arm. It was quite a change from gunnery and none the worse for that. One of the RAF pilots was a young officer called Ken Porter, with whom I served years later when he was an air vice-marshal, and still suffering from a limp which he attributed to damage caused by the Navy during his time in *Eagle* in 1937. Eventually he became a Commander-in-Chief, the first electrical engineer in his service to rise so high.

As *Birmingham* had not returned by the time our fortnight in *Eagle* was over, Cleeve and I went again to *Dainty* and underwent some unofficial destroyer time. Captain (D), a great player named Harold Hickling in *Duncan*, was in company, and we were thrown all over the sea, fired torpedoes, did all kinds of general drills, and so forth. Then back to *Birmingham* and gunnery it was, but the ship was our own, we were very fond of it, and glad in many ways to be home.

It was now nine months since we had left England, and for many, the commission had another 15 months away from home to run. There was no airmail to speak of, papers and letters took six weeks or more to reach us at Wei-Hai-Wei, and the ship's company, many of whom were married with young families, had only the most tenuous links with home. Just a few officers had been able to afford to bring their wives out to the China Station, and some of these took passage to Wei-Hai-Wei in Fleet auxiliaries. Yet morale seemed to be good, leave-breaking was not very prevalent, drunkenness (as always) was bad, but not so bad, to my eye, as it had been in the Home Fleet. The chief health and disciplinary problem on the China Station was the incidence of venereal disease. *Birmingham* was less afflicted in this respect, but there was a great deal around. In Hong Kong the prostitutes would gather outside the China Fleet Club waiting for custom. Sailors would be accosted, mobbed almost, as they left the club. The girls' services were cheap, nearly all were infected, and they were, like many young Chinese girls, extremely attractive. The disease, or catching it, was not treated as a major punishable offence lest this should foster concealment, but men's leave and some part of their pay was stopped while they were suffering from it. Concealment by officer or man was regarded seriously and, in an officer, disease blocked promotion till cured. (It was also an offence to get so sunburnt as to be unfit for duty.)

All things considered, the enthusiasm, spirit and general contentedness of the ship's company were absolutely remarkable. It helped, I think, to have the umbilical cord cut: you couldn't be rung up by your wife or telephone her, letters took so long to come, the weekly *Daily Mirror* with 'Jane' was 13 weeks old when it reached the ship. There was nothing to be done but to get on with life as a ship's company doing a job, to hope to belong to a good mess, to have good petty officers, a good divisional officer, a good skipper and a ship to be proud of. The average age of the men was about 27, a good deal higher than it became during the war, though we did have a boys' division of 16-year-olds on board the cruisers. The average age of the officers was probably about 32. We were proud of our role and of the Royal Navy, and competitiveness in sport was a very strong motivator. Punishment for misdoing was prompt, arbitrary rather than harsh, and usually met with cheerful acceptance. As a midshipman, one would attend as assistant divisional officer at the commander's 'table', where cases which he could either deal with or remand to the captain were tried. Lees made it obvious that what he wanted most was to find out why a particular offence was alleged, often being convinced – and rightly – that it had occurred. The most wonderful stories were produced and were handled with cheerful aplomb. It was a very important part of one's education as a future divisional officer to listen to this two-way exercise in applied psychology.

In the relative calm of Wei-Hai-Wei, whether sailing, in the motorboat, working down below in the engine room, on the upper deck or at action stations, we came to know sailors pretty well, and their resilence, cheerfulness and loyalty never failed to impress. There were other standards learnt on that China Station before the war in terms of smartness and drill; of the importance of entering harbour in a seamanlike way – the lower booms out together, the boats properly lowered – the practice of calling the away all boats to lay off during 'Colours', sending a boat to the senior officer on arrival, the etiquette requiring one to request permission of the senior officer present to proceed when sailing: all these were matters of some importance in the pre-war Navy, but irrelevant in war. I drew on my recollection of them greatly in later years to help to instil some extra pride in service in the ships – and later, Fleets – I was to have the honour to command.

It was now September 1938, and I remember general anxiety everywhere about the deteriorating world situation, of which we were kept pretty well informed. Father's ship, *Kent*, was due to come to Wei-Hai-Wei to work up, but this was cancelled, and the Commander-in-Chief, then flying his flag in *Cumberland*, sailed for Hong Kong. *Cumberland* was going home to pay off after her two-year commission, and I remember we cheered her out and were astonished to see the Japanese manning ship on our old watchdog, *Kuma*, and also cheering. I really believe that that Japanese admiral thought that we were all leaving the station for good, and, afterwards, the rest of us did leave Wei-Hai-Wei in two convoys, with Brind in charge, little *Grimsby* remaining as guardship.

My last boat trip was into the mainland with a letter for the consul, who met me on the jetty with two naval wireless operators to come back to the ship. Warships had been spotted passing by Wei-Hai-Wei earlier and Brind sent an aircraft to investigate. They turned out to be American, under Admiral Harry Yarnell, also leaving the Yellow Sea for Tsingtao, where, after turning our convoys over to another cruiser off the Saddle Islands, we repaired too. Tsingtao was a good place for a run ashore. It was a great place for riding, and a party of us went out once or twice. This led to a rather unfortunate incident. The countryside was thronged by Japanese soldiers, and on one of our excursions we passed through a group of them. A couple of minutes later, up rode Baillie-Grohman, white as a sheet: his horse had knocked over a Japanese soldier, and I think he expected to be instantly executed, as well he might have been. Fortunately, however, the other Japanese soldiers roared with laughter, and that was the end of the matter as we cantered off as insouciantly as we could manage.

Ashigara, the Japanese Fleet flagship, had entered harbour and anchored close by when, suddenly, we were told to weigh and proceed 'with despatch' to Shanghai to embark a battalion of Seaforth Highlanders and evacuate them to Hong Kong. We sailed at 2 a.m., crossed the Yangtze Bar in the dark that evening, and anchored at Woosung, waiting for the soldiers to come downriver. I remember seeing them approach in a string of tugs, which secured alongside us, and they were soon on board. We sailed and crossed the Yangtze Bar at 28 knots with about 4 ft of water to spare. I was on deck, and could see how our stern went down in the shallows, an enormous mound of yellow river water piling up behind it. *Birmingham* held her course well, and about a day later we came alongside the dockyard wall in Hong Kong, astern of Father's ship, *Kent*. The soldiers were met by a general, and disembarked. I went over to *Kent* to call on her captain! Hitler had just issued his ultimatum to the Czechs, and Munich had yet to happen. I remember Father greeting me and saying, 'Dear boy, I had no idea that the next time we met it would be in circumstances like these. Come and have a drink.' We had supper together in his cabin; he looked well and happy, and obviously thoroughly loved his ship. He had had a good passage out, and was expecting Mousse to get to us before Christmas. Peter was well, and all the news seemed fine except on the political front. There was no time to see much of one another then – he was very busy and nobody knew what was going to happen, whether we might not be at war quite soon.

It was the peak typhoon season, and warnings were frequent, but I think we did get one walk together. The Munich Agreement took the pressure off, and I wrote in my journal at the time: 'It has been a case of peace at any price rather than of peace with honour, but there is little doubt as to which was most acceptable, the peace that has been made or war.' The typhoon warnings continued, junks were forever moving to their special anchorages and out again, and the warships were shifted from alongside to buoys and back, as the weather changed. *Birmingham* spent some time in the Hong Kong exercise areas, as did *Kent*, and occasionally we were in company, which was pleasant for me. Munich had lifted the threat of war in Europe, but then the long-expected invasion of South China by the Japanese took place. On 15 October they landed at Bias Bay, where expected, and not far from Hong Kong. Four days later came *Birmingham*'s turn to go to Shanghai, the best run ashore on the station, and very much looked forward to by all hands.

On our passage to Shanghai we passed two Japanese aircraft carriers, presumably covering the invasion of South China, and then were ordered into the enormous outer harbour of Amoy. This was on Trafalgar Day. All available officers and midshipmen were stationed on deck, the ship's company were fallen in for entering harbour, lining the upper deck, all the armament was unmanned, as were the turrets fore and aft, and the captain took us in at about 8 knots. It was a lovely day, and I shall never forget it. We passed between two lines of Japanese battleships, continued through a tremendous number of cruisers and destroyers, two flotillas of submarines, eight submarines in each – through, in fact, the main force of the Imperial Japanese Fleet. We made sketches, took photographs and tried to copy the characters on the sides of their ships as we passed them, finally coming to anchor not far from the island of Kulangsu on which the International Settlement was situated. At Japanese request, no calls were exchanged, and no doubt they were on a war footing. We all mustered in the wardroom before the departure run and were briefed by the commander and captain in person on what to look for on the way out. We left harbour in the dog watches, as slowly as before, compiling what must have been a most comprehensive intelligence report, and obtaining at the same time a very shrewd idea of what the China Squadron would face should there be a war with Japan.

We berthed between the British buoys in the Whampoa, which were close abreast the Bund. At that time the International Settlement and French Concession at Shanghai were invested by the Japanese Army, which had seized control of the city. Their old armoured cruiser, the *Idzumo*, lay alongside in the river below us. Guardships from the other treaty powers were also at buoys in mid-river – the French cruiser *Lamotte Picquet*, the Italian *Raimondo Montecuccoli* and the American *Augusta* – so there was a great deal of boatwork to be done under very difficult conditions. The current was fast, up to 8 knots, and the river was cluttered, not only with sampans, but with great barges full of most odoriferous 'night soil' on its way from the city to the Yangtze and the sea. Crossing this traffic, mostly unlit, was difficult, particularly at night, and on one occasion I very nearly got caught by one of those filthy barges. I had the Resident Naval Officer at Shanghai, Commander Ralph Edwards, in my boat at the time, about 2 a.m. He came to see 'Daddy' Brind, as the SNO afloat, a great deal, to keep him briefed on the situation ashore and in general. He became an admiral later, was a signal officer, and a delightful man.

Shanghai was a crowded, amoral city with extremes of wealth and misery plain to see, but time here passed merrily enough, and we were sad to leave the day after Armistice Day and the Remembrance Day Parade on the Bund. We saw little of the Americans. There were no midshipmen approaching our age on board their ships, as indeed there were none in any of the foreign ships, and my chief recollection of the American presence is, I am sorry to say, of their libertymen laid out in rows, horizontal on the Bund at almost any time of the day or night, drunk and waiting to be taken back to their ship by their patrols. They had no idea of how to hold their liquor. The US Marine patrols seemed to handle the sailors pretty brutally and our own men would certainly never have stood for that kind of treatment. The British sailors behaved very well by comparison: there were the usual troubles, but I do not think that the incidence of defaulters was all that dreadful; apart from anything else, people did not want to get their leave stopped while they were in Shanghai.

We called into a largely deserted Amoy on the way down to Hong Kong (only three Japanese cruisers present), and when we came finally to Hong Kong we heard the good news that four of us were to do our destroyer time. Cleeve and I were going together to *Diamond* for a two-month course and she sailed almost immediately for Swatow. On the way, during the morning watch when I was on the bridge, we passed through a Fleet of some 1,000 sailing fishing junks. In pairs, with their nets slung between them, they were not manoeuvrable, or were disinclined to be so, and it was quite a fascinating business threading one's way through them all. I had often seen fishing junks inshore from *Birmingham*, but this was the first time I had really felt part of the scene, a scene now gone for ever, of sail upon square sail as far as the eye could see on a calm, misty morning.

The British Consul at Swatow had a good, verandahed house with a tennis court on a small island at the entrance to the harbour off which we anchored. I went ashore and played tennis the first afternoon. It was now November, the weather was apt to blow up a bit, and our berth was fairly exposed. During our second night there a tragedy occurred. The ship's motorboat, due to bring libertymen off shore from the consul's island, broke down; some 13 men tried to come off by sampan, and in a series of accidents involving fishing nets and stakes, four men drowned. *Diamond* was a happy ship with a fine captain, Terence Robinson, and First Lieutenant, John Hodges. The whole ship's company was plunged into grief by this episode, and as newcomers I think Cleeve and I felt a little out of it. A court of inquiry was held at once, and we played our part in that with the navigating officer, trying to trace exactly how the sampan had drifted, charting the fishing stakes on which it had capsized, and so forth. Eventually, the bodies were recovered, and there was a naval funeral ashore, to which *Asheville*, an American sloop in harbour, sent a contingent. The whole ship's company, except a few on watch, took part. The Mayor of Swatow was there, as were the British Consul and the American Consul. *Diamond*'s firing party, bearers and mourners did extraordinarily well, watched by swarms of uncharacteristically silent Chinese. It was my first service funeral in an appropriately far-off place for our far-flung service, and I remember it well.

We remained at Swatow until the beginning of December. A good many drills and exercises were carried out, and we learned much about destroyers in this harbour period. Two or three times a day, Japanese seaplanes would alight nearby in the harbour and sampans would come out from the shore of the mainland, each with a bomb. The bombs would be strapped onto the racks on the lower wing of the biplanes, which would then take off, disappear for a couple of hours or so, and come back for re-arming. There was no Chinese retaliation, noticeable or practicable. From Swatow, we went on a reasonably calm voyage down to Hong Kong to rejoin the Fleet. Our first job was to attend on *Eagle* for day and night flying, with the seaboat manned as a crash boat. This was very interesting, as it was the first time I had seen carrier flying at night, night torpedo attacks and flare-dropping exercises. Also very interesting were the flotilla exercises, including a night-encounter exercise with our own *Birmingham*. On one occasion we made a divisional torpedo attack on Father's ship, *Kent*, and retired under smoke, later forming a screen on her. Some motor torpedo boats had come out to Hong Kong by sea from England by then, and they did some attacking, but the snag about them was that they were big and too noisy.

On 23 December I was given Christmas leave until the 27th, and returned to a different life. Mousse had arrived in Hong Kong on 9 December, they had a splendid flat at the May Road level, No. 9 Branksome Towers, and a Ford V8 car with a delightful Indian driver called Shurzaman. I was back in the home atmosphere with home catering and in plain clothes for days on end. Peter had obtained a first-class pass out of the training cruiser *Vindictive*, and was being appointed to *Dorsetshire*, a cruiser due to join the

China Station, but wouldn't be with us for a while yet. Then it was back to *Diamond* for more of the usual training and exercises, culminating in our destroyer exams in early January.

Cleeve and I rejoined *Birmingham*, which sailed to Manila for a change of weather before going to Wei-Hai-Wei once more as guardship. It was bitterly cold at Wei-Hai-Wei, the *Kuma* was there, and the chief recreation ashore was skating on the pond. Our sailors had a monopoly of the Fleet canteen, and we had the officers' club to ourselves. There was a hospital on the island, run by the Navy, and the resident officer in charge of the whole affair was a surgeon commander called Pomfret. He had his family with him, and it must have been a rather pleasant job, despite the Japanese who periodically came to see him. We were working a winter routine, which meant getting up later in the morning (I don't think we started until 8 a.m., 7.30 perhaps), and we ceased work soon after lunch. It was a welcome change from the busy life and enervating climates we had become used to in the south.

The idyll was interrupted by sudden orders to raise steam and proceed with all despatch to Tsingtao. I landed at about 8.30 p.m. to tell the officers ashore what was going on, and all came off by a special boat sent in two hours later, leaving several wondering wives to watch us sail. The next morning we anchored between a Japanese destroyer, a Norwegian merchant ship and the British-registered *St Vincent de Paul*, which had been arrested by the Japanese on the high seas and ordered into Tsingtao. *Ashigara* was also in harbour. *St Vincent de Paul*'s illegal arrest was the reason we had been despatched.

An officer went over to find out from her master his version of what it was all about, and came back and reported. I then went over to see the master and tell him that a boat would be sent for him at 11 a.m. and he was to bring the ship's log, a written statement of his complaints and any other evidence. I was prevented from going alongside by a Japanese customs launch, but was able to talk to the master, shouting up to him on the bridge. I was eventually allowed aboard, being heavily photographed by the Japanese who were lying off. By the time I got back to *Birmingham*, however, the Japanese had hoisted a quarantine flag on board the ship, so the master was unable to leave for *Birmingham*.

Arguments went on most of the day, with the Japanese officers going to and fro, the Consul-General coming off from shore and the Norwegian Consul coming too. Eventually, I was sent for by the commander, who said that we were going to place an armed guard on board *St Vincent de Paul* for the night and a midshipman volunteer was wanted to take charge of it. This was easy, and I volunteered at once. It sounded as though it might be interesting, and sure enough, before it got dark, I drew a pistol, was sent with four armed ratings and a petty officer (one of the ratings being a signalman), with instructions to make certain that the Japanese did not board the ship in strength during the night. If they tried to do so, I was told to refer them to *Birmingham* and if they refused to go away I was to signal for assistance.

I hoisted the gangway so that not even a Japanese monkey could get aboard, and posted armed sentries. 'Daddy' Brind, who was faced with a potentially serious international incident, took a very strong line and told the admiral in *Ashigara* that he was going to sail in the morning and take *St Vincent de Paul* with him. Early in the morning, I had to lower the gangway to let a telegraphist rating from *Birmingham* come on board; a Japanese customs launch came alongside at once, and three officials came up the gangway demanding to see the master. I met them at the top with my revolver, not brandished but handy. It was a long argument, I kept referring them to *Birmingham*, saying, 'Go and see my captain in the Birmingham,' but they refused to do that. I therefore left them there, with my petty officer and an armed rating in charge, and went to find out from the master what he thought about it all. He was lying on his bunk in his cabin when I came in, and when I explained the position he rolled over and said 'Your bloody captain has taken over my ship, you're now in charge and I'm not going to give you any advice, it's entirely up to you.' – Clear, if not helpful!

I went back to the Japanese, who then asked if *Birmingham* had commandeered the ship, and I told them to go and talk to the captain of *Birmingham* and ask him. They then asked again to see the master, but I said that I was in charge, and he was not available. They then left. Soon after, a boat came from *Birmingham* (which was now under way) for me and my party; *St Vincent de Paul* weighed, and we left harbour together. The Japanese admiral then made a last attempt at intimidation, and as we sailed at action stations with *Birmingham* between *St Vincent de Paul* and *Ashigara*, her 8 in broadside was trained on us. 'Daddy' Brind at once trained our 6 in guns on the Japanese flagship. Fortunately, no one was stupid enough to go further, and we escorted *St Vincent de Paul* as far as the entrance to the Yangtze before returning to Wei-Hai-Wei. Brind kindly showed me a copy of his 'Report of Proceedings' to the Commander-in-Chief, in which he had said something quite nice about 'my officer in charge of the boarding party', so I was very proud. Brind's nerve should not be underestimated: the Japanese were at war in China, trigger-happy and unpredictable.

Back in Wei-Hai, it was still cold-weather routine, lots of work, and instruction and Chinese New Year, when we made a special effort for our gunroom stewards. We were eventually relieved by another ship and removed down to Hong Kong, where we were due to have our mid-commission refit at the Taikoo dockyard. *Kent* was in Hong Kong and I had a weekend's leave, so I was back in the family atmosphere again for a short time.

About this time, the Commander-in-Chief went south in *Kent* to visit Admiral le Bigot at Saigon, and also the Dutch in Batavia. Lady Noble, my mother and various other ladies went in his despatch vessel, *Falmouth*. Before the Commander-in-Chief left, I had made my application for permission to go home on the Trans-Siberian Railway. This was approved, so it remained to get to Shanghai and apply for a transit visa to cross the Soviet Union.

Our time as midshipmen was drawing to a close for both Cleeve and myself. We faced our final board of examination for the rank of lieutenant in June, and we had other examinations, such as ship construction, to take in between. We had also to make certain that our navigation workbooks were full of the astronomical observations and fixes required of us. We had to do several exercises called 'A day's work', which consisted of a sun sight, a meridian altitude and either an evening or early morning star sight. The ship undocked shortly after Easter, and not long after that *Kent* returned, and also *Falmouth* with Mousse on board. Peter was on his way, but hadn't arrived when the Commander-in-Chief transferred his flag to *Birmingham* and we sailed for Amoy.

There was a crisis involving the International Settlement on Kulangsu. The Japanese had landed 400 sailors on the island, and were threatening to seize the International Concession in contravention of all the current treaties. Admiral Noble took charge, with the agreement of the American, French and other foreign representatives. He ordered the Japanese to withdraw or said he would land 500 bluejackets. In response, the Japanese reduced their force to 42, and were joined by similar detachments from ourselves, the French and the Americans.

There was a series of meetings on board *Birmingham*, and as midshipman of the watch on the quarterdeck I saw many of these occur, with consuls-general, a French admiral and US captains coming on board and, eventually, the local Japanese admiral. Japanese officers never left their menacing, curved swords behind, so he found some difficulty in negotiating the hatch down off the quarterdeck to the admiral's quarters. I shall not forget his return, about four hours later. I have never seen a man so angry in my life. I do not know what Percy had said to him, but in the twilight between peace and war in which we were then living with the Japanese, I think straight talking never went amiss.

Before we left Amoy, *Myoko*, with a vice-admiral on board, entered harbour, as did our new Rear Admiral Murray in *Cornwall*. All being settled, we sailed, with the British Ambassador to China also embarked. Our destination was off Sharp Peak at the mouth of the Min River, and *Birmingham* anchored offshore, with *Diamond* near the Pagoda Anchorage inshore. The area was still under Chinese control, and Foochow, about 70 miles further up the Min River, was the seat of a Chinese Army headquarters with an important general in command, whom the ambassador, Sir Archibald Clark Kerr, with the Commander-in-Chief, had arranged to visit. They were to make the passage in the admiral's barge, and I was lucky enough to have my motorboat selected as anti-aircraft escort for these two great men. Accordingly, a Union Jack was painted on the canopy, a Lewis gun was mounted aft, and off we went early one morning.

The Chinese had sunk a number of merchant ships and piled stones on top of them to blockade the entrance to the river to stop the Japanese Fleet getting through, but there was a small gap about 30 yards wide, and we followed the barge through that, buffeting against a 10 knot current. The pagoda, after which the anchorage was named, was high on a hill to starboard, and it was a fascinating journey for me, the farthest into China proper that I have ever been to this day. There was tremendous activity along the river banks: fishing boats, barges, all kinds of evidence of a flourishing rural economy. The brown hills on either side of the river were intricately terraced and all beautifully cultivated. As we drew nearer to the city, the river narrowed and the stream became stronger, but we were still able to make quite reasonable headway. When, after 3½ hours, we reached the Jardine Matheson Jetty at Foochow, the admiral and the ambassador went off to their conference, having been met by the governor, an Admiral Lee and the General. We busied ourselves with refuelling the barge and my motorboat, both of which were showing signs of strain. Eventually, I was free to go with the consul's daughter on a conducted tour of the city, which was on high ground either side of the river. Then suddenly came the wailing of sirens, and as we hurried out from a lacquer factory high above the city, I saw people like ants scurrying everywhere and clearing the bridges. Sure enough, bombs – Japanese ones – were being dropped. It was my first air-raid experience, and I did not know then how many more there were to come.

The consul's wife gave us lunch in the Foochow Club, and at about 4 p.m. we returned and manned the boats ready for the Commander-in-Chief and the Ambassador. We set off downriver with the benefit of the stream under us. However, about two-thirds of the way back, the barge broke down, so we stood by her, being the anti-aircraft escort. Efforts to get her going again were failing, as was the light, and the Commander-in-Chief decided to go back to the ship in my boat with the ambassador and leave the Flag Lieutenant in charge of the barge in the hope that something could be done about it. So off we set. Because of the delay, it was dark by then, and I had the problem of finding the unlit gap in the boom of sunken ships in order to get safely out of the river and to *Diamond* in Pagoda Anchorage. I approached it very gingerly, but with the stream under me, speed was necessary to maintain steerageway. The Commander-in-Chief and the ambassador decided to come up and stand either side of my cockpit to con me through. When this had been done to everybody's satisfaction, they went aft and sat down on the bench abaft the canopy on the smart, white, blue-piped cushions provided. However, I distinguished myself in a moment of euphoria, having seen the lights of *Diamond* ahead, by pushing the throttles hard forward, putting on speed and steering straight towards her. Unfortunately, there was a lop on. There was a shout from aft, and I had succeeded in drenching both the great men. They were fortunately very forgiving, and I always remember coming alongside the starboard accommodation ladder in *Birmingham* later, with quite a difficult alongside to do because there was a nasty swell, to be greeted by a number of the ship's company, who had lined the side of the ship wondering what was going on, giving a great cheer when they saw that the VIPs were coming back in the ship's boat and not in the barge.

We next visited Shanghai and the day before we left Shanghai, I crossed the Rubicon, went to the Soviet Consulate-General and filled in my transit visa form. One question, of many, asked if I had any relations in the USSR. On Mousse's advice, I said 'no'. The day after we arrived back at Hong Kong, Peter was there in *Dorsetshire*, so we met as a complete family on 8 June, the only time we were all together in Hong Kong, as on the 9th *Dorsetshire* left for Amoy to relieve *Cornwall*. Then it was Wei-Hai-Wei again for *Birmingham*, and Cleeve and I were on positively the last lap, getting ready for our board of examination for the rank of lieutenant. We were three months ahead of the others, who had not had the advantage of the time we had served in the Home Fleet and had joined *Birmingham* straight from the training cruiser. This Seamanship Board was the culmination of all the time as a midshipman, and you went to it with a document called 'A Record of Training' (which I still have). This you presented to the President of the Board, who, in my case, was Captain Hammill of *Cornwall*. In it were the remarks of all the officers who had reported on me since I first went to sea in the Fleet. You also had to have with you your captain's recommendation for promotion to acting sub-lieutenant.

Mousse was in Wei-Hai-Wei at that time, having come up in *Falmouth*, and, pending the arrival of *Kent*, she was staying with Lady Noble in Admiralty House. *Birmingham* had to go to sea, so I stayed there too, and on 28 June went off to my board in *Cornwall*'s motorboat from the jetty at Admiralty House at Wei-Hai-Wei. I hoped this might bring me luck. It was an anxious occasion, and Cleeve and I were really put through it. No captain could have taken more interest in his midshipmen than 'Daddy' Brind, and both of us were awarded First Class Certificates at the end of the day. This was very important as, like the 'passing out' results from Dartmouth and *Frobisher*, it affected one's seniority as a sub-lieutenant.

Cleeve left for Shanghai to join SS *Rawalpindi* for his voyage home, taking my baggage with him. I stayed at Wei-Hai-Wei for most of my summer leave, and hoped that my Russian transit visa would come through in time. Father arrived in *Kent*, and we moved into No. 7 Bungalow, which, though small, had everything we needed, and we were admirably looked after by the Chinese stewards from *Kent*. Although the time there was relaxing and enjoyable, I did not know when I should see Peter again before I had to go back to England, added to which the Soviet transit visa had still not arrived and the last P&O liner which would get me back in time for my sub-lieutenant's courses had sailed. I kept rather quiet about all this. At last the visa came through, and then I had to get down to Shanghai in order to catch a ship to Manchukuo to board the railway. This all fell out happily, the General Officer Commanding in China, Major-General Grasett, came to visit Wei-Hai-Wei and was bound for Shanghai thereafter. The Commander-in-Chief produced a destroyer for him, *Defender*, sailing on 15 July, and I took passage in her. After some interesting days with my aunt and uncle in Shanghai, I sailed in the SS *Tsingtao Maru*, a Japanese merchant ship, for Dairen near Port Arthur. Going from the port at Dairen to the station for the South Manchurian Railway was quite a skylark. I do not think my passport has ever been inspected and stamped so often before or since. The officials were all Japanese, incomprehensible, abrupt, and often, it seemed to me, downright rude. However, I got through with a few other people bound for the same destination.

In Manchukuo, the Japanese occupation was very much in evidence. I shared a compartment with a Japanese man who gave no trouble, but it was disappointing that as we approached the Siberian border and were just penetrating the Valdai Hills, which promised to be a beautiful landscape, all the blinds were drawn and armed Japanese soldiers were posted outside the door of every compartment. Although Japan was not at war with the Soviet Union, there was no love lost on the frontier, and there had been quite a considerable 'incident' a week or so before we approached it. On the way, we stopped for only a couple of hours in Mukden, but spent 24 hours in Harbin. I wandered round the streets of this thriving city with its large Russian population, looking incongruous in a blazer and grey flannels, and took a few photographs.

We reached the frontier in the evening, and all had to get out of the train at the Japanese frontier post for our passports to be examined, our luggage checked, and so on. We then climbed into a special broad gauge train with a large contingent of Japanese Army on it and moved towards Russia. When we reached the frontier, the train stopped with half of it in the Soviet Union and half still in Manchukuo. The Japanese soldiers marched out of the after end, and the Red Army marched into the forward end. Then we went on our way and arrived at the Soviet frontier post at Manchouli. There followed the customs examination to end all customs examinations in a large wooden shed. Everything was unpacked and examined; my camera, as I knew it would be, was sealed, and some of my books were taken away. I was trying to keep a diary of the journey; that was taken away, and I was told that one was not allowed to write in the Soviet Union. Eventually, however, deprived of my writing materials, some of my reading matter and my camera, but allowed to keep the pineapple chunks, corned beef and other hard tack I had taken with me for the journey, I was allowed to embark. However, my passport was retained by the Russians, and I was told that I would get it back when I left the Soviet Union. This, I know now, was the standard drill but it was very uncomfortable at that particular moment.

The engine of the train was fired by wood, and the carriages were pre-Revolutionary wagons-lits. I shared a compartment with a man called Smythe, about twice my age, who was a businessman from Chungking. Fortunately, although he had no pineapple chunks, he had beer, which came in very handy later. Our compartment consisted of a longish settee and a short seat opposite, flanking the door to a washing compartment shared with the adjacent compartment. During the evening the *provodnik* would come along and lower down a bunk overhead, so one of you slept on the settee and one of you (in this case, me) on the top bunk. It was pretty comfortable, and vastly cleaner than I had expected. There was always a samovar bubbling under the care of the *provodnik* at the end of the corridor and, unfortunately, there was near-incessant, modern Soviet music, raucous speeches and almost incomprehensible news broadcasts coming at strength five from the loudspeaker despite our frequent attempts to have it switched off. The restaurant cars were at the back and invariably full of Russians, smoking and talking at the tops of their voices. I was determined to make the maximum use of my first-category meal tickets, but after the first three or four days, I could stomach no more caviare. The food was very good, Russian-style but fatty, indigestible unless one took plenty of vodka with it, and of course, I was getting very little exercise. I was grateful indeed for the pineapple chunks and beer. Neither Smythe nor I was very talkative, so I spent a lot of time reading, and looking out of the window. I had been briefed to watch for certain things, like double-tracking of the line and interesting loads travelling east towards Vladivostock, and I did spot sections of submarine being shipped along the railway.

Apart from meals, which soon lost much of their attraction for me, the main events of the day were the stops at stations *en route*. It was a chance to take some exercise, and I would walk up and down, talk to the missionaries, and sometimes to a young German couple who were also in the train in a first-class compartment. We stopped at what seemed already to be great cities, like Chita, Omsk, Irkutsk, and also at a delightful little halt called Baikal on the shores of the lake of that name. Here, a wonderful view stretched across the lake to the mountains in the distance. As we drew nearer the Urals, the country changed, with a feeling that we were approaching Europe. We stopped for quite a while at Sverdlovsk (which used to be called Yekaterinberg), and there I left the station and went for about an hour's walk into the town, trying to get the feel of where it might have been that the imperial family was murdered in 1918.

Then it was on across the steppe to Moscow, where we arrived early one morning, sadly passing the old cities of medieval Russia during the silent hours. I had a full and sunny day in Moscow, because the luggage had to be moved from the train we had come so far in to another at the station for Minsk and Smolensk going west. The naval attaché, whom Father knew, Captain Clanchy, sent his car for me and looked after me during the day. I had a meeting at the British Embassy, a lovely building on the banks of the Moskva, was debriefed on my journey so far, and was told what to look out for during the next run from Moscow to Warsaw. I was then shown the sights. Everyone was awaiting the arrival of the British Military Mission under Admiral Drax, and so were very busy, but I was given a good rundown on the international situation, which was to be helpful to me on the next lap of my journey home when staying in Germany.

I set off that night from Moscow, bound for Poland. This was a different train, and I was fortunate enough to share a compartment with a King's Messenger on his way home with bags of despatches, so we had the compartment entirely to ourselves. I had already been in the Soviet Union about six-and-a-half days, and there was just a day-and-a-half to go. The train to Poland didn't stop until we reached Niegoreloye, where the procedure experienced at the Soviet frontier with Manchukuo was now re-enacted, the Red Army dismounting off one end and the Polish Frontier Police climbing in at the other as the wide gauge train stopped half across the frontier. Then we went over into Poland, my passport was returned, and I drew a sigh of relief to feel I was back in Europe.

The atmosphere at the Polish customs post was quite different from that in the Soviet Union, as you would expect, the only jarring note being to see everybody's hand held out for money (tips were illegal under Stalin). We went through Warsaw in the dark, and I retain clearly the impression of a lovely city of lights reflected in the Vistula on a glorious late summer's evening. There was no time to leave the railway platform at Warsaw and explore as on we pressed, and the next thing I remember is being woken up at the German frontier post, and being treated with the proper respect due to someone who was the travelling companion of the King's Messenger. I was to stay with Nina Lucke (my aunt and godmother) in Berlin, but first I had to go to the British Embassy and report to the naval attaché. I expected to stay just over a week, and my instructions were that I was to ring him or his office every day and find out if it was all right to stay on. In addition, my aunt's husband had to inform the police of my presence just as often. This was just before the Molotov-Ribbentrop Agreement, and there was still hope that a peaceful solution might occur, but Berlin was packed with men in uniform, each saluting the other. Private soldiers saluted one another, everybody saluted the officers, and the officers saluted everybody else, or so it seemed to me. They had the choice of using the Nazi salute (with the right arm stretched out at 45°), the less formal Nazi salute (where you just lifted your right hand above your shoulder), or a military salute. It all seemed quite indiscriminate, and I kept my trilby firmly on my head. There was no doubt that morale was very high: they felt on top of the world and were raring to get cracking at something.

On 21 August I said goodbye to my aunt and uncle, and set off for Brussels. I never saw them again. They both committed suicide when the Red Army entered Berlin at the end of the war. My aunt had told me that if there was another war she didn't want to live, but I am afraid she had to live through a very great deal. It was a quiet trip to Brussels to visit great-aunt Alexandra Phipps, my other godmother. At last, I arrived back in England on 26 August 1939 (which, in retrospect, was cutting it a great deal too fine to be sensible) and had a week or so's leave before starting my sub-lieutenant's courses. There was much to be done: collecting my gear from SS *Rawalpindi*, which had arrived from China; having my sub-lieutenant's uniform fitted, buying a sword, and so on. They were anxious days. Then, in the drawing room at Castle Hill, I heard Neville Chamberlain's speech telling us that we were now at war with Germany. Then, coming over the wireless, I heard the first air-raid siren since those in Foochow. It seemed a world away and an age ago.

CHAPTER TWO

War – from Hull Docks to Tokyo Bay

1939–45

On promotion to acting sub-lieutenant, all officers normally underwent a series of courses at the naval specialist schools and at the Royal Naval College, Greenwich. This used to take about a year but, because of the war, Greenwich was cancelled, and our training – as well as being much abbreviated – was spent partly in slit trenches as nightly air raid alerts in Portsmouth tore us from our beds. Some of us were appointed to sea, but the majority completed everything in three months flat, including the exams, which, as usual, had a seniority 'carrot' attached. I managed 'five ones', as it was called, and so, subject to getting a watchkeeping certificate, could expect promotion to lieutenant after the minimum 12 months, the maximum being two years.

While most of us were still on course and were together as a term again for the last time, our first to die was killed in command of a small trawler off the east coast, which was attacked by aircraft and sunk. His name was Searles-Wood. Some six Greynviles in all did not survive the war, and of *Birmingham*'s gunroom, just under half were lost. While still on course, I was told that my next appointment would be as sub-lieutenant of *Jupiter*, a new J Class destroyer built by Yarrow, which was commissioned in August 1939. I joined on 3 January 1940, after my last Christmas for a good many years at Castle Hill. My captain was a very experienced destroyer officer, Derek Wyburd, and I joined the ship at Hull. As regular officers, we had the captain, first lieutenant, engineer officer, 2nd lieutenant, sub-lieutenant (myself) and a gunner. We also had two RNVR sub-lieutenants, under training to begin with, and an RNVR doctor.

The 'sub' of a destroyer in those days helped the captain with the navigation and maintained the charts, light lists, and lists of radio signals. In addition to corrections from Notices to Mariners notifying wrecks, changes in buoys, lights, beacons and so on, a most arduous task off the east coast, where we were operating, was plotting the minefields and the channels through them when swept. The mine campaign was in full swing, and 'Q' messages came by the sackful from the Admiralty, telling us where all these various hazards were thought to be. Every chart then had to be plotted with this information, since you could not know whether or not you were going to need it at short notice. It was long and hard work. Charts would become soaked with sea water and would need replacing, but new ones drawn from the Chart Depot would have none of the temporary data on them. I was also in charge of the signals department and responsible for the confidential books. Time in harbour was short and usually spent on 'corrections' in the little chart house. Coloured pencils were essential to keep charts comprehensible. Only Coloroll pencil could be erased, and these were not naval stores, so all my friends and I dipped into our own pockets as part of our war work. (I have cast a critical eye on naval stores ever since.)

Wyburd had studied Russian in Tallinn, knew Uncle Corney and although rather forbidding, he was a very good captain indeed. My first hurdle was to obtain a Watchkeeping Certificate, which would allow me to take charge of the ship at sea on my own, and next to get a Certificate of Competency as in all respects fit to be a lieutenant. We had no radar in destroyers in those days, and a sharp look-out on the bridge, especially at night, was essential, so we normally ran two officers of the watch. Wyburd made me stand watch with Mr Jones, the gunner, who already had a Watchkeeping Certificate. He told both the gunner and me that I was to be in charge of the watch. Somewhat to my surprise, Jones was thankful to be relieved of that responsibility by me. I thought it odd at the time but I understand his point of view better now, for then there was a great gap – not only social – between the aspiring cadet entry and those who, to their credit, had been promoted from the lower deck and so had fulfilled every reasonable ambition.

We were in and out of Immingham a great deal, on patrol up and down our own coast and occasionally over towards that of Holland. We were also a regular escort of convoys of coastal shipping from the Norfolk coast off Orford Ness to Flamborough Head. The threats were from aircraft, E-boats, the odd submarine and, above all, from the ever-present mine. The convoys, in the main, had to keep in single file through the swept channels and could never move in a mass of columns as could the ocean convoys. The ships' masters were unaccustomed to travelling in close company, and station-keeping was often appalling. There were channel buoys, lighthouses and light vessels, but the latter two would be inactive until switched on at pre-arranged times to help our ships as they passed. We were as much shepherd as defender, and at night and in foul weather the risk of collision was high. It was very good training in acquiring a seaman's eye.

I remember well being in charge of the watch on a northbound leg and failing to sight the East Dudgeon light vessel. It should have been lit, as we were not late. I slowed, looked around, spotted a buoy flashing very faintly, took the ship up to it, put a signalling projector onto it and read 'Wreck'. I called the captain by his emergency bell. 'Really, Ashmore,' Wyburd said, 'You must not do this kind of thing.' (We heard later from the BBC that the East Dudgeon light vessel had only recently been sunk, and the buoy had been laid to mark the spot.)

E-Boat attacks tended to occur further south off the Norfolk coast, but rather ineffective air attacks were frequent. We had a system of 'Help' messages to the sector operations centres of the RAF but seldom, if ever, were able to give them the warning they needed to intervene in time. Fighter patrols, which would have been effective, were quite beyond their resources.

The Royal Navy was losing a destroyer a week at this time from one form of enemy action or another. *Jupiter* and others were often ordered suddenly to Scapa if the Home Fleet needed more Fleet destroyers, and we were in and out of that base a good deal. The first time we had to sail at night through the Hoxa Gate (the main gate from the Flow for the big ships), I got lost and had to tell the captain so. This was a great humiliation, as he knew the way and took over at once. My mistake had been that there were strong lights switched on for ten minutes for our passage which were some distance off and which I confused with others much closer, so getting into a total muddle. Had the land not been so low-lying I would have been less bewildered. Another lesson learnt, of course, and another mark to the captain!

Jupiter was pretty uncomfortable in a rough sea, as any destroyer is bound to be. She washed down heavily forward and over the bridge. The officers' cabins were all aft, yet we had to sleep forward at sea unless in a very relaxed state of readiness. We ate aft, and coming forward in a high sea at night was difficult and dangerous. The ten torpedo tubes would be swung outboard at readiness, and men had either to climb over them or skirt them outboard along the iron deck, holding on to a man rope. If the timing was wrong there was real danger of being swept overboard, and we did lose people that way. Later, a long catwalk overall was added to the ship. This, with the splinter mats and plating fitted to protect bridge personnel, and ready use ammunition created a top-weight problem, adversely affecting stability.

The worst weather we encountered was on Norwegian convoy escort duties. We would be at defence stations in two watches, watch on, watch off, for the ten days or more required to take one convoy across the North Sea and bring the return convoy home. There was a constant threat of air attack, and in daylight hours one's head was seldom down for long. As navigator, I found it additionally troublesome because we had to plough through this heavy weather at the speed of the merchant ships, maybe 8 knots, and a tremendous amount of drifting would occur. You always hoped that you wouldn't miss the UK altogether on return.

Once the Norwegian Campaign began, following the German invasion, we were shifted to Fleet duties and *Jupiter* was on the screen of destroyers ahead of *Rodney* when the Commander-in-Chief, Admiral Sir Charles Forbes (unkindly known as 'Wrong Way Charlie') was again trying to find the German Fleet, which was ahead, far to the north. When the Luftwaffe came in to attack us we found that *Jupiter*'s 4.7-in guns, which could not elevate above 45°, were useless in the anti-aircraft role. As the Fleet steamed south under continuous air attack to cover a cruiser bombardment of Stavanger airfield I remember seeing a bomb from a Heinkel hit *Rodney* two miles astern of us and a great plume of black smoke rise up. I learned later that it had exploded in the gunroom flat I knew so well and had killed some of the midshipmen. Other destroyers then relieved us to go back to Scapa to refuel. (Fuelling at sea had not yet been mastered by the Royal Navy, although some exciting experiments, in which one laid back on a spring and invariably hit the oiler, were in progress.)

One evening in Gutter Sound, Dannreuther, 'sub' of *Cossack*, asked me over. She had recently distinguished herself in the *Altmark* incident, but the reason their tails were up that night was that their brilliant tyrant, Captain Philip Vian, was leaving in the morning. It was interesting to see his terrifying eyebrows for the first time when he joined us for a drink, bestriding the club fender in the wardroom as if he owned the place (which, in effect, he did).

After the second battle of Narvik, *Jupiter* went north up Vestfjord into a deep, well-sheltered and hidden anchorage called Sjell Fjord (known locally by then as 'Cripples Creek'). In it, alongside a German merchant ship prize, lay *Eskimo* with her bows blown off and several other destroyers which had been damaged in one battle or the other. We were troubled by the odd air raid, but the fjord was so steep-sided that there was no chance of a reasonable sortie on the ships within it. An oiler was anchored there, and was our base for the days of patrolling until the time came to go home after Hitler had attacked the Low Countries and the decision was taken to evacuate our forces from Narvik. We accordingly sailed with some merchant ships towards the end of May. It was still cold, and we kept to the northern edge of Vestfjord through the Lofoten Islands. I asked the captain to take us northabout through a channel called the Maelstrom, rather wanting to see what it was like. Half-way through, we were beset by a violent snow flurry, and lost all visibility. There was a very strong current running, but we came through without any real trouble, relieved and curiosity satisfied. We escorted our charges to the Clyde and then went into Gourock for a boiler clean lasting some five days.

Father had returned home, having been taken extremely ill soon after the war began, and only thanks to Mousse's determined efforts to get him proper treatment in the civilian hospital on the Peak, for which she had to obtain permission from the Commander-in-Chief himself, did he survive. However, he had recovered sufficiently for shore service and joined Admiral Ramsay's headquarters in Dover Castle for OPERATION DYNAMO. After three days he was carried out in great pain with feet so swollen that his shoes had to be cut off him. All he could say to my mother was, 'Thank God Edward's ship is boiler cleaning.' Peter was ashore at the time, *Dorsetshire* having come home.

Of those of our flotilla at Dunkirk, one was sunk and another badly damaged. I had a brief spell at Bletchingly, and saw Father and Peter for a short time, the first time we had all been together with Mousse since before the war in Wei-Hai-Wei. Peter had been appointed as sub-lieutenant of *Kipling*, a ship very like my own, having achieved his five first-class certificates.

Jupiter's boiler cleaning had been extended because of the complaint known as 'condenseritis' in both boilers, but by the end of June 1940 we were back in service and, finding that the Home Fleet had moved from Scapa to Rosyth, joined them there. So many destroyers had been sunk by now that the Js and Ks were amalgamated into one flotilla, the 5th, under Captain Lord Louis Mountbatten (who was not an experienced destroyer officer, although, of course, distinguished in other respects). Philip Mack, our splendid Captain of the 7th Flotilla, was eventually to be promoted and killed as a rear-admiral, and we were very sad to see him go. 'Dickie' Mountbatten was full of theories, and had us change our camouflage paint to the colour used on the hulls of Union Castle liners, which he had found difficult to see in the dark. It was known as 'Mountbatten pink' thereafter, but no other flotilla followed suit. The threat of invasion and air raids was ever-present and the flotilla was moved down to Immingham again to operate on patrol out of the Humber.

One of the principal activities of naval light forces at this time was the laying of mine barriers off the east coast of Britain, and also as close as we could get them off the coasts of Europe. Destroyers were involved both in laying mines and in covering minelayers. Because the *Kelly*, which was Mountbatten's ship, was (not for the first time) out of action, 'Dickie' embarked in *Jupiter* to command a covering force off the Dutch coast at the end of August. The minelaying force hit trouble. *Esk* and another ship were sunk, and *Express* had her stern blown off. We moved in to close and in the early hours took *Express* in tow and towed her stern first back to the Humber. Her captain had been killed and she was conned by the second-in-command, standing on the after conning platform, although there was little enough he could do, poor chap. I remember this because it was the only time I was on the bridge in an operational situation with Mountbatten and some of his staff: Signal Officer Dunsterville, who became a good friend of mine, and Navigator Butler-Bowden, for whom I also formed a great respect.

'Dickie' sat in the captain's chair for very nearly 24 hours, staying awake most of the time, and I thought he did well – as indeed did Wyburd, to whom the handling of *Jupiter*, picking up tow and such tasks were delegated. If I had any inner comment, it was perhaps that Mountbatten's persistence was a little excessive, that my captain could have done with time in his own chair for a spell, and that Mountbatten's constant presence on the bridge was not strictly necessary. Now, perhaps, I understand rather better how he felt.

By that time Mountbatten had a reputation among the sailors for being unlucky. They attributed it, so the story ran, to his black medal ribbon, the Order of St John of Jerusalem. Certainly, there seemed to be trouble when he was around, if not for *Kelly* then for whichever ship he happened to honour with his presence. But one could not help admiring and liking his tremendous enthusiasm. He used to hold a war game from time to time for ranks such as sub-lieutenants in his cabin in *Kelly*, and was never slow to give advice, which we appreciated. We were all exercised on 'The Mountbatten Station Keeping Device' and had to use it, though I don't think we found it helped a great deal. It certainly wasn't conducive to fuel economy and if used badly to recover station would strip the brickwork off your boiler quicker than anything because of the acceleration demanded to restore the indicator needle smartly to the central 'in station' position.

Soon after the incident with *Express*, the whole flotilla of eight destroyers, which had again briefly joined the Fleet at Rosyth, was ordered south through the Thames Estuary to Plymouth, the invasion scare having intensified and the decision having been taken to reinforce the West Country.

We were told, I think, to proceed 'with moderate despatch', and went overnight through the searched channels, across the Thames Estuary and down to our destination. I was still navigating *Jupiter*, and I have never known such a hair-raising passage. Mountbatten took his ships, 1½ cables (300 yards) apart, in what was then known as 'close order', at 28 knots all the way. Destroyers were like gold dust at that time, and in my judgement then, as well as since, it was a highly irresponsible action. Wyburd, of course, never left the bridge, nor did I, my head forever in the chart table calling out the buoys as we approached and the various course changes. Wyburd kept his night sight adapted to enable him to watch everything and avert the imminent hazards of collision and grounding. Although we were following 'Dickie', who expected the kind of station-keeping intended for a torpedo attack, not an inshore passage, ship safety remains the individual captain's responsibility. 'Dickie' and Butler-Bowden pulled it off, and all went well, so perhaps one could claim it as an achievement by the flotilla as a whole.

Towards the end of September it was decided that it would be worth bombarding the invasion craft that were reckoned to be accumulating in the port of Cherbourg behind its big breakwater, and we set off with *Revenge*, an available battleship, and seven of us destroyers. *Revenge* stood some way out with her 15-in guns, and we closed in to the breakwater and fired fairly rapidly for, I suppose, five minutes or so, then retiring on *Revenge*. It was only as she finished her bombardment and we were setting quietly off towards England again that the enemy shore batteries opened up. None of us was hit, but it was an extraordinary sensation as enormous plumes of water appeared among us and there was nothing whatever to be done about them.

Not long after that, we set off again for the French coast because there had been some German destroyers patrolling which we were to find and sink. We had with us two E Class cruisers (which I had last seen in the East Indies Station pre-war livery of white with yellow topsides), *Emerald* and *Enterprise*. In the chase that ensued, they showed our brand new destroyers a clean pair of heels. However, we did not bring the German destroyers to close action, and the operation is memorable to me for two things. The first is that we were under air attack by Heinkels to begin with, and then by RAF Blenheims, at which, at length, we had to open fire. Fortunately, some Messerschmitts then appeared and put an end to a rather embarrassing situation. Secondly, there were French fishing boats in the area, and 'Dickie' thought that some of them must know something and might indeed have warned off the Germans. *Jupiter* was ordered to board one, so I, as boarding officer, was sent away in a seaboat. I felt fairly confident in French, but not about my reception, and climbed over the guard-rails of the fishing trawler with my revolver at the ready. I was met by the captain, and was treated to a furious tirade. Never, never in his life did he ever expect to have a pistol aimed at him by a British officer. He had fought in the last war, he hated the Boche, and so on – with me feeling smaller and smaller. However, I explained what I was about and that I had to search his ship, and he agreed with a reasonably good grace.

At the end of it all I thought he was clean, and so informed Wyburd.

Nevertheless, I was ordered to bring her into Plymouth, which, with the reluctant acquiescence of the skipper, I proceeded to do. I think our intelligence people wanted to have a good look at him and a good talk with him and his crew, but I had a frightful conscience about it and after I had rejoined *Jupiter* in port, I decided to find out what was going to happen. It transpired that the Frenchman was to be released and allowed to go home, and the next morning I went on board to see how they were and, I hoped, patched things up a little.

Derek Wyburd left us for another command on 21 October 1940 and was relieved by Lieutenant-Commander 'Pug' Thew, so that we then became message boy of the flotilla, even though 'Pug' was an extremely experienced, well-known destroyer officer, and renowned as a great 'player' or party man. Leaving harbour after a lunchtime 'session' was sometimes an adventure. About this time the 2nd lieutenant left us for a command and I replaced him, although I do not recollect my special duties changing and was still navigator, torpedo control officer and signal officer of the ship.

Towards the end of November, five of the flotilla were on a unusual patrol off the English coast with 'Dickie' in *Javelin* (because *Kelly* was, for some reason, again out of action). It was a clear, calm night, and we all saw gun flashes well to the east of us when off the Lizard. 'Dickie', of course, wheeled at once and charged off at high speed in the direction of the flashes. We then heard from shore that there were merchant ships being shelled off the Eddystone by German destroyers, and proceeded to intercept.

We crashed along in close order in the direction of the enemy, keeping between them and the French coast, but instead of leading us round, 'Dickie' turned us and put us into quarter-line on practically the opposite course to intercept. Unfortunately (as happened sometimes), not everybody received the succession of urgent, complex signals, and the second division failed to turn with the first. Therefore, close astern of *Javelin*, with her on our port bow because we were in line of bearing, we became separated from *Jackal* and *Kashmir*.

We bore down on the enemy, using star shells and searchlights to illuminate, and seemed to be very close; I could hear shells going overhead as we opened fire. I asked the captain if I could fire torpedoes. We used to have a broadside of ten in two sets of tubes, but only a few weeks earlier the after tubes had been removed to put in a 4 in star shell gun, so I only had five torpedoes, but it seemed worth firing. Thew hesitated and then agreed and swung the ship to port as I fired, aiming at the second German destroyer using a 'fast fixed-sight' setting, hoping in this way to have the best average chance with the small salvo. As I pulled up my last firing lever and heard the torpedo whoosh out, I saw the enemy turning away and so had no great expectations. About 30 seconds later there was the most enormous explosion just on our starboard bow, and an RAF officer from Coastal Command, Domville by name, who was aboard 'for the trip', threw his arms round me and said, 'Was that the enemy?', to which I had to say, 'No, it's Captain "D".' The Germans had fired just before *Jupiter*, and my shots had all missed ahead, but I sometimes think that the turn away to bring the tubes to bear might have spared us from being hit too.

By this time *Jackal* and her consort were coming up through the smoke and we could see them. Thew, who was brand new to the flotilla and junior, decided to reduce speed to let *Jackal* overhaul. *Javelin*, of course, was dead in the water and well astern by now. We heard later that *Jackal*, thinking it was *Jupiter* that had been torpedoed and that 'Dickie' had reduced speed, followed suit, and there was a delay which let the Germans get ahead before things were sorted out. We were still within range and shooting but though we chased them unrelentingly all night, they drew away and we lost them near the French coast. We returned after dawn under heavy air attack to find *Javelin* stopped but upright, with nothing forward of B gun and nothing aft of X. She had been hit by two torpedoes, but retained buoyancy and stability in what seemed a miraculous fashion. We escorted *Javelin* under tow safely into harbour, being attacked heavily from the air. Eventually, after a long refit in the south yard at Devonport, she returned to service.

There has been controversy over this inglorious action ever since. We had a *Daily Mirror* cameraman on board *Jupiter*, and from his photographs we were able to estimate the distance apart of ships when we were in close action – it was hundreds of yards, not thousands: 600, I believe. I was happy to be unscathed, but felt that 'my DSC' had gone west with the torpedo miss.

We continued operating in and out of Plymouth for the next few months. The most memorable events were the concentrated mass air attacks. When they began we were at a wardroom thrash in the Royal Hotel. After the sirens had been followed by several bombs, we decided we had better make our way back to the ship and did this independently to minimise casualties. In those days sacks of sand were stationed handily around the streets and I put out four incendiary bombs myself on the way back to the ship, putting sacks on top of them as they lay alongside houses – also being narrowly missed by one flung out of an upstairs window by some vigilant householder. There were casualties outside the main gate of the dockyard, but they were being looked after, and I hurried back on board to action stations. On that night or the next, the Royal Hotel was totally destroyed, as was most of the centre of the city.

The attacks took place at night, mainly fire-bombing, and at action stations in harbour, special parties were detailed off to assist in fire-fighting and salvage ashore in the dockyard. I remember lying on the fo'c'sle in my tin hat with my party, comforted by the fact that we had some rather convenient splinterproof plating round the bottom of the guard rails (not to protect us, but to protect the ready-use ammunition for the guns), and looking up to see Rame Head at the western entrance to the harbour covered with glittering points of light. Several aircraft must have unloaded their entire cargo of incendiary bombs in quite the wrong place. However, enough bombs of various kinds landed near us to give us plenty to do, and a couple of our sailors who had been too lazy to get out of their hammocks and lie on the deck received splinter wounds from fragments passing through the ship's side.

The invasion scare had receded after the Battle of Britain, and for a change we were put on convoy duty in the Atlantic for a while. Fleet destroyers were not specially suitable as escorts, being short-legged as well as less efficient anti-submarine craft than the purpose-built corvettes and converted escort destroyers.

To our delight, in February 1941 we were detached to join Force H under Admiral Somerville in Gibraltar, and I was able, for the first time in all my visits there, to go ashore. We were there to provide additional light forces to escort Force H for the bombardment of Genoa, and this we duly did. When the heavy ships went in, we laid off and found some islands to bombard rather more quietly on our own. There was also a submarine scare. However, it was comforting to be in warmer waters should anything go wrong and the customary air attacks did not appear in daylight. This interlude over, we returned home. About that time, *Scharnhorst* and *Gneisenau* took shelter in Brest. The flotilla was therefore kept based in the West Country, and we patrolled pretty constantly, ready to intercept should they come out.

By now we had our first radar fitted. The little set told you the range of anything, providing it was more or less ahead. It was an ex-aircraft air-to-surface vessel search equipment that had been replaced by something rather better in the air. It could not give a range accurate enough for gunfire, but we found it helpful and vastly interesting. In May 1941 I remember, vividly, deciphering the *Prince of Wales*'s signal, 'Hood sunk', and following the operations which destroyed the *Bismarck*, which we were unfit to join, for *Jupiter*'s boilers were still giving trouble. When the rest of the flotilla sailed for the Mediterranean, including Peter's ship, *Kipling*, we were sadly left behind.

On 16 June 1941 my time in *Jupiter* was up, and I said goodbye to my friends on board. (She was to be lost eight months later in the Battle of the Java Sea, and some of my friends went down with her. Thew was captured by the Japanese. 'Pug's' qualities of leadership were, by all accounts, outstanding during his purgatory as a prisoner of war.) I reported to the Admiralty, where I was told that I was being appointed as the senior executive officer at a Hunt Class destroyer, *Tetcott* (then building at Samuel White's yard at Cowes in the Isle of Wight), and that I was to be First Lieutenant when she was commissioned in about four months' time. After a short spell of leave, I went to Cowes and put up in great comfort in the Gloucester Hotel as almost the only guest. Practically my first duty was to attend the launching of the ship. It seemed perfectly clear to me that there was no hope of her being ready on schedule and that I was going to be away from the war for rather a long time. I therefore went back to the Admiralty and asked to be transferred to a ship that had been building longer and was more likely to get to sea quickly.

They saw my point, and sent me to *Middleton*, building at Walker-on-Tyne and due to complete by the middle of November. Father had a great friend, Matthew Slattery, who was standing by *Cleopatra*, an anti-aircraft cruiser building at Hawthorn Leslie's, as her captain, and he introduced me to the Northern Counties' Club, which was kind enough to give me a room and make me an honorary member.

Every day I went to the ship by tram, to work in a small office at the dockside. There was a great deal of work to be done. *Middleton*'s construction was not as advanced as all that, and the practice then for siting life rafts, hawser reels, furniture, and so on, was to walk round with the foreman of the ship with a piece of chalk and mark exactly where you would like the various fittings sited; up top, in the mess decks, in the officers' cabins, even the location of the chart-table on the bridge. You also had a decisive voice in more momentous matters in which your practical knowledge of seamanship in destroyers could be of use. As the time for commissioning the ship approached, I heard that my captain was to be David Kinloch, who had been a Term Officer at Dartmouth when I had been a cadet there and was a fairly senior lieutenant-commander. I knew him to be an extremely kind and pleasant person. Senior ratings and advance parties then started to arrive, and I began to hear who our ship's company were to be.

As Senior Executive Officer, I had to write the ship's orders, which covered virtually every activity, evolution and eventuality, and had to draw up the 'Watch and Quarter Bill', giving people their duties, special duties, action stations, and so forth, indicating which mess they were to be in and making sure that everything formed a consistent pattern. To my delight, who should turn up as chief boatswain's mate but Crockford, my old friend from *Birmingham*, and we got on famously together. The ship was being 'tropicalised', which took time, and then, suddenly, about the beginning of December, the powers that be decided to 'arcticise' her. In the end, though I could hardly credit it, *Tetcott* got to sea before *Middleton*. However, it is an ill wind that blows no good, and the wind blew very well for me at this time.

Father was working at the Admiralty, still not fit for sea service, but getting better all the time, and he and Mother had a small flat in Little St James's Street in London, where I used to go down for fairly frequent weekends, mostly standing in the corridors of crowded trains. Mousse was working on comforts of various descriptions in Eaton Square with some other naval ladies. Among them was Lady Sturdee, who was an old friend from the Saltash days. Sturdee was a retired rear-admiral, son of the victor of the Falklands Battle, and working in the Censorship Department in a senior post. Their daughter, Elizabeth, was a Wren in London, at Flag Officer Submarines HQ. We were introduced, hit it off very well, and we used to go out a lot together. Father and Mother were looking for a house in the country, and sometimes, when petrol allowed, Elizabeth and I would go out in the car with them on these expeditions. We were with them when they found the house they decided to buy at Godden Green, near Sevenoaks in Kent. We were also able to join them for the first weekend they had together in it, in December 1941.

Father was fit for sea again by then, and had been appointed to command the battleship *Barham* in the Mediterranean. As he was about to leave to join her, she was torpedoed and sank with heavy loss of life. He was next appointed to *Valiant*, and this gave him a little more time at home than they expected. Elizabeth had shifted her job to Wren HQ, also in London, where she worked in the Officers' Appointments Department and came to know a great many people.

In Newcastle, the great day of commissioning *Middleton* was approaching, and our evenings out in London, which were such fun, had come to an end.

I was in the directors' dining room at Walker-on-Tyne when the shocking news came on the BBC that *Prince of Wales* and *Repulse* had been sunk; *Jupiter*, on their screen, had survived. *Prince of Wales* had been built at the yard, and I was surrounded by those who had built her. Their concern and distress was plain to see, and brought home to me their sense of commitment.

I could not get away from the north for Christmas because of pressure of work, and commissioning took place on 31 December 1941. Commissioning day was fraught with significance for the First Lieutenant, because it was everyone's first impression and first chance to see if anything was going to work at all. The acid test to the sailor was supposed to be the quality and temperature of the food the cooks brought to each mess for the first meal on board. A tremendous number of young sailors were 'hostilities only' men (HOs, as we called them). I was just 22, and the average age of the ship's company was probably under 20. Our main armament was six 4-in guns in three mountings, which made the organisation of the seamen comparatively easy. You could run them in three watches – red, white and blue – for cruising, which meant that you always had a twin-mounting closed up, usually the forward mounting; or in two watches – port and starboard – for defence watches, when you could have three mountings closed up, one gun manned at each. We had a complement of about 180, and apart from the captain and myself, Sub-Lt. Catchpole as navigator, the warrant engineer and the gunner, the other officers were RNVR, two sub-lieutenants and a doctor. One 'sub', Berryman, who was appointed as the gunnery control officer, had a Watchkeeping Certificate and had done a Gunnery Control Officer's (GCO's) course. Until Thornton, the other, got his certificate, I had to stand my watch as well as being second-in-command and gunnery officer of the ship. I normally kept the last dog and the morning. As *Middleton* was a wartime design, the officers' cabins were forward, near the bridge, unlike those in the *Jupiter*, and this was a great blessing. We carried depth-charges and Asdic, and had much improved radar, including one with a modest anti-aircraft capability.

Father had talked to me in the most helpful way when I was going through the throes of preparing the Ship's Orders and wondering what particular line one might take, and he was full of all sorts of advice and hints. I chiefly remember his views on the treatment of petty officers. The social gulf in those days was very great, and Father had devised, and tried in *Kent*, various ways of narrowing it for those who played so crucial a part in the discipline and efficiency of a ship. Accordingly, soon after commissioning, I obtained the captain's permission to fall in the petty officers specially and separately from everybody else, and introduce each one of them by name to Kinloch, who shook hands with them. Father had done this in *Kent*, and in the bigger ship, where it was possible, he always provided a separate brow when alongside for the petty officers' sole use. I could not do that, but I did what little I could to provide and emphasise their privileges, and I believe it had a very great effect and helped us all in the hard times that lay ahead.

We left the Tyne in mid-January and went up the searched channels to Scapa to work up under the Rear-Admiral Destroyers, Admiral Hamilton, who was an old friend of Father's. A destroyer 'work up' was strenuous anyway, but in winter weather it was brutally hard work, and I remember having awful trouble and failing to satisfy the Rear-Admiral Destroyers' gunnery staff with my attempts at analysis of our various firings. In the early weeks of the commission I was also fo'c'sle officer, which was a cold and often wet job.

Gradually, everything shook down into place, enormously helped by our very experienced and wise captain. We had a good anti-aircraft capability for those days. Thornton proved a sound anti-submarine warfare control officer, with a good ear for the noises coming out of the Asdic, but the other 'sub' had so much difficulty with the gunnery control officer's duties in the director that the captain eventually told me that I must take that on myself. The ship's full speed was 27 knots, which was only just enough to keep up with the Fleet in reasonable weather, but we often seemed to be detailed off for Fleet escort duties, and I later discovered this was because there was a flotilla of Fleet destroyers known as the 'M Class', consisting of *Marne*, *Matchless* and others, and that because our name began with an 'M', the Fleet staff became somewhat confused about our performance.

When the time came for Admiral Hamilton to be relieved by Admiral Burnett, who was commanding the minelayers then operating out of Loch Ewe, we were sent down to pick up his personal gear and bring it to Scapa. This we did in absolutely filthy weather, in the course of which what I suspect was a treasured possession of his, a kind of wall map of his term showing how well or badly they had all done, with him at its top, got badly damaged by sea water. He was a bluff, tough, rather red-faced man, who had delivered a 'blood and thunder' speech to our ship's company when he had visited us on taking command of the destroyers. This had not gone down well. No ship's company appreciates an admiral who seems to want to see the scuppers running with their blood. However, there was nothing for it but for me to go and call on the great man myself and apologise for the damage to his chart. I remember my trepidation when the Flag Lieutenant showed me in, and I remember too how very understanding, generous and kind was Bob Burnett, although he was not naturally a patient man.

Apart from containment of the surface units of the German Fleet and their armed merchant cruisers, the main job of the British Fleet in home waters at this time was covering the Atlantic convoys and those to North Russia. Convoys would assemble to the south with a local escort, often provided from the Western Approaches Command. A Fleet detachment would provide an ocean escort for the Russian convoys, probably led by a cruiser, but otherwise consisting of destroyers, frigates and corvettes. The Battle Fleet would provide a covering force to the north and east. *Middleton*, in her role of masquerading as a Fleet destroyer, would often find herself on the screen of this covering force, which involved refuelling, usually at Seidisfjord in Iceland. Sometimes other destroyers would then take on, and we would wait at Seidisfjord to take over from them as the Fleet returned towards Scapa. There was not much for us to do ashore except walk to the post office, which was a good way up the fjord, exchange smiles with the pretty Icelandic girl in it and walk back towards the ship again.

I remember one dreadful occasion on the bridge in the middle watch when the destroyer screen ahead of *King George V* was being moved round because the force was about to change course. *Punjabi*, to starboard of us on the screen, missed a signal or miscalculated her manoeuvre and the *King George V* struck her. As she sank, her depth charges blew up under the bow of the battleship, killing most of the destroyer's ship's company. *King George V* remained seaworthy but in Seidisfjord two days later, her bow displayed a row of jagged serrations horrible to see.

Once back at Scapa, we would first go alongside the oiler to fuel and pick up fresh provisions and mail, and then, if we were not to go out again at once, to a buoy in Gutter Sound unless bad weather compelled us to anchor in the Flow. Then it was a question of anchor watch at ten minutes' notice for steam, as the ship dragged until there was no more room, when she would weigh, move up to the windward side of the Flow, anchor again and repeat the process.

Sea service in these northern waters in winter was arduous in the extreme for the men. Destroyers tried to keep the armament in operation with steam jets, but the steam frequently removed the heavy grease and froze, so there was no substitute for moving all essential exposed machinery through its limits every fifteen minutes or so. A gun's crew – their sheepskin coats and gloves, their balaclavas, and often their beards, caked with ice – had to be closed up, and often could find little shelter. Decks and guard rails had to be kept clear of ice in the interests of stability, and the ship would alter course to stop washing down and to allow this to be done, only to see the ice accumulate again on resuming course into sea. Fog, in the guise of Arctic sea smoke, was a particular hazard, since masts often showed above it, attracting air attack. Below, the mess decks were damp and rank with drying garments, and hammocks could not be aired. Our light plating frequently developed deckhead leaks to add to the discomfort. Tuberculosis was a real hazard to exhausted, very young, often seasick men. Their spirit was amazing.

Elizabeth and I were writing to each other, and she had just been given a marvellous appointment: to go, with two more senior officers, to set up the Royal Canadian Wrens. This was in February, and in May Father went off by air to join *Valiant* at Durban. When refuelling in Khartoum, he heard that Peter's ship, *Kipling* (which had picked up the survivors of *Kelly* and *Kashmir* in March when Peter won his DSC), had been sunk in the Mediterranean with *Jackal* and *Lively*. It was not until he arrived at Durban that he heard that Peter was one of those safely rescued by *Jervis*. One can only imagine what Mousse, with three of us at sea, was going through, and she quickly sent me a telegram to say that Peter was all right.

Father had to commission *Valiant* from the survivors of *Dorsetshire*, *Hermes* and *Cornwall*, all of which had been sunk by the Japanese off Ceylon. The remnants of their ships' companies had expected to be sent home, yet many were now commissioning *Valiant* in Durban for the Eastern Fleet again.

Father met the problem head-on, and fell his ship's company in on the quarter deck with the men facing inboard and the officers and petty officers fallen in in front of him, facing the men. He then talked to them as only he could. He told me that there was one incident, and one rating had to be seized and marched off the quarterdeck, but no action was taken against him thereafter. *Valiant* proved a happy commission, distinguished herself at Salerno (where her bombardment, with *Warspite*, turned the tide ashore), and survived glider bomb attacks to escort the crippled *Warspite*, broadside on through the Straits of Messina, safely back to Malta. In *Valiant*, Father eventually led the surrendered Italian Fleet into the Grand Harbour at Malta.

Back in Scapa, *Middleton* and some others, including our chummy ship, another Hunt Class destroyer, *Blankney*, received very welcome orders to go to Gibraltar and reinforce Force H for a special operation. We conducted a practice firing or two as we left, and the fuse-keeping clock which controlled our anti-aircraft fire became defective. I remember spending most of the passage to Gibraltar sitting in the transmitting station with the ordnance artificer, the electrical artificer and the drawings, trying to make the thing work again. The operation took place in the middle of June 1942 and was an attempt to relieve the blockade of Malta, which had reached critical proportions. Almost simultaneously, Admiral Vian sailed from Alexandria with some 11 merchant ships and a strong covering force (Operation VIGOROUS) and Admiral Curteis (who, as Captain of the Fleet in *Rodney* before the war, we had always known as 'The Old Toad') sailed from Gibraltar with quite a large covering force including *Middleton*, five merchant ships and a tanker (Operation HARPOON). The water was warm and the weather lovely – good for spotting periscopes, but also ideal for air attack.

There came a time when *Eagle* and our covering force had to turn back and we had to go on alone. By then the cruiser *Liverpool* had been seriously damaged, and we had lost one merchant ship. The air attacks from dawn to dusk by Italian torpedo and high-level bombers and German Heinkels and Junkers 88s intensified the nearer we came to Sicily, and they reached a sustained crescendo when the short-range Stukas could reach us. These performed spectacularly, throwing themselves into a high, near-vertical dive straight at their targets, aiming the bomb with the aircraft and pulling out very low.

The close escort consisted of five Fleet destroyers and four Hunt Class destroyers in the charge of an anti-aircraft cruiser, *Cairo*, whose captain, Hardy, had been the Physical Training Officer at Dartmouth. We were thankful that we had embarked as much anti-aircraft ammunition as we could possibly stow before leaving Gibraltar.

We passed through the Cape Bon Channel at night, and were at action stations again before dawn. I was scanning the horizon from the director when I sighted to the north what I thought were two battleships and five destroyers. So we made a signal to *Cairo*, conventional in the circumstances, saying 'Attention is called to such and such a bearing.' Back came the reply 'Aircraft in sight are friendly' (there was Beaufighter with us from Malta), so my captain made an enemy report straight to the Admiralty. This was re-broadcast generally, as was the custom, and Father saw it at his breakfast table and spent an anxious day. Once Hardy appreciated this new threat, he ordered us out in groups, Fleet destroyers, Hunts and *Cairo* separately, directly towards the enemy at full speed to close the range, making smoke to screen the convoy, which was left with some minesweepers as close escort. Our best hope, of course, were the torpedoes in the Fleet destroyers, and as we closed they moved ahead of us, having the legs of the Hunts. Fire was then opened at extreme range by both sides.

Early on, my director layer, who had a grandstand view of the enemy and whose steady hands were vital to effective fire, had had hiccups, which I could hear coming over the intercommunication system, but fortunately, by now, he had calmed down. As we got nearer, it became apparent that the enemy consisted of two Italian cruisers and five large destroyers. At least there were no battleships. *Bedouin* and *Partridge* were hit and stopped, but then, to our great surprise and delight, we saw the Italians turn away. The convoy by now was under heavy air attack by Stukas, against which it had precious little defence. As we moved back to support it, the enemy turned towards us again, and we checked and turned at them. They showed no sign themselves of closing the range, so we rejoined our convoy, which, by then, had suffered severely. *Kentucky*, the tanker, was ablaze and was sunk later by enemy aircraft with another damaged merchantman. Fighter aircraft from Malta eventually joined us, and with two surviving merchantmen, we made for the island.

Early the next morning, the merchant ships led us in. One hit a mine, but made her berth safely with most of her cargo intact. As we destroyers followed, *Badsworth*, astern of *Middleton*, was mined and stopped. Next, the Polish Hunt Class *Kujawiak*, bringing up the rear, hit another and sank. Finally, *Matchless*, our next astern, was mined, but made harbour safely. The captain said 'I'm not going back, No. 1,' to which, I hope encouragingly, I said 'No, Sir.' A series of errors was responsible, and the minesweepers and, gallantly, *Blankney* picked up survivors.

The sun was rising, and I shall never forget Grand Harbour as we entered it that morning. There were people everywhere, cheering and waving from the familiar battlements. The harbour itself was littered with wrecked or damaged ships, *Penelope* the 'pepper pot' among them, and there were few berths vacant. *Middleton* went alongside at Parlatorio, the ammunition jetty. Commanding officers were called to a conference, and we stood down from action stations and tried to get clean and fed. True to form, and very heartwarming, a Maltese dghaisaman came alongside and asked if he could take the officers' laundry. I thanked him very much, but said I did not think we would be there quite long enough for that.

The next excitement was an air-raid warning, and I was getting the ship ready to move - as it did not seem that the ammunition jetty was the right place to sit alongside during an air raid – when to my great relief the captain came back and moved her for us. Those of us fit for sea were to leave at once through a new channel, and unencumbered by the merchant ships, to make a quick passage back to Gibraltar! We had broken the siege, if not raised it.

The return voyage was marked by the interception of *Seawulf*, under Polish command, from whom we embarked some brave men for passage to Gibraltar. Here again we were cheered in, securing in the destroyer pens alongside *Blankney*. Both captains went ashore together, I stayed as duty officer for the two ships. We all had our heads down that afternoon when who should arrive but 'The Old Toad' himself, who put his arm round my shoulder and asked me, as their senior officer, if he could address the ships' companies. So we cleared lower deck and fell them in on the fo'c'sle of *Middleton*, and he congratulated them and thanked them very nicely. I thought him near to tears, and realised how dreadful he must have felt when the covering force had had to turn back and he could only read the signals reporting our trials and tribulations. He told me that the convoy from Alexandria had had to turn back completely. At that time Malta needed a ship a month to keep going. We got in two, and the next convoy, 'Pedestal' in August, relieved the siege.

Because of the state of our fuse-keeping clock (which was even worse than I had thought), we had conducted most of our anti-aircraft firing in barrage fire, a method I had devised and practised using three types of barrage, depending on whether dive-bombers, torpedo bombers or high-level bombers were attacking us. The ship's company were convinced that we had shot down six aircraft, but I think we claimed three. I learnt subsequently that I had been awarded the DSC, and I am glad to say there were several awards for the ship's company. There was leave for each watch and much shopping, after which we sailed back to Scapa Flow.

We arrived in time to join the Fleet covering force for the tragic Russian convoy, PQ 17. Off Iceland, on the Fleet screen, we heard that the convoy ocean escort had been recalled by the Admiralty and the convoy ordered to scatter. Soon the distress signals from the merchant ships, all in plain language, started coming in. This went on over several days as we went slowly back to Scapa, and was heart-rending. Only the local escort of corvettes and armed trawlers had been allowed to stay with the merchant ships, and we were in Scapa when the destroyers of the ocean escort entered harbour, bitter and dismayed. Matters were not helped when all the commanding officers were sent for by Bob Burnett, who in his talk to them said, 'Gentlemen, I want you to know that I never thought you ran away.' Nor had they, they were only obeying orders which they heartily disliked, which went against all their training and every tradition in their book. Until their admiral used those words, it had never entered their heads that anyone might think that they were running away. Kinloch, who knew many of them well, could hardly speak on the subject.

There were now some 1,400 survivors, British and Allied merchant seamen, in North Russia. The Russians could not feed them properly, and accordingly, *Middleton*, *Blankney* and two Fleet destroyers were detailed off to take provisions and stores to North Russia for these people. We were also to take Rear-Admiral Fisher and his small staff, who were going to Polyarnoe to assume the duties of Senior British Naval Officer North Russia. We embarked them in the Clyde and, with them, two couriers from the Soviet Embassy in

London on their way home with large bundles of documents. We went north of Bear Island in order to keep as far as possible out of range of the German shore-based aircraft. They must have been resting on their laurels after the destruction of the convoy because we had a good passage, keeping well east until in sight of Novaya Zemlya before heading for the Kola Inlet.

While the two Fleet destroyers of our group returned to the Orkneys, we two Hunts remained in North Russia to form part of the escort for the next homeward convoy. We anchored at first off Vaenga, below Murmansk. We spent about a week there, getting to know the crew of a Soviet destroyer alongside and her huge 1st Lieutenant Rudakov, and going for walks, avoiding the many sentries. We then moved alongside at Polyarnoe, the main naval base of the Soviet Northern Fleet. Calls were made on Admiral Golovko, the Commander-in-Chief Soviet Northern Fleet, for which I accompanied the captain, the Commander of the Base and various other people. These were mostly conducted in an atmosphere of mutual incomprehension, accompanied by glasses of tea without milk. Rear-Admiral Fisher was meanwhile establishing himself ashore and trying to find some kind of decent quarters in which to exist. However, the ship's liaison went quite well and we were offered a Northern Fleet concert party on board *Middleton*. Everybody foregathered in the main seamen's mess deck forward, which was pretty crowded as a result, and the captain and I sat in front. The concert party came on board and proceeded to perform in the cramped space available. It was all a great success.

After about ten days at Polyarnoe, three short visits to Archangel and an abortive submarine hunt in the Kara Sea, we were told that we were to move base to Archangel, where the ships that had survived convoy PQ 17 were mostly berthed. The survivors were now provisioned and under the eye of Admiral Fisher, and could be assumed to be all right. They were to be shipped to Archangel rather nearer the time of departure of QP 14, the next home-bound convoy.

So, under the command of our senior officer in *Blankney*, Commander Powlett, we departed for the White Sea. On passage, near somewhere with the unforgettable name of Cape Orloff Terski Tonki, we became aware of activity inshore and went to action stations. There is little real darkness in early August in those high latitudes, and we discerned four or five destroyers, large ones, inshore of us, doubtless laying mines which German destroyers often carried on rails aft. Powlett, thank God, decided that our duty was to press on to Archangel to provide part of the escort for QP 14, and we passed by on the other side. In the surprise attack open to us, we could no doubt have exacted a heavy price for our own destruction, although that would certainly have been part of the outcome. Years later, Powlett told me how much this prudent decision weighed on his conscience, but I am sure that he was right and desperate measures were not called for in the East Barents Sea at that particular time.

We went through the entrance to the White Sea in daylight, entered the Dvina in good order and came to anchor opposite the town, where the river was broad and relatively empty of ships. The problem now was twofold:

first, to keep the sailors happy, and second, to keep them fed (which is, of course, part of the same struggle). The First Lieutenant was also ship's victualling officer. We were already baking our own bread, I having made the first batch to give the supply petty officer confidence which he lacked, certainly before he had his daily tot, after which he was sleepy. The Russians had remarkably little except fresh reindeer meat. The British sailor is not accustomed to reindeer but it was the only meat available and I had to conserve our tinned stocks. The wardroom officers set an example. The result was that the ship's company were adequately fed, if not entirely to their taste, and thanks to our stock of dehydrated vegetables, we had far fewer boils and skin complaints than *Blankney*'s company suffered.

Shore leave was difficult. There was nothing to buy in the shops, the restaurants were few and far between, and everything was very expensive. According to the official rate of exchange, we could get 20 roubles to the pound, but any local would proffer 60 roubles for a twopenny bar of nutty milk chocolate. Trading illegally could get one into dreadful trouble, however, and all the sailors were warned against it.

I had been pondering my future all this time, with Elizabeth in Canada, and eventually decided that there was no time like the present. I went ashore to the post office and sent a telegram to her in Ottawa, asking her if she would consider marrying me. Having taken that decision made the rest of the spell in Archangel rather easier.

Meanwhile, we were kept informed of the massive preparations for PQ 18, the next Russian convoy, which everyone was determined should not suffer the fate of its predecessor. QP 14's sailing was delayed until the Russia-bound convoy's escort could support us in the Barents Sea. There were German surface ships at Narvik, a pocket battleship and two cruisers at least, so we expected no picnic and felt rather out of training, having sat in harbour for so long with no practice facilities. We left Archangel, without regret, on 13 September, with our long line of 15 merchant ships, minesweepers, corvettes and trawlers filing down the Dvina to the open sea. Some days later we met up with Admiral Burnett and his cruiser and destroyer force. They had an escort carrier, *Avenger*, with them, whose aircraft had performed well against mass German torpedo attacks. Fortunately, the weather changed and was now thick, restricting enemy air operations. But on skirting Spitzbergen, steering north towards the ice edge, the sun shone for us and the high crags still covered with snow made a beautiful sight.

Then the submarines found us, and three of our merchant ships were sunk very quickly, all of them survivors of PQ 17. Earlier, we had lost a minesweeper and, as we were nearing Iceland, *Somali* was torpedoed. Though taken in tow by another destroyer, she sank later in heavy weather and poor Catchpole, who had been 'sub' of *Jupiter* when I took over from Keddie, was lost. Even in August, no one could last long in those northern waters.

The rest of us came home safely and there was mail for *Middleton* in the oiler at Scapa. There was no word from Elizabeth, but a very nice letter from her mother saying how delighted she was to hear the news, so I assumed things would be all right, although we were not going to be allowed to make any announcement until we had met each other again. This would depend first on how and when Elizabeth could get back to England from Canada, and secondly on when *Middleton* would have a suitable boiler-cleaning period.

I think none of *Middleton*'s crew ever wanted to see North Russia again, but I was quite pleased that our provisions and so forth had held out so well, and that although I'd had to embark rum on passage from one of the oilers, we had not actually had to broach it. I gathered *Blankney* had broached her cask and found it was Army rum and not a patch on the real stuff, so my sailors felt one up. In the conditions in which the men were living and working in those ships in those days, with a high incidence of tuberculosis, the daily tonic provided by the spirit ration was undoubtedly beneficial. There were few entitled who did not draw it, and those who did consumed their own tot, I am sure. Things were to change in the post-war Navy.

Soon after our arrival in Scapa, David Kinloch left us for *Obedient*, and a well-earned DSO in the Battle of the Barents Sea. Our new captain was a delightful man, a Lieutenant Battersby, known as 'Shelly'. With years of destroyer experience, he could well have changed all sorts of things, and I am sure he probably wanted to, but he was nothing but helpful to me and the other officers, and great fun as well.

The great news reached me that Elizabeth was due back at the end of November in a convoy from Halifax, and that *Middleton* would begin a short refit in Hull in early December. All seemed set, providing we had not changed our minds. I was given leave as soon as we berthed, and nipped down to Kings Cross on the first available train, to be met by Elizabeth. We decided we were doing the right thing, and an announcement was put in the paper. Since no banns had been or could be called, I got a special licence from the registrar at Westminster Abbey at vast expense, rivalling the cost of the engagement ring.

We had a marvellous, small wedding in the Chapel Royal at St James's Palace on 11 December, my 23rd birthday. Lin Pirie, ex-*Jupiter*, was my best man. Because of a shortage of brother officers who could come, Elizabeth had arranged a guard of honour of Wrens, and very nice they looked. It was sad, specially for Mousse, that neither Father nor Peter could be there. Mousse moved to Bletchingly and lent us Godden Green Lodge for our honeymoon after one luxurious night in the Dorchester. Then it was back to the ship, and Elizabeth awaited her next appointment. She was by then a 2nd officer, which I think she felt was a bit of a come-down from having been an acting lieutenant in the Royal Canadian Navy.

Back north, the familiar in and out of Scapa routine continued but, after a short time, I heard that I was to be relieved by a lieutenant-commander RNVR called Lawson. He duly arrived on 13 January, and, after a quick turnover, the ship dropped me and all my luggage off into a drifter and so to a wet and cold jetty in Aberdeen. She then disappeared north in heavy weather, leaving me to look for a train. I hoped for a spell of leave and then to be sent as First Lieutenant of a Fleet destroyer, which would be the normal progression towards getting a command. However, the Admiralty thought otherwise, and instead, I was appointed to join *King Alfred* on 2 February 1943. This was a training establishment for 'hostilities only' officers, and I was sent there as one of the divisional officers. Men of all ages, who had at least six months' sea time in the Fleet and shown themselves educationally and otherwise likely to make reasonable officers, were sent to this establishment for eleven weeks. The first six were spent in the Lancing College building, and the remaining five in a converted swimming pool complex at Brighton. To qualify for this training, men had completed six months at sea as officer candidates, wearing white cap bands to mark them out from their fellows, and had then passed an interview board presided over by one of two admirals. Each week's intake formed a division and was assigned a divisional officer and a field training officer. The Admiralty at that time required *King Alfred* to produce 100 officers each week. My division, the Jervis Division, which joined a couple of weeks after me, started only 80 strong.

As well as extremely hard work, it was a great ordeal for the candidates, as any who failed at any time during the course of the eleven weeks went straight back to sea as ordinary sailors. It was the divisional officer's responsibility to make sure that no one unsuitable to be a wartime officer was allowed to qualify. In addition to the past divisional records of the man concerned from his previous naval service, one had access to a report by an industrial psychologist. I felt I had some non-starters, whom I kept under my close personal observation and was determined should suffer as little as possible and, therefore, should go as soon as practicable. The system allowed you to bring men up 'for review' before the admiral of the board who had admitted them. In this case, it was Admiral Davenport and, nice chap that he was, it was not easy to hear from some whippersnapper of a lieutenant that someone whom you thought three weeks earlier was suitable should no longer continue training. But we were all on the same side, and the system worked pretty well.

So did the Training Establishment, largely because we had the most splendid executive officer in Dick Jessel, once captain of *Havock*, whose wreck I had seen as *Middleton* passed through the Cape Bon Channel on the way to Malta. He was heavily decorated and a born leader. If the candidates were chased, so were we, the divisional officers. As well as my field training officer, Eason, who took charge of the normal drills and smartening up, I had a good seamanship officer RNVR, a schoolmaster called Newth, who taught them buoyage, coastal navigation, how to work out tides, and so on. I had very little formal instruction to do myself, but I do remember, to my horror, having to give a lecture on leadership, which is not the easiest subject to expound. For the Jervis Division, I chose Lord St Vincent as my exemplar, and I fear I frightened the life out of them.

Best of all, however, was that a kind and civilised Admiralty, as well as appointing me to *King Alfred*, had earlier appointed Elizabeth as the Wren officer in charge of the Combined Operations Establishment, *Lizard*, at Hove. We were therefore able to set up married life together in a bedsit with a small gas burner in a house on First Avenue, Hove. At this time I felt I had to make a decision about my future career in the Navy. The normal tour of duty at *King Alfred* was at least a year. If I did that and subsequently obtained a job as First Lieutenant of a Fleet destroyer for, say, 18 months, it would be, I thought, at least three years before I could expect a command. I found it difficult at that time to believe that the war would last so long. At the end of our midshipman's time in China, we had all been asked to make a statement as to whether we wished to specialise or not, the options being gunnery, torpedo, communications, and so forth. Other alternatives were aviation, submarines or general service. I had a feeling that I might like to specialise in navigation, and talked to Father about it. He thought that it was a nonsense, and that any naval officer ought to be able to navigate. He suggested that unless I wanted something else in particular, I ought to put down general service as first choice, which I did. Now I judged that if, at the end of the war, I was not to find myself a 'salt horse' pacing the teak on the quarter deck of some cruiser or other, I had better make up my mind to specialise. I chose signals because it seemed to me that it was possible that I might find out rather more about the war if I was in a signal job. I therefore put in my application to the Admiralty and as they were short of signal officers I was relieved at the end of my first divisional term at *King Alfred*.

Nevertheless, I enjoyed my time there. It was interesting and daunting on one occasion to take battalion drill, comprising the five divisions at Brighton, and keep them in formation while drilling in the space available. Finally, I had the satisfaction of seeing the 60 or so chaps left in my division change into uniform – midshipmen RNVR with red tabs if they were under 20, acting sub-lieutenants RNVR if they were older – and enjoy a tremendous farewell party that they all threw. The brightest ones went as fighter direction officers, the next brightest to coastal forces, and the others mainly as First Lieutenants of the landing craft that were being built in quantity up and down the country in aid of the forthcoming operation to invade Europe. They left merrily enough, and I hope that their casualty rate was not high later on.

We had a great family occasion in March 1943, when, Peter leading, he and I had the DSC pinned on us by the King himself in Buckingham Palace. Mousse and Liz were there, and Father came to a lunch at the United Services Club given by Lionel Sturdee to celebrate the occasion. Later in the war, such investitures could not be held for medals such as ours, so we were very lucky. By now, Elizabeth was expecting our first child and, once this was proved to the satisfaction of the Admiralty, she was discharged from the Wrens and we were free to find somewhere to live together near the Signal School. This had been moved some six months earlier to a large house called 'Leydene', which belonged to a Lady Peel, high above East Meon, where we rented a small but cheap cottage owned by an eccentric retired architect.

The Long Course began in June and lasted six months. It was very hard work. We had to learn the theory of wireless, intricate details of most of the transmitters and receivers then in service, the signal procedures for use both on radio and by light, an intimate knowledge of the tactical Bible of the time, *The Conduct of the Fleet*, and a pretty thorough knowledge of the Fleet Signal Book and the 'groups' in it, so that these would be interpreted properly by ships when we were advising our captain or admiral on how to conduct manoeuvres. We used to spend quite a time equipped with 'answering pendants', acting the part of ships in what were known as 'marching manoeuvres'. We did a great deal of flag-hoisting, and had to know by heart, and instantly, the colours and meanings of all the flags, including the emergency alarm signals. We had to work up to something like 12 words a minute in semaphore, 15 words a minute with flashing light and 22 words a minute sending, 25 receiving, with a buzzer in Morse code. I was a permanent member of the backward buzzer class (but I was not alone).

Finally, we had to complete a short radar course in the Navigation School. We were then ready for appointment to the Fleet as signal officers, where a variety of jobs were available to us, either as signal officer of a big ship such as an aircraft carrier, signal officer of a destroyer flotilla, or on the staff of a Commander-in-Chief or some other admiral. The dunce of the party, we always said to one another, would go as signal officer to Addu Atoll in the Maldives, which was just opening up as a wireless station. There was a whole array of examinations to contend with at the end of the course but, fortunately, for many of them we were allowed to use our notebooks, and Elizabeth was a tremendous help in typing out my wireless technical notes. The high-powered transmitters of that day had enormous valves and inductance coils within safety gates that clanged behind the unwary, leaving you, you felt, open to every kind of electric shock. All sorts of tricks were played on us in our passing-out exam on this hardware, but we all came through unscathed.

We were very professionally taught, covering the ground at twice the speed of that expected in peacetime and, indeed, there was more ground to cover, not least on the cryptographic side. There were nine of us on the course, destroyer officers mainly. I somehow qualified top, and received the Jackson Everett prize for doing so.

Our daughter, Susan, was born just as the Short Radar Course was starting. This delayed my arrival slightly, but after visiting the Middlesex Hospital, I was able to go down Portsmouth with a reasonably quiet mind, thrilled with our child.

The course lasted ten days, and I received my first appointment as a signal communications officer at its conclusion. I was to go as Fleet Wireless Assistant on the staff of Admiral Sir Bruce Fraser, C.-in-C. Home Fleet. If I had wanted a change from destroyers, I had certainly got it. Happily, I was not required to join until after Christmas, and I was able to be there when Liz and Sue left hospital and came to Godden Green. The area was then a good deal safer than London and, with Mousse's help, we found a small flat across the green and Elizabeth and the baby moved in. All too soon I had to go, and caught what was known as the Jellicoe Express to Thurso for Scapa at the end of December. After ten months of married life ashore, it was pretty hard to leave. It was also strange to be going back to a battleship, albeit a very different one from *Rodney*, and to a staff job, having had so long in destroyers with little or no paperwork since my chart-correcting days. As I remember it, the journey took about 24 hours to Thurso, and then we caught a ferry to Lyness, where *Duke of York*'s boat picked us up. The journey was greatly enlivened by one or two other staff officers travelling back from leave, among them the Fleet Gunnery Assistant, Michael Le Fanu, who was particularly kind and cheerful. I little knew how much our paths were to cross in the future, or how sadly at the end.

I arrived in *Duke of York* only a day or so after she had entered harbour having contributed immensely to the sinking of *Scharnhorst*. We were in the classic position of 'the ones who weren't there', and everybody on board was naturally very cock-a-hoop and full of the action. So it was a very cheerful, if enormous, wardroom that I joined, relieving an RNVR signal officer called Norman Beale, who had completed the usual nine months' or so stint as Fleet Wireless Assistant. I always described myself as the lowest form of animal life on the Commander-in-Chief's staff, and in physical terms, that was certainly true: I spent a great deal of my time in the Main Communication Office far below deck as among my responsibilities was the routing of all the 'flag' signals wherever they had to go. As many of them had very long addresses, the achievement of the correct and most economical route and the avoidance of breaches of security, was very much an officer's job. I also had to cipher and decipher quite a number of the 'Officers' Eyes Only' messages and it was exceptional for me to leave the MCO to turn in before 11 p.m. in harbour. I was also directly responsible for the training and discipline of the Fleet in all forms of radio-operating. This meant organising and conducting exercises, usually through the medium of a particularly skilful leading telegraphist called Collins, but sometimes with my own hand on the key.

A particular difficulty occurred in tuning the Fleet to the Fleet Wave, when we tried to operate clandestinely on 210 kHz at very low power, using an extraordinary contraption, rather like a breadboard set, called the 4-D. Try as one would, someone sooner or later invariably increased power to make themselves heard, and when one re-entered harbour, the shore listening stations would report with delight all the Fleet transgressions on the air. When the Fleet went to sea, wireless silence would be maintained, except on our low-powered Fleet Wave, unless in contact with the enemy. This meant that we had to leave behind a great deal of dummy traffic to be transmitted on the various shore broadcasts to make it look as though the Commander-in-Chief was still in harbour and controlling the Fleet from Scapa. The preparation of these messages in vast quantities of appropriate lengths and priorities and with appropriate address groups was also my responsibility, so it was a very hard-working spring and early summer, made even busier by radio telephone training for officers designated for the forthcoming Normandy landings.

I remember in particular one dreadful oversight, as a result of which the orders for a big convoy to Russia, instead of going by landline everywhere, were transmitted on the broadcasts. As soon as I saw the messages beginning to come out, I knew the mistake I had made and reported to Peter Dawnay, the Fleet Wireless Officer, about my ghastly error. He told me to report personally to the Commander-in-Chief, and did not offer to come with me. At about 10 p.m. I went aft to Bruce Fraser's cabin, knocked on the door and went in. The little man was sitting on his sofa tinkering with a balalaika which Admiral Levchenko, who had been sent to collect *Royal Sovereign*, which was being lent to the Russians for the duration of the war, had given him. 'Yes, laddie, what is it?' said Bruce. I told him. 'What does that mean?' he asked. 'Sir,' I said, 'I think it's possible that the enemy may be able to deduce that a new convoy is about to sail.' 'Oh,' he said, 'What a pity. Thank you, laddie, good night.' I spent some very unhappy days, and was thankful when that particular convoy had a fairly normal passage through, but my admiration and affection for the admiral soared.

I well remember reporting to the Commander-in-Chief, whether in the middle of the night or at some other time. You'd see, in the small sea cabin that he occupied near the bridge, the hump over his tummy and the red glow of his pipe burning quietly as he lay on his bunk, pondering, no doubt, the ebb and flow of war but alert for his next call and decision. There was always a very calm rejoinder to the report you made, whereas his successor, Admiral Sir Henry Moore (known for his stature as 'Twiglet' by the staff), would, as soon as you knocked on the door, be half out of his bunk and on his way to the bridge. Both attitudes deserve praise, but the contrast was considerable for somebody of my age and experience, and never forgotten in the years ahead.

Rather glumly, with eyes glued to the signals coming in, we sat in Scapa Flow as a covering force in case of an enemy sortie from Norway or Germany while Normandy was invaded. Admiral Moore had relieved Fraser by then, and we had learnt that Bruce was to be Commander-in-Chief of a British Pacific Fleet. I was in the Main Communications Office at about 1.30 a.m. when I was rung by Peter White, a midshipman in *Birmingham* and now secretary to 'Daddy' Brind, Assistant Chief of Naval Staff Operations Home. He said that the admiral wanted to talk to me. This was reminiscent of being caught coming back late from leave at Tsingtao, but I was delighted to learn that he was going to the Pacific as admiral commanding the cruisers and wanted me to be his flag lieutenant and squadron signal officer. There could only be one answer to that, as I so much liked him and Peter. I was also extremely junior for the job, which I heard later had been offered to me only over the dead body of the Signal School, which had proposed a senior nominee. So it was clear that my days of hard labour in the bowels of the Fleet Flagship of the Home Fleet were numbered, and I can't say that I was particularly sorry.

I hope this account has conveyed something of my respect and affection for Bruce Fraser, but more about his relationship with the Russians is worth putting on paper. As I mentioned above, Britain had agreed to lend them *Royal Sovereign* for the duration of the war, and they had decided to change her name to *Archangelsk* and sent Admiral Levchenko and a captain or two to take her on and sail her to North Russia, hoping that we would provide an escort to ensure her a safe passage. This we agreed to do, reluctantly, because there were plenty of Russian destroyers, as I well knew, sitting in North Russia doing nothing. But this project was always referred to by Bill Slater, Chief of Staff, in the presence of the Russians, as their 'Death Ride'. They obviously regarded it in that light, and the situation became somewhat fraught. I happened to be on the compass platform once when this particular problem was being discussed by the Commander-in-Chief, Admiral Slater, and Guy Russell, captain of *Duke of York*. I think Admiral Fraser was complaining about the Soviet sense of humour, or lack of it, and Guy Russell interjected a remark that I had not heard before. 'Oh well, Sir,' he said, 'Niggers begin at Calais.' However, Fraser, having taken *Duke of York* almost to the Kola Inlet and met Golovko, C.-in-C. Soviet Northern Fleet, had earned the great admiration and liking of the Russians, and this stood him in good stead with Levchenko, who was, in fact, a commissar – a political admiral.

So I was thrilled to be going out with 'Daddy' Brind to the Pacific in a job 'well above my station' but one which I felt reasonably confident of carrying out, and to know that my late and greatly admired Commander-in-Chief, Bruce Fraser, was to be in charge of whatever effort we put into the Far East. It was a marvellous prospect climatically too, after so long in the northern seas. It meant more separation from my family, perhaps for longer, as the war in Europe was going well but the war in the Pacific at that time was anybody's guess, but it was a professional opportunity not to be disregarded, and who knew what was going to happen anyway. In due course, Duncan Knight, from the latest Long Course, came to relieve me, and I left on 8 September 1944 and went home for some leave and to make ready for the war against Japan.

So, in September 1944, I came back to Godden Green and the family and spent a happy six weeks or so. I called on Brind, who seemed to me to be very tired, learned that our flagship for the passage out was to be *Swiftsure*, a brand new cruiser, and tried with Elizabeth to prepare ourselves mentally for quite a long time apart. Father was at home, having been promoted to rear-admiral and appointed as Director of Naval Training, and it was lovely to see something of him. He was more tired and depressed than I realised at the time, although showing the strain of his long period at sea in command of *Valiant* and *Malaya*. Peter had been sent as 1st Lieutenant of a Hunt Class destroyer, *Melbreak*, and was to go on as 1st Lieutenant of *Tartar*, one of the surviving Fleet Tribal Class destroyers. He was clearly doing brilliantly, and was soon to win 18 months' additional seniority, which put him over my head for a matter of six months or so until I was granted a year, which just redressed the balance.

The time passed all too quickly, and in November I joined *Swiftsure* and met the other members of staff. Peter White, the secretary, I knew very well, and we also had Ian McGeoch, a distinguished submariner, as staff officer operations and an RNVR staff officer intelligence called Gowing, who had completed a course in Japanese in the United States. *Swiftsure* had a very senior captain, R.D. Oliver, another gunnery officer, who messed in the 'Cuddy' (as the admiral's mess was called) with Brind and his personal staff – Peter and myself. 'Daddy' Brind was most welcoming and kind. He was now a widower, his poor wife having died some while before of her affliction of asthma, which had from time to time made her very ill in China. Again I was most fortunate in my own team: John Ellis, the signal boatswain, was to prove absolutely outstanding, and Willie Parkin, the warrant telegraphist, was indefatigable. Fortunately, they hit it off very well together. Brind's title at that time was Admiral Commanding the Cruisers of the British Pacific Fleet (we were the only one!). *Swiftsure* faced a fast passage to Australia, where Admiral Fraser, the Commander-in-Chief designate, had gone on ahead by air. A clash of personalities between Oliver and Brind was made more unfortunate when Oliver was promoted to rear-admiral while we were on passage, particularly as the ship had no admiral's bridge and the two men had to share the same compass platform. It made no great problems for me as I was so much on Brind's side anyway, but there were occasional embarrassing moments for everyone.

We called at Alexandria, fuelled at Aden and paused at Colombo for two days. I went with Brind to call on my ex-captain, 'Dickie' Mountbatten, now Supreme Allied Commander South East Asia, at Kandy. The Flag Lieutenant rang up to find out which of us had served with 'Supremo' before, and if so, where; a car was sent, and off we drove through the lovely Ceylon countryside. The large headquarters was in the Botanical Gardens at Peredeniya, and calls were first made on the Naval Chief of Staff, Douglas-Pennant – the commander being Admiral Layton in Colombo – and General Wheeler, US Army, the Land Force Commander; then to the 'theatre', where, before a staff of unconscionable size, there ensued a parade of briefing officers on a large stage with panels, maps and diagrams being slid to and fro in, to me, a thoroughly unaccustomed manner. 'Dickie' Mountbatten may have asked a few questions – we visitors were all speechless. Much later, of course, I have seen this kind of thing often at SHAPE, SACLANT and other big headquarters (though I have tried to have less elaboration at my own), but it was, in modern jargon, a 'culture shock' at the time. We then moved to a large senior staff dining room, had a drink and waited. A whisper, 'Supremo', ran round the gathering, and then in bounced Mountbatten on the balls of his feet, straight up to Brind: 'Daddy, how nice to see you here,' and to me, 'Ah, Ashmore – *Jupiter*, wasn't it?' (Knowing he had been briefed made it less impressive, I'm afraid.)

We went straight on to Australia, called in at Fremantle, where American and British submarine squadrons were based, and then crossed the great Australian Bight, making a quick passage to Hobart for a break over Christmas. We were admirably looked after, mostly by the Young Victoria League, and after a great party, saw the sun rise on Christmas morning from the top of Mt Wellington. We then went north to Sydney, and duly secured alongside at Woollamaloo in another beautiful but very empty harbour. I went with Brind to call on the Commander-in-Chief, Sir Bruce Fraser, and it was nice to catch a glimpse of him again and have a chat with Vernon Merry, his Flag Lieutenant, and Dicky Courage, the Fleet Communications Officer. Bruce had just come back from a most successful visit to Pearl Harbor, where he had hit it off admirably with the C.-in-C. Pacific Fleet and Pacific Ocean Area, Admiral Chester Nimitz. As a result of this, all risks of the British Fleet, soon to come out, being diverted to work for General Macarthur in South East Asia had been averted, and we were to play our part as best we could in the main American offensive against Japan. As a result, the British ships were to be equipped with American transceivers for tactical use, one using very high frequencies, the other frequency modulation in the 40 MHz band. We were to carry an American cipher team in our flagships and were to adopt US Navy methods of flag signalling and manoeuvring. In essence, all that I had learnt during my Long Course except for the Morse code, wireless and cryptographic theory, and the international code of signal flags was to be discarded. Hard though this was for me, it was much harder for those who had been longer qualified and were more practised in the British art of signalling at sea, and especially, of course, for people like my excellent signal boatswain and warrant telegraphist, who were experts in their trade in the old ways.

Almost immediately after our arrival, Brind in *Swiftsure* was sent north to Ulithi, where Admiral Spruance and the 5th Fleet were foregathered pending their next operation. His task was to make contact with that Fleet, and in particular with Spruance, and also to acquaint himself as best he could with American methods of operation in the Pacific. I was specially briefed by Dicky Courage (whom I knew from the *Duke of York*) on my role. This was to familiarise myself thoroughly with the American methods of signalling and manoeuvring at that time, and to report on any difficulties which could be foreseen in adopting them. We were given trunkloads of operation orders and the American signal books, notably their General Signal Book and something called PAC70B, which I had to absorb and teach my staff thoroughly about during the passage. All kinds of things were different, even the phonetic alphabet changed – it was my third! Because of the absence of a Japanese submarine threat in the wide expanses of the Pacific, conventional British screening systems had been discarded. Circular screens, arranged about an axis centred on some point in the middle of the formation, which might or might not be occupied by a ship, but round which the heavy units would be disposed, had been adopted. We embarked an experienced US Navy captain for the passage, and he was the greatest possible help to me as, reading through the books, I came upon points that defied my comprehension. The weather was perfect, and we were in our tropical white shirts and shorts. This became a strong bone of contention with the Americans, who all wore khaki, and who felt that the white would make us more visible at night to the Japanese, who were renowned for the strength and optical efficiency of their binoculars, as well as for their general alertness.

Swiftsure's arrival at Ulithi is unforgettable. The large expanse of water within the coral atoll was crammed with ships. As we entered, people were flashing at us from all directions, and my staff could only take some of the messages. One I remember was, 'Welcome from the signal gang of USS *Columbia*,' another was, 'Hello *Swiftsure* – where is the other half of the British Fleet?' No reply was needed or possible, though the main body of the Fleet had just about sailed from Colombo on its way to attack Sumatra and then join the Commander-in-Chief at Sydney. I attended on Brind for his call on Spruance in *Indianapolis*, the flagship, and was warmly greeted by 'Red' Armstrong, the Fleet Communications Officer. Back on board *Swiftsure*, I studied yet more piles of orders, communication orders mainly, and also the Fleet list, which included no fewer than 40 rear-admirals. This was because, in addition to carrier and battleship force and group commanders, the whole of the Service Force Pacific – tankers, supply ships, and so forth – was also in harbour. It was quickly brought home to us how immensely difficult it was going to be for the British Fleet to maintain itself at sea, thousands of miles from its base, without a service force or Fleet train. This had to be put together from practically nothing before a British contribution could make sense.

'Daddy' Brind was enormously impressed by Admiral Spruance, and there is no doubt that the two men were alike in character and temperament and hit it off extraordinarily well. They went for long walks together along the atoll, and the friendship that they struck up permeated down the line. All of us on the staff found nothing but kindness and help from people who had been through tremendous battles in the course of turning near defeat into near victory and could be forgiven for thinking that they wished to lick the Japanese on their own and hardly needed 'limey' help. Personally, I found this friendliness most evident at a meeting of the communications officers of the Carrier Force run by Cdr. Armstrong, at which there were some 50 officers, of whom I was certainly the youngest and also the junior in rank. At lunch in Spruance's flagship, where the fruit cocktail was definitely fruit only, it was also obvious how Michael Le Fanu had already made his distinctive mark. Of all his many great services to the Royal Navy, his time at sea in the Pacific Fleet as Fraser's liaison officer with Spruance and Halsey was undoubtedly one of the most significant, and one of which he was rightly very proud.

Our visit to Ulithi over, we were not allowed to return to Sydney, much as the ship's company would have preferred it, but instead went to Manus in the Admiralty Islands. This was to be the forward base of the British Fleet, where, as well as an excellent anchorage, there were limited airfield facilities and a small American naval facility, including, I remember, a Coca-Cola factory, of which they were inordinately proud and round which we were shown. Meanwhile, the rest of the British Fleet, joined at Fremantle by Vice-Admiral Rawlings as second-in-command to Fraser, was arriving at Sydney and preparing to come north and rejoin the war. The climate at Manus was hot and very humid, the temperature in my cabin by day was 120°F. There was a mass of work for me to do, much of it because the British Fleet radio broadcasts had not yet begun, and we had to read the American 'Fox', as they called it. This was alive with information, most of it irrelevant to our immediate needs, but also carried essential messages. The only way of sifting it properly was for me to scan every signal myself; there was no other qualified filter. Most of us by then had prickly heat – I was no exception. I shall always associate Manus with sitting in a very hot cabin surrounded by bits of paper, some of them incomprehensible, with nothing on except underpants and prickly heat powder.

We had now learned that the British ships were to operate as a single task force and integral component of the American Pacific Fleet at sea. There was a great deal for us to understand in implementing the American task force organisation, which seemed an eminently practical but novel system. We had to learn how they made up their call signs, how they encrypted their manoeuvring signals, how they controlled their radio telephone nets, and many other details. I was singularly fortunate in having time alone to assimilate US Fleet practice and train my staff while the other British signal officers were busily engaged with ships in company still operating the British system until departure from Sydney. I was able to get a distinct lap ahead and I hoped that this would be of general help.

There was not much to do at Manus by way of a run ashore. We occasionally went for a walk, and once I remember going with the admiral and the flag captain, Admiral Oliver, in a jeep along a road to a coral airstrip, both being built by the 'Sea Bees' (as the construction battalions were called). It was the first time I had seen modern earth-moving equipment in quantity in action, and it was extraordinary to witness a road of crushed coral being driven towards its destination through primary jungle at the rate of perhaps 50 yards an hour. We drove as far as we could, had supper with the American base commander, and then came off after dark by barge.

On the way back (and I suspect I was responsible for the navigation), we hit a coral head in the harbour and stuck. The only thing to do was to lighten the boat, so, led by the admiral, we all jumped out onto the coral, pushed her off and scrambled in quickly. Unfortunately (but somewhat to my secret satisfaction as relations between him and Brind then were at a very low ebb), Oliver was left on the coral head, bleating like a lost sheep. We went back, nosed onto the head, and he was hauled on board over the bow. It was a very wet party that went up the starboard after accommodation ladder into *Swiftsure*.

Very soon after this, Oliver was relieved by the cheerful and outgoing Pat McLaughlin, which made for a much happier mess in the 'Cuddy', and a livelier and a more cheerful ship. It was, I am sure, also a relief for Brind, who had been visibly exhausted by his long stint as Assistant Chief of Naval Staff Operations at the Admiralty, and whose determination to master every detail of the unfamiliar situations in which we now found ourselves was taking up a great deal of his mental and nervous energy.

We went south at last to meet the cruisers of our squadron, which were assembling at Sydney. There were some seven others, of various sorts and sizes, including *Achilles* and *Black Prince* from New Zealand, eventually *Uganda* from Canada, and the initial UK contingent, *Newfoundland, Gambia, Argonaut* and *Euryalus*. My old commander, Lees, had *Black Prince*, and Edwards of Shanghai days commanded *Gambia*, so Brind, Peter White and I found good friends. All Australian cruisers were already heavily engaged under General MacArthur in the South West Pacific. Much work had to be compressed into a small compass while we were at Sydney, including meeting the signals staffs and, as a flag lieutenant should, organising the admiral's programme and his entertaining. We sailed again for Manus at the end of February, arriving in early March to find the Fleet train, or part of it, already there, a mobile naval airbase established on one of the coral atolls fringing the lagoon, and some damaged American cruisers in harbour. Our task force commander, Vice-Admiral Bernard Rawlings, reported for duty to Spruance in the American way, and after ten hot and sweaty days we sailed north.

The Americans were launching an attack on Okinawa, the first piece of historic Japanese territory to come within their grasp, and the British force's job was to support these operations by suppressing the Japanese airfields on Sakishima Gunto. We were therefore operating in a degree of isolation from the main American task force, which provided an excellent opportunity for us to familiarise ourselves with their systems and practices. The drill was that in the combat area, when our strikes were being flown off the carriers and we were under heavier attack from the Japanese, Rear-Admiral Vian in *Indomitable*, as Carrier Task Group Commander, took tactical command, whereas in the rear area, Rear-Admiral Brind took tactical command for the replenishment. Rawlings in *King George V* was in overall command, and tactical command was delegated from him. This gave Brind and his staff a very demanding job. There were not many of us, and it was more or less 'watch on, stop on'.

Replenishment consisted mainly of the embarkation of fuel oil and aviation spirit at sea from tankers, whose pumping rate at that time was very very low indeed, and whose gear was far from familiar. A big carrier, *Victorious*, for example, with Captain Denny in charge, might therefore be alongside refuelling for something like 12 hours, with the captain on the bridge throughout, as he would also have been during the days and nights of combat operations. In addition, the battleships and cruisers had to be refuelled and stores and ammunition had to be embarked. (Loading cases of beer also took up some time, but there was little reluctance shown about this.)

The escort carriers came up with replacement aircraft from Manus, and the 'flyable duds' (as we called damaged aircraft which could still fly) had to be flown off the carriers to them and new aircraft embarked. One had to ensure that destroyers fuelled as often as necessary, so that when we left for the combat area they were fully topped up. All in all, it was a complicated business, there was always a danger of air attack, and in our British way, we half expected submarine attack too. Fortunately we were generally left in peace to replenish, as the Japanese had their work cut out to deal with the American assault on Okinawa.

Brind was always keen to visit his other cruisers; from time to time he was called to conferences by Rawlings, and as usual, I went with him, finding it useful to talk to their signals people and to Cdr. Stopford, the Task Force Communications Officer. A destroyer would be sent, and we would transfer by jackstay to her, and then from her to whatever ship was our destination. (Being hauled up from a destroyer to the cliff edge of a carrier's flight deck was quite an experience.) The admiral insisted on going first, so the jackstay was always well tested before I got on the quaint seat that was then our idea of the best method of transfer. Later, we found that a stirrup was better, and indeed safer, because you could get out of it more quickly if you ditched, as would happen if the transferring ships came too close together.

My more through knowledge of the American signal books came in handy, and twice a destroyer was sent to take me to talk to one of my 'oppos' on another admiral's staff to explain personally the intricacies of unfamiliar manoeuvres. I also found that there were so many ships on the tactical net and the British regional accents were sometimes so difficult to distinguish that when we were in charge of a replenishment, it was important for me to control the net myself for anything other than the most routine messages. This also became the practice in the combat area, and I well remember, as a kamikaze was approaching Vian's flagship (then *Victorious*), hearing David Milford Haven's voice on the TBS (tactical net), going ever faster to get his message away before the enemy hit her deck and burst into flames. Thanks to the armour plating on our carrier decks, the damage was nothing like as catastrophic as it would have been had the ship been American and thin-skinned. *Victorious* was launching aircraft again about 40 minutes later; a US carrier would have been a major casualty. During these operations, *Formidable*, *Indefatigable* and *Indomitable* were also hit, some of them more than once, always by kamikazes, who seemed to bear a charmed life as they came lumbering through the gunfire of battleships, cruisers and destroyers.

The British part in the Okinawa operations kept us at sea for nearly 90 days. We left the combat area towards the end of May, and moved to Manus, whence the rest of the force left for Sydney. We stayed on with *Implacable*, which had just come out from home and needed working up. Brind had been given the job of conducting an attack on the Japanese island of Truk in the Carolines as a run-in for her air group, and this was to be combined with a substantial bombardment by some of our cruisers. So *Swiftsure* sailed for Sydney and the flag transferred to *Implacable*, whose captain was a splendid raconteur called 'Trunky' Hughes-Hallett, who kept us in fits of laughter in the 'Cuddy'. I was given a berth in a cabin right alongside the funnel, sharing with the gunnery officer and another when at sea, and off we set.

I suggested to 'Daddy' Brind that it would be an excellent idea, as he was now commanding an operation in which the main thrust was air attack, if he could do a flight or two from *Implacable*'s flight deck, and he agreed. I went with him, and we took off in an Avenger on a dummy run for the attack on Truk. We had not been in the air for more than ten minutes before acrid smoke began to permeate the whole aircraft. Brind was sitting in the observer's seat behind the pilot and I was further aft under the plastic bubble covering the air gunner's position. It all began to feel rather dicey, and I was choking when we sighted a coral airstrip and the aircraft landed safely. Out we scrambled, coughing and gasping, to find out what had happened: the maintenance staff, realising that the admiral was going to fly in this aircraft, had painted the engine with Silverine to make it look smart; when this burnt off, it had produced the noxious fumes. By now it was too late to accompany the dummy strike and we had to return rather ignominiously, but greatly relieved, to *Implacable*. I later investigated how I should have got that plastic bubble off my seat in order to get out, and was told that it could be done, but since one could not then get out with a parachute on, there was very little point in doing it. I asked how I was supposed to get out with my parachute on, and was shown a miserable little tunnel from under the seat towards the back of the aircraft where there was some kind of hatch. Clearly, one had much better have died or drowned with dignity in one's seat, but the briefing was a good deal less than adequate.

The air attacks on what had once been a very substantial Japanese base were a success, and there were no tragedies except that one of our aircraft on return missed her wire, caught the barrier and 'pecked' (her nose came down and her airscrew hit the deck and shattered). A fragment caught the popular flight deck officer, Lamb, who was lucky to survive. We transferred to a cruiser for the bombardment, and this went reasonably well though, unfortunately, the British very high frequency communication sets on which we were relying for controlling the aircraft spotting the bombardment proved thoroughly unreliable, and I endured a good deal of justified stick from the gunnery officer as a result. The trouble, I am now sure, was that vibration at high speed dislodged the tuning controls, causing an intermittent loss of communication and a considerable loss of confidence on the part of the users. Unfortunately, the much more reliable American equipment was incompatible with our aircraft sets.

We returned uneventfully to Manus in *Implacable*, then flew by Dakota to Sydney. Mail took a while to reach us in the British Pacific Fleet. In March I had a telegram from Mousse saying that Father had been extremely ill. In fact, he had suffered a massive coronary early in the New Year and had taken a great deal of time to pull through but was now getting better.

The war in Europe was soon over, and gradually more resources were being made available to us in the Pacific, but it was still hard to see how Japan could be brought down. We British all sailed north from Sydney on 28 June, after a good long spell for most people, during which all of us had enjoyed great hospitality. About this time, *Illustrious* left us, and at her farewell party I met her captain, Charles Lambe, for the first time, little knowing how greatly he would one day influence my future. On this deployment, we were to join Admiral Halsey's 3rd Fleet, and Rawlings, in due course, reported for duty as Commander Task Force 37. This time we operated in close conjunction with the Fleet itself as its 4th Task Group, usually on the right flank of the other three. This was a wonderful opportunity to see the US Fleet at peak efficiency in action. I accompanied Brind on his call on Halsey, to be greeted again by the inimitable Mike Le Fanu, and to find that the fruit cocktails were not quite the same as those of Admiral Spruance, nor were his staff quite so serious-minded, efficient though they were. The staff secretary was Harold Stassen, who was later to run unsuccessfully for US president. Brind also visited a couple of the carrier group commanders: Mitscher, who was also commanding the carrier task force under Halsey, and notably, Admiral Radford's task group, where we spent most of the whole visit in the flag plot seeing how they did it all.

Their friendliness towards the British by now was tinged with respect. They admired the way our carriers took the punishment they received from the kamikazes and our aviators, with their rather less effective aircraft, had made a great reputation for themselves with their professionalism and courage. We had got the hang of their communications and our Force Fighter Direction Officer, 'Drunky' Lewin, had taught his American opposite numbers a great deal in disciplined and orderly methods of control, which they were quick to learn. This resulted in a notable improvement in the efficiency of aircraft direction across the whole Fleet.

Throughout July, in glorious weather, a pattern of operations similar to that off Sakishima Gunto was observed: air strikes and air battles as the Fleet came under kamikaze attack for three or four days, followed by passage to a replenishment area, two or three days' replenishing, and then return to the combat area. Our Fleet Train had been somewhat improved, pumping rates were a little higher, and time alongside was therefore not so long, though longer by far than that needed by the Americans with their fast Fleet oilers. By this time we had 18 cruisers assigned to our squadron, and the flag was shifted to *Newfoundland* under Captain Ravenhill, as *Swiftsure* was detached with some others towards the South-East Asian Theatre. A major cause for sadness was the departure of *Uganda*. With the end of the war in Europe, the Canadian government had indicated that any of its servicemen who did not wish to continue fighting in the Pacific war could express a preference for going home. Captain Mainguy was thoroughly downcast when his ship's company rather naturally volunteered to go home instead of seeing the thing through to the end. When Brind went on board to say goodbye, it was embarrassing for both officers, although wholly understandable in view of the particular line taken by the government of Canada.

In early August, we were detached in *Newfoundland*, with some other British ships and American cruisers and battleships, to carry out a bombardment of the forts at the entrance to Tokyo Bay. It was to be the first time I would see Japan. Twenty-four hours before this was due to take place, we received a signal ordering all ships to be 300 miles from the Inland Sea by 4 a.m. the following morning, 6 August, as 'special missiles' were to be dropped. So we turned about, postponed our operation and made for the south. Ever since joining Brind's staff I had been on the 'Ultra' list which gave access to intelligence derived from breaking enemy ciphers, but neither he nor I had any inkling of what was to occur.

Then we heard that an 'atomic' bomb had been dropped on Hiroshima. Thereafter, intelligence gave us some indication of the turmoil in Japan, but the war was still on and the Fleet air attacks continued, although our bombardment was cancelled and we rejoined the Task Force. On 9 August a second bomb was dropped on Nagasaki, and on the 11th I heard on the radio the Emperor's voice calling on his people to surrender. One could hardly believe that the war was over at last.

In the British Task Force, the signal 'Cease hostilities against Japan' was hoisted by flags, and we prepared for a broadcast to the Fleet by Admiral Halsey. I produced my camera and took a photograph of the hoist just before it was executed. As it was, by hauling down, a kamikaze splashed into the sea 300 yards astern of *Indefatigable*. The Fleet remained under practically continuous air attack, and Admiral Halsey's broadcast was made, warning us of the likelihood of continued attack, and instructing everybody that the end of hostilities meant that Japanese aircraft were now to be shot down 'in a friendly manner'.

The situation clarified: the irreconcilable kamikazes were dead, there was a magnificent flypast of some 500 naval aircraft, and on 12 August the main body of the British Fleet departed for Sydney. We stayed because Brind had been detailed off to be the Senior British Naval Officer Afloat in Japan after the formal surrender had taken place. Vian went with the carriers, but Rawlings in *King George V* stayed, and soon afterwards Sir Bruce Fraser joined in *Duke of York*, having left Guam immediately after the ceasefire. The situation sounded calmer ashore and we anchored with American ships in a large bay just to the west and south of the entrance to Tokyo Bay itself. Somehow, a couple of British prisoners of war, who were released by their guards in the turmoil rather than suffering the massacre that some Japanese had intended, made their way out to us, and some American prisoners of war likewise found their way to their ships. Ours said they knew we were British because they had found a couple of Players cigarette packets washed up on the beach. Unfortunately, one of them was not placed under medical supervision, and very nearly died from celebrating his freedom.

On 27 August, in the early morning, we entered Tokyo Bay, following astern of *King George V* and *Duke of York*, all led in by *Missouri*. The forts which we were so short a time ago to have bombarded were flying white flags as we passed them, at action stations, to anchor in Yokosuka Bay, not far from a surrendered Japanese cruiser. Some Allied forces were soon ashore, and our prisoners of war were collected as fast as practicable. The condition of most of them was deplorable, though not always as bad, I was told, as that of those who had been held by the Japanese further south in Indonesia and Hong Kong. The most important prisoners had been kept in Manchuria and had been flown out in the face of the Soviet invasion. I took a walk round the Japanese cruiser, which was interesting: all the ladders, hatches and doors were clearly made for people a good deal smaller than ourselves. The equipment lacked the sophistication of ours, even in those days, and one had to admire the fight they had put up.

On the morning of Sunday 2 September the delegates for the surrender assembled on the verandah deck of *Missouri* and I was most fortunate to go with Brind to represent the British Pacific Fleet with Vice-Admiral Rawlings and two others. We all went in our working uniform, the British in white tropical shorts, the Americans in their khaki, and milled around on *Missouri*'s deck while people completed the scaffolding outboard, from which the press were to photograph the proceedings. It was like the end of a school term and the beginning of the holidays, and the Americans, with their delightful volatility, were meeting old friends, slapping each other on the back in great excitement, soldiers and sailors alike. Some, like General Doolittle, 'Vinegar Joe' Stillwell and others, I could recognise; General Blamey was there for the Australians, General Le Clerc for France, Derevyanko for the USSR, and others besides.

A table was laid out with a chair each side of it, obviously for the surrender ceremony. Eventually, the carnival atmosphere was brought to an end as a boat came alongside with the Japanese delegates on board, the press sprang into action, and we all grouped ourselves round, leaving a clear space between the head of the gangway and that long table. As they came to the top of the gangway, led by Shigemitsu, the Foreign Minister, in a black morning coat and top hat, limping and carrying a stick, a hush fell as people gazed on the enemy. He was followed by several others, some officers representing the Imperial High Command in white mourning uniforms.

When they had been arranged in front of the table, General MacArthur, who was to sign for the United Nations, walked with Admiral Nimitz, for the USA, to their place behind the table. MacArthur read the surrender terms aloud, and the documents were produced. The Japanese, Shigemitsu and General Umezo, came forward and signed. MacArthur then signed, flanked by General Wainwright, whom he had left behind at Corregidor, and General Percival, the last commander of Singapore. Both these officers had been flown out of prison in Manchuria, and were thin as rakes and swaying on their feet (whether from emotion or from exhaustion and illness I do not know). MacArthur used two pens, and gave one to each. After Nimitz and his team, Admiral Fraser signed for Great Britain, with Rawlings and Brind flanking him as he did so. He pocketed his pen and told me, years later, that it had been against the rules to do so. As the signing took place, aircraft from the Fleet flew over us in formation – not least among the instruments of victory. When all was done, MacArthur led the Allied representatives away, and the rest of us started chatting and talking, laughing and finding our friends as before. Only the Japanese remained fallen in, silent in their humiliation in their place on deck. They were eventually shepherded into a boat and away, but nobody bothered with them any longer – they had done what they had come to do.

We had all been invited into *Missouri*'s officers' mess, where there was a cold collation of sorts but, of course, no alcohol. There were photographers there, and my photograph was taken with MacArthur, one arm round my shoulder and the other round the shoulder of a young American enlisted man. (Unfortunately, I never managed to get a copy of it, although I have a good many photographs of that day.) I wondered whether to talk to General Percival and tell him that my uncle, Colonel Ashmore, had escaped safely to rejoin the war, but decided not to because one really did not know what had happened in Singapore. Brenton was very cross with me later for not having done so. Eventually, I went back with my admiral to *Newfoundland*, where we could have a drink and celebrate the occasion properly. It was the end of a long haul from Kingston-upon-Hull.

CHAPTER THREE

To Moscow and Back

1945–53

The other British ships sailed, but *Newfoundland* remained off Yokosuka as she was now our guardship in Japanese waters and Brind was Senior British Naval Officer Afloat. Commodore Collins of the Royal Australian Navy took over naval officer ashore duties in the British Embassy in Tokyo, John Robertson, his signal officer, with him.

Meanwhile, the poor prisoners of war who were not well enough to be flown out by air to Manila were being embarked in hospital ships in Tokyo Bay. Those from Manila were being ferried home to England, the British in our aircraft carriers (whose return was delayed by Bruce Fraser to permit this). Those in Tokyo Bay had to wait, and our Church of Scotland minister in *Newfoundland*, a man called Husbands, arranged visits to them, on one of which I went. All were suffering from deficiency diseases or worse, and looked dreadful. They were so anxious to pour out their woes that it was not difficult just to listen, in as sympathetic a way as possible, for long periods. One heard nothing to reduce one's revulsion for the Japanese.

By now I had two assistants, John Rushbrooke, a regular naval signal officer, and Jim Dennits, an RNVR officer, both quite excellent. John went to Tokyo to help there and act as a shore link. It was a tremendous problem to select the signal traffic intended for the Admiral and *Newfoundland* from a whole plethora of American 'Foxes'. It was nose to the grindstone again for me, since I felt the only satisfactory approach was to thumb through all the messages we were receiving in bulk from shore myself, in the hope of finding the occasional nugget of value to us in the mass of information which we were being sent. The Manus problem was compounded, but happily in cooler weather, and eventually, Hong Kong opened up to pass on our own messages from Australia.

Brind was very tired, and so was Peter White who had done a magnificent job as his secretary and kept us all straight. He had been awarded the MBE, and I received a Mention in Despatches for my service. I think, now the war was over, Brind's widowerhood was weighing heavily on him and he was not happy. The situation had become so difficult towards the end of the second operating period that Pat McLaughlin, the flag captain, had sent for me and told me that since the admiral was taking so long to make up his mind on the bridge, I was to make the signals when McLaughlin told me to, and not to wait for the admiral's decision. To this I said, 'Aye, aye, Sir,' though I found it best to use my own judgement and, knowing the admiral so well by then, to anticipate his decision if the situation seemed to require it. This seemed to me to save a possible scene between the captain and the admiral. However, Peter White now asked to be allowed home, as he had a plan to go east-about via the United States. This he eventually did, being relieved by John Bradbury around the beginning of October.

Brind, with his great gift for dealing with people, and now relieved of his self-imposed duty of trying to mediate between Rawlings and Vian, made a point of making friends with General Eichelburger, who was the American land commander in the Tokyo district, and established excellent inter-service and international relations with him, as also with General Gairdner, the British soldier ashore. As well as the signals grind, therefore, there was a certain amount of quiet entertaining to do and, in addition, from time to time, I used to drive up by jeep to Tokyo to see John Robertson and the team there. It was a journey of some 12 miles, and the entire route passed through ruins. I have never seen anything so flat (apart from the atomic bomb damage I saw later), and I remember the sides of the route being littered with office safes – nothing much else seemed to survive.

In October we moved south of the Inland Sea to Sasebo in Kyushu, where, had the war had to take that course, some of the initial landings would have been made. There, after meeting some US Army Air Force officers ashore, Ian McGeoch and I made our way to the airport and thumbed a lift on a couple of Piper Cubs to go and see Nagasaki, the site of the second atomic bomb, which was not far away. The town lies in two valleys between mountain ridges, and I shall never forget coming up to the edge of the first ridge and seeing all the trees lying flat, rank upon rank of them. We flew low over the devastation of one arm of the city, and then back to Sasebo. Soon afterwards, *Newfoundland* anchored off Nagasaki Harbour itself, and leave was granted on request. I went ashore and walked alone up the main road of the city, through the valley, towards its head. I had never seen factory chimneys bent before. The hospital still stood, but scorched and with no windows, the Mitsubishi arms works were blown in and everything else seemed to be knee-high.

Other visits were more pleasant, but I had been away from Elizabeth and home for over a year, and it had been a long war. I was unsure what I wanted to do next, but noticed in an Admiralty Fleet Order that Russian courses for servicemen were being started at the School of Slavonic Studies in Cambridge. This offered the change of environment I needed, and I asked 'Daddy' Brind to put my name forward for the first one of these, which he agreed to do.

Early during this time, reports on signals experience in the British Pacific Fleet were called for. With the help of Ellis and Parkin, I produced one on the manoeuvring and operating aspect, and another on wireless procedures and practice. In these, which Brind endorsed, we strongly recommended that the British Fleet should adopt procedures similar to those the Americans had used in the Pacific for our future peacetime use, and that our signal books should accordingly be considerably re-written in the light of experience in that theatre. I believe these reports found favour; certainly, a

Signal Books Committee was set up, and Brind was appointed to be its chairman. I was worried that this might be the end of my chance to learn Russian, but it was not so: Brind let me stick to my guns on that, although from time to time during the Russian course I received a Signal Books Committee paper and was asked to comment.

In early December we were relieved by Admiral Servaes and his team in time to reach Sydney in *Newfoundland* for Christmas. We had breakfast at separate tables from our admirals in Servaes's 'Cuddy' – much to my disgust! Admiral Brind was told that he was to fly home to get the Signal Books Committee under way. He very kindly said that he would take me with him, but there was no flight available until early January. Jim Dennitts and I therefore went to the hospitality hut on the Cathedral domain, and there found an invitation from a Dr Thompson and his wife to spend Christmas at their beach hut at Terrigal on the north shore from Sydney. Off we went, and we had a marvellous, relaxed time with a delightful family and their friends. Then, one fine Saturday morning, Brind and I boarded a Lancastrian at Mascot airfield in Sydney. I sent a telegram to Elizabeth saying, 'Expect me on Monday for tea.' In those days, this was phenomenal: it was a 65 hour journey in all, of which 58 were to be flying time.

The aircraft carried six passengers, sitting on seats along one side and looking across to the other, where there were small windows at intervals. At night a flap came down overhead, reminiscent of the Trans-Siberian Railway. This allowed us to double bunk, lie down and sleep. The aircraft was unpressurised and did not fly very high, although there was oxygen available if required. The noise of the four engines driving the airscrews was a relentless thunder to which one became inured, mainly through becoming temporarily deaf.

All did not go according to plan. On take-off an aircraft hatch, which had not been properly secured, blew off, so we had to circle Mascot for three hours to use up enough fuel to make it safe to land. This we did, stopping (it seemed to me) perilously close to a hangar, and we left again some six hours later. As a result, in places where we were supposed to have landed in daylight, we came down at night, and vice versa. Then, on what should have been the final leg, from Lydda to London we ran into a violent storm and failed to make it across the Alps. During the bouncing, lurching struggle, we discovered one of the oxygen masks was not working, and I gave mine to an elderly gentleman who was in some distress. We turned back after a very hairy time, and landed at Marignane near Marseilles. On the approach one of the engines failed, and it was found that we were in no condition to take off again.

The admiral had to decide what to do. He knew that he had to be back in England pretty quickly and he knew how badly I wanted to be there. After a call to the embassy, he decided to catch a train to Paris and go on by car and ferry. Little did we know that Peter White, who was looking after our interests in London, had arranged for a relief aircraft to be sent out to pick us up; but by then we were on the train. We spent a very comfortable night at the Hotel George V in Paris, and went on by embassy car to board the ferry at Dieppe. Two blow-outs delayed us, and the admiral almost turned back, but I had other ideas and managed to persuade him that undoubtedly the ferry would be waiting for him and he could not possibly turn round until he had got to Dieppe and found out whether this was the case or not. So on we pressed, reached Dieppe and, miraculously, the ferry was waiting. We scrambled on board and made our way across the Channel, reaching London to meet Elizabeth in time for 'Daddy' Brind to give us supper and present her with a sheepskin coat bought for her in Australia.

I owe him a great deal – for example, for his patience and never-failing kindness, as well as for his interest in my career. Later, when he went as the first Allied C.-in-C. Northern Europe, and again to the Far East as Naval C.-in-C., he asked for me, but the Admiralty had other plans. He distinguished himself in both appointments, helped then, and in his all too short retirement, by a new wife, the widow of Admiral Blagrove, who had been lost in *Royal Oak*. From midshipman to quasi-permanent lieutenant-commander (to which rank I was about to be promoted), he was, after Father, the dominant influence of my naval life.

Susan was staying with Mousse and Father at Godden Green, where we soon went. The whole family, including Peter, who had been appointed an equerry to the King, were together again: we had survived the war! Father had made a remarkable recovery, and had been appointed as Flag Officer Commanding the Reserve Fleet based at Chatham, so he could commute quite readily to and from Godden Green. Elizabeth was living with friends in Sevenoaks, and we now had to decide what to do. This was not difficult because Elizabeth's parents had a large house at Cambridge on Parker's Piece, whose attic flat they very kindly said we could use. I had known of this possibility at the time I took the decision to learn Russian at Cambridge and knew, too, that to find a house that we could afford in England immediately after the war would be extremely difficult. So all was fine, and leaving Susan safely with her grandparents at Godden Green, we shot off on a holiday together to St Mary's in the Scilly Islands – and absolutely lovely it was.

The Russian course began in April. There were about 60 of us enrolled on it, though the naval contingent consisted only of Major Kirby, RM, who was the senior officer, myself and three other lieutenants, Dobbs, Harvey-Jones and Kaye. The rest were Army and RAF, other ranks as well as officers. Our teacher was a formidable lady of some 50 summers called Lisa Hill, an Anglo-Russian of demonic energy.

Having learnt the alphabet from Hugo's *Russian Grammar Simplified* and heard the language spoken sometimes, I was a slight lap ahead at the beginning and, having Liz there to look after me properly and to hear my words at night, I managed to keep just ahead of the game. However, it was enormously hard work to master the language and obtain an interpretership in just six months. We were advised to adopt the Japanese student practice of using white cards, like visiting cards, to accumulate our vocabulary. One wrote the English word on one side and the Russian on the other, and then went through the English words and checked you could remember the Russian word – you at least knew when you cheated by having to turn the card over. We had oral practice in the evenings, and a good many set lessons trying to grasp the complicated grammar of this fully inflected and beautiful language. Poetry was a help, often read to us by an old *émigré* actor, Ranevski, whose rendering of Pushkin's 'I loved you' I shall not forget. The Russian songs that Lisa Hill used to sing with us in the evenings were a tremendous help, too.

I was able to walk to work and back from the house on Parker's Piece, and the weekends were our own except for the homework to be done. We went to Bletchingly at Easter and I heard from Peter that a VIP plane went weekly from London to Nuremberg, taking bigwigs, mostly politicians, to witness the War Crimes Tribunal then in progress. As I was trying to become an interpreter and the tribunal had the first simultaneous interpreting system in the world in operation, I thought I might have a case for a back seat in someone's aircraft. Sure enough, Peter worked the oracle, and in mid-course, off I went. Sir Orme Sargent, then head civil servant in the Foreign Office, was the VIP, and tagging along as I was, it was delightful to hear nice Lady Lawrence, wife of the senior British judge on the tribunal, say how sorry they were not to be able to put me up, too. However, the American-run German hotel for visitors was comfortable enough for two vividly-remembered days, mostly in court, but also visiting Brigadier-General Schreiber, US Army, in charge of the exhibits for the prosecution. This was a 'Chamber of Horrors', but real ones. I returned to Cambridge, sadder and wiser and better disposed to sympathise with the Soviet sufferings under the German invasion.

In October I learned that I alone had qualified as a first-class interpreter, but I was not wholly pleased to hear that my job was to go to Moscow as interpreter and assistant to the naval attaché, since Elizabeth by then was well on the way to having our second baby and everybody told me that it would be madness to take her to Moscow. We found a house in Hambledon, which we rented from some nice Foreign Office people at the princely sum of 4½ guineas a week. I could afford this because my arrangements for pay in Moscow would be such that living costs would be looked after 'by the King' and would make no demands on pay. I only expected to be away for a year this time, but it was hard to part so soon after the long absence in the Pacific, particularly as war was now at an end. However, I was still uncertain about my future in the Navy, and the opportunity to improve my Russian and learn something of the USSR had to be seized.

There was briefing from the Naval Intelligence Division, whose head was a signal officer called Tony Courtney, and my passage was booked in a Russian ship, *Byeloostrov*, sailing from London in early December. I was told that the naval attaché's clerk would meet me on arrival at Leningrad, so eventually, off I set. My cabin in the ship was comfortable and she was half-full of Russian officers in uniform, returning home after delivering back some minesweepers we had lent them. These chaps were great chess experts, and played constantly in the saloon of the ship. I used to watch and eventually joined in, to be soundly beaten. However, relations were very good, and it was useful practice for my Russian since they spoke not a word of English.

We stopped briefly in Stockholm *en route*, and the British naval attaché there invited me to supper, which was very decent of him. I had been told how careful I had to be of 'bugs' – hidden microphones – everywhere in Russia, but was surprised when he showed me one hidden behind his fireplace in the British Embassy flat in Stockholm. My view of 'neutral' Sweden had been naive, but living as they do, cheek by jowl with the Soviet Union, Swedes cannot be greatly blamed for taking every kind of precaution to safeguard their neutrality.

As we neared the Soviet Union, a boat came out with the frontier guards and a shiver ran through the Russians on board at seeing them. As you can imagine, passports were scrupulously inspected, and so was the luggage. It took a long time, and I was more than pleased to be a British citizen, not a Soviet one, and now, thanks to my diplomatic visa, to retain my passport. At last we entered the Gulf of Finland, passed by the Fortress of Kronstadt and into the River Neva, pushing through the brash ice in the grey afternoon light. Once alongside, Mr Plummer, the naval attaché's clerk, came on board to see me. He was a little man, extremely friendly, and his fluent Russian, much squeakier than any I had heard before, seemed to be well understood. Eventually, we went ashore just after dark and Plummer took me by taxi to the hotel where we were to spend the night, the old Astoria, on the square by St Isaac's Cathedral. It was dusty, the windows would not open, and I had a four-poster bed curtained in the plush with which all the furniture was covered. I turned in early since the Moscow train required a prompt morning start. It was light before I left and the view from my window over St Isaac's golden dome towards the ice-bound river was superb. It was extraordinary to find oneself in Mousse's home city at last, to glimpse the frozen river and to wonder what lay ahead.

The journey down to Moscow was long, noisy and uneventful, passing a succession of snow-covered plains with the odd little village perched here and there. The train was rather more comfortable than the Trans-Siberian Railway had been, but not much faster. However, there was a great deal to talk about with Plummer, and I learned that David Chance, my precedessor, had already left, and that I was to take over his apartment at one end of the naval attaché's flat in the Arbat. I knew my new boss, Captain Duncan Hill, by repute, since during the war he had spent part of his service starting up a Damage Control School in London, which was soon reckoned to be the best wartime course available. Duncan regarded it as a 'run ashore', as well as an instructional period for officers back from the sea. As a result, damage control doctrine spread like wildfire. He had married a Wren officer called Maureen Uprichard, whom Elizabeth knew. They were most welcoming and kind, although it was perfectly clear that they much regretted the departure of David Chance, who had been a great favourite. I think they feared, probably rightly, that I was going to be very pukkah and rather hard to jolly along. Their flat was large, and my quarters at the end of the passage comprised a very nice bedroom and bathroom and a large sitting room, partitioned off from the room that the Hills used as a dining room. At parties, the partition was apt to go and I might have to be elsewhere, unless invited (which was, generously, often the case). There were a great many people to get to know, and the Hills could not have been more helpful, introducing me to their particular friends.

Work in the office, some 20 minutes' walk away, consisted of helping Duncan Hill compile his reports. We had intelligence targets set for us by the Joint Intelligence Bureau and the Naval Intelligence Department, although we were very restricted in what we should do in order to obtain this information. One of my contributions was to read the Russian newspapers and try to put two and two together and make four from the snippets that one could cull from them. Obituary notices were particularly useful. The signatures published in the papers below them gave an excellent idea of the pecking order in the Politburo at the time. There were also professional magazines like *Red Star* and *Red Fleet* that had to be digested, and I was given, as a particular project, orders to find out what I could and write a report on the navigability, development and use of the Great Northern Sea Route from the Bering Strait to the Barents, about which the Soviet authorities were making a great fuss at the time. I would go to the bookshops, too, and often wished that the Russian word for 'oceanography' was less easy to stumble over. In addition, from time to time there were meetings of the Three Bs Mine Clearance Board (the 'Three Bs' standing for the Baltic, Barents and Black Seas). I was its interpreter, and Duncan Hill was the British member, the chairman being a Russian captain first rank. This was all good Russian practice for me. In the evenings, two or three times a week, I had Russian lessons, at my own expense, from a lady called Vera Petrovna, about twice my age, married to a Frenchman who was now locked up by the Bolsheviks.

Our normal routine was to leave for the office at about 9 a.m. in the winter, earlier in summer, come home for lunch, and go back to the office again until about 4 p.m. In the evening I might have a Russian lesson and then go out, either to a party or to the Students' Opera with embassy friends. Sometimes I would set off alone to any little Russian restaurant, find a table somewhere near a band, and sit down. Sooner or later I would be joined by some Russian who would know that I was a foreigner (that, I am afraid, was obvious) and who perhaps had had enough to drink to embolden him to accost me, but not so much that I was unable to understand a word he was saying. I would then have conversation, very often of interest, always depressing to anyone who felt sympathetic towards Soviet people and occasionally containing some element of intelligence.

Once, for example, one man declared that he was a scientist, and told me that Kapitza was under a cloud because he had flatly refused to help the Soviet government make an atomic weapon. I believe this to have been true. On one excursion only were I and the man who had been sitting at my table stopped as we left the restaurant. I, addressed as 'citizen', was told to go on my way, and the Russian was taken off by the police. I knew it was important to strike a balance and not put anybody in an impossible position. The man with me that night was a simple soul and would not, I am sure, have come to harm, though I felt uncomfortable about him for days. It was also very important to avoid Soviet women: 1946 and 1947 were some of the worst years of the Stalin regime, and caution was our watchword. It was not easy to obtain tickets for the Bolshoi Theatre for the magnificent opera and ballet, and from time to time I risked going to the steps of the theatre and buying tickets there from one of the many 'hand-traders'. This was against the rules, but not dangerously so, as it was, in a way, paying a compliment. The black market price was fairly moderate in the circumstances. Although the official exchange rates was 22 roubles to the pound, we could change money at a diplomatic rate of 48, which helped.

Among the hazards of Moscow diplomatic life were the National Days and Russian parties, and I formed the habit of swilling olive oil before I went, and again, to settle the fumes, when I came back. In that way, and through eating a mass of *zakuski* (Russian small eats) while drinking, I managed to survive comfortably. It was important to be able to do this, as one gained face – certainly, those who did not stand the pace lost it.

Letters from home were regular and I was able to telephone Elizabeth. I did this about once a fortnight, though we were both conscious that every word was being overheard, if not recorded. I remember coming in one day and finding Vera, the young housemaid, piecing together the contents of my wastepaper basket on the bedspread. She scuttled off at once, and would have found nothing had she had time to finish.

I went into the country once or twice, and it was a pleasant change to walk through the birch woods in the snow. It was cold, 20–30 degrees of frost was usual, but quite tolerable unless there was a wind, when one had to watch out for frostbite. I was issued with an Astrakhan fur hat, which looked rather dishy with a naval metal cap badge sewn on, and had a pair of naval fleece-lined flying boots on loan for this particular appointment. Otherwise, the naval greatcoat (or 'British warm') and some lined gloves sufficed, backed up by a scarf over the lower part of the face if there was a breeze.

Soon after Christmas, Field Marshal Montgomery came to receive the Order of Suvorov from Stalin and it so happened, to my great good fortune, that Duncan Hill was sick at the time, so I took his place in many of the various ceremonies and festivities. I was, therefore, with many others at the airport, stamping about in the cold evening, when the little man arrived, stepped out of his aeroplane and inspected the Soviet honour guard. This is a formidable affair of men six feet or more tall, holding their rifles at the 'present' and following with heads and eyes as the inspecting officer walked past the ranks. 'Monty' then went to the microphone and made a speech. He said, of course, how glad he was to be there, but where he scored over other visitors of his kind in the Soviet Union at that time was by his lavish praise of the contribution of the Red Army to victory and his outspoken sympathy with the privations and sufferings endured by the Soviet people as a result of Hitler's attack. In this way he got off on absolutely the right foot, and by all accounts his visit was the most successful of them all.

General Gatehouse, the military attaché, held a reception for the Field Marshal, to which I went and was presented to him. He looked at me and said, 'Ashmore! We've met before, haven't we?' and I said, 'Yes, Sir.'

He then said, 'In the Home Fleet wasn't it?' and I said, 'Yes, Sir, you asked me about radar.' 'Ah, yes,' he said, 'I remember.' So I went on my way. We had indeed met before D-Day, in *Duke of York*, and I asked George Cole, his military assistant, remembering the episode with Mountbatten, how they managed to brief the Field Marshal so well. He replied that they never did, and 'Monty' became very angry if they tried, but that he just had a remarkable memory for faces.

I did not go with him for his call on Stalin, but I was the Royal Navy guest at the banquet given for him by the Soviet Armed Forces headed by General Vassilievski, with their Foreign Office represented by Gusev. I found it of absorbing interest, as so many of the great names of the Red Army were there. 'Monty', who drank water throughout, made another splendid speech, but did say that he wondered where Marshal Zhukov was, and how sad he was not to see his old friend, Marshal Rokossovski. These two were among the most distinguished of the Soviet Marshals of the war, and extremely popular with the Red Army. As a result, they had fallen upon evil times and been exiled by Stalin. It was brave and typical of 'Monty' to refer to them on this occasion. The party went on after the field marshal left, and I was grateful for the olive oil when I got back to my flat.

The next day I went with Monty on a conducted tour of the Kremlin, which at that time was not open to the public. This was hosted by General Slavin, Commander of the Moscow Garrison. We all drove in through the great gate and ended up on the enormous square outside the cathedrals and palaces on which stands the Great Kremlin Gun, the Tsar Cannon. Everything was beautiful, covered with snow and glinting in the early morning sunshine. The temperature was about 35 degrees of frost, and there was no wind. Monty immediately said he would like to have a look inside the churches. The guide mentioned something to Slavin and I moved closer. Slavin told the field marshal, through his interpreter, that unfortunately the cathedrals were closed for repair and they were not open for inspection. 'Ah,' said Monty, 'How interesting that you are repairing your cathedrals, I should very much like to see the work in progress, let's go in.' Slavin replied that he was sorry, but they were locked. 'Oh that's all right,' said Monty, 'Find the key.' So somebody was sent off to get the key, and we stamped up and down trying to keep warm for about a quarter of an hour. A man then came back and spoke to Slavin, who looked upset and turned round to the Field Marshal and said, 'I am very sorry, Field Marshal, but we have lost the key.' Monty did not look best pleased, and said abruptly, 'All right, I'll stay here until you find it.' Some ten minutes later we started going into the cathedrals. I heard subsequently that Eisenhower, on his similar visit, had expressed the same wish but had not shown the same determination, so this was a very British victory (if one can call such discourteous behaviour by a guest by that name). Sure enough, the churches were under repair, there was scaffolding up by all the frescoes and round the iconostasis, but the workmen had been sent out of the way and the churches had indeed been locked.

Very shortly afterwards, I heard Elizabeth had given birth on 19 January

1947 to a little girl, whom we were going to call Tamara, and that all was well. A kind Admiralty ordered me home for a meeting, and Hill sent me off with an extra few days' leave so that I could see Elizabeth, Susan and the new baby. It was a bitterly cold winter throughout Europe. I had a flight in an Aeroflot Dakota from Moscow to Berlin, an exit visa (otherwise I should not have been able to get out of the Soviet Union), and a re-entry visa through Leningrad, as I was to come back by sea. I sat in that aeroplane on Moscow airfield, with the door open, in something like 25 degrees of frost, for nearly half an hour before it was ready to take off. We then flew, gradually warming up, to Kaliningrad (once called Königsberg), in what used to be East Prussia, and came down in the dark to refuel. There was an enormous bonfire blazing, of timbers from houses that had been destroyed when the city was taken by the Red Army, and we stood around it trying to keep warm while the aircraft was refuelled. The fuelling bowsers and the aircraft were far too close to the bonfire for my comfort. We eventually flew on, and landed at Schönefeldt Airport in East Berlin around 11 p.m. It took me longer to get from the airport into West Berlin than it had taken to come from Moscow to Berlin. I remember getting very tired and cross about it all. Eventually, I was greeted in West Berlin by John Rennie, a naval officer who was assistant secretary to General Sir Brian Robertson, commanding the British forces. I was put up at one of the officers' messes; there was a shortage of fuel, and I found I had to jump up and down to get warm enough to get into bed, and then jump up and down and do exercises in the morning to get warm enough to face the day. I was due to fly on to England, but because of the weather no flying was possible, and in Berlin I stayed.

One morning I walked into the Russian sector, joined up with an American journalist, and entered the ruined Reichschancellery. I relished the contrast with August 1939. We saw a fire, approached, and found a man with a torch. So we entered Hitler's bunker, saw where he, Eva Braun and, in another room, the Goebbels family died, and did not feel credibility stretched on being shown two shallow depressions where the bodies of Hitler and Braun had been burnt. (Sensibly, the Russians blew all this up later on.) I visited the Allied Mission at Potsdam, where the British naval member, Tupper-Carey, had been on Fraser's staff in the Pacific Fleet. He took me on a tour of Frederick the Great's Palace at Sans Souci. I also went to a meeting of the Coordinating Committee. This was a regular session in which the commanders of the Allied Occupation Forces met and discussed the affairs of the Occupation. Brian Robertson was there for us, Lucius Clay for the Americans, Koenig for the French and Marshal Sokolovski, whom I had met in Moscow, for the Soviet Union. I do not remember what they talked about, but I do remember the distinction with which Brian Robertson discharged his particular part in the proceedings. He spoke little and, if he could, last, and therefore to very great effect.

At length, I decided the only way to get home was to go by train and this I did, through the snow out of Berlin to the Hook of Holland, across to Harwich, and then from Harwich up to London, and so to Godden Green to see the family. This was a treat, and England, though cold in February 1947, was not quite as cold as the places I had become used to. To my great good fortune, it transpired that there was to be a meeting of Foreign Ministers in Moscow in March, therefore I was to go out on the special train with the Foreign Secretary and his entourage rather than taking the long haul, which I had done already once, by sea to Leningrad.

We set off in considerable comfort from Victoria to witness first the signing of the Treaty of Dunkirk by Ernest Bevin, our Foreign Secretary, and Bidault, his French opposite number. I had a grandstand seat at this ceremony, which marked the beginning of Western European Union and the defence cooperation from which so much has since stemmed. The French laid on a champagne buffet and then we boarded our special train and went on our way. The next stop I remember is Warsaw, where we spent the best part of a day and had a conducted tour of the city, which was in a pitiful state. It was still cold, and the people looked poor and ill fed. Horse-drawn carts with bricks and debris from the ruins were the only traffic to be seen, and the whole impression was sadly different from the glorious, lit buildings along the Vistula that I had glimpsed from the train in 1939.

Then on we went to encounter the customs formalities for entering the Soviet Union, the point of entry being Brest Litovsk. I ran into trouble because my re-entry visa was for Leningrad, and here was I trying to come in through Brest. No customs officer was prepared to stamp my passport, and I thought that I might have to enlist the aid of the Foreign Secretary himself. One of the passengers, a well-known Russian-speaker and author, Edward Crankshaw, came to my aid, and we had an animated argument with these officials. As a result, while resolutely refusing to stamp the visa, they did agree to stamp a blank page in the passport. (This was just as well, because if it had not been done I felt that, when the time would come for me to leave Russia, I might have gone along to the department dealing with the foreign military for weeks on end with my passport, and been refused an exit visa on the grounds that I was not there at all.)

On arrival in Moscow, Ernest Bevin and most of his party went to the British Embassy at Sofiskaya, and I returned to my quarters on Arbatskaya. Later, I attended one or two of the foreign ministers' meetings when a naval subject was being discussed. I remember most clearly one where the subject of discussion was the future of the Japanese fishing fleet. The ministers there besides Bevin were Bidault, Molotov, and Marshall from the United States. There was a rather complicated technical discussion about the use of fishing vessels for minelaying, minesweeping, for coastal patrol, and so forth, which went on for quite a while. Bevin sat there, saying nothing. When the discussions seemed to have reached an end, he said, 'Can anybody please tell me what the Japanese eat?' Someone, who had obviously been prepared for this in advance, said that before the war something like 70 per cent of the protein in their diet came from fish that they caught. 'Right,' said Bevin, 'are we going to let them starve?' Everybody shook their heads. Then he said, 'If they don't catch their own fish, which of us is going to catch the fish for them?' In the event, of course, the Japanese retained their fishing Fleet, and again I was impressed by the performance of the British representative at a meeting like this, and also by the value of being last to speak.

There were great receptions, of course, and a Gala Performance at the Bolshoi of *Romeo and Juliet*, with Ulanova, to which I went and glimpsed Stalin. The reception at the British Embassy I remember particularly well because Bevin was buttonholed by the Soviet Deputy Foreign Minister, a nasty piece of work called Vishinsky, a very plausible lawyer who had been responsible for the State Prosecution at many of Stalin's most brutal trials. Bevin was visibly displeased, and barely concealed his distaste for the man. Full marks again.

The good news came that a squadron of the Mediterranean Fleet was to visit Sevastopol in the Crimea after Red Navy Day in August. This meant that the naval attaché would have to go down there, with me as his interpreter, and that a programme for the Commander-in-Chief, Admiral Sir Algernon Willis would have to be prepared and agreed, as well as arrangements made for such entertainment as the Russians could offer to the ships' companies of *Liverpool* and the destroyers who were to accompany her. I heard also that my relief, Tony Howard, was to come out in *Liverpool*, and this was good news in itself. A mass of administrative work was involved with the Ministry of the Armed Forces Naval Section. As part of the pleasant preliminaries of the Fleet visit, the Admiralty sent out a selection of volumes about a Russian admiral called Bellingshausen, who had been a great explorer of the Southern Seas. These Duncan Hill was to present to the Chief of Staff of the Soviet Navy, Admiral Golovko, and I went, too, to interpret. Golovko was a delightful person who spoke very highly of Admiral Fraser and others whom he had met when he was C.-in-C. Northern Fleet during the war, and it was altogether an unusually enjoyable occasion.

It was decided that we were to fly down to the Crimea and live in railway carriages on a siding at the railway station at Sevastopol for the duration of the Fleet visit. Hill and I were invited to go down earlier to be present for Red Navy Day. Accordingly, we embarked with our baggage in the inevitable Russian Dakota for the flight to Simferopol, only to discover there was trouble. We had our swords with us, and we were not allowed to take them, these being regarded as military weapons and therefore prohibited in any civil aircraft. Eventually, a compromise was reached, and our swords flew with the pilot in the cockpit. We landed in Simferopol around 2 p.m., and then drove through rather barren mountains to our railway carriages at Sevastopol. We found, to our dismay, that we were sharing them with a number of Russian officers, including some sent down from Moscow, and this, as you might expect, meant a choice of vodka or brandy for breakfast and at any other time of the day at which they could persuade you to have a drink with them. It was hot and not very comfortable, but we did have time to see some of the sights, and in particular, to go up to a marvellous panorama on top of the Malakov Redoubt which displays the Siege of Sevastopol and the battles around it during the Crimean War of 1854.

There was a large number of ships in harbour, including an incredibly ancient battleship called *October Revolution*.

As guests of the Soviet Navy at Red Navy Day, we were well placed to see what there was to be seen. The chief festivity seemed to be a Fleet swim. This was an extraordinary affair whereby, at a given signal, officers, petty officers and men from all the ships in harbour jumped into the water in bathing suits and started to swim towards the main jetty above which we and the high-ups were sitting, pushing before them floats and rafts sporting large banners glorifying Stalin, the Soviet Motherland, the Great Patriotic War and, of course, the Soviet Fleet. The men wore skull caps of different colours, one for officers, one for petty officers and one for the rest, and swam relentlessly towards us in formation, pushing their floats. One would have thought the exercise ludicrous except for the fact that all these fellows were swimming with apparent enjoyment a far longer distance than I would have ever have thought it possible to attempt. There was a reception ashore in the evening, and the ships were all lit up – not floodlit, but with fairy lights, as in the old days – and very pretty they looked.

The next day, just before the British squadron was due to arrive, the more modern ships slipped and went to sea. *Liverpool* and her destroyers arrived on time and in good order, and the naval attaché and I went off to meet Algy Willis. We then accompanied him on his call on Admiral Oktyabrsky, C.-in-C. Black Sea Fleet, at his headquarters in the very same building that was once the Kist Hotel in which Father and Mousse had lived until they had had to leave Russia in 1919. By some miracle it had survived the wholesale damage caused by the Siege of Sevastopol, and was therefore a natural choice for the headquarters. I met my opposite number, Oktyabrsky's English interpreter, Yevleev, and we came to a gentleman's agreement that at the lunch that was to follow, he would translate Admiral Willis's speech into Russian and I would translate Oktyabrksy's into English, this being much easier for both of us. All went well and we repeated the same thing at the return lunch on board *Liverpool*.

Algy's programme included a trip along the coast to Yalta, and a number of receptions, including one given by Admiral Fadeev, the commander of the port. We drove out along a good road towards Yalta and as we came through one particular valley, I could see to the right the approach to the little port of Balaclava where Mousse and her family had sought refuge during the Revolution. We passed the single-track narrow gauge railway that had been built from Balaclava to the lines outside Sevastopol to supply the British Army in that war long ago and also saw quite clearly the valley up which the Light Brigade had charged the Russian guns. We came to Yalta past the Livadia Palace, where Father had been on their wedding day to deliver the king's letter to the dowager empress, and so to a place called Massandra. Here a wine tasting was being held in honour of the British Commander-in-Chief, who was notorious in the Royal Navy for his dislike of all things alcoholic. Since this does not apply to me, I quite enjoyed myself. The interpreting was not particularly difficult, but I noticed during the course of the session that, from time to time, as the Commander-in-Chief raised his glass to admire the colour of its contents, holding it up to the light, his eyes closed in patient resignation behind it.

A swim on the 'Golden Beach' (which turned out to be made of black pumice-stone) was next on the programme after lunch. This meant going down in convoy through a very steep-sided valley, but we all reached the beach, and the British started to swim. The next item on the agenda was something of which Russians are very fond: ice-cream. It was due to be delivered to the beach so that we could enjoy it before going back to Sevastopol for Fadeev's reception. A worried liaison officer came up and explained that the cars were short of petrol, so the Commander-in-Chief said, 'Well, in that case, forget the ice-cream. Fill up with petrol and come back. We will then be in time to change and be ready for the admiral's reception.' So off they went, and after about an hour, when we were getting impatient, back they came with ice-cream, having failed to fill up with petrol. The Commander-in-Chief's face was a study. He knew he was going to be late and he felt, I am sure, that this was not the sort of country in which he wished to stay a moment longer than he had to. Fortunately, Duncan Hill's car had enough petrol, just, to get the two of us back to Sevastopol, so we set off, driven by a young Russian sailor, up the steep road from the beach, armed with a message to say that the Commander-in-Chief would arrive as soon as he could but, through no fault of his own, would be late. As we went up, our driver missed his gears and we started rolling down backwards. Quick as a flash, Duncan Hill had the door open and was out of the car onto the hillside. I was nothing like so quick. Fortunately, the sailor then came to his senses, turned his steering-wheel, and the car stopped, with its back stuck into the hillside. (I have always thought with admiration of Hill's reactions, and felt guilty about my own much slower ones.) We pushed the car back on the road, and reached Sevastopol without further incident. The message delivered, we nipped down to the railway carriage, changed, and made it on time to the party, where Admiral Willis eventually arrived an hour late (not that the Russians minded very much, since their views on punctuality are not ours).

We returned to Moscow by train, stopping at Kharkov, which was a ruin, and seeing quite a bit of the Ukrainian countryside as we went. The train paused at all sorts of halts, and there were always people on the platform with produce to sell, reminiscent for me of the stations on the Trans-Siberian Railway. I was able to complete most of my turnover to Tony Howard on the train and once back in Moscow there were only a few days of packing up and goodbyes before I travelled to Leningrad for eight days' holiday before catching the ship for home.

I again stayed in the Astoria, but by myself, speaking better Russian now and being able to make my way around and see the sights that nowadays are well on the tourist beat. One day I went to a tourist office and asked for a complimentary ticket for a trip on the River Neva, and this was given to me without any difficulty at all. I think my Russian accent at that time was rather like that of someone visiting from the Baltic States. So, armed with my complimentary ticket, I caught a boat and went down through the river as far as Kronstadt, and then back in the evening. This gave me a clear view of various naval dockyards and construction, the details of which I tried hard to commit to memory. Back in my hotel, I wrote them down and guarded the paper with my life until I was safely off the Soviet ship, *Sestroretsk*, and in England.

We were unable to disembark on the night of arrival, but Liz came to collect me the next day, and we spent the night in London. It was good to be home again, and doubts about a continuing future for the armed forces and a useful career in them had been set at rest by my Soviet experience.

Their Lordships' sense of humour had got the better of them, and despite my very different activities in Moscow, I was to be sent to the Signal School, HMS *Mercury*, as T4 (previously W2), the staff officer to whom was entrusted technical training in wireless – not my preferred subject. However, I was thankful not to have been consigned to the recesses of the Naval Intelligence Division in the Admiralty, where one could easily have spent the rest of one's days. This meant a return to 'Leydene' at Petersfield, and we faced a financial problem because, now that I was not living free, so to speak, in Moscow, we could no longer afford to rent the house in Hambledon, of which the family had become very fond. I talked it over with Father, who said he could lend me some money, and we decided to find a house to buy. This we did, with great luck, in Sussex Road at Petersfield. It suited us extraordinarily well. We had a car by then (by which hangs a long tale of enterprise and initiative on Elizabeth's part), and there was enough petrol to go on the odd excursion, providing we were careful with our ration coupons.

Learning technical wireless was the first thing I had to do before I could teach it, and fortunately, I had time before the Long Course of which I was to take charge began. I enjoyed being back in the signals world again, but I was not to escape Russians entirely. During my time at *Mercury*, the Soviets returned *Royal Sovereign*, the battleship which they had renamed *Arkhangelsk*, to Rosyth with some four submarines, and I was detailed off as one of the interpreters for this event. Who should I discover among the Russian side but my old friend Rudakov, the destroyer 1st Lieutenant from the Northern Fleet, now walking round as a captain. In fact, he was a rather more impressive personality than the captain first rank in charge. As well as dealing with *Royal Sovereign*, I went round the four submarines with a Lieutenant-Commander Varley, who had been in the term above me at Dartmouth and whose father had been in submarines with mine. They were in a pretty dreadful state, and the switchgear, which is most important, had clearly not been maintained at all. *Royal Sovereign*, on the other hand, was clean, except for the heads, which were very Russian indeed, and we were all impressed by the way her captain brought her in and secured to his buoy.

Eventually, the Royal Navy Long Course at *Mercury* which was to put me to the acid test arrived, and we got down to it. In those days one taught details to component level of the various wireless equipments in the syllabus, which were those currently in use in the Fleet. The course was taught theory by an Instructor Commander and his team and my senior ratings would take them in most of their 'practical'. They had to have a detailed knowledge of the circuitry and understand how everything worked; I felt like the blind leading the blind. For one particular subject, radio propagation, which seemed to me of immense importance; the science was developing fast, and I found it easier to take them to the Admiralty Signals and Radar Establishment at Haslemere to hear the gospel direct from the lips of Fred Kitchen, the expert there. I could then handle the tactical applications of that kind of knowledge at sea.

On the equipment side, I managed to sort most of it out with lots of help, but one particular problem arose when I found I could not fathom how a particular circuit in a new receiver, the B40 it was called, worked. So I went to see the theory expert, the Instructor Commander, who gave me an explanation which he found entirely satisfactory and which I still failed to grasp. So I went to Haslemere to see the designer, and I said, 'Would you please, I am so sorry to be so stupid, explain to me how your noise limiter circuit works?' 'Why?' he said. 'It works, doesn't it?' I said, 'I suppose so,' and he said, 'Well, that's why it's like that.' He had apparently tried various combinations of components and selected the one that seemed to him to give the best results.

My opinion of the Instructor Commander's theoretical knowledge sank abruptly and I was provided with ammunition, which was very satisfactory from my point of view, to use with the Long Course. This lasted a year in those days, and since I had been in the establishment some six months before these officers arrived, I felt the one thing I did not want to do was to have to take another RN Long Course through *Mercury*, for this would mean being ashore for almost three years in one place. No one else seemed to share my apprehension, so I took the decision to volunteer for the Staff Course at Greenwich. This is not something I would have done normally, because Father had brought us up to have a pretty healthy contempt for most courses, but it did work the oracle. I was duly selected and relieved by somebody else in time for him to prepare for the next Long Course. By that time, however, a revolution had occurred in the technical side of the Navy, the Electrical Branch had been established, and Lieutenant-Commander Bill Alder of the new specialisation had arrived in *Mercury*. My senior ratings, who had been chief petty officer telegraphists, had mostly volunteered to become chief radio electricians, and the officers who formed the next Signals Long Course were no longer to learn details of the equipments, but only roughly how they functioned on a block diagram basis, and of course, how to operate them. Circuitry, maintenance and the correction of faults was now a matter for the Electrical Branch. I felt I was fortunate in a way to have been part of the old regime, and also to have had a key role in *Mercury* during the transition. Indeed, the first course of electrical officers from *Collingwood* had to come to me to be examined in wireless technical, and included another friend from Dartmouth days, George Crane, of the same term as Varley. Despite the hard work, it had been a very happy time in *Mercury*, we had made a tremendous number of friends and enjoyed the summer balls and the Christmas festivities, even the produce of the market garden and, occasionally, the shoot.

In the spring, just before leaving to join the Staff Course, I was detailed as liaison officer between the C.-in-C. Portsmouth, Algy Willis, and the Russian cruiser *Murmansk*, which had been the American *Milwaukee*, and was calling at Portsmouth on her way back to the United States. On this occasion, unlike with *Royal Sovereign*, I was the only interpreter present and it was very hard work. I went out by boat to meet the ship. With the captain, sure enough, was Rudakov, greeting me like a long-lost friend, and disappointed that I would not have a drink on the strength of it. *Murmansk* anchored at Spithead, and the visit went fairly satisfactorily. Algy knew me well from the Crimea and performed admirably, giving me ample time to interpret sentence by sentence. The Russians were exuberant with their hospitality, as usual, and I had to conduct the odd rescue operation with some of Algy's staff who did not know the form. They were relieved while still manageable, and I had hopes of getting away, when an invitation to the Russians arrived from the captain and officers of *King George V*. This was greeted with enthusiasm, a team was assembled, and I had to accompany them. There was a tour of the ship, during which I remember deliberately misinterpreting the answer to a Russian question on the range of the 14 in guns. At long last, they were poured into their boat, and I came ashore and turned in in the staff officers' mess guest room for what was left of the night. Next morning, an early start found me boarding *Murmansk* with Algy's wishes for a good voyage, happy to see Rudakov thoroughly bleary-eyed and off form.

However, from the career point of view, it was essential to shrug off both a 'technical' and an 'intelligence' aura, and the Staff Course, living at Greenwich and coming home for weekends, was well calculated to achieve this. Most of the officers were commanders, I was one of three 'two-and-a-halfs', and the senior officer was Bill Beloe. He was a most delightful person, so the atmosphere was excellent. The course lasted six months, and was followed by a short tactical course at Woolwich. During it, I heard that my next appointment was to be at sea as signal officer of *Gambia* in the Home Fleet, and, although not yet senior enough, to be 1st Lieutenant later on. I felt this was a frightful let-down, having been signal officer of a squadron of 18 cruisers at the end of the war, although I recognised that things had to change in peacetime. Fortunately, the commander of the Signals School, Lord Cairns, who had proposed my 'nomination', was relieved by James Stopford, who had been the signal officer to Rawlings in the British Pacific Fleet and knew me better, and my appointment, for some reason or another, was changed. I was instead to go as signal officer of *Vengeance*, a light Fleet aircraft carrier and part of the 3rd Aircraft Carrier Squadron, relieving Colin Robertson, whom I knew.

I joined *Vengeance* at Portsmouth in October 1949. It was strange no longer to be a flag lieutenant but a ship's officer again, as I had not lived in a wardroom since *Duke of York*, nor had I had anything to do with the Fleet Air Arm except in spells in *Eagle* and *Implacable*. It was high time that I had further experience of naval aviation. I had a sizeable ship department to run, and one that was vital, not only to the ship's operations, but to flying as well. There were air signal officers in the squadrons, some of whom I had taught at *Mercury*, but their responsibilities were restricted to aircraft equipment, and I answered for communications as a whole. With the operations officer, I would attend all briefings and de-briefings, and give a brief myself on my subject. I maintained a very close liaison with the electrical officer and his assistants on the maintenance of all radio equipment. *Vengeance* was a very happy ship, with a superb captain in John Cuthbert. The air group commander, Nigel Ball, was a born leader, as were the squadron commanders, Andrew Lindsay and Pete London. Fireflies and Seafires were our normal complement (although Sea Vampires were sometimes carried). I had a great deal to learn.

By the greatest of good fortune, no sooner had I joined than the flag of the 3rd Aircraft Carrier Squadron transferred from *Theseus* to *Vengeance*, and I became, as ship's signal officer, the squadron communications officer of the 3rd Aircraft Carrier Squadron. My predecessor, Henry Hanrahan, gave me a splendid turnover, but that was only the beginning of my good luck. The admiral concerned was Charles Lambe, his staff officer air was Percy Gick, and the flag lieutenant was John Edmondson, who became a great friend, as did Jimmy Pack, the secretary. This all took time. The admiral and his personal staff, though kindness itself, were a very close-knit little team of their own. But happily for me, John was a member of the naval ski team, and for the impending Combined Fleet Spring Exercises he was busy away skiing. His job as flag lieutenant therefore fell to me, in addition to my ship and squadron responsibilities. In fact, this made my job rather easier. I could go to the admiral direct, advising on manoeuvres and so forth, attend him both on the admiral's bridge and in the operations room, and generally speaking, keep in the eye of whatever storm was brewing. Lambe was highly intelligent and a dedicated officer; he had held a private pilot's licence for years, and was one of the most charming and cultured people it has ever been my good fortune to meet, let alone serve.

A serious deficiency in the Fleet's equipment in those days was in methods of intercepting and taking bearings of hostile radar transmissions – a form of what is known as 'electronic warfare' – and although development of suitable equipment was proceeding apace at the Admiralty Signals and Weapons Establishment, which had now transferred from Haslemere to Portsdown, there was nothing in use at sea. So when I went to Lambe with an idea for converting an airborne search radar pod into a radar search receiver, I was given enthusiastic support. (This was very essential, as the powers that be at ASWE were averse to 'short cuts'.) With the help of a friendly scientist called Hawkins at the Services Electronic Research Laboratory at Baldock, and Bob Grayson, a young lieutenant of the Electrical Branch in *Vengeance*, I was allowed to 'lose' one of these pods at SERL, have it converted to a receiver, mount it on the forward pom-pom mounting on the deck of the ship and put it into action. The results were excellent. Submarines were using their radar freely, so were the coastal forces in some of the night attacks they carried out on the carrier squadron.

We detected them all, and this extravagant success was enjoyed by the admiral as much as by anybody. Reports were written, more pods were provided, and 'Dumb-Bell', as I called it, was approved for interim Fleet use. It was disappointing only in that our modification did not stand up to the shock of deck landing, and airborne trials were mostly unsuccessful. However, its main virtue lay in causing those who had thought that they could use radar with impunity to think again. Bob and I each received some money, I think it was £20 for him and £30 for me, out of the Herbert Lott Fund for Inventors, which seemed very reasonable in those days.

The C.-in-C. Home Fleet when I joined had been Admiral McGrigor ('Wee Mac'), once chief staff officer to Percy Noble in China. He was succeeded by Philip Vian. After some six months in *Vengeance*, I was sent for by my captain and told that he had given me a very good report, but that Vian had sent all the confidential reports for promotion to commander and captain back to their point of origin, saying that he could not believe that the Fleet had so many outstanding officers and all were to be revised. John Cuthbert told me that I was still given a pretty good report, and later, the Admiral told me (which he should not have done) that I had been high on the Fleet list for selection for promotion. It was comforting to feel that I was doing well, and Alan Seymour Haydon, the Fleet Communications Officer, was a good and loyal friend.

During the Combined Fleet Exercises in the Mediterranean in the Spring of 1950, we were allowed to exercise radio warfare, including deception, providing we did not cheat. By careful scrutiny of call signs and traffic in *Vengeance*, we were able to establish enough information to play a conspicuous role in this. I was able, legitimately, to instruct two 'orange' submarines (they were, in fact, foreign ones) to report their positions, and to intercept their reports, and on three occasions to turn back reconnaissance aircraft based on North Africa that could have found us. I finally blew it when I ordered part of the enemy air force to attack their own Fleet, and they then realised that they were being spoofed. Charles delighted in this kind of thing and the exercise outcome vindicated what we had done, with lessons learnt for various aspects of communications security for the future.

That autumn, the confidential reports on officers eligible for promotion went in. The admiral told me that I was second on the Fleet list, and sure enough, on 31 December 1950, I was promoted to commander – quite an expensive caper in the wardroom of *Vengeance*. To my delight, Alan Seymour Haydon was promoted at the same time: it would have been dreadful to have gone over his head. Having just turned 30, I was the youngest commander in the Navy, and had recovered, in terms of sea time, from the Russian interlude. I wondered what would happen next. Although the Navy in the 1950s had many more ships than in later years, and the headquarters establishment at the Admiralty then (before unification of the services' headquarters caused an increase in naval staff to keep up with the Joneses) was reasonably small, the probability of an appointment to headquarters became pretty high on promotion to commander.

Liz and I had decided it would be best to move house and we were looking around. Given this promotion, I felt that the future was a good deal more assured and also that if we could not find a house near Petersfield which we very much liked, we should look nearer London rather than further away. After much searching we found 'South Cottage' at Headley Down near Bordon, offered for it at once, and bought it in very quick time. While all this was happening, I received my new appointment as Assistant Director of Radio Equipment for Communications in the Admiralty, and I started work after ten days' leave. Although it was just possible to commute comfortably in the summer, it was really necessary to have somewhere to live in London, and I went to lodge in Eaton Terrace, sharing a flat with Peter who was then 'planning' in the Second Sea Lord's office.

I took over in the Radio Equipment Department from Raymond Dreyer, whom I had previously relieved in the technical teaching job at the Signals School, and found it pretty daunting. The department was the interface between the staff, in the shape of the director of the Signals Division, and the research establishment, which also handled procurement (my old sparring partner, the Admiralty Signals and Radar Establishment). There were three assistant directors as well as the director and the deputy director in the department: myself, one for radar and one for navigation. The Radio Equipment Department was in the Controllerate of the Navy. The Controller was Ralph Edwards (who always reminded me that I had nearly killed him by taking him in my motorboat in front of one of those dreadful night soil barges in the Whampoa at Shanghai). He was a splendid officer, and I remember meeting him walking from his club (the Senior, to which Father had joined me long before) down the Duke of York's steps to the office after lunch, and saying something to him about being a little unhappy at being on the material side of life rather than in a division of the staff. I was told in no uncertain terms that I was bloody lucky to be there at all. He was relieved during my time by Admiral Sir Michael Denny, whose secretary was Peter White and whose naval assistant was Michael Le Fanu, so I had good friends 'at court'.

The work involved a host of different subjects. All the naval shore wireless stations had to be modernised after the war, and since the Navy operated world-wide at that time, there were large numbers of them. I remember those in Singapore, South Africa and Ceylon in particular. (In Malta, the work was well ahead by the time I joined.) My main preoccupation, however, was the conversion of the Fleet tactical communications from very high frequencies ($c.$100–156 MHz) to ultra high frequencies (200–400 MHz). This may sound simple, but it had to be effected without interrupting the operational readiness of the Fleet. The equipment was never quite ready by the time that ASRE said it would be, the ships had to be brought into the dockyard when capacity was available and their other duties allowed, and a great deal of coordination was required.

The director of ASRE was Laurie Durlacher, who had been a midshipman of Father's in *Ramillies* long ago, and we came to know him and his Russian wife. I used to go to the Controller's annual meeting on ASRE's programme, and I well remember once some suggestion coming up, because of the nuclear threat at sea, that in future, radar aerials should be designed to be retractable. There was some discussion of this until Laurie Durlacher said, 'Of course, it could be done; but it does pose the problem of when to retract.' This remark reminded me of Ernie Bevin saying, 'What do the Japanese eat?', and needless to say, no one spent any more money or time trying to design retractable radar aerials. The hours were quite long, but I used to get away around 6 p.m., earlier perhaps on a Friday to go home. It was my first office job, the forerunner of many, and lasted the full two years: the first time since I had joined the Navy that I had ever spent so long in one appointment.

In about November 1952 I was rung up from the Signals School by the commander, Robert Phillimore, and told that the captain wished to know my reaction to going next to Washington to relieve John Trechman as signal officer in the British Naval Mission there. I found the prospect appalling. I knew that if I went, I would stay at least two years – probably more because of the cost of changing somebody over in an expensive city like Washington. At the end of this, I would have spent five years ashore after promotion to commander, and would have to serve at least two years at sea – if I could get to sea – before hoping to be promoted to captain. This would mean a pedestrian career, even if promotion to captain came. I talked to Father about it, and he agreed. He told me that no naval officer can be held in contempt of anybody if he asks to go to sea. When I rang back, Phillimore was upset. 'Oh dear,' he said, 'When the captain asked for your reaction he didn't expect you to say you didn't want to go, he just wanted to know whether it would upset you domestically.' I said, 'I'm sorry, but I do not want to go to Washington, I would like to go to sea. Would you please tell the Captain?' So Robert, who was a very nice chap, said yes, of course he would. Next, the Captain of the Signals School himself descended on me in my office, told me not to be stupid, and that I was to go to Washington. I said I would like to speak to my director, Keith Walter, about it, and he had to agree to this. Then, in the club at lunchtime, the director of the Signal Division, Foster Brown, got hold of me, sat me down, had at me, and told me that of course I should go to Washington. Still no one had talked to Keith Walter, yet the meeting for the nominations, which involved signal officers and was nothing to do with the appointing authority (the Naval Assistant to the Second Sea Lord), was imminent. I asked to see Keith Walter. I told him what I felt, and told him about the problems that would be caused by the near simultaneous departure of James Wood from ASRE and myself (this as my final shot). He said he would see what he could do to help. I understand that my name never came up at the meeting; somebody else was sent to Washington.

As part of my 'struggle for freedom', I had written to congratulate Admiral Lambe, who had just been appointed as C.-in-C. Far East Fleet, and said that I hoped that if ever I had a chance to serve under him again, he would remember me. I received a nice letter back. Then, before Christmas, I was summoned to the Second Sea Lord's office to see the naval assistant, Captain St John Tyrwhitt, to be told that I was to go to sea. This was in spite of the Signals School, and it turned on my confidential reports being sufficiently good to mark me a likely candidate for early promotion, which meant that I had to go to sea next. Tyrwhitt told me that he had had me down for command of *Scorpion*, a brand new Weapon Class destroyer, and that Admiral Robson, Flag Officer Flotillas in the Mediterranean, had accepted me for the job. However, he said, he had now received a request from Admiral Lambe that I should go to command *Alert*, a converted Bay Class frigate and the despatch vessel – in effect the Admiral's Yacht – on the Far East Station. 'Well, Ashmore,' he said, 'which would you like to do?' I asked, 'How long can I have to think it over?' 'Oh,' he said, 'Come back after lunch.'

I went to see Peter and told him about this, but he could not advise me, and I had to decide myself. Because I had written to Charles Lambe and asked to serve under him again, I felt I was honour bound to take *Alert*, which indeed attracted me greatly. So, after lunch, I went back to Tyrwhitt. 'Have you made up your mind?' 'Yes, Sir,' I said. 'What is it to be?' '*Alert*.' He looked at me as though I was something the cat had brought in: clearly turning down a first-rate modern destroyer in favour of going around in the admiral's yacht was just what he expected a signal officer to do. However, the die was cast, and months later, when he came out to Singapore as captain of *Newcastle* on his way to the war in Korea and I went to call on him from *Alert*, he very kindly gave me a drink in his cabin and was good enough to say, 'Well, Ashmore, I think you made the right decision after all.' I felt he then realised that what I had was an independent command – as opposed to being one of a flotilla – working directly to the Commander-in-Chief, though administered by the Rear-Admiral commanding the Malayan Area, and enjoying a great deal of autonomy. *Scorpion* went to Raymond Dreyer instead and, sadly, a run of bad luck in her finished his career.

CHAPTER FOUR

South-East Asia to Northern Europe

1953–9

I left the Admiralty in the middle of January 1953, being summoned unexpectedly by Admiral Denny, my 'Superintending Lord', for a fireside chat in which he was good enough to say I had the ball at my feet and to advise me to read conscientiously and with discrimination to prepare for the future. I felt greatly honoured and somewhat shaken.

I had expected to go out to *Alert* quite soon, but in fact there was something like four months' holiday before I was wanted, so the family had a lovely time, and were able to plan our journey. This was by troopship, in *Empire Clyde*, all the family together for the whole trip. Because *Alert* was styled 'locally-based', the officers were allowed to have their wives on the station, although the sailors could not. We were not entitled to the family overseas allowances that people ashore enjoyed, nor to a married quarter, but I did receive a seagoing allowance, like all officers and men afloat. This allowance, which was very much smaller, had to maintain the family, and this meant living pretty rough.

I relieved a nice man called John Moore, and we decided to take on his house and as much as he and his family could spare from their possessions. The Moores met us at Singapore and showed us our new home, 'Fifteenth Mile Bungalow' in Sembawang Village, right outside the fence of the Naval Base. It was an old, wooden bungalow on stilts. There were no glass windows, but 'chicks' (blinds) that could be let down over various openings to keep out the sun or the monsoon and to give privacy at night when the oil lamps were lit – there was no electricity. Water was heated by the sun in a tank topped up by a handpump. We had a shower, but no bath. There were two bedrooms, and a large verandah served as a sitting/dining room. The kitchen and servants' quarters were 20 or so yards away in the garden. It had belonged to the assistant manager of the Sembawang Rubber Plantation, but had been condemned as unfit for European habitation some six years earlier, since when naval officers had lived in it. We were delighted with it and its wonderful view of the Johore Straits. There were all sorts of plants growing in the tropical garden. We later planted pineapples to back up the bananas. We had one problem, in that Elizabeth had to negotiate fairly firmly with the powers that be for the children to be allowed to enter the Dockyard School.

This was eventually achieved, and despite a convenient hole in the fence near us through which they could scramble, official transport was provided.

I had to go straight into action, calling on all sorts of people. The Dockyard Commodore was Walton, commander of *Dainty* on the China Station when I served in her. The Flag Officer Malaya, my administrative authority, was Rear-Admiral Pugsley, who commanded *Javelin* when she was torpedoed with Mountbatten on board off the Eddystone, and the Commander-in-Chief was Charles Lambe. His Chief of Staff was Laurie Durlacher, ex-midshipman in *Ramillies* with Father as 'nurse', then Commodore Superintendent ASRE, and now another friend close at hand. (I mention all these names because it does give a flavour of the family atmosphere in what was still quite a large Navy.)

Alert herself was in a bit of a pickle, I thought: the sailors were out there unaccompanied for up to two years, and I was the third Commanding Officer that some of them had had to endure. John Moore had served about 15 months, and now here was I, another new broom determined to shine at sea. Because sea time was so precious from the career point of view, the other officers also served less time than the sailors, so that a rating might have not only several Commanding Officers, but more than one 1st Lieutenant, more than one Divisional Officer and so on. Also, the climate in Singapore is enervating, as I remembered from my days there in *Birmingham*, and there was still no question of air-conditioned ships. Costs ashore were very high compared with Hong Kong, and there was a general air of lassitude, which did not accord with my vision of a Commander-in-Chief's Despatch Vessel.

I now drew on my recollections as the commander's 'doggie' in *Birmingham* before the war to recall how a ship entered harbour smartly, how ceremonial drills should be carried out, and the various refinements by which the boats, booms and ladders of a smart ship were distinguished. Edwards, the pleasant First Lieutenant, was ex-Royal Indian Navy, and some of my ideas, including my determination to stop people scrubbing the deck and smoking at the same time – indeed, to stop all smoking in working hours except at stand-easy – were pretty difficult for him. As there was also a squadron of Algerine Class minesweepers based nearby in Singapore, I could not change the smoking practice in my ship without their cooperation. This was achieved, so far as the officers were concerned (how effectively it was put into practice I am not sure), but it was enforced for all in *Alert*.

The requirements of the Commander-in-Chief for the ship were outlined by the Fleet Operations Officer, but within them I had great flexibility in arranging my own programme and this was of enormous value to me. I was able to take her away into the Singapore exercise areas or up one of the coasts, depending on the monsoon, lie up somewhere quietly and organise our drills, painting and other maintenance, as well as expeditions and banyans ashore. The more we were out of Singapore, the better it was for the ship's company. This was the time of the Korean War, and ships were constantly passing through Singapore on their way to or from that theatre of operations. The Naval General Service Medal was awarded, subject to a qualifying period, for 'operations' in Malaya. Time at sea seldom qualified, although time in a hospital ashore for whatever reason, even VD, did. Partly in reaction to such nonsense, I set my face against arranging the ship's programme to enhance our so-called 'qualifying days'.

Alert had a very good navigator, Michael Rogers, part of whose job it was to keep up to date a 'cruise book' in the despatch vessel, showing where good beaches or interesting sights existed, and generally recording data to help us lay on a good programme for the Commander-in-Chief or any guests whom he might send to us. In order to put some flesh on all this from my point of view, soon after joining I took her independently up the east coast to call on the various sultans.

Back in Singapore, there was time to see the family, but then we had to prepare for the Commander-in-Chief's first cruise in the ship with me in command. This was to be to Saigon, to call on the French, and then to Bangkok towards the end of September. Admiral and Lady Lambe embarked, and off we went. It was a good trip up the Mekong to Saigon, from where the war with the Communists was being conducted. I remembered how Father had taken *Kent* right upriver before the war, and was delighted to be following in his wake. On approaching the jetty at Saigon itself, there was a French military band playing us in on the pontoon on which I had to berth, and I had two very excitable French pilots on my bridge. At various stages, they gesticulated to me to stop or go astern or go round again, but I paid no attention and brought the ship alongside rather smartly, causing the band to start clearing off the jetty because of the fast approach, justified by the astern power available. *Alert* was a very different cup of tea from the 30 ft motorboat I had been used to handling in *Birmingham*, but had reciprocating engines. This meant that providing you could rely on the engineer officer, and indeed I could, you could apply a great deal of astern power very quickly. This made for smart handling of the ship. Charles Lambe said afterwards that he was pleased I had paid no attention to the pilots and had got on with it, so I left the bridge with a sheepish grin on my face, which I did my best to hide till in my cabin.

Saigon, as I saw it then in 1953, was a beautiful city – the best type of French colonial civilisation, I suppose, flourishing in a rich, welcoming and friendly country. Charles Lambe was very impressed with Bao Dai, the so-called Emperor. It was a most successful visit, before the battle of Dien Bien Phu and the dreadful catastrophe which converted a well-run, prosperous country into a disaster area.

I then sailed for Bangkok, turning the ship in a fast manoeuvre where the larger *Kent* had had to hold her bow in the bank and be pushed round. The Lambes and personal staff flew to Angkor to see the great temples. After a two-day passage, enlivened by the sight of basking turtles in the Gulf of Siam, *Alert* arrived at the bar at the entrance to the Chao Phraya River. There was just enough water to cross, providing we maintained our speed. We then embarked a pilot and made our way up to the city. I turned the ship in the river in fairly slack water, and secured alongside at a naval berth not far below the royal palace. The Lambes moved on board, and we prepared for the round of political and social engagements awaiting the Commander-in-Chief. This British naval visit was made the occasion for a reconciliation between the Dictator of Siam at that time, General Pibul Pibulsonggram, and the Royal Thai Navy. (Reconciliation was necessary because, during an unsuccessful attempted coup about 18 months previously, the Thai Navy had thrown Pibul into the Chao Phraya, from which he had barely escaped with his life.) We had a great river picnic with the Thai Navy, whose admirals were accompanied by very pretty wives, and whose names, always about six syllables long, were abbreviated to one, such as 'Nit' or 'Tik'.

After leaving Bangkok, we went down to Huahin, Sonkhla, and back down the coast, passing those lovely islands, to Singapore. It had been a memorable cruise for me, and very good for the ship's company who had rarely seen the Commander-in-Chief on board and now realised that high standards were required for someone of his stature. Everyone had also enjoyed some of the bright lights in Saigon and Bangkok. Soon after our return, the ship was inspected by Admiral Pugsley, a renowned destroyer officer who I feared would wreak havoc on my strange command, which had to be a yacht at one moment and a warship the next. He took us to sea, the gunnery passed muster and we had the usual drills, steering breakdowns, and so forth, in the Singapore exercise areas. On return, I was told to berth at the east side of the dockyard. Being inexperienced, instead of stopping the ship and manoeuvring her to point in the right direction towards the berth, I put on wheel and went straight in. I saw Pugsley look at me. Fortunately, God was on my side and it was a very good alongside. (I know now that in my confidential report he said I handled my ship confidently and well. This was more good luck than good judgement but I value it as high praise coming from such a source.) The Inspection Report was quite good from the ship's point of view, and so tails were now fairly well up.

As time went on, *Alert* was lent by the Commander-in-Chief to various people: one was the High Commissioner, Sir Ian MacGillivray, who, with his wife and his staff, came up the East Coast with us. It was a success, and I was given a Sakai blowpipe by his staff later (the wardroom already had a Dyak one). The Durlachers went on a short trip up the east coast with their son, Peter, and pretty daughter, Sasha. An east coast trip depended very largely on finding places on the beaches where the giant leatherback turtles laid their eggs. I knew roughly where to go, and this first attempt was a great success.

When the Commander-in-Chief went to Hong Kong, he and Lady Lambe would usually go by air. I would take Elizabeth, if invited, any staff wives and the Lambe children and their nanny up in *Alert*. On one occasion, I took Charles to Macao to call on the Portuguese governor. This was all the more interesting because the previous frigate to visit, *Modeste*, had run aground. I was anxious not to do the same with the Commander-in-Chief on board, so I placed leadsmen in the chains all the way across the Pearl River, and took precautions beforehand to lighten the ship as far as I could. We had the minimum of fuel on board, and had trimmed down by the bow so that the screws were drawing as little as practicable. On passage and in mid-river, a sounding of 'less a quarter three' was called: just about the draught of my ship aft. However, there was nothing then to be done except press on through what I hoped was silt, and this indeed worked. I anchored perhaps rather too far off Macao, being anxious not to stay there forever, and accompanied the Commander-in-Chief in the barge when he went ashore, where there was a marvellous Portuguese naval guard waiting for him, graced by a number of sailors with magnificent moustaches.

One return voyage from Hong Kong was made in company with a frigate squadron commanded by Captain Brian Durant, *Alert* making the fourth ship for the run south. He put us all through our paces, with exercises and manoeuvres, jackstay transfers, and so forth. He invited me to transfer the Commander-in-Chief's children by jackstay to his ship, but I am afraid that I compromised by keeping them on board and letting the nanny go, which was far more popular. On return to Singapore, he went to see the Chief of Staff and said he thought that *Alert* would make a fine addition to his outfit, and it would be much better for me and my ship to be part of a properly-administered squadron and spend more time in company, and so on. Laurie Durlacher was asked to put this to me by the Commander-in-Chief next time he took passage in *Alert,* and was very understanding when I said that I considered my independence worth more than almost anything else and that the last thing I wanted was to be part of anybody's squadron. I am thankful to say that the suggestion was quietly dropped.

Borneo was part of the command, and I had conducted a private expedition there in *Alert* to look around and see what it was like before taking Pugsley's replacement as Flag Officer Malayan Area, Ernie Shattock, a renowned naval aviator (and member of the Magic Circle), to visit Borneo. He very sensibly asked Elizabeth to go with him as his hostess. A main object of the trip was to visit Kuching, the capital of Sarawak, way up the Sarawak river. A trek to a longhouse and the game of blowpipe darts organised by the governor made their mark.

Alert then sailed for Brunei, moving slowly up a long, narrow channel in the clear water of the bay with a masthead look-out posted to make certain I didn't hit the sand on either side. We moored just below a barrier that had been made long ago by sinking junks across the entrance to the Brunei River to keep pirates out. The admiral and I called on the Sultan, and the Resident, a delightful person, ex-Rajah Service from Sarawak, looked after us all well. Elizabeth and I went to the Kampong Ayer, the village on stilts in the middle of the river for which Brunei is justly famous. Jesselton, capital of North Borneo, was the next port of call. My new navigator, Selous, who had relieved Michael Rogers, very rightly and properly turned round to me as we were approaching through the islands and said, 'Sir, I think I am lost, I don't know the way in.' I was delighted to be able to say, 'Well I do, I'll take her,' and at the same time felt that I was exorcising the ghost of my failure in *Jupiter* at the Hoxa Gate long ago. Jesselton's unspoilt and beautiful harbour with miles of golden beaches on the islands round it, on one of which we had a barge picnic, was the fitting last visit of a lovely cruise.

The Fleet worked to tropical routine in Singapore, which meant starting fairly early in the morning and finishing work at 12.30 p.m., allowing an afternoon siesta. I usually had lunch at home, where it was very much cooler than in the ship. After a quiet afternoon, we would go swimming, using a Dyak dug-out canoe brought back from Sarawak. There was just enough buoyancy for all four of us with an inch of freeboard, and with practice, we seldom capsized. We did a certain amount of entertaining ashore in our oddly exotic house. It gave parties a certain cachet, and people were pleased to come – the exceptions being those allergic to large insects, such as the praying mantises which were attracted by our paraffin pressure lamps.

We had a quite excellent Chinese 'boy' called Ah Sang, whose wife was Amah. Ah Sang looked after our interests when Elizabeth promised Admiral Shattock some banana trees from our garden before we went off on a trip and told Ah Sang to provide them. She received a very nice letter from the admiral when we returned, thanking her for the banana trees, but we could not see any change in our grove. Ah Sang, it transpired, had decided that rather than us providing the banana trees, they should come from the garden of someone for whom one of his friends worked, so the admiral got his banana trees, and we were given the credit.

Ernie Shattock had a sizeable swimming pool at Rodney House in the naval base with a bottom of black-and-white tiles. He devised a merciless game of 'underwater draughts' which, of course, we all had to play. This was a usual Sunday morning after-Church do. Each team was assigned a draught. Members took turns to stay underwater as long as possible, keeping near the bottom without weights. You could then push your draught forward one tile's worth, push the other fellow's back one, and so on. Eventually, one surfaced, out of breath, and one's team mate could dive in and take up the struggle until the first team reached the end of the 'board' and won. Susan and Tamara were excellent at this, and I am sure that their prowess did a great deal for my prospects of promotion.

All this time, the ship kept busy. We went again to Trengganu, wearing Ernie Shattock's flag, and landed a company to march past the Sultan on his birthday. We had yet another inspection, which I chiefly remember for Ernie conducting my sea inspection in the Straits of Johore, breaking down my steering gear and inducing what I thought was a hazardous situation. Fortunately, we survived without mishap, since to have anchored would have risked picking up heaven knows what by way of expensive submarine cables in the area he had chosen.

The wardroom decided to give a great 'summer' dance in *Alert* and invite the Lambes and all our friends as guests. We could take, I suppose, about 150 people. At Elizabeth's suggestion, we very bravely decided not to spread the quarterdeck awning, and this kept us open to the elements and in danger of a nocturnal rainshower. Although we had a standby venue organised in the Dockyard Police Hall, it would have made a pretty miserable alternative. As it turned out, the gamble paid off, and the open-air ball was pronounced a tremendous success.

In June 1954, Ernie Shattock again hoisted his flag in *Alert*, and I took him to call on the Indonesian Navy at Jakarta. His daughter, Janice, was on board for the trip, and was a notable attraction when being ducked in the crossing the line ceremony. Although I had crossed the equator many times before, I had no certificate to prove it, so I had to go through it again, and was mercifully kindly treated by the 'Bears', who presented me with a plastic turtle badge. Ernie's host was Admiral Martadinata, married to a delightful Sulu princess. Ours was the first visit by a British warship to Jakarta since the war, and I think Father, in *Kent*, had been the last British warship (certainly the last flagship) to visit before it. The harbour at Jakarta was a shambles, but fortunately there was a Dutch harbourmaster and a Dutch pilot, who eventually found a clear berth for me. The admiral was well received, and we had a very successful cocktail party on board, as well as good official ones ashore.

The Commander-in-Chief had invited Elizabeth and the children on a final trip to Hong Kong, and this was a great treat. Susan and Tamara were put in charge of Petty Officer Chapman, the captain of the quarterdeck, who was a vastly experienced seaman and petty officer, and a great dear. The ship, when converted to a despatch vessel, had lost its after gun, so we had a very substantial quarterdeck aft, on which you could parade a full guard, which was often necessary with an admiral on board. This was fine for the children and deck games. There was a wonderful teak taffrail around it, and I was delighted when the last captain of *Alert* before she was scrapped, gave me a piece of this made into a pencil box.

Dunbar-Nasmith of Peter's term had been appointed to relieve me, and was soon to arrive. When he joined, poor chap, *Alert* was in dry dock, looking absolutely dreadful, the battle against rust having been temporarily suspended. He was very good about it and took a lot on trust. We held our brief turnover in Admiralty House. It had been a variegated, happy commission, with a vast store of experience gained, both professional and political. Charles Lambe let me run a night encounter exercise, for example, which could never have happened except with him, and I had been able to attain a considerable insight into the politics and geography of South-East Asia at a difficult and crucial period, with war in Indo-China and an emergency in Malaya. Malcolm MacDonald was the Commissioner-General at that time, and the Malay Chinese Alliance, the party that was eventually to take over from us on the independence of Malaya, was formed one night in the admiral's cabin in my ship in considerable secrecy. I was on the quarterdeck for the comings and goings and remember the event well.

The passage home by troopship was pleasant and uneventful, and we found 'South Cottage' in good order, but I was to go as commander and executive officer of *Mercury*, which meant that I had to live on site, and a quarter was provided near the establishment. I had very little leave between appointments, and the change of climate had given me an unpleasant attack of skin trouble, so I had to join *Mercury* unshaven and covered in boils. Fortunately, the doctor took one look and gave me a large injection of penicillin, which sorted things out pretty smartly.

About this time I received an invaluable letter from Charles Lambe from the Far East, in which he quoted my confidential report from Shattock, where he had remarked that I would have a splendid future in the service unless increased responsibilities made me too rigid. Lambe endorsed this, and said that I must be careful not to take life too seriously, adding, 'I expect Elizabeth would agree with me!' There was no one except Father whose judgement I respected more, and I did my best, I hope, to take this advice.

It was certainly needed at *Mercury*, where my captain, a well-known signal officer whom I had not met before, was John Longden (known throughout the branch, for obvious reasons, as 'All Night Longden'). He was a very gregarious and intelligent person, who got through his work quickly and then found time on his hands. As his second-in-command in the next office, I would be called in at least half an hour before lunch to start drinking gin with him and generally pass the time of day. I enjoyed this and liked him, but was not getting through my work at quite the same pace as he. An extremely able training commander, Rae McKaig, ran the signals side of life.

My job was to run the establishment, and also to advise the captain, who was 'nominating authority' on the appointment of signal officers. Appointments were made by the Admiralty through the Second Sea Lord and his assistants. Only they had access to an officer's confidential reports, which should govern the appointment, but unofficial records were maintained in the commander's office at the Signal School, with remarks by my own and Longden's predecessors written on them in pencil. (Someone had written on mine, 'Will do anything well,' just before I had objected to going to Washington!) The commander had a Wren officer assistant – Susan Rigby was mine – who sat in the same office, where people were liable to call in before seeing the captain in the hope of finding out what was likely to happen to them. When I had last been at *Mercury*, strongly influenced by Father who thought the system of the schools making nominations without access to officers' confidential reports was iniquitous, I had determined to remove the Wren from the Commander's Office, and also to see what I could do to change the nominating system if ever I became commander of the place. With Susan's loyal cooperation, I did move her from the office, and established her in a little lobby, which had been a bathroom, between my office and that of the captain. Sue took the change well, understanding my reasons for it, but did not enjoy it much. I saw Longden and asked permission to erase all the pencilled marks on the officers' records. He said he would think about it, but turned my request over to his successor. (I don't remember whether I received authority to do so or not, but I know for certain that I added no unofficial comments of my own.)

The bulk of the job was concerned with the discipline and security of the establishment, and also with works matters, which were all new to me. I had an excellent barrack master, and Duncan Knight was First Lieutenant, who, from the saddle of his official bicycle, saw as much of the establishment as anybody. He was also in charge of our 'swill disposal unit': the pig farm. As we were a New Entry Boys' Training Establishment, standards had to be the highest, with full Divisions on Fridays now that Divine Service had been made optional and Sunday church parade was no longer appropriate.

The mid-1950s saw a major reorganisation of officer structure in the Royal Navy. This had many ramifications: some positive, others less so. The Committee on Officer Structure and Training recommended that the list of seaman officers of commander's and captain's rank should be split into two, between those who would go to sea and those who, on promotion to commander, would be most unlikely ever to receive a sea appointment again. This split was made on the basis of officers' confidential reports. The schools were not consulted, and I, thankfully, was not involved. I did have a preview of the list the day before it was published so that the Captain could tell his officers in *Mercury* which way they were going – 'wet' or 'dry' – in advance of publication. Obviously, both lists had to contain a number of the more exceptional officers, and it was a great sadness to find that although I was 'wet', both Rae McKaig and Jake Laughton, a good friend, were to be 'dry'; so were Walter Wells of my Long Course and many others. It caused deep division and bitter disappointments and many officers came to see me at that time to ask for advice on what they should do – advice that I could not and would not give. I am still, to this day, of the opinion that it was a mistaken move on the part of the Admiralty, and that the responsibility for deciding officers' appointments and their future was in no way mitigated by a manoeuvre so divisive of the seaman branch on which the Fleet so much depends.

For some reason, when the time came for the confidential reports and recommendations for the half-yearly promotions to be forwarded, Longden sent for me and showed me mine, which was very kind, but said that I should not be promoted this time. I was not best pleased, and in retrospect I believe that he had made a gentleman's agreement with 'Sandy' Gordon Lennox, who was to relieve him before the promotions came out, that I would be there for at least six months to see 'Sandy' in. John Longden left us, after a tremendous farewell party, to go and command the cruiser *Birmingham*, and my surprise was complete when, on the morning of 30 June, before the signals had been received, 'Sandy' walked into my office and said, 'Let me be the first to congratulate Captain Ashmore.' There were other promotions in *Mercury*, and we had a party at lunchtime in the wardroom, during the course of which Longden rang up. He asked if one particular chap had been promoted, and I said, 'Yes.' He then said, 'Are there any other promotions?' I said, 'Yes, Sir, me.' There was dead silence at the end of the telephone. (In retrospect, I think Longden was right, and I subsequently served nine-and-a-half years as a captain, rather than the usual nine.) At 35, I was the youngest captain since Beatty, two years younger on promotion than 'Dickie' Mountbatten, who very kindly rang up and congratulated me from the Admiralty, where he was then Fourth Sea Lord. Kit James came to relieve me, and despite an abrupt move out of our quarter, we were all pleased to go back to 'South Cottage'.

To find out what I was to do next, I went up to London and reported to the naval secretary, Admiral Luce. He told me that I was to do a Joint Services' Staff Course at Latimer, a six-month affair. I was dismayed, as I knew that this would reduce any chance I might have of going to the Imperial Defence College unless far too much of my captain's time was to be spent on courses. So I said, 'But, Sir, I've already done the Staff Course.' 'Yes, Ashmore,' he said, 'I know,' and that was the end of that particular conversation. So Latimer it was, and I thoroughly enjoyed it and learned a great deal about the other two services. I happened to be the senior officer of the course, which, like being senior midshipman of a gunroom, was a disadvantage: most of the other students were a good deal older than me and I also had to make the 'speeches'. However, the work was interesting, and I enjoyed the syndicate work in particular. I also made some good friends and played bridge most evenings.

At the beginning of October, I was summoned to the Admiralty and told that I was to be personal liaison officer between C.-in-C. Portsmouth, Admiral of the Fleet Sir George Creasy, and Golovko, C.-in-C. Soviet Baltic Fleet, who was to pay him a visit between 11 and 17 October. I dropped all schemes, stopped playing bridge, put a wet towel round my head, dusted off my Russian books and tried to catch up on what I once knew. Then it was down to Portsmouth the day before the Russians' arrival to meet Admiral Creasy and find out what it was he wanted of me. I was very kindly invited to stay in Admiralty House, which made things much easier, and learned that my first assignment was to meet the Russian ships at Spithead and call on their commander as soon as they anchored. I was glad to know that he was an old acquaintance. I went to see the assistant harbourmaster to find out what arrangements had been made. I was to go out in a motor torpedo boat at, I think, 7.30 a.m. It was typical October weather of autumn mists and calms, and this boat had no radar. I therefore laid on a standby, a harbour auxiliary craft with radar, and decided to set off half-an-hour early. This was just as well – there was thick fog in the morning.

I was much impressed by the way the Russian squadron made its way up to Spithead and anchored more or less on time. It consisted of the cruisers *Sverdlov*, *Ordzhonikidze* and four destroyers. The fog was so thick that I could see sections of the flagship five minutes before the whole ship became visible. A Jacob's ladder was thrown over for me, and I climbed on board *Sverdlov* to be taken to the bridge to present Admiral Creasy's compliments to Golovko. He was still in his seagoing kit, unshaven, and had obviously had an anxious night, but I found him friendly and welcoming. I had brought an operator with a wireless set with me, and established communications with C.-in-C. ashore to reschedule the first call because of the weather. I then went ashore again, leaving the pilot and an interpreter on board, and was on the quayside when *Sverdlov* and *Ordzhonikidze* berthed safely and well at South Railway Jetty.

Golovko was accompanied on his calls by his Chief of Staff, Vice-Admiral Abashvili and who but Rudakov, now a Rear Admiral, was left in charge of the ships. I had other officers working for me who spoke some Russian and I established a liaison office in the *Sverdlov* while the whole command staff swung into action to make certain that the visit would be a success. There was much ceremonial, a welcome lunch in *Victory* attended by all the Russian commanding officers, and the usual exchange of dinners and other functions.

The four Soviet destroyers were brought neatly alongside while the *Victory* lunch was in progress. This was an impressive display of seamanship by the four 1st lieutenants. Golovko laid a wreath on the war memorial at Southsea, to which I escorted him, and I remember, coming back in the car, he said what an impressive occasion it had been and, in the course of conversation, remarking that the submarine was the weapon of the weaker naval power. Although far from an original thought, I was interested that he saw fit to utter it. Golvoko was clearly impressed, and rightly so, by George Creasy, but even more so by Lady Creasy and Lady Cazalet, who were present at the Admiralty House functions. The Russians, 'Soviet men' as they were, had no idea that such poised, cultivated and charming ladies even existed.

The First Lord, Sir Rhoderick McGrigor, came down for the dinner in *Sverdlov*, and I remember him best for heeding my advice as interpreter and delivering his speech in shortish sentences which I could more easily handle. Admiral Creasy, on the other hand, rattled through his, and all I could do was give a summary at the end, which I hope was adequate. (Actually, this was rather less demanding than having to translate the First Lord phrase by phrase.) A Russian officer translated for Golovko, as I had thought that on home ground I ought not suggest the exchange of role that had worked so well at Sevastopol.

One morning I was in the liaison officer's cabin in *Sverdlov* when I heard a loud noise outside. I ran on deck, to see one of the dockyard workmen writhing in agony on the jetty. The Russians had been shifting the brows in order to arrange a better route for when the ship was open to visitors that afternoon and in doing so had let one run away, knocking over this poor chap and breaking his leg. I told the liaison officer to ring for an ambulance, and ran down to the victim just in time to stop the Russians picking him up and lugging him on board out of sight. They were upset and very excited, and I had to stand astride him while doing my best to explain that an ambulance was on the way and he would be treated in a proper hospital as soon as possible. Once he was safely in the ambulance, I went back on board, where I was confronted by Rudakov, very angry, shouting that it was all the fault of the British. This I repudiated at once, and asked to see the Commander-in-Chief. Eventually, I was allowed to see Admiral Golovko, and I explained my version of what had happened. I reported the affair to George Creasy before we all went to a ball given by the Lord Mayor of Portsmouth that evening. Soon after Golovko arrived, he asked me to take him formally to the Commander-in-Chief. I did so, whereupon he stood to attention and made a full apology for what had happened to one of our people. Creasy, of course, took it very well and said 'Accidents will happen.' I was absolutely astounded at a Soviet officer apologising to anybody, but Golovko was not only determined that nothing should mar his visit, he was, I think, also a genuinely nice man. I stood by his side for the 'Beating of the Retreat' by the Royal Marines on the jetty alongside *Sverdlov*, and at the end of it he turned to me, with tears in his eyes, and said what a wonderful spectacle it had been, and how, when he returned to Russia, he would try to arrange something similar there.

On Golovko's programme, for some reason, was a visit to 'Broadlands' for lunch with the Mountbattens, and I took him there. The Russians arrived bearing gifts – an amber box for her, and a *palekh* box for the Earl. The Mountbattens had no presents for the Russians, but as we went in to lunch, 'Dickie' took me to one side, pointed to the books of matches on the table which had 'Mountbatten of Burma' and a crest on them, and said, 'If they would like to take a book of matches when they leave, please make certain they do so.' I found that embarrassing (and still do), and when the end of the meal came, I turned to Golovko, pointed out the books of matches and said, 'I'm going to take one of these, why don't you?', and handed him one.

I hope the Russians enjoyed themselves. They certainly did enjoy their trip to London, where again I had to look after them. They called, unescorted, on their Embassy as a preliminary to Madame Tussaud's, which was always top of the list for Soviet visitors to London. First, however, I had to take them to Highgate Cemetery to lay a wreath on the tomb of Karl Marx. This they did, and I, although escort officer, felt no obligation to salute with them before the monument to the chap who, after all, had started what eventually deprived my grandparents of everything in this world. As an addition to the programme, I suggested to Golovko that he should write his name in the Queen's Book at Buckingham Palace. He was tickled at the idea, although rather nervous. Out came the usual combs, and careful hair-combing went on as the car approached the palace gates. We found the book, and he signed it, as did Abashvili and I. I think that it was a gesture worth suggesting to them, although I had done it partly to find out their reaction.

One night in *Sverdlov*, Golovko held an informal reunion party for senior British naval officers whom he had known during the war when he was C.-in-C. Northern Fleet. Only Bruce Fraser could not make it, but Harold Burroughs, Bob Burnett, Geoffrey Miles and Douglas Fisher were there. I was the only interpreter, and we dined and drank in the admiral's modest cabin. I remember it as a delightful evening with everybody enjoying themselves, Golovko visibly warming to his guests and they departing over the side clasping a bottle of vodka or brandy each.

Better still, however, was the appearance of Admiral of the Fleet Lord Fraser of North Cape one afternoon. I looked after him on the quarterdeck, where he was surrounded by young Russian sailors, and his unaffected charm and genuine interest clearly captivated them. Many of them had cameras, and we were much photographed. They were a delightful, cheerful lot. (So, Father told me later, were the sailors in the Russian Fleet before the Revolution who were later to slaughter the officers almost before the eyes of their British messmates.)

When the visit came to an end, Golovko said, 'I have a present for your wife,' and handed me a *palekh* box inscribed inside 'From the Soviet Naval Sailors in Memory of the Visit to Portsmouth in October 1955', with which Elizabeth was delighted. It had undoubtedly been a very successful occasion, and George Creasy kindly wrote a charming letter to Father about my part in it, which gave great pleasure to us both.

The rest of the Joint Services Staff Course seemed almost relaxing after that rather heavy week. The Naval Secretary now offered me a choice of two shore appointments, both signal jobs: either as Chief Signal Officer to C.-in-C. Allied Forces Northern Europe, or in the same capacity to C.-in-C. Allied Forces Mediterranean. Both were pleasant prospects, but I had no hesitation in chosing Norway, which was a 'three-service' appointment. It seemed clear that the way ahead lay more and more in joint service as well as NATO activities, and the fact that so good a position could be combined with making the acquaintance of Norway and Denmark was exciting indeed. By then we had Tom, at whose arrival, on 24 November, I was lucky enough to be present: not in the room, as is the modern way, but at least in the house. I was soon allowed up to the bedroom and it was a most thrilling moment.

There was time in hand before going to Norway and at the suggestion of the Admiralty, I took part in a seminar at All Souls College, Oxford, conducted by the Chichele Professor of Military History, Norman Gibb. I spent a couple of nights a week in college but otherwise was at home on leave. There were some interesting lectures, one from the Joint Intelligence Bureau, one from Professor Max Beloff, all concerned mainly with the Soviet Union and its future. Since this was a subject in which I had taken a lifelong interest and about which I had done much reading, I was able to make the occasional contribution. No memorable conclusions were reached, but it was an educational exercise, certainly for me.

Eventually, the time came to go to Norway to relieve Robert Phillimore as Chief Signal Officer (or, as some preferred pompously to call it, Assistant Chief of Staff Communications) to General Sugden, the newly arrived Allied Commander-in-Chief. Accommodation in Oslo was difficult to find, and as we were to take over the Phillimores' house, I had to go ahead of the family and stay in a hotel until I had taken on the job and Robert and his family were able to leave. Although I was responsible to the general, there were two subordinate regional commanders, and I was delighted to find that the admiral was an old friend from the Far East, Gerald Gladstone. The airman was an American general called Sanders (known to all and sundry as 'Tex'). Although the admiral had his own signal officer and Tex had Group Captain Boon, RAF, I still had what seemed to me an enormous staff, made up of British, American, Norwegian and Danish officers of all three services. As well as the staff, I also commanded the Signal Support Regiment, quite the best in NATO, run by a Royal Signals officer called 'Lucky' Fenton. This was a combination of men and women, some of them Danish *Lotte* (female soldiers).

It was all unlike anything I had faced before, and involved a great deal of NATO theology as well as dealings with the two host nations of the region, Norway and Denmark. There was a mass of people to meet and visit in both countries. Robert took me down to Copenhagen as part of the indoctrin-ation process. I met a number of eminent and slow-speaking people in the Chief of Defence's Department in Kastellet, in particular the Chief Signal Officer. This was a Danish naval officer, Commodore Weilbach, a marvellous, rather elderly gentleman, and an education in himself. In Norway, the Chief Signal Officer was Colonel Palmstrom, a very distinguished officer indeed of some 70 summers, with a staff that was ornamented by a wartime hero called Rorholt, who was as much distrusted as he was admired by the NATO officers who dealt with him.

Robert Phillimore piloted me round this new world in the nicest possible way, and also turned over to me Sis Aasen, his Norwegian secretary, and a Wren signal officer called Simone Goldring as personal assistant, who turned out to be a tower of strength. The British element of the headquarters included a national cell, which came under me, looking after the confidential books and run by Maj. the Honourable Mary Anderson, WRAC. This embraced an intelligence unit which was 'UK eyes only'. Thanks to Robert, it was nothing like as confusing as it sounds and, thanks also to the extremely nice people I had to deal with in the two Scandinavian countries, it was not hard to settle in.

My deputy was an American called Cuphaver, a skilful engineer who was devoting all his energies at that time to a project for installing the headquarters signals below 300 metres of rock cover in the heart of the rock at Kolsas outside which our offices had been built. The project was well advanced, although the final staff requirements had still to be settled and were to prove one of my early worries.

It was a very busy time for the headquarters, which had been established about five years earlier by 'Daddy' Brind, no less, as first Allied C.-in-C. Northern Europe. He was followed by a general, Sir Rodney Moore, now relieved by Sugden. As a result of its naval initiation and the limited resources of the region, the headquarters was less large and populous than any other major headquarters in NATO, and this was a great advantage. The papers came through quicker, and we reckoned we knew our business better. My specialist superior was the Chief Signal Officer at Supreme Headquarters, Allied Powers Europe, outside Paris: a US Air Force general, later relieved by General Conrad, US Army. Once a quarter, there were meetings of the SHAPE Communications Electronics Board, held in alternation at SHAPE and the three major subordinate commands, AFNORTH, AFCENT and AFSOUTH. I went to all these and enjoyed seeing how the other half lived.

At the time we were in Norway, 1956-8, a great deal of money was being spent on what was known as 'communications infrastructure', building up the communications and radar systems of the countries of NATO. Norway and Denmark were my particular concern. The object was not only to enable the efficient operation of the host nation forces, but also to support the reinforcement forces that would arrive in the event of a war with the Soviet Union, all this being vital to the peacetime deterrent 'posture' (as the jargon had it) of the command. Because so much money was involved, the Chief Signal Officer was considered a VIP by the host nations' staffs. This was convenient and pleasant, but the other side of the medal was that one was liable to be involved in internal politics. For example, a number of new switching stations had to be positioned in Norway, and there was a battle between the national interest and that of NATO as to where they should go. This arose from a general feeling on the part of the host nation that they should be positioned so as best to perform a dual role, with a bias towards helping the national economy in peacetime. Time and again, I had cause to remember Charles Lambe's letter about the need to avoid rigidity – often sadly late in the day.

It was indeed difficult to reconcile the interests of the host nations, Norway or Denmark, with the strict, rather badly set out, military requirements from SHAPE where American jargon was endemic. I feel, in retrospect, that my instinct to support the pure military solution often went beyond the call of duty and resulted in delays. Once I was asked to go and see Palmstrom to hear him express his heartfelt disappointment with my attitude. In the end, the host nation, which had to implement the project, often did precisely what it wanted. On the other hand, I feel that my standing up for the Allied military position was good for the reputation of the headquarters.

A more difficult situation arose over the plans for the layout of the Regional Communication Centre in the rock at Kolsas. My American deputy, and many others on the staff, had been beavering away for years to produce the best layout, and had, in my opinion, done an extraordinarily good job. It was based, as far as practicable, on common-user circuits, but this had so far failed to receive the assent of the air commander, supported by his own Chief Signal Officer. This position of theirs was also in contravention of the SHAPE criteria. Feeling pretty strongly about it, and under great pressure from below, I took the whole matter to the Commander-in-Chief himself, and had a meeting with Sugden, General Sanders, Admiral Gladstone and Dan Boon, as a result of which I was overruled. Sanders said that communications were a function of command, and he was damned (or worse) if he was going to share his communications on vital matters of air operations with anybody from any other service. General Sugden said. 'Well if you feel like that, there's nothing more to be done,' and Ashmore retired hurt. After a day or so's reflection, I asked to see Admiral Gladstone on a personal matter. He saw me, and I said, 'Sir, do you remember the meeting we had on the common user communications, and the Commander-in-Chief's decision? I would like your advice on what the good naval officer does now? Should I, having been overruled in this way, ask to be relieved?' Gerald Gladstone was quite clear on the subject: 'Some people would think that Tex Sanders is an ape. He's not, he's a Texan. You've caused the Commander-in-Chief quite enough embarrassment already by bringing this thing up to his level, and you're to do nothing more about it except accept his decision.' This was not said unsympathetically and, indeed, we were so happy in Norway that I was very glad that that was the line he took. It was the first, but not the last, time that I was to become embroiled in conflicts between what seemed rational and sensible to two of the services and nonsense to the third, which too often, and wrongly, regarded such suggestions as veiled attacks on its independence.

Generally speaking, I encountered no such difficulties within or between the Norwegian Armed Services, in particular because their signals were already comfortably established as a Norwegian Joint Signal Service led by Palmstrom, and the sharp end of their forces, Brigade North and the 6th Division, based in Harstad, were under a single Task Force Commander North Norway, on whom it was my business to make a very early call. He was General Lindbeck Larsen, who had been Task Force Commander North Norway for many years, and was almost a folk hero. Under him there was a very good Joint Command and Operations Centre in a mountain somewhere near Bodo, and he was quite rightly the focal point for the forward defence of Norway, and indeed of the links between Norway, the British amphibious forces and the Allied Atlantic Fleet.

I made many visits to the far north, summer and winter, in the course of furthering these particular links, as well as taking part in the siting of some of the mountaintop stations of the NATO early-warning radar chain which was then being established. This was great fun, as my helicopter pilot was quite addicted to helping the Lapps to round up their reindeer herds, and any Norwegian engineer was perfectly happy either to take you puffing up a mountain behind him to look at a site or to spend half the night with you in your hotel bedroom drinking your whisky. (I learned never to have more than a half bottle of whisky visible at a time.)

From the strictly communications point of view, the high latitudes are a difficult operating area, and various stratagems, including multi-frequency transmissions from the Striking Fleet Atlantic, were tried in order to effect some improvement. I remember once going to the north with General Sugden in his own aircraft to meet an infuriated Supreme Allied Commander Atlantic, who had found, in the middle of the current exercise, that the communications between the Fleet and the shore were, to put it mildly, imperfect. He said he had done everything he could to make them effective, including sending an admiral around the world, who indeed had been to see me at Kolsas. Having done this, he said, still his communications did not work. To this, the only reply I could make, was, 'Well, Sir, did anybody ever lead you to expect that they would work?' My Commander-in-Chief backed me up, and we got away with it – quite properly, because with the technology at the time, we were still very much at the mercy of propagation conditions in the ionosphere.

A year later, in the next big autumn Striking Fleet Atlantic exercise, my own signal support unit at AFNORTH HQ was in error on the same subject. We had a large tape relay centre, in those days using torn tape, and were radiating multi-frequency, high-frequency transmissions to the Striking Fleet in the Norwegian Sea. Owing to a mistake by one of my technicians, all transmissions were cut off for some five hours so that nothing went out at all, although messages were pouring out from the staff and subordinate commands addressed to the Fleet. At the Commander-in-Chief's staff meeting in the morning, some eight hours after all this had happened, I had to confess our failure, which was, naturally, somewhat sternly received. It did, however, give me a chance to let out for a moment the bee I always had in my bonnet about there being far too many signals around, and to say to the Commander-in-Chief and staff: 'It is of some interest, Sir, that in spite of this failure on our part, there has not been a single complaint from the staff about non-delivery of any message or of no reply being received, nor any complaint from the Striking Fleet of lack of information.' I was allowed to get away with this. It was not really fair in detail but in general terms an absolutely reasonable point to make.

Although communication with the Fleet, which was vital to the defence of the region in time of a war, provided quite the most difficult technical problem which we faced, there were plenty of other problems. These were mostly organisational, and many of them stemmed from the multiplicity of messages and staffs of the various Allied headquarters, as well as from a proliferation of headquarters through the need to give proper representation in the command chain to both national and Allied officers. Within the Northern Region, comparatively small in terms of population, there must have been some 12 subordinate, though major, headquarters. The distances, of course, are great. From Oslo to North Cape is the same distance as from Oslo to Rome. The length of the Norwegian coastline, if one went in and out all along it, amounts to some 25,000 miles. But the forces under command were minimal, though you would hardly have thought so from the fuss that some of the people that we had to deal with made. This fussiness was nearly always at a civilian level, and often rather pronounced in Denmark, especially in connection with military priorities and control of PTT resources in emergency. Here, a great empire-builder with political ambitions was at work.

One of the fascinations of the job, which required me to travel widely over both countries, always with some major NATO project to discuss, was in distinguishing the very different attitudes and characteristics of Norwegians and Danes. Both were polite, but the Norwegian was a master of understatement and seldom acknowledged any requirement for flexibility in his approach. The Dane, on the other hand, was charming, more volatile, far more political, and had a very keen financial and business mind. The two defence headquarters were organised differently. The Norwegians had a chief of defence staff, with service commanders under him. The Danes had a chief of defence, to whom everybody was subordinate. In Norway, therefore, the services had more voice, and matters progressed, usually surely but slowly. In Denmark, there was great rivalry and unhappiness between the services and the staff at the Ministry of Defence, most of whom seemed to be professional 'Kastellet warriors'. Difficulties very often seemed not to come to a head at all, but to remain submerged in a welter of rival paperwork.

Signals, however, fared a good deal better than most branches. This was due to three things: one was the importance the Danes attached to making full use of the NATO money available for infrastructure; another was that in the aftermath of their experience during the war, the services were more ready to come together in joint command and operations centres in their much smaller geographical area; the third was the personality, experience and connections with the Royal family of Commander Weilbach, with whom I usually had to deal. A bachelor, he had been captain of the Royal Yacht and was still an ADC to the King, and had been in his job a very long time indeed. No one could fail to like him, and I am glad to say that he and I hit it off, and I still treasure a charming letter that he wrote to me after I had left. (Unfortunately, some three or four years later, he was taken ill, in the Royal Yacht, I think, with the King, and died very quickly.) Spurred on by my staff and by my own interest, I was usually full of ideas and Weilbach would listen patiently and say, 'Yes, Captain

Ashmore, I think that's a very good idea. Now let me see, when was it that I heard that idea before?' With his help, however, much was achieved.

In neither country had people yet become reconciled to Germany, and the thought of having German officers in the Allied HQ in the Northern Region was anathema to the 'regionals'. However, the new C.-in-C. Central Europe was a German officer, General Speidel, who was to visit AFNORTH to call on Cuthbert Sugden. Sugden arrived at the Oslo airport, Fornebu, 24 hours before Speidel was due, and the word went round that it was not Sugden but Speidel who was coming in. Demonstrators gathered, the airport was stormed, and our Commander-in-Chief had to take refuge in the control tower. He was rescued in a towering rage: not because people had tried to throw stones at him, but because they had thought that he was a German general.

The converse of this attitude to the Germans was the Scandinavian attitude to us, which was openly pro-British. At the time of the Anglo-French invasion of Suez, I happened to be coming back from Bergen by train and met in my compartment the head of the Norwegian Women's Services, who was greatly upset. 'Captain Ashmore,' she said 'We have always trusted the British, but what are you doing now?' In the Allied HQ, one had no special information on national policy, and all I could say was, 'Please, just go on trusting us a little longer.' Our friends, in general, were undoubtedly very worried and upset, not only by the attempt but, in many cases, more so by its failure. However, the fiasco of the withdrawal elicited much unspoken sympathy on the part of Norwegian and Danish service colleagues.

In the second half of my time, America and the UK decided to release to NATO rather more information than had been given so far on electronic warfare and it was my duty to launch it at high level in the Northern Command. With the support of the Commander-in-Chief and of the regional signal staffs, this was not difficult, and I well remember giving a talk in Copenhagen to more generals than I imagined existed in the Danish Army. Everyone was very receptive and a very long haul was off to a good beginning.

I also went to the NATO Special Weapons School at Oberammergau for a course on the tactical exploitation of nuclear weapons. The course was all the more interesting because it was the first on which German generals had appeared. They took a great interest, and I said to my brigadier friend, after listening to one of them 'appreciate the situation', that hearing him speak so brilliantly, one wondered how they had lost the war. 'Yes,' he said, 'so do they.'

Just before my relief, Tony McCrum, arrived, I learned that my next job was to be at sea, as Captain of a Frigate Squadron. This was the best possible news from the career point of view. There were farewell parties in both countries, as well as in the headquarters, with some nice speeches made. I was very happy to be turning over to Tony: we were boys in Alverstoke together, and his father had been in submarines with mine in the First World War. It made a great difference to us to have such a nice person take over a job in which we had made so many friends.

We finally left at the end of May 1958, full of intentions of returning to Norway again whenever we could, and travelled across a calm North Sea in the *Blenheim*, a larger ship than either of us had used for the passage out. Then to Godden Green, and Susan came out from West Heath, where she was now at school. Mousse was well, but Father was suffering agonies from his back: the same pain which had ruined for him a short visit to us in Norway some time before. He was becoming increasingly incapacitated and more and more ready to face an orthopaedic operation if necessary. Then we went to Dartmoor to see the Sturdees, and back, finally, to 'South Cottage' and home for the rest of the summer holidays.

Apart from the joys of Norway, the introduction to NATO at senior staff level had been invaluable, and the 'three-service' nature of the work had consolidated the knowledge gained at Latimer. I felt very grateful for the experience, which would stand me in good stead for the future.

CHAPTER FIVE

Mediterranean to Caribbean via Whitehall

1959–65

My command was to be *Blackpool*, a brand new Type 12 frigate, and the 6th Frigate Squadron, the balance of which was made up of three Type 15 frigates, *Undine*, *Ulysses* and *Undaunted* which I had previously seen as destroyers of the British Pacific Fleet. Before joining the ship, I was required to attend a tactical course at Woolwich for six weeks and had to live-in most of the time, going home for the weekends and, occasionally, to Godden Green for an evening.

The course was essential as I was very rusty and had much to learn, in particular how to operate with some of the new equipment that I would find in the operations room. One particular problem was that the ship was the first in the Fleet to go to sea equipped with the ship-launched anti-submarine torpedo. The limitations of these torpedoes were such that I could not discern what realistic tactical purpose they could have. No one at Woolwich seemed to be able to tell me, so I made a mental note to try to establish a tactical doctrine as soon as I got the ship to sea. The course, on the whole, was efficiently run and of great value to me. This was just as well, because while I was on it, I missed the commissioning of *Blackpool* and her visit to Blackpool town, as well as her initial trials. For this, Tony Diamond, another signal officer and a friend, took command, which gave a wonderful opportunity to him as a young commander. Before taking over the ship, I went down to see the then 'F6', Ray Hart, in *Undine* at Portsmouth, and received a great welcome from him. I knew his First Lieutenant, Roger Morgan, but had not met Ray before, although he had a reputation to conjure with as a much-decorated Escort Group commander during the war. I knew that any advice he gave me would be first rate, but I felt somewhat daunted at taking over from such a distinguished small-ship operator.

I relieved Tony in *Blackpool* at Chatham, her homeport, on completion of her weapon trials. The work-up was to take place in Malta. While the ship's company were having leave before deployment to the Mediterranean, I went to Northwood and called on Sir William Davis, C.-in-C. Home Fleet, saw his staff, and arranged, by dint of juggling a few programmes, that I should be able to sail with the whole squadron in company for passage to the Mediterranean. This achieved, we foregathered at Portsmouth, where I met the other three ships, and in particular their commanding officers, Lloyd Foster of *Undine*, Jock Cunningham (who was divisional commander) of *Ulysses* and Roger de la Pasture of *Undaunted*. We then set off in fine style, all four together, making our way towards Gibraltar. After some manoeuvres and exercises, I ordered them into column (or 'line ahead', as it used to be called) for the first night passage at standard distance apart of 2 cables. As we settled down for the night, I signalled 'Optional to disconnect the second boiler', which gave discretion to economise on fuel and watch-keepers, but kept my own connected. I came on deck around 1 a.m. to order an alteration of course for rounding Finisterre, and signalled the alteration by wheeling in succession from the front. As the executive signal was made, I went out to the bridge wing, looked aft to watch the ships astern comply, and to my horror, saw a scatter of bright points of light across the surface of the sea. I had seen that sight before, and I knew what it meant. The wireless office then reported that *Ulysses* was not answering (she had, in fact, lost boiler power and – correctly – hauled out of the line to starboard). An inexperienced sub-lieutenant, officer of the watch in *Undine* astern of her, not realising what was happening, had tried to turn inside, and hit her aft. So we had an early crisis on our hands. Mercifully, as signals came through, it became apparent that no one had been injured, and also that the watertight integrity of both ships could be ensured.

The weather was kind, and instead of steaming with a smart squadron towards Gibraltar, *Undaunted* and I escorted the two damaged ships back to Devonport Dockyard. There, I saw the Commander-in-Chief. A Board of Enquiry was convened, but I obtained permission to continue to Gibraltar with the two remaining ships. That passage was uneventful, but I did not enjoy entering harbour at the Rock with half a squadron when a whole one had been expected. The Flag Officer Flotillas on whom I called, Roy Wright (once my divisional officer long ago in *Frobisher*), was nothing but sympathetic. Repairs did not take very long, and the two ships then joined me in the Mediterranean. However, I think that what I wrote in my report on the incident earned me a reasonably justified censure from the Admiralty for not having made my intentions about boiler power clear. I had signalled 'Optional close down second boiler' on the assumption that ships where officers of the watch were too inexperienced for it to be sensible to reduce astern power by closing down a boiler would not do so. My assumption was wrong, and only *Blackpool*, which had least reason to do so as head of the line, had kept two boilers connected. It was an uncomfortable black mark at the beginning of my most important seagoing command.

My morale was sustained by Christopher Bonham Carter, Chief of Staff to C.-in-C. Mediterranean, and by the Flag Officers Flotillas, all of whom had the same sort of destroyer wartime background as I. They were much concerned that the accident in the 6th Frigate Squadron should not result in a pussy-footing attitude on the part of authority to the handling of destroyers and frigates in the peacetime Fleet. There was, therefore, no particular disposition to criticise me for the formation which I was using, which was a convenient one in waters busy with merchant ships and fishing vessels, and I think it was held that I had done well immediately after the incident and in the towing of *Undine* back to Devonport. But it remains an episode I shall not forget.

The work-up in Malta was under the auspices of Rear-Admiral Madden, Flag Officer Malta, who ran a pretty efficient working-up base, although the facilities were not comparable with those to be established under Flag Officer Sea Training at Portland. The Mediterranean Fleet at that time consisted of a carrier, some cruisers, including my old ship *Birmingham*, and a couple of squadrons of destroyers commanded by Otto Steiner and Colin Madden, as well as a squadron of Daring Class ships, each of which had a captain in command. *Triumph*, the Fleet repair ship, was there with Walter Wells as the executive officer (at sea despite being on the 'dry' list). A term-mate of Peter's, Tony Griffin, commanded the minesweeping squadron with its own support ship, *Meon*, which allowed it to operate as far afield as necessary. These, a submarine flotilla and a number of Royal Fleet Auxiliaries made up a sizeable force. There were many calls to be exchanged, and plenty of people to meet. I reported directly to the Flag Officer Flotillas Mediterranean, Rear-Admiral Alistair Ewing, and most important of all, the Commander-in-Chief was Charles Lambe, who was friendliness itself, and I was often included in picnics and so on when in Malta.

The destroyers and frigates were berthed in Sliema Creek, and a legendary hurdle confronted their commanding officers in berthing there. It had to be achieved stern first, day or night, bringing the ship to rest smartly between the two buoys assigned, and securing to them, head and stern, with the minimum of fuss and bother. The turn before entering the creek had to be made using a great deal of power, because there was very little space in sheltered water at its entrance. One then had to go astern at something like 10 or 12 knots in order to maintain good steerageway, and pass between the ships already berthed in lines all down the creek. On approaching one's buoy, the engines were put half ahead and, if late, to full power, to end up stopped so that the picking-up rope could be quickly secured to the head buoy. One then manoeuvred, using as much power as was necessary, to make the stern wire fast. The Flag Officer Flotilla's office overlooked the scene and you could be sure of being watched. It was one of the hallmarks of a smart commanding officer and a smart ship that this manoeuvre was carried out properly whatever the weather.

I remember approaching Sliema Creek on one perfectly filthy afternoon when it was gusting hard, as it often did in Malta during the autumn equinox, and receiving a signal from Colin Madden in *Trafalgar*, to say that he had arranged an extra 'tid' (a small tug) for me, but would quite understand if I thought the weather was unsuitable for entering harbour. It was one of those moments for a personal decision. I decided to take her in, and thankfully, all went well. I was very grateful to Colin for the consideration he showed, and the episode naturally did me nothing but good with my ship's company, who would not otherwise have had shore leave.

The submarines berthed in Msida, a parallel creek the other side of HMS *Phoenicia*, the shore base at Malta for the smaller ships, where the canteen and playing fields, as well as the stores, and so forth, were. A large part of our work-up as an anti-submarine ship and squadron involved exercises with submarines. These usually took place to the south of Malta, reached via the Comino Channel. Gunnery was carried out there too, including bombardment practice at a small island called Filfla, which must have been carpeted with steel. The great advantage of these exercise areas over those at Portland was the comparative absence of merchant traffic or interference from aircraft but, as at Portland, the weather was often unkind.

Blackpool rolled phenomenally, 25–30° according to the pendulum indicator on the bridge, and I became concerned about her top weight. I remembered that Father had had a problem in *Cyclamen* which required one of his masts to be cut down. So we embarked the Fleet Construction Officer for a day, made him seasick, and took him back to do his calculations. He reported reassuringly that all was well, and we continued to roll like hell unless I engaged the stabilisers, whose thumping was almost as disturbing. This did not improve our living conditions nor our performance as a gunnery platform.

We were having constant trouble with the new-design turret, in particular the hydraulic rammers which loaded the shells into the guns. As the gyro-rate unit in the fire control system also seemed to be performing very oddly, we seldom managed a successful firing run. This was very depressing for my staff gunnery officer, John Steel, who coped admirably, and also for the ship's company, many of whom would be closed-up for hours for shoots and then find that, owing either to the GRU or the rammers, the shoot could not take place or, if started, be completed. (It transpired later that the rammer pins being sent to us were not made of the proper metal, something we were quite incapable of sorting out ourselves.)

This particular saga culminated when we were on passage some time later to the eastern Mediterranean with Flag Officer Flotillas for an important exercise and a shell became jammed in one of the barrels of my turret. To avoid being put out of action, from the gunnery point of view, for the whole exercise, I talked with the engineer officer and gunnery officer and decided to remove the shell from the gun. To do this, we tapped its base, screwed in an eyebolt, turned the turret so that it faced aft, secured a wire hawser to the eye-bolt in the base of the shell, rove it round the centre line capstan and heaved. The gun cleared, to the entire satisfaction of everybody on board. I got frightful stick for this afterwards, and at our next docking and defects period, new inner linings were ordered to be fitted to both barrels. I made things worse by including a rather naughty remark in an appendix to a report to the Flag Officer Flotillas, in which I said that if this had been the wrong way of clearing the gun, could I please be informed what would have been the right way? Soon after Admiral Ewing received this letter, I was sent a signal ordering me to 'repair on board', so knew something was going to happen. He was very good, and told me I had no business to write a letter like that. I said, 'I was not writing to you, Sir, it was an appendix intended for the staff.' He said, 'It makes no difference, they are my staff.' I apologised, and he gave me back my letter and told me to write again, omitting the offending remark. That was the end of the incident, for which I was very grateful to Ewing, but the episode is worth recounting as a sign of the frustration under which many of us laboured owing to design defects in some of our weapon systems. By contrast, our anti-submarine work-up and training and subsequent performance were very satisfactory. We took part in frequent exercises when in harbour, at the anti-submarine attack trainer ashore at *Phoenicia*, where I was pleased to see, once, one or two of *Blackpool*'s runs pinned up on the school wall as examples of how to do it.

Life was full of incident, and every day brought a new experience of some kind. I had a first-rate team of officers, the two most important being the commander (ME), Herbert Gardner, who was also squadron engineer officer, and the First Lieutenant, Edwards, an ex-submariner to whom nothing was so trivial as not to attract his personal attention. It seemed (and I have heard so since) that it was a happy ship, as well as a good example to the rest of the squadron.

We were a foursome again before Christmas, and I had already completed my first Cyprus Patrol with two ships and some minesweepers. This patrol was the standing operational task of the frigates and destroyers on the station at this time. It involved reporting to the flag officer Middle East, who was a famous submariner, 'Crap' Miers, VC, whose headquarters were at Episkopi. Under his operational command, ships patrolled round the coast of the entire island day and night in an endeavour to intercept caiques bringing arms for EOKA from Greece. Patrols were well organised, and liaison and communications with the Army ashore were good, so one spent weeks patrolling round the lovely island with practically no opportunity to go ashore, except for an occasional liaison lunch with the Black Watch at Xeros or the Argylls at Dhekelia. I anchored once at Kyrenia, about half a mile offshore in 20 fathoms on a sloping shelf, went ashore for a walk, and determined to come back again one day if I could.

The Cyprus Patrol, and indeed some of the other long passages on the station, required destroyers and frigates to refuel at sea from an oiler, and one was assigned to each patrol. Somewhat unwisely, perhaps (but I think we all enjoyed it, and it certainly sharpened us up), a competition was run throughout the Fleet to achieve the fastest time on the refuelling evolution. The time taking on board fuel did not count, because that depended almost as much on the oiler as on the ship, but what was competed for was 'dead time'. This was the time taken by a ship between her arrival half a mile astern of the oiler and the time at which pumping over began. To this was added the time between the order to stop pumping and the time that the last line was cast off from the oiler, which was responsible for keeping an independent record for the Fleet staff. This was right up Edwards's street, and also Gardner's. All I had to do was to make certain that the time taken for the approach was as short as possible. This meant coming in at 20 knots, and going half astern when the bow was abreast the oiler's stern, so as to end up, with luck, in the right position for the hoses to come over and be connected, at the same speed as the oiler and about 30 yards off. With a splendidly worked-up engine room and upper-deck team, we came top of the Fleet list. One or two ships used full power astern to stop abreast the oiler, and sometimes, I think, my approach time was bettered, but I regarded this as unwise, as it left nothing in reserve. (After we had left the Mediterranean, I understand that the whole competition was cancelled by a later flag officer flotillas.)

The 6th Frigate Squadron spent Christmas in Malta, and I was the guest of the Steiner family for Christmas Day itself, Otto being away on Cyprus Patrol, where he had relieved us. With the cooperation, and indeed, applause of Bertie Lyddon, the captain of *Phoenicia*, we held a highly competitive squadron carnival in his establishment to celebrate Christmas, won by *Ulysses*. On Boxing Day, playing hockey against Flag Officer Flotilla's team, I put my back out for the first time – so badly I could not pick up my hockey stick. (A few days flat on my back sorted this out, but I have had to watch it ever since.) About this time, I was offered the opportunity of an exercise with USS *Skipjack*, the newest US nuclear submarine, which was engaged in trials in the Mediterranean. *Undaunted* had the first long-range sonar in the Fleet, so I felt it could be made an exercise of particular interest. The problem was that *Skipjack*'s maximum speed and acceleration exceeded that of any of my ships. I therefore designed the exercise round a reversal of the usual roles: in other words, I asked *Skipjack* to attack us, rather than trying to attack him. This allowed him to make various passes at us, disengage and come in again. It maximised contact time, and gave us an opportunity to measure our performance against that of a nuclear submarine. The exercise took place at night, since that suited *Skipjack*'s passage plans, and I adopted a diamond formation for my ships. The exercise had a good write-up from everybody, I am glad to say, but there is no doubt that the submarine was master of the field. *Undaunted* had carried out the first Fleet trials with a Dragonfly helicopter embarked before leaving the UK, but we had no sonar-equipped helicopter with us. If this exercise showed anything, it showed the need for these aircraft in frigates. About this time, I managed to write the detailed paper necessary to get my anti-submarine torpedoes, which I had reckoned to be useless at the Tactical School, approved for removal from *Blackpool* at the next opportunity. We were all glad about this, as in addition to being tactically futile, they were very difficult to maintain.

After *Skipjack*, we had a day or two in Gibraltar, and during the passage back to Malta I received a signal offering a couple of us visits to the Greek Islands, and asking which islands we would choose. The message told me nothing about the various islands' advantages, so I sent back a parody of Byron, asking Richard Gledhow, the Fleet Operations Officer, to choose: 'The Isles of Greece, / an isle apiece, / let Gledhow choose and I'll comply.' I then was sent to Syra, seat of the Nomarch of the Cyclades, as that seemed the sensible place for the senior officer, whereas *Undine* went to Mykinos, which was much the better visit from the tourist point of view. However, the two days in Syra, although quiet, were fun, and I was looked after by a Greek merchant captain and the harbourmaster, who were extremely friendly. The Nomarch was courteous, the usual wreath was laid in the town square on the war memorial, and nobody seemed to mind that we were going straight on to Cyprus Patrol thereafter. At this time, the garrison in Nicosia included the Lancashire Fusiliers, a natural for a special relationship with *Blackpool*. Tom Lash, the commanding officer, was a delightful person, and we exchanged parties. This was slightly dangerous for my officers, since the Lancashire Fusiliers' after-dinner game was some kind of rugger in the mess, and they were much bigger and fitter than us.

Undine and *Blackpool* knew, during this particular patrol, that we were to make a visit to Venice afterwards, a very welcome prospect of some bright lights for everybody, and I did my best to learn a little Italian in the long hours spent circling Cyprus. When we arrived in April, we were told to moor stern first close by Santa Maria De La Salute, at the entrance to the Grand Canal. As the senior ship, I went in first, to be nearest to the wall to which we would have a 'walkashore' (a kind of small bridge). I picked up my buoy satisfactorily, but was unable to bring my stern close in to the shore. Eventually, I sent a leadsman aft, who found far less water than I had been led to expect. *Blackpool*'s stern, happily, was resolutely refusing to be manoeuvred into the mud. So we settled as close as we could, and libertymen had to use a dinghy on a double line and haul themselves ashore and back to the ship. (I have been a little distrustful of Italian harbourmasters ever since.) Lloyd Foster brought his ship nicely alongside outside me.

Then it was back to Malta and exercises, followed by *Blackpool*'s docking and essential defects period. Elizabeth and Tom came out from England for six weeks during the course of it. This was absolutely marvellous, and I have the clearest recollection of little Tom rushing across the apron at Luqa to greet me. I always remember my first night ashore, before the ship went into dock. She was berthed in Sliema Creek, and it blew very hard, or seemed to. Sleep became impossible, wondering if everything was all right (as of course it was).

Elizabeth and Tom went home, but the back of my separation from the family had been broken, as the rest of the commission was only partly to be in the Mediterranean. It was, however, an extremely interesting part, as Alastair Ewing took a team of us, exercising *en route*, eastwards to Istanbul. On the way, *Tiger*, *Blackpool* and *Ulysses* visited Beirut for three or four days. This was a fascinating experience. I was admirably looked after by the naval attaché, Charles Wheen, and had some excellent runs ashore with Jock Cunningham.

On our last evening, before a cocktail party, it unfortunately started to blow up hard from the north-west, and *Tiger* wisely sailed. We were berthed inside a jetty, with *Ulysses* astern of *Blackpool*. It had been a difficult manoeuvre to berth and mercifully I had put down an anchor off so that we could haul the ship out on it if necessary. There was little room to turn, and merchant ships lay ahead. (It would have been wiser to have turned before berthing, and I cannot now remember the reason why I did not do so – perhaps time was short.) We had to cancel the cocktail party, though a few hardy spirits, mostly female, came on board just the same. We got them ashore just in time, more or less dry-shod, but soon afterwards, waves, beating back from the further shore of the bay, began breaking over the jetty, and the ship rolled heavily. *Ulysses* astern was more sheltered, but the ship ahead, an empty Chinese freighter, was beating and banging herself to pieces as we watched. Herbert Gardner came to see me and said that he did not believe it was safe for *Blackpool* to remain alongside.

I had raised steam, and it must have been about 10 p.m. when I went up on the bridge to take her out. With luck, some of *Ulysses*'s ship's company in life jackets were able to cast off our hawsers without being washed into the harbour. It was a very anxious moment, and I remember my voice sounded (to me, anyway – I hope not to everybody) quite unnatural as I 'rang on' and gave the first engine orders, at the same time heaving in on the anchor to drag the bow away from the jetty. The anchor held, and then came up clear. By use of a great deal of power, I turned the ship and pointed in the right direction without hitting anything. We moved out into the bay and safety, with the cable party on the fo'c'sle securing anchors and cables for sea. In my relief, I failed to realise that I was by then doing about 12 knots, until, by the grace of God, the navigator, a splendid Australian called Bertie Richards, said to me, 'Sir, you should reduce speed at once,' which I did. In the euphoria of having extricated us from this pickle, I had been in danger of sending a wave over the fo'c'sle and washing some of the cable party into the bay.

During this visit, the admiral detailed me off to give a lecture on NATO strategy to the Turkish Defence College – a very silent, polite and senior collection. I remember being asked what I thought would comprise an adequate nuclear deterrent. I replied, 'One nuclear weapon which Khrushchev is certain would land on him,' and that seemed to satisfy them.

I was then allowed, by dint of having asked pretty persistently some time before, to fulfil a long-held ambition to take some ships into the Black Sea. *Blackpool* led *Ulysses* through the Bosphorus and on: a wonderful trip on a lovely, clear day. I had wanted to go to Trabzon, but this the Turks would not allow. I was, however, able to take *Blackpool* to Samsun, while *Ulysses* went in to Zonguldak. Samsun is famous for tobacco; Zonguldak is famous for coalmines, and was, I'm afraid, the less attractive of the two. That over, it was back to Malta to see friends and prepare for the passage home. There was a new Commander-in-Chief, Admiral Bingley, Charles Lambe having left to go as First Sea Lord just before we had sailed. On his departure from Malta, we had all cheered ship, and I received a charming signal saying how much he had appreciated the cheering from *Blackpool*.

We went home by divisions, and I took *Undine* with me to Setubal, just south of Lisbon, a delightful little town at the base of a beautiful peninsula. We had a Portuguese interpreter with us, whose Portuguese, learnt in Brazil, was somewhat archaic and different from that of the Setubalese, but we were given a great welcome by Britain's oldest ally and thoroughly enjoyed ourselves. The usual crisis occurred. This time it was due to rice-grass coming down river and blocking the condenser inlets in *Blackpool* disabling the engines. However, our motor cutter, with *Undine*'s and the harbourmaster's launch, together managed, somewhat to my surprise, to pull her clear of the jetty. I had half expected to have to lay out an anchor and kedge her off. We anchored in midstream near *Undine*, where the rice-grass swept harmlessly by, cleared the inlets with divers, weighed and sailed, late but not badly so.

We then entered Chatham, our base port, for refit. We had done a great deal of work to prepare a thorough defect list ready for this and I hoped it would be the moment when we could get our gunnery system properly set to work. At that time the UK dockyards were having their organisation revised and, among other measures, officers were being appointed to individual ships refitting in the dockyard to act as project officers to help expedite the refit. I had a very good one (whose name I forget), and asked him if everything was all right, if we had done our homework properly, and so on. 'Yes, Sir,' he said, 'but I don't think anyone at Chatham is looking forward to refitting *Blackpool*.' I said, 'Why not?'. He replied, 'I don't think I want to say any more.' 'You've said too much already, tell me.' 'I think I can put it best like this: people feel that the ship's officers are taking too much interest in the refit.' Horrified, I decided to press him no further, and drew my own conclusions.

A major concern, at the refit conference and thereafter, became the dockyard's refusal to take a root and branch attitude to refitting the gyro-rate unit because the ship was unable to identify the particular defects from which it was suffering. All I could say was that it was unreliable and did not work, and I lost the battle to have a new one installed. During the refit, which included the removal of the torpedo tubes, we stayed several times at Godden Green, from where I could drive to and fro easily. It was a pleasant relaxation from time at sea, although one hated to see the ship become filthy, as was inevitable with the work to be done and the ship's company accommodated ashore. I visited the rest of the squadron from time to time.

Eventually, the refit ended and we went down the Channel, having arranged a practice shoot *en route*. This was an abysmal failure. I entered Portsmouth Dockyard, and their experts on our fire control system came on board, listened to the newly-refitted gyro-rate unit being run up, and said at once: 'Your GRU's no good, you need a new one.' So much for the efforts of Chatham Dockyard, and there we returned for another protracted spell to fit a new GRU.

I saw the Commander-in-Chief and asked for a court of inquiry. This was held, conducted by the Chief Staff Officer (Technical) to the Commander-in-Chief, and I gave my evidence in writing as well as orally, as I thought it important to be on the record. We sailed in due course, did some more firings and found the system at last worked – practically at the end of my commission. The story ended some months later, when I was in the Admiralty. I was unexpectedly sent for by Admiral Sir Peter Reid, the Controller of the Navy. I reported to his office, and he said, 'Ashmore, I have sent for you on behalf of the Board to tell you that you still enjoy the confidence of their Lordships.' 'But Sir,' I said, 'I had no idea I was in any danger of forfeiting it. What is this all about?' He told me. Apparently, the court of inquiry had found in favour of the ship, and had heavily criticised Chatham over the business of my GRU. The Admiral Superintendent of the dockyard, who reported directly to the Controller rather than to the Commander-in-Chief, had then appealed on behalf of the dockyard officers. The Controller had sent the report of the inquiry to the Naval Law Division to weigh the evidence. They had ruled in favour of the Commander-in-Chief and the ship, and the dockyard had been so informed. Not realising that I was in ignorance of all these goings-on in high places, the Controller had kindly seen fit to send for me and interview me. You could have knocked me down with a feather.

Blackpool now had a jaunt up to Londonderry, to the Joint School of Anti-Submarine Warfare. As I went upriver with my squadron, we ran into fog. The ships ahead of me anchored, but *Blackpool* managed to slip past and reach Derry itself, where the weather was clearer. It was a short visit, and then it was back to the south coast and into Portsmouth. I misjudged my approach to my jetty, just in from the flagship's berth at South Railway Jetty, and gave the ship the worst knock of the whole commission, putting a small wrinkle in the bow. The dockyard were nothing but helpful, the damage was assessed at £60, and was put right, as far as it could be, the same day. No change to my programme was required, nor was there any particular reaction to my report of the incident. (However, I fear *Blackpool*, whose eventual destination was New Zealand, bore a slightly whimsical look to part of her stem for the rest of her life.) I have since heard that the jetty I hit is notorious for the inward surge that caught me. I wish I had known at the time.

I now knew that my next job was at the Admiralty, as deputy director of plans, so I would be serving pretty close to Charles Lambe again. I was to relieve Ray Hart, from whom I had taken over the squadron only some 18 months earlier. I gathered that his face had not fitted with John Bush, the very energetic and dogmatic director of plans. I felt this might help me, since if he was losing one deputy, he might find it wise to be more tolerant of a second. I called on the Commander-in-Chief to say goodbye and turned over *Blackpool* to Duncan Knight, whom I already knew so well, with complete confidence that he would look after the ship as she deserved. I thanked my lucky stars for having come through the many hazards everyone meets at sea with reasonable success, as well as making many new friends – and, I fear, also some enemies.

This brief account of my time in *Blackpool*, with some of the various concerns and incidents in both ship and squadron, gives evidence typical, I believe, of the vicissitudes of life at sea in the Royal Navy in peacetime. It is never dull, never without challenge or anxiety. The commanding officer – 'sole master under God' – feels his responsibilities keenly. Competition with his peers, though never to be acknowledged, is ever-present and, to the credit of almost every officer in the Fleet, is seldom evident. Luck has much to do with success or failure, but nothing occurs that bearing in adversity cannot greatly mitigate. The life is physically hard, in small ships especially, and the hours demanding at sea, and frequently in harbour, too. In my annual inspections of ships, when it was important to temper the exaction of the highest standards with understanding of the pressures on individuals, I made it my practice to hold an immediate 'wash-up' in the presence of my staff and all the ship's officers. No adverse comment in writing the report was permitted by me unless it had first been aired at that meeting. Human relationships are the essence of leadership and confidence and are the vital threads running through all time at sea.

It is easy to understand why the professional direction of the Navy attaches so much importance to views and recommendations from sea, and why those who have endured the privilege of command at sea expect, and merit, appointments of the highest responsibility and influence in the service. There is always a shortage of sea command experience, but in a fighting sea service, there is no substitute for it. Brains, for which the Navy is rightly not renowned, are no substitute either. A great Chief of the Air Staff, Andrew Humphrey, once said to me, 'The problem with my service, Edward, is that only the officers fight.' In the Navy, we are fortunate in being all of one company in the ship, sharing experience and danger in common. That sense of community is engendered, commission by commission, in conditions no less intimate, and often more exacting, than those of the regimental system by which the Army rightly sets much store. It is no less needed in Whitehall, where I again returned.

Plans Division had a fearsome reputation for long hours and hard work. As deputy director to John Bush on the naval side, as opposed to the joint planning side, I would be responsible for papers concerning the size and shape of the Fleet and could expect a good many of both. The first task was to find somewhere to live in London during the week and I was fortunate indeed to be able to go again to 35 Eaton Terrace and rent two small rooms, with the use of a bathroom and kitchenette, which suited me admirably and allowed Elizabeth to come up when, rarely, she was able. I always had lunches at the United Service Club in Waterloo Place, which provided ten minutes' walk each way.

There was a large number of divisions in the naval staff, among which Plans worked directly to the vice-chief of the naval staff (VCNS); Operations, through a rear-admiral assistant chief of the naval staff, worked to the VCNS also; Tactical and Weapons Policy, with the bulk of the Weapon Divisions, answered to the deputy chief of the naval staff (DCNS). The First Sea Lord, as chief of naval staff (CNS), superintended all these divisions, subject to the collective responsibility of board members. John Bush had two deputies: myself (on relieving Ray Hart) and Bill O'Brien, deputy director for joint plans, who ran the naval organisation within the joint planning staff, working to the Chiefs of Staffs Committee chaired by the chief of defence staff (CDS). We were all captains, as were the four assistant directors of plans, three of whom worked to me: one for Logistics, one for Fleet Air matters and the other for Ships and Submarines. There were, of course, a number of commanders, the hardest-worked of whom was George Kitchin, of Peter's term, in the 'Size and Shape' area, which covered not only numbers, but deployment, refitting, organisation and long-term plans for the Fleet. He was to be relieved by Jimmy Syms, of Western Province and Yardley Court days. Much was expected of me, and I was conscious not only of John Bush's intellect and reputation as a driver, but also of the fact that Ray Hart, a brilliant sea officer if ever there was one, had found him intolerable. It was the royal road, but a rough one.

I had hardly joined, nor had time to call on Sir Charles Lambe, when he was stricken. I visited him in the Millbank Hospital, and found him pale but composed. He said: 'Edward, they say that you never feel the coronary that kills you. I have had so much pain that I should live for a thousand years.' He had discussed the situation with his friend, 'Dickie' Mountbatten, who was his predecessor and now CDS. He told me that he was to take a sabbatical year and then come back and see what he could do, but that he would not stay on as First Sea Lord, although as Admiral of the Fleet, he would never retire. He felt that there were a great many things he could still hope to do. He said what great fun it would have been to have worked together again, and regretted this would not happen. Less than a year later, while shaving at 'Knock Hill', his house in Fife, he suffered a fatal coronary thrombosis. A senior civil servant in the naval staff, Nigel Abercrombie, said to me that Charles Lambe would have been a great First Sea Lord. Fraser, he said, was a great First Sea Lord, 'Dickie' was not. (Indeed, the story runs that after 'Dickie' had been CDS for six weeks or so, Charles sent him a rubber stamp which said 'Forgive me for interfering, but . . .'.) The loss, not only to the Navy but to inter-service cooperation as a whole, was inestimable. Lambe's combination of brilliance, charm and modesty was unique.

His successor was Caspar John, a noted naval pilot, and the talented son of Augustus. He had taken over the 3rd Aircraft Carrier Squadron from Lambe, and had recently borne the burden of being VCNS to 'Dickie' Mountbatten. The transition, therefore, was quite easy for him, and for the staff who knew him well, but to face another three years in Whitehall could hardly have been welcome to him. John's successor as VCNS was another aviator, Walter Couchman, who had never served in Whitehall before, and who found the going hard indeed with a boss who knew it all and whose relationship with John Bush, who had been effectively his No. 2 when he was VCNS, was extremely close; indeed, it seemed to me that Bush was really doing the VCNS's job while doing his best to keep Couchman fully informed.

My own hours were about 9 a.m. to 7.30 p.m., and Bush was always there when I left the office. My particular task was strictly single-service in the darkest of dark-blue, trying to make the naval case for use in inter-service discussions later and also, of course, arguing within the naval staff to keep the right balance within the Fleet; this, together with the other forces, was being reduced in size because of the reasonable and necessary constraints on resources which were being applied to us all.

The two big questions facing the Navy and the RAF were, on the one hand, the fact that all the aircraft carriers which had been built during the war were nearing the end of their useful lives, and on the other that the deterrent provided by Bomber Command with nuclear weapons was also rapidly reaching the limit of its credibility. There was plenty to learn, mostly from Bush, and much to do, as few position papers were accepted at first sight, and revisions were always requested – of course, the day before yesterday. I learned that I was much better at criticising other people's work than producing screeds of my own, particularly since only Bush had a shorthand secretary and I used to find that, unless dictated, my sentences became cluttered and complicated.

After six months in the job, I was told that I was shortly to relieve John Bush, and knew then what I was in for. This had, I feel sure, been Charles Lambe's plot, but he was no longer there. Caspar, however, obviously enjoyed John Bush's confidence, and vice versa, so I assumed they must both think I was up to it. Bill O'Brien was senior to me, having been a chief cadet captain

Tamara with her sons Edward (left) and Peter in about 1926.

Cadets Ashmore, with the future First Sea Lord on the left, 1934.

Dartmouth; the Greynvile Term marches past the Prince of Wales, with Admiral Sir Lionel Halsey on his left. Cadet E. Ashmore is in the fourth rank from the rear, on the far right.

The 1935 Jubilee Review, with a model of HMS *Victory* passing the battleship HMS *Nelson*.

The Home Fleet in 1938, photographed by the author from *Rodney*.

HMS *Birmingham* on the China station.

One of HMS *Birmingham*'s exciting 35-ft motor boats, photographed in the destroyer anchorage at Wei-Hai-Wei.

Captain L.H. Ashmore, Royal
Navy, 1938.

The China Squadron at Wei-Hai-Wei in 1938. HMS *Birmingham* is in her normal anchorage
on the far right.

Returning to HMS *Eagle* in one of her Swordfish after taking part in a dummy torpedo attack on HMS *Birmingham*.

My 1938 photograph of the impressive Japanese cruiser *Ashigara*; she was sunk by the British submarine HMS *Trenchant* seven years later, in June 1945.

HMS *Kent* (Captain L.H. Ashmore), the flagship of Vice Admiral Noble in Hong Kong. My parents' flat at May Road level is above the central funnel.

The Ashmore family briefly united in Hong Kong in 1939.

The Seventh Destroyer Flotilla, 1940.

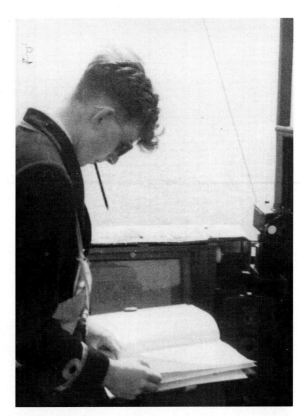

'Vasco' at work in HMS
Jupiter.

HMS *Middleton.*

Chapel Royal, St James's Palace, 11 December 1942.

The King's visit to the Home Fleet shortly before it dispersed in readiness for the invasion in 1944. He is flanked by Admiral Fraser, the C.-in-C., on his right and Vice-Admiral Dalrymple Hamilton on his left. I am behind the Chief of Staff, Commodore Slater, on the left of the picture.

Rear Admiral E.J.P. ('Daddy') Brind, Flag Officer Commanding Cruisers of the British Pacific Fleet, 1944–5.

HMS *Swiftsure*, wearing Brind's flag.

Signals Officer, CSBPF, June 1945.

HMS *Alert* at Kuching in 1953, wearing the flag of Rear Admiral E.T. Shattock, Flag Officer Malayan Area.

Admiral Sir Charles Lambe, C.-in-C.
Far East Fleet; he was my Admiral in
HMS *Vengeance* and HMS *Alert* was his
Despatch Vessel.

With Admiral Golovko, C.-in-C.
Baltic Fleet, at Portsmouth in 1955.

The Sixth Frigate Squadron, 1958–9; left to right, HM Ships *Blackpool* (leader), *Undine*, *Ulysses* and *Undaunted*.

St George's, Grenada, with HMS *Londonderry*, 1963.

Hard at work, 1963.

HMS *Victorious* and HMS *Hermes* at Aden, May 1967.

when I was a junior cadet at Dartmouth, but, nice chap that he was, seemed not in the least put out. My relief as my deputy was to be Tony Griffin, one of the brightest members of Peter's term. It was also clear that in the ordinary course of events – after a year as Director of Plans Navy, and in that capacity, also one of the directors on the Joint Planning Staff – it would be for me to take over as the director of plans to the CDS and as chairman of the directors of plans. Such appointments then worked to a normal rotation between the services, a system much inveighed against as being 'Buggins's turn' but one which did allow the services to plan ahead and produce someone suitable, in the right place at the right time. I felt sure that my NATO and joint service experience in Oslo had something to do with my suitability for this particular post. Also, of course, I did know Mountbatten.

I found it a good deal easier being director of plans than deputy. For one thing, such original thoughts as I was able to produce were for somebody else to put down in papers, which I could then criticise and, one hoped, improve. I saw more of the First Sea Lord and of the First Lord, who was then Peter Carrington in the Macmillan government. I had met him first when deputy director, one of whose duties is to sit in the officials' box in parliament with the civil servants during debates in which the minister is heavily involved. I was accordingly in the box for the first Navy Estimates Debate that Carrington had to take. He came up in the middle, rested his arms on the edge of the box, and said 'Isn't this fun?' before walking off. I have seen him many times since, always with pleasure.

I also found that I thoroughly enjoyed the work of the joint planning staff and the meetings of the directors of plans. The system was designed to process policy or plans, usually originating in the Chiefs of Staffs' Committee and issued through their secretary. At that time this was Major-General George Cole, whom I had met in Moscow as Monty's military assistant.

Occasionally, although we were never short of work, the directors of plans would initiate some subject and suggest terms of reference for it for approval by the Chiefs of Staff. In every instance, a preliminary draft was produced at commander or assistant director level, then revised by the deputies, mine being Bill O'Brien, who would in turn produce a draft. This was then considered by the directors of plans, who would write a final version and submit this to the Chiefs of Staff in committee. The director of plans for the Navy was in the strongest possible position, because he combined in his own person the jobs of director for joint matters and director for single-service matters. On any paper that I signed, therefore, I was responsible for briefing the First Sea Lord or, if it was being taken by the Vice-Chiefs, the VCNS. My colleagues, a brigadier and an air commodore, had to brief 'briefers' in their respective departments, and the briefers then briefed the board member – a rotten system which they seemed to take for granted; and, it seemed to me, they went often more in awe of their briefers than they ought.

It was a busy time, our main preoccupation being the aircraft carrier replacement programme. Helped by Val Bailey and Tony Griffin, I had put forward a strong case, I thought, for smaller ships, the size of the present

Invincible Class, to be built in greater numbers than we could possibly hope to obtain with big aircraft carriers. We failed to convince the board, in spite of the support of the very newly-arrived VCNS, Sir Varyl Begg. This was because of the opposition of the DCNS, an old friend, Laurie Durlacher, who supported the view of the Tactical and Weapons Policy Division, and above all because the First Sea Lord himself was wedded to the large carrier, the very high-performance aircraft that only a large carrier could embark, and a force-projection role for the Royal Navy. About this time Skybolt, the US-built air-launched ballistic missile, lapsed, and the Polaris Agreement was made between Macmillan and Kennedy at Nassau; the Navy, therefore, was to take on the strategic nuclear deterrent. My RAF colleagues found this hard to take, and were inclined (wrongly) to attribute machinations to Mountbatten.

A critical task for the directors of plans during my year was a paper for the Chiefs of Staff to define a strategy for the 1960s at acceptable cost. This had to reflect a report by very high-level officials chaired by Sir Norman Brooke, Secretary of the Cabinet, written during Charles Lambe's time as First Sea Lord. Known as the 'Future Policy Review', it reflected on Britain's place in the world, on the realities of its power, and on the economic burdens that the country could afford to bear. It was approved by the Cabinet and Chiefs of Staff, and became the Bible from which to draw conclusions about the size and shape of our defence forces and what the country could expect from them. A principal constraint was the cost in foreign currency of large overseas bases, and this, of course, opened the way to a formidable argument between the Navy and the RAF as to how power could best be exerted without such bases. We saw the carrier task force with adequate amphibious support as the obvious way to exert power and provide the ability to establish air bases which could then deploy shore-based aircraft. The RAF concept envisaged a chain of island air bases through which the sinews of war could be staged to meet whatever contingency might arise.

The battle ranged between these extreme views, with the Army generally content to await the outcome. Some of the more obscure islands, Aldabra and Marion, for example, had to be found on maps and then checked to make certain that the RAF figures were right. (There were those in the naval staff who thought otherwise.) Then there was the cost of ensuring the security of the islands, if of strategic value. In the event, the directors of plans approved a paper, JP(61)91, entitled 'Limitation of the Future Cost of Defence', which examined UK defence commitments outside NATO. The examination, according to its terms of reference, was 'to include the concept of reducing or replacing the present overseas garrisons by maintaining larger forces in the United Kingdom and/or afloat, accepting in either case a reduction in the scale of facilities immediately available at existing overseas bases'. This document recommended a Navy including six large aircraft carriers, able to maintain three or four carrier groups always in service. I remember my RAF colleague, Derek Stapleton, white in the face as he signed the final version. When I briefed the First Sea Lord, he said, 'I've waited ten years for this,' so I felt very pleased – wrongly. The Chiefs of Staff threw the paper straight out, with a direction to rewrite it. It was considered too 'dark-blue'. In January 1962, the chiefs eventually approved a strategic paper, COS (62)1, 'British Strategy in the Sixties', which I think we all felt struck a reasonable balance between the services, much though I regretted the failure to emasculate the expensive overseas bases, which were potential hostages to fortune.

I was relieved as director of plans, Royal Navy, by Andrew Lewis, and became director of plans to the CDS and *ex officio* chairman of the directors of plans, relieving Brig. Powell-Jones, a delightful and energetic Welshman, but rather too excitable for the job he had had to perform. The First Sea Lord took me out to lunch, a traditional privilege enjoyed only by the director of plans among the naval staff captains, but I was sad to lose another privilege of the job, that of using the VCNS's car to go home at night. Since my working hours usually extended to 9 p.m., this had been a very welcome help. However, I found that the new job was far less exacting and really rather up my street.

I got off to a lucky start. During my call on 'Dickie' Mountbatten, he was very friendly, sat me down and started telling me how to do my job. It went on a bit, and then the telephone rang. It was Princess Ashraf, sister of the Shah of Persia, ringing up about some forthcoming visit to London and asking his advice which he, of course, gave. I sat listening, riveted by this long conversation. When it ended, 'Dickie' turned round to me and said, 'Ashmore, where was I?' I had not the slightest idea, so I said, 'Well, Sir, you were saying . . .'. 'Ah, Yes,' he said, and off he went again for the next quarter of an hour while I breathed a long sigh of relief. He was an interesting character, of whom so much has been written that it's hardly necessary for me to add to it in this account. I found him always very kind, and not overtly manipulative in any of his dealings with the directors of plans, although I believe he deliberately treated our rather key committee with kid gloves. He had a sense of humour and could laugh at himself if necessary, but I thought him capricious and vain, and felt that many of his manoeuvrings, usually unnecessary, arose from an inability to recognise early enough that he could, in fact, be wrong. He worked quickly, with a certain fitful brilliance, but his high opinion of his own abilities made him a difficult colleague for the Chiefs of Staff. He also met in cabal with Sir Robert Scott, Permanent Under-Secretary at the MoD, and Solly Zuckerman, the Chief Scientific Adviser to the Government, a practice which I believe to have been harmless, if not beneficial. But it created so much suspicion that it perhaps had better been avoided.

At that time he was bent on centralisation of the MoD, including the replacement of service ministers by a functional system. I was grateful not to be involved, or to have the directors of plans involved, in it. I was, however, shown the paper, and asked for my personal comments on it, which were to welcome co-location and the maintenance intact of the Chiefs of Staff system, but to be wary of 'functional' organisation, especially at ministerial level. Proliferation of ministers does not lead to clarity or speed of decision, rather the reverse in my experience, and the downgrading of the service ministers to parliamentary under-secretary level in aid of establishing functional ministers of state did not, in my view, help parliament, the services or defence. (It was not immediately adopted, but came in later in 1967, under Denis Healey.)

As far as my particular job was concerned, I had to run the Joint Planning Staff Secretariat and so forth, chair the Directors of Plans Committee, and contribute to the balance of the final papers which were sent to the Chiefs of Staff. I would, among others, brief the CDS on those papers and attend the Chiefs of Staffs Meetings, at the bottom of the table, in case some query was raised that the cohorts of briefers had not foreseen. After a couple of months in the job, 'Dickie' ticked me off for not being a commodore, and I was made one. I was against this; in the Navy, any captain of six years' seniority or more ranks with a brigadier or air commodore, and there was therefore no reason I could see why I should not do my job adequately as a senior captain. The rank of commodore in the Navy is not substantive, and was only assigned if it was necessary at sea to make one commanding officer senior to others for some purpose that the flag officer concerned had in mind. A good example of this, as in bygone days, was the Commodore West Indies, who, being a commodore and with a station responsibility, comfortably took command of any ships commanded by officers senior to himself, other than flag officers, who might arrive on the station. It seemed to me a nonsense to have to introduce this into the MoD. I could afford a high-falutin' view as it did not affect my pay, only uniform, which I seldom wore. However, 'promoted' temporarily I was, and there was nothing more to be done about it. I had at least made my point, but the appellation has since spread to designated naval members of staffs in the more unified MoD of today – a regrettable 'rounding up'.

A great deal of our work at that time was concerned with events in what were known as the 'Protocol States' – remnants of the old French Empire of Indo-China – as Britain, with her vast base at Singapore, was an important member of the then South-East Asia Treaty Organisation. We were also heavily involved with the Central Treaty Organisation (CENTO, ourselves, Iran, Turkey and Pakistan) and, of course, NATO, although much of the NATO planning had properly slipped out of national hands into those of the Standing Group, the Supreme Allied Commanders Atlantic and Europe and of the Channel Committee. Not long after taking over, I found that, apart from Andrew Lewis, neither of my colleagues, Stapleton of the RAF or Strickland of the Army, had been as far east even as Aden, so I determined on a directors of plans' tour. This, I am sure, was a good idea, although in the course of it a particularly close relationship was struck up between the Army and RAF members of the committee, of which I felt myself, at times, to be the target. However, it did disabuse them of the ideas that they had kept fielding in committee, as though conditions in South-East Asia were suitable for a NATO-type alliance, with the kind of unqualified commitments that the members of that alliance give. We visited the major headquarters and were very kindly looked after, particularly by Elworthy in Aden, who made a great impression on us all. It was fun to see Hong Kong again, and also to go to Cyprus and spend more than an hour or two at a time on dry land there. We visited Germany and met with the joint

Commanders-in-Chief to learn their problems, and this was of special value to me.

Back in Whitehall we continued with the usual chores of preparing reinforcement plans, evacuation plans, contingency plans, and so forth, aided by Peter Wilkinson, our excellent Foreign Office colleague, who sat with us. (He was relieved by Peter Ramsbotham towards the end of my time.) Unified commands were being set up overseas, and a certain amount of work was involved in doing this. The pattern was that of the Middle East, where Aden was already headquarters of a unified commander, responsible to the CDS. It was, on Mountbatten's insistence, emulated widely: in Hong Kong, Singapore and, finally, in the West Indies, where the senior naval officer West Indies was made Commander British forces Caribbean Area, towards the end of 1962. Only in the UK itself was it found impossible to set up a single, unified command, and therefore a Commander-in-Chiefs' Committee was established at Wilton, where Cs-in-C. Home Fleet, UK Land Forces and Bomber Command RAF could commune together and masquerade as a unified outfit.

My time was coming to an end, and another appointment had to be found. I was told that they had command of a cruiser, *Blake*, in mind for me, and I did not think too much of that. The aircraft carrier available, *Ark Royal*, had been given to Tony Griffin, and I therefore talked to Bertie Padfield, the assistant to the Naval Secretary, who let met know that after my hard grind in Plans, I would be allowed a certain amount of discretion in what I might want to do. I therefore opted, at once and strongly, for the newly-created post of Commander British Forces Caribbean Area and Senior Naval Officer West Indies, and this appointment was confirmed. Father had been in the West Indies as a sub-lieutenant and Peter as a midshipman and again as captain of the Dartmouth Training Squadron. It was a station full of naval history which I longed to see, and it was exciting to be going in charge there.

My time with CDS ended, and I was relieved by Derek Stapleton in January 1963. A rather silly episode occurred when one of the staff said, 'Of course, you would like a picture of CDS wouldn't you?', to which I said, 'Well, it's up to him, if he likes to give me one that's fine,' and nothing happened. I certainly was not going to indent for one, and one did not arrive, which worried me not at all. 'Dickie' was, as usual, charming when he said goodbye, and I think that the job really had gone very satisfactorily; I had certainly acquired a firsthand knowledge of the functioning of the Chiefs of Staff system, which had changed little since it was set out by Lord Hankey of Committee of Imperial Defence fame, and seemed to me to function wisely, if unimaginatively.

John Martin in the West Indies was not due for relief until mid-summer, so we had a splendid spell of leave ahead of us in which to prepare for the trip to Bermuda, where the family would be based while I was in the Caribbean. I was delighted with the thought of another three-service job, and felt that my experience in the Chiefs of Staff organisation and the many friends and acquaintances I now had in the other two services would stand me in excellent stead. It would have been fine and right to have been given another ship to command, but I would be at sea a great deal in the West Indies anyway, where there promised to be plenty of action.

Before taking up my appointment as CBFCA, I had to make calls in the MoD and also on the commanders-in-chief, who would be providing the forces that I would have under command. There was Sir Charles Madden, C.-in-C. Home Fleet and C.-in-C. Coastal Command at Northwood, and then General Bray at Bulford, who, as C.-in-C. UK Land Forces, provided the garrisons in British Guiana and British Honduras, as well as some troops in the Bahamas. Elizabeth came with me, and very pleasant it was at both places. While at Fleet HQ, the Chief of Staff, Vice-Admiral Clutterbuck, told me that as captain of *Tiger*, he had recently been to Bermuda and what a shocking mess the naval dockyard was. He called it a disgrace to the Royal Navy and said something ought to be done. I therefore saw Peter White, who was engaged at that time in the Second Sea Lord's Office concerned with bricks and mortar. He introduced me to a surveyor of lands called Alan Fairley. We made a plot that if I found things were as bad as Clutterbuck had said they were, I would send the necessary report home and they would hope to come out to do something about it.

Since there was plenty of time, we were able to go out with Tom in the SS *Pizarro*, in great luxury in the best cabins, taking our gear with us. The voyage was quiet, and the first sight of Bermuda, with its white roofs and blue seas in the sunshine, was unforgettable. At Hamilton, John and Rosemary Martin were there to meet us and give us the best possible turnover. I took over the station and staff in good heart, and received excellent advice from John, who had been made the first Commander British Forces abut two-thirds through his time as Senior Naval Officer West Indies. One was also Island Commander Bermuda in the NATO hierarchy, working to CINCWESTLANT. The United States dominated the military situation in the Caribbean. They had an admiral in Puerto Rico responsible for whatever local operations there might be and for extensive US Fleet training in the general Caribbean area; another as Commander Key West Force, at Key West in Florida, who had few ships but a good many jet aircraft at his disposal; an Admiral Commanding the South Atlantic in Trinidad; and a four-star general, C.-in-C. South, in Panama, with some 12,000 troops, who was their man for the Isthmus, Central and South America. Their chief concern then was the containment of Communism, and in particular of Castro's Cuba. The American Coastguard was also very active in the area, operating under Admiral Daniels of Coastguard District 7, based at Key West.

Clearly, my job was to meet and get to know all these various dignitaries, and to operate as far as possible in conjunction with them, but at the same time to ensure that British interests, as Britain saw them, were properly maintained. I was also responsible for aid to the civil power in British territory and territorial sea. I was the immediate military adviser to five governors – Bermuda, Bahamas, Barbados, British Guiana and British Honduras – to numerous administrators, to the high commissioners in Jamaica, Trinidad and Tobago, and also, if required, to ambassadors on the periphery of the

Caribbean. The forces in the area were under the full command of each Commander-in-Chief back in the UK, but under my operational command while on my station. They consisted of three frigates, a resident battalion in British Guiana and a reinforced company group in British Honduras. There were also reconnaissance Canberras helping to map British Honduras and the interior of British Guiana, although, naturally enough, I had little to say about their activities. I also had a certain responsibility for advising on the efficiency of the defence forces of the islands and liaison with their police forces. So there were plenty of people to see and meet in learning all I could about the station.

Since the failure of the attempt to federate the British Islands and Territories in the Caribbean, the area was in a state of transition, and the frigates' job was a varied one. With three ships on station, I tried to keep two fully operational at all times; the third might be resting or carrying out assisted maintenance in Bermuda, Trinidad or, more rarely, a US port. One would always be within reach of the Eastern Caribbean, another almost certainly on patrol in the Bahamas Channel, where illegal activity on the part of the Cubans was endemic, and during the hurricane season, either or both would be acting as hurricane guardship, ready to bring immediate aid to the smaller territories which had very little capacity to look after themselves when hit by a hurricane. Fuel was available ashore and a dash via Jamaica to British Honduras had to be provided for. In the event of any internal security difficulties, the governor or the administrator of the territory concerned would almost certainly require a frigate to be hull down on the horizon, ready to appear and perhaps land her Royal Marine detachment, augmented if necessary by sailors, should he think the situation required it. I had a resident naval officer in Bermuda with the small base of which Clutterbuck had spoken, and ships would normally join and leave the station through it, embarking or returning hurricane stores, and being fully briefed on the special tasks of a West Indies Station ship. To ensure that the station could be properly reinforced if necessary, one also had to prepare reinforcement plans and have them agreed with the staff of the Commanders-in-Chiefs' Committee at home and approved by the Chiefs of Staff. As Commander British Forces, I was directly responsible to the CDS himself.

There were wireless stations of various degrees of efficiency in Bermuda, in British Honduras, in British Guiana and in the Bahamas, though communications were not the strongest feature of the Caribbean area at that time and much reliance was placed on the contribution made to them by the frigates on station. My headquarters was wherever I happened to be at the time. To assist me I had a small but very pleasant staff: a secretary, Oscar Bayley, a splendid major of marines, Gerald Roberts, an Army staff officer, John Pine-Coffin, normally stationed in Nassau where there was also a resident naval officer, Lieutenant-Commander John Stedman, and – the key member of the staff – flag lieutenant, staff operations officer and staff communications officer combined, Hugh Faulkner. (He did not know it, but his parents' pages at their wedding in Malta long ago had been Peter and myself: I always liked to think that this gave me a slight moral advantage, but perhaps it was the other way round!) These officers, like myself, had their wives on the station and were all well up to their jobs and thoroughly enjoying them.

No sooner had I taken over, called briefly on the governor of Bermuda, General Sir Julian Gascoigne, and met *Londonderry*, *Ursa* and *Caprice* (as well as Nick Rutherford, the RNO, to whom, having confirmed the unspeakable state of the dockyard, I gave the task of preparing a report about it and of illustrating it with photographs), than the internal security situation in British Guiana took a turn very much for the worse. It was necessary for me to go down there immediately and size up the situation. I therefore flew to Nassau, picked up the Army staff officer, Pine-Coffin, and continued to Georgetown.

The commander of the battalion in residence, the Second Coldstream, turned out to be a splendidly calm and capable officer called Alan Pemberton. I met the governor, Sir Ralph Grey, and the commissioner of police, Peter Owen, sniffed around for a bit, listened to Pine-Coffin's advice, and decided without too much difficulty that a reinforcement battalion really had to be called for. The necessary signals were made and the reaction was quick. The emergency battalion, kept at 48 hours' notice in the UK in those days, was despatched, together with a skeleton brigade headquarters and, rather to Pemberton's dismay, a brigadier. We decided to pitch tents in the grounds of garrison headquarters to accommodate the brigadier and his team when they arrived and to allow for his proper briefing. I did not know the Army and their ways then as well as I do now – within precisely 24 hours of the arrival of the Greenjackets and of Ken Trevor, a splendid brigadier, the colonel was in the tents and the brigadier in the building.

The morning before the reinforcements arrived, I went, on behalf of the Governor, to call on the Prime Minister of British Guiana to tell him what was going on. It must have been about 8.30 a.m. I knocked on the door of the Red House where Cheddi Jagan and his wife lived, and the door was opened by Cheddi in an Indian pyjama outfit. I explained who I was, and he very politely asked me upstairs and sat me down on the sofa alongside Janet, who was a well-known Communist. I explained that I had advised the governor that it was necessary in present circumstances to reinforce the garrison because people were being bullied, if not terrorised, in the villages, and we needed more troops to help the police. I told him that a brigadier was coming to take charge of the reinforced garrison, and as soon as he arrived I would be going elsewhere about my business on the station. The Jagans could not have been more charming or understanding, and I reported as much to the governor. He was not surprised; indeed, had he expected a different reaction, I am sure he would not have asked me to go alone to make the announcement to the prime minister.

On the ground in British Guiana, relations with the Jagans were a great deal better than was usually assumed at home, where the Communist taint (associated particularly with Janet, an American citizen by birth) was given great prominence, no doubt under pressure from the United States. In fact, in the extraordinary mirror-image society of British Guiana – where the blacks were the shopkeepers and toughies, and the East Indians, as they were called, were the farmers and labourers – Cheddi, on the whole, was not a bad compromise. Nevertheless, politically-inspired inter-communal violence was rife, funerals of victims of this were always a security hazard, and the effective policemen, although there were some expatriate and 'white' local officers, were predominantly black: hence the need for disinterested troops. The Greenjackets in particular were excellent with the villagers, many of them being country boys themselves.

A day or so later, I drove the 20 miles to Anderson's Field along a road liberally painted with anti-British slogans, dropped Pine-Coffin at Nassau, and returned to Bermuda to take stock. Tom had mumps, but nevertheless Elizabeth had managed to move into 'Broad Reefs', the Martins' house at Devonshire Bay. Susan, having left her job at Worcester College, plus Tamara, ex-West Heath and A-levels, had flown out and we were settling in. I had ten busy days of introducing myself in Bermuda – to the speaker, premier, chief justice, bishop, colonial secretary, the Bermuda Rifles, the Bermuda Regiment and many others. Hugh Faulkner had meanwhile planned and cleared an inaugural cruise in *Londonderry*. Her commanding officer, Darby George, ran a splendid ship, whose exemplary standards withstood the ordeal of transporting a new commodore on his 'getting to know you' round so soon after taking his predecessor for his farewells – an ordeal I had underestimated, especially for the sailors.

I embarked with my staff and retinue (whom Elizabeth had now to do without) – a petty officer steward, a leading steward and a cook – and sailed at the end of July for Jamaica. Hugh Faulkner, as flag lieutenant, always came with me, and usually the staff Royal Marines officer as well. Oscar Bayley, the secretary, came occasionally, but otherwise was the anchor man in Bermuda. I frequently came under pressure from the authorities at home to increase my staff: they wanted me to have a planning staff officer, and later, when Shackletons and helicopters came, the RAF were very keen that I should have an RAF officer. I was allowed to refuse both. The whole essence of the command was to be able to travel light and to combine one's operational duties with showing the flag in a ship whenever one could. In the case of the cruise in *Londonderry*, she was acting at the same time as hurricane guardship in the eastern Caribbean, the hurricane season being well under way now in August. *Ursa* was on Bahamas Patrol, *Caprice* about to be relieved.

The 'haul-up' report on the dockyard had been despatched before sailing, and Elizabeth and I had decided, particularly after Gerald Roberts had been run in for speeding (for doing more than 20 m.p.h.) while coming to our house at Devonshire Bay with an 'immediate' signal for me, that we should move closer to the dockyard on Ireland Island. Through Guy Ridgeway (a contemporary of Father who had been a lieutenant in *Cornwall* on the West Indies Station before the First World War and whose watches Father had kept from time to time while Guy courted his Bermudan wife), we met Stan Moore, representative of Pepsi-Cola in the Middle East, who was, for some reason, based in Bermuda. He was moving house, and the one that he had earlier rented from Harding Mott (an American, and son of the extremely wealthy Executive Vice-President of General Motors) was becoming available.

Called 'Enfield', it was situated on the edge of Ely's Harbour, with its own dock, about 10 acres of beautiful grounds, and enjoying one of the best views in Bermuda. It was only ten minutes' drive from the dockyard. Stan suggested how to go about approaching Harding Mott, and before sailing I wrote a careful letter, having first established with the Admiralty what the limits of rent I could offer would be. One day, the telephone rang at 'Broad Reefs' and Susan answered it. It was Harding Mott on the phone. He said, 'You can tell your father that he can have "Enfield" on the terms he suggested.' Susan (which was pretty bright for a girl of her age) said, 'Thank you very much, can we please have it in writing?' The new house was a great thrill for them, although with me away and Tom with mumps, the move, room by room as the Moores evacuated, was a major operation for Elizabeth and the girls.

Once arrived in Kingston, whose harbour entrance was still complicated by the ruins of old Port Royal, I called on the high commissioner, Sir Alexander Morley, and the prime minister. Alexander Bustamente had begun life as a bus conductor, became a trade union leader, and then the undisputed political leader of Jamaica on independence. At lunch, I sat next to Lady 'Busta' and opposite the great man himself, whose flow of anecdote never ceased. The Jamaica Defence Force was run by an ex-brigadier, British Army, Paul Crook, and I stayed with him and his wife at what must have been the house of the garrison commander in colonial days. He was most enthusiastic about his outfit, which consisted of an Army, an Air Force and a Navy (which, he explained with mock apologies, wore khaki like the rest). All seemed to me to be in good nick, and Crook was dedicated to producing indigenous officers as fast as was possible.

Jamaica was our stepping stone to British Honduras, where a reinforced company group garrisoned the colony against a Guatemalan threat. I detached *Londonderry* to Nassau, and flew with Faulkner by Costa Rican Airlines via Miami to Stanley Field. The KSLI formed the garrison at that time, and the swift movements of the quarter guard took me slightly aback. The troops were deployed to protect the airfield, through which all rapid reinforcement must pass, and in addition manned certain observation posts and a more substantial outpost on the main road to the border with Guatemala. According to local judgement, the threat was heavily qualified by their assessment of the opposition, and soldiers from the small garrison were able to take advantage of the excellent training areas available. Still it was isolated duty and the fleshpots of Belize City, decorated by very attractive ladies, were (perhaps fortunately) some way downriver. The garrison commander and his wife managed their comparatively long tour in so enervating a climate, and in accommodation very different from that enjoyed by the Crooks in Jamaica, with dedication. I learned how important it was to improve our communications with this isolated 'outpost of the Empire', one less likely than others to engage sympathetic support from the United States, and whose airport was limited to accepting Hastings or similar aircraft – even the Comet could not land. However, I did not rate the threat at the time highly enough to recommend vast expenditure on extending the runway, preferring to let sleeping 'Guats' lie.

While staying with the governor, Sir Peter Stallard, I received a signal telling me that a Cuban expedition had landed on one of our small islands in the Bahamas, Cay Sal, and had abducted a party of Cuban 'refugees' on the island. The Bahamas Patrol was powerless to do more than support the police in restoring the situation on the Cay, but it was a flagrant violation of British territory and it turned out to be of great concern to the Americans, who, I think, had more than a little to do with the 'refugees'. I decided that the only thing to do was to consult immediately with Sir Robert Stapledon, Governor of the Bahamas, and flew to Nassau via Miami. He agreed to American help in reinforcing our deterrent against future forays of this sort, and the next day I flew back to Miami and drove down the Florida Keys to Key West. There, Rear-Admiral Lou Kirn, Commander Key West Force, and kindness itself, organised a meeting between me and the head of Coastguard District 7, Rear-Admiral Daniels. It was readily agreed to act in concert, and that the British must be seen to be in the driving seat because their territory had been violated. I suggested to Stapledon that I should come over with Daniels and debrief. This we did in an aircraft of the US Coastguard. An excellent working arrangement was evolved with the Bahamian authorities, including the Bahamas Police, for whom I was able to make a strong case for an air wing to augment the Royal Navy patrol.

In the event, the result was a satisfactory arrangement which improved the security of the Bahamas as a joint Anglo-American effort, backed, in the last resort, by Lou Kirn's jets. I also requested and received the temporary detachment of a flight of Shackletons to my command to improve air surveillance in the Bahamas area. They settled in happily, and Pine-Coffin was made responsible for their liaison with the police. I then re-embarked in *Londonderry* to resume my cruise.

It was now mid-August, and I took *Londonderry* first to Key West, to consolidate relations with Lou and Ray Kirn and return some of the hospitality of a couple who have become life-long friends. Lou, a US Navy aviator of great repute, gained my entire confidence. He was strongly in support of our confidential agreement and although tough as they come could be trusted never to engage in any 'gung-ho' adventure which would have caused political difficulties. Stapledon soon asked them to stay at Government House, Nassau, and the unofficial alliance was sealed. I next sailed to Puerto Rico, to meet US Rear-Admiral Caldwell, commander of the Caribbean Sea Frontier. He was a friend of Lou's, and therefore of mine. The weapon facilities and ranges off San Juan were of importance to my ships since we had no equivalent west of Gibraltar and throw-off shoots were all we could otherwise manage whenever I could collect two of my frigates together. (These facilities have since developed into an important resource for the missile-equipped ships of the modern British Fleet.) After a short stop there and some sight-seeing, we left San Juan and set off for the British Antilles.

Barbados had a governor, Sir John Stow. He, Stapledon, and Ralph Grey had all been cadets together in Nigeria years before, but because of local sensitivities about the defunct West Indies federation, could see very little of one another. It was therefore pleasant for me to be able to visit them all from time to time to carry news between them. The other islands had administrators, all welcoming and friendly, and all quite different from one another, as indeed were the islands.

The cruise pattern was to spend one or two nights at each island, leaving one in the morning and arriving at the next probably the same afternoon. On arrival, I would call on His Honour, the administrator, who would take me to call on the premier. In the course of the visit, security plans would be reviewed and we would meet the police chief and the commander of the local defence force or militia. I would give a lunch or dinner party for the premier, the administrator and their wives, and there would be a cocktail party on board and an evening reception, usually with a dance, for the officers ashore. Some islands were able to offer trips for the sailors, whose shore leave was otherwise often aimless. It was an exhausting regime for myself and the officers from some points of view, but pretty dull for most of the ship's company, certainly for the less enterprising members. The staff had been to the islands before, if only on John Martin's farewell cruise in *Londonderry*, and they and the ships' officers had many acquaintances ashore, which helped me.

Antigua, with Ian Turbott, a New Zealander, as administrator, was the first port of call. It rated a full visit as a large island with a wonderfully-preserved naval dockyard at one end of it. Every 'White Ensign' ship sent a working party to do something to help restore the place, from which one or two yacht charter companies were already beginning to work. There was no deepwater port at that time, so we anchored off. (Indeed, an alongside berth was only available at Barbados and St Lucia of the smaller British islands, although construction of a deepwater jetty at St Vincent was about to begin.) All went well at Antigua, though I did not particularly take to Mr V.C. Bird, the premier, a large and forbidding-looking gentleman. Like nearly all the island premiers, he had made his way to the top as a trades union leader, and there seemed to be very little prospect of significant opposition to him in political terms, given the power of the union. Here, as elsewhere, I was intent on finding out the administrator's views in the event that some internal security problem arose in which, on police advice, he might want naval or military support and the CDS would expect my recommendation.

Then it was Montserrat, Dominica, St Lucia, Barbados, St Vincent and Grenada, always staying ashore in Government House. The response to the letter proposing the programme always asked what I wanted to do in each island, and I invariably replied, 'see the island and take photographs'. This was convenient for everybody, a form of reconnaissance, and it was very nice for me when I returned to Bermuda to have slides to show the family what it had all been like. (I was also keeping my weather eye open for the islands of greatest interest, so that if one day Elizabeth could make a tour of them, we should know which to choose.)

Trinidad was an important visit, as the dormant US naval base at Chaguarramas provided an excellent location for assisted self-maintenance periods for my ships – south of the hurricane zone, near the British Guiana troublespot and with good recreational facilities. The US Commander South Atlantic was away, but Sir Norman Costar, the high commissioner, ensured I met the governor-general, Sir Solomon Ho Choi, and the formidable prime minister, Eric Williams (who wore dark glasses and a hearing aid, but was reputed to have excellent vision and acute hearing). I visited the sizeable defence force, and inspected with pleasure the coastguard, run with enormous enthusiasm and energy by Loftus Peyton Jones, a retired naval officer. (In the not very distant future, their disciplined and decisive reaction to a mutiny in the defence force was to save the government.)

A return visit to British Guiana was now due. I flew down from Trinidad, leaving *Londonderry* to go north to rejoin the Bahamas Patrol, relieving *Ursa*. The brigadier had settled in, and had the internal security situation well under control. He felt that it would be sensible to have a permanent garrison commander, and this I agreed. The nightly meetings with the governor, Ralph Grey, were worth a guinea a minute. Every other evening we would get a telegram from Duncan Sandys, Secretary of State for Commonwealth Relations and the Colonies. This would be read aloud by the governor, starting, 'We, Duncan Sandys, Secretary of State for the Commonwealth Relations and the Colonies . . .', and we would hear what the great man or his office wanted us to hear. Then there would be a report from the internal security commander, the brigadier, and from the chief of police, and the bones of a telegram back to head office would be settled. Ralph Grey would then press the bell, glasses of whisky would be brought in for all of us, and he would sit down at his own typewriter and hammer out the return telegram. This would then be read over, amended or agreed, we would drink our whisky and go about our business; for me, this usually meant going back to stay at Government House.

During this visit, Peter Owen, the commissioner of police, was making one of his periodic inspections up-country in a twin-engined Cessna aircraft with room for one passenger apart from himself, and invited me to go too. He became a good friend. I visited the two battalions in the colony, the Coldstream having been relieved as garrison battalion by the 1st Battalion the Grenadier Guards, who, as sensible people should, were making themselves extremely comfortable. I suggested that some of the facilities that they enjoyed as the resident unit should be made available to the Greenjackets and later reinforcement battalions as they came and went, but this did not fall on particularly fertile ground. However, all were in good heart, although I formed the impression, then and later, that the guards battalion was perhaps less adaptable and flexible in dealing with villagers than country regiments like the Greenjackets, the Devon and Dorsets and the Queen's Own Buffs, who were to follow. They were invariably kind and responsive to me – a fish out of water, but nevertheless saddled with the responsibility for their showing in the colony.

Because so much of the trouble was in the streets of Georgetown, there was clearly great advantage in the availability of air surveillance, particularly with helicopters, to observe the way crowds were massing in the streets, often on occasions of a political funeral (and few were not), and to direct the police – and, if necessary, troops – to wherever they were most likely to be needed. I wrote accordingly to the CDS for the Chiefs of Staff, and received a rather dusty answer.

After some seven weeks' absence, in late September I was able to fly back to Bermuda, with my mind's eye full of the bright colours of the islands and their peoples and of the ever-changing patterns of a variegated command. Apart from the odd visit to Nassau, where a new wireless station had been established, I was now able to get to know Bermuda better. Peter White and Alan Fairley, the surveyor of lands from the Admiralty, came out in response to my report to try to negotiate with the Bermuda government a final solution to the chaos in the dockyard. They succeeded brilliantly. In return for the surrender of British sovereignty over the remaining dockyard area, replaced by a 99-year lease at a peppercorn rent, they obtained enough money for Britain to allow me to extract what I needed from the Admiralty to rationalise that part of the dockyard area that we still wanted and to make it a credit to the Royal Navy.

As part of the agreement, the Bermuda government themselves paid for the rehabilitation of Prince Alfred Terrace, just outside the gate of the dockyard, and its conversion into married quarters for naval ratings and their families. I obtained the agreement of the officers on the station to transfer the officers' club to ratings, and this allowed us to dispose of the old canteen, which had once been the Parsonage, and to concentrate everything round the Royal Naval dockyard berths. We turned the cells into lay-apart stores for frigates, which, when they joined the station, had to disembark various Arctic stores in order to embark hurricane guardship kit. We were able to acquire from Alcoholics Anonymous, which had ceased to be interested, the old superintending civil engineer's house as offices for the commander British forces and the resident naval officer. We removed the debris of an old fish-meal fire, re-opened and gilded the badges on the south gate and, all in all, had a high old time.

Of course, this did not happen at once, and on the way to its achievement there was a sad and unfortunate decision which I felt I had to take. It was sad because it consisted of relieving the resident naval officer early as I felt he was ill and unable to face and carry through all the changes necessary. First, I saw the governor, told him what I intended to do, and established that he would have no objection. I think he remarked, 'If you feel like that, Ashmore, it's entirely a matter for you.' When I gave the news to the officer, he was extremely upset, and asked if he could appeal to the governor. I said, 'No, it's my affair,' and added, unfortunately, 'in any case the governor agrees with what I am doing.' The officer's wife then rang a friend of theirs, the governor's nephew and ADC, asking how the governor could possibly agree with such a dreadful suggestion. The governor blew up, sent for me, said that he had not 'agreed', it was entirely my affair, nothing to do with him, and disgraceful of me to bring his name into it at all. At the time I did not feel that I had done this, but in retrospect I reckon that I was wrong to say what I did to my officer. I also failed to recognise that the governor was having quite enough trouble locally with the bishop, an ex-naval parson, who had made the mistake of firing a locally respected canon.

This excited a hornets' nest of Church politics which the governor also, naturally, wished to keep at arm's length. As a good guardsman, he must have felt that the Navy were an intolerable nuisance, and sadly, he never came to our house again. Moreover, he wrote to the Second Sea Lord complaining of my conduct and asking for me to be removed, but this did not occur.

In mid-November I hoisted my Broad Pendant in *Londonderry* for the last time, to visit Georgetown. I called on Forbes Burnham, the mayor, already a brilliant lawyer with a fearsome reputation. This was a chance to bid farewell to Ralph and Lady Grey, and also Ken Trevor, a Colonel King having been appointed as garrison commander. It was good to have a ship under me and be able to return much hospitality. On the passage to Trinidad, before my transfer to *Ursa*, the *Londonderry* wardroom dined me out. In his speech, the First Lieutenant said, not unreasonably, that they often wondered what the 'M' was doing in my name. They gave me a photograph of a sloth which the ship had adopted as mascot in British Honduras. I hoped the memento was not a comment on my industry.

After shifting my Broad Pendant, I flew to Nassau, stayed with the governor, and joined *Ursa* when relieved on Bahamas Patrol by *Tartar*. One of the problems for ships on the West Indies Station was lack of consorts. I therefore tried to arrange, as far as possible, that the turnover of Bahamas Patrol should take place on site, and allow a short spell in harbour with the two ships together. In this way social and sporting exchanges could take place between ships' companies. The station was fun for the officers, but pretty deadly for the men.

Ursa, commanded by Douglas Baker, an aviator, was now the designated hurricane guardship, but late in the season, so I could take her further afield. I came south to the islands, passed *Londonderry* off St Vincent, and continued through the Grenadines to Carriacou, the southernmost of the group. I reckoned that I now had a feel for much of the British part of my station, and sailed west for Curaçao to call on Admiral Baay, the Commander Netherlands Antilles at Willemstadt. On approaching the town to reach the inner harbour, we paused until a couple of motorboats had hauled open the pontoon bridge closing the neck of the entrance. The Dutch, as always, were cordial. There was business to be done in arranging joint exercises with their maritime aircraft and a submarine, when available, but time also for duty-free shopping and some sightseeing in the wonderful old eighteenth-century town (later much damaged by fire). After the usual two days we sailed for Colón, a port at the eastern entrance to the Panama Canal, not far from Nombre de Dios Bay where Francis Drake died. I drove to Panama City, on the way passing the Panama Canal, stopping to admire the locomotives made in England which still haul ships up towards the Pacific. I stayed the night with the British ambassador before making my call on the US C.-in-C. South, at his large headquarters. Although a four-star general, he welcomed an exchange of views, and I had the usual American-style briefing. The objective of establishing contact with the US armed forces, the source of power in the area of my command, was to put my resources and responsibilities into some perspective for them and, in passing, establish a personal liaison.

On return to Colón, I sailed *Ursa* to Puerto Limón on the Caribbean Coast of Costa Rica. I had heard that this was an interesting place to visit, and that there was a delightful British boss of the Costa Rican railway known as 'Tiny' Taylor, who was always pleased to see the Navy. So it proved. From Costa Rica, it was a short voyage to Belize City, to meet the new garrison from the 'Duke of Wellington's', and find them tough but very burnt by the still unaccustomed sun. I joined some on a jungle warfare exercise, and visited another detachment in the Mountain Pine Ridge training area. I also drove to Stan Creek, a small, very poor fishing port near the Honduran frontier, down the 'Hummingbird Highway' (so called because it never follows a straight line, preferring to dart this way and that). I came back by aircraft, allowing a good look at our observation posts along the Guatemalan frontier on the way. I then left *Ursa* to her patrol and flew to Bermuda. It was now December, and time for Christmas.

Early in 1964, a new constitution was to be inaugurated in the Bahamas, and the Bahamian government had kindly asked Liz and me to attend the ceremony. This was made an occasion for tremendous celebrations by the whole Cabinet (known as the 'Bay Street Boys'), most of whom had known cousin Guy Henderson since they were youngsters. I had first met Ted Symonette, the premier, on a visit to his birthplace, Harbour Island, when representing the governor on the occasion of a transfer of land from the Commoners of Harbour Island to the British Admiralty to help equip the Atlantic Underwater Test and Evaluation Centre. This is based on Andros, but configured around the 'Tongue of the Ocean', a great stretch of deep-blue water dividing the coral islands which makes an ideal site for underwater weapons testing. (It is a facility that we could hardly have afforded on our own, but the Americans, generous as ever, recognising the real estate around it as ours by ancient title, allow our forces to share fully in the use of the instrumentation ranges now established there.)

For the handover I had to wear full whites, sword and medals. To my dismay, my white uniform trousers parted at the crotch as I tried to fight my way through the starch to get them on. Since they had been made of sailor's white drill, purchased cheap by Father at the end of the First World War and given to me when he retired, this was not altogether surprising. A merciful providence, however, had provided that the governor's ADC was an ex-lieutenant-commander in the Royal Navy. He had a spare pair of trousers, and into those I climbed without doing more damage. So off I set for Harbour Island, in an open boat with the local member of parliament and the prime minister. On landing, we walked to a dais somewhere off the middle of the high street, where speeches were to be made to record and applaud the generosity of the Commoners. I had a speech ready in my pocket, but luckily, I was not to speak first. After I had listened to the first two very charismatic speeches, one by Ted Symonette and one by the chairman of the Commoners, I mentally tore up my own and did my best to respond in kind without bringing tears to my eyes or anybody else's. After a very successful rum and curry lunch, we marched in procession back to the jetty to catch a boat for New Providence. The member for Harbour Island, one of the Commoners, the prime minister and I, almost arm-in-arm, were preceded by three black ladies dancing jigs and followed by the band and sundry members of the Harbour Island community. As we went, we sang 'Pack up your troubles', 'It's a long way to Tipperary' and other songs of that ilk. We arrived to board the market boat, full of ladies with cabbages, chickens and fish, onto which we piled and made our way merrily back to Nassau. It was a very Bahamian occasion, one that I fondly remember feeling that the Commoners' gift to the Admiralty Board had been duly celebrated.

The British government was represented on Constitution Day by a junior minister. The ceremonies went off without a hitch in lovely weather, with everybody congratulating everybody else.

We then returned to Bermuda to await the visit of Field Marshal Sir Richard Hull, CDS Designate, who kindly asked Elizabeth to come with him on part of his 'acquaintance tour' of the station. This proved a highlight of our time in the West Indies. We went first to Jamaica, to witness a very smart parade of Paul's Jamaica Defence Force, and then to Georgetown, where we stayed with the garrison commander. The Grenadier Guards gave a splendid dinner for Dick Hull, and also a picnic, in which we were included, to the Kaietur Falls in the interior. On our return to Bermuda, we had the doubtful benefit of a visit from delegates to the Commonwealth Parliamentary Conference. Elizabeth and I were roped in by the governor and colonial secretary to do what we could to help with their entertainment. Those from Britain consisted of Sir Edward Boyle, leading the Conservative team, and the shadow foreign secretary, Patrick Gordon Walker, leading the Socialist team, which included Denis Healey. The first time we met, he and I stood side by side in pouring rain for a parade in their honour, which he never forgot. We also had a long talk, in the course of which I found him entirely sound on aircraft carriers. (Needless to say, he changed his mind about them later, as about so many other things.)

In March I sailed in *Tartar*, Brian Hutchings in command, for a rather delayed official visit to Washington, DC. After a beautiful approach up the Potomac, Brian had to berth at the Naval Annexe. This was a hair-raising affair for him, with *Tartar*'s large single screw and twin rudders rendering her near unmanoeuvrable at slow speed. The narrow navigable channel is crossed by a number of low bridges carrying traffic. These are supposed to open as you approach them, but for the minimum time. Brian carried steadily on and, sure enough, in the nick of time, each bridge stopped its traffic and opened to let us through. Had any been late, requiring *Tartar* to apply stern power, there would inevitably have been some manoeuvring difficulty, if not a grounding. The ambassador was Lord Harlech, and he and his wife had lunch on board and charmed us all. Calls included the Mayor of the District of Colombia and various authorities in the US Navy, as well as the heads of the British Joint Services Staff and British Naval

Mission in Washington. It made a pleasant change from my last flying visit. This had occurred after an episode in the Bahamas Channel when *Londonderry* was still with us. She was the ship involved, and fortunately, the one I knew best and in which I had absolute confidence.

While on patrol in the Bahamas, she had been given a station by me with a view to intercepting illegal traffic between Cuba and the Bahamas or via the Bahamas to the United States. This station was known to the UK Chiefs of Staff. In the middle of the night in Bermuda, I suddenly received an urgent message telling me that she was to vacate her station. I accordingly shifted her to the southern part of the Bahamas Channel, reporting this to London. During the following night, she carried out a classic interception of a boat crammed with armed men operating illegally in British waters. She seized and disarmed the lot, interviewed them, and reported this to the Bahamas Police (then under Nigel Morris). Under the eye of the 1st Lieutenant, the weapons and most of their personal gear were duly confiscated, but a careful list was made and receipts were given. The next day the balloon went up. I received an infuriated signal from the Chiefs of Staff asking what I was at. Why had I intercepted something I should not have known anything about? What had happened was that the Central Intelligence Agency had warned British Intelligence of an operation planned for the northern area of *Londonderry*'s patrol, but had failed to mention that they intended a similar operation in the south, which – very efficiently and somewhat to my satisfaction – we caught red-handed. There then followed bitter American complaints about the conduct of the officers and ship's company of the ship that made the interception. Fortunately, knowing *Londonderry* so well, I was able to defend them to the hilt. The Bahamas Police confirmed that they had done all the right things and the Americans eventually had to admit that they were not entitled to any redress. However, in the outcome (which is why this story comes into the narrative here), I was ordered to fly to Washington and report to the Embassy. There, I was met by Maurice Oldfield, head of our Security Liaison Staff. He took me to CIA Headquarters and introduced me, hoping to persuade them that I was on their side after all. As far as I know, this worked but it was nice now to be in Washington without a cloud in the sky and to visit sights like Mt Vernon and Williamsburg and enjoy the social round of a ship visit.

I now made time to call on Admiral Smith, USN (the Supreme Allied Commander Atlantic), at Norfolk, Virginia and, as Island Commander Bermuda, to receive the first of many comprehensive SACLANT briefings. I stayed with Bill Beloe, now Deputy SACLANT, and a good friend from Staff Course days. The admiral returned my call in *Tartar*, which was good of him. She was a smart, good-looking ship, whose teak quarterdeck no doubt convinced the Americans that we had yet to grow up. Beloe was an admirable officer for the job, his charm, sense of humour and quiet common sense being just what was needed – not only by his supreme commander, but also by the many British officers serving in an unfamiliar environment.

The demands of the station were never-ending. I needed to follow up my earlier visit to the Dutch Navy and plan some kind of joint exercise using their resources with ours. So *Tartar* took me to Curaçao and Willemstadt once more, after which, as it was her turn to take hurricane watch, we sailed east to the Turks and Caicos Islands, through the desolate, dry and sparsely-populated coral islands, calling at Providenciales on our way to the rendezvous off Nassau. I then flew to Bermuda for a quick visit to the family and headquarters, and was able to stay over Easter. I was there to see the famous flower festival in Hamilton and welcome *Devonshire*, a guided-missile destroyer, commanded by David Williams (an Old Yardley Courtier of my vintage), which was to do a spell on the station. They gave a splendid party, which was almost Susan's last social appearance in Bermuda before sailing to work in Washington, DC. Tamara was working for the Bermuda Library and proving a great help to us, as Susan had also been, when officers came to 'Enfield' in the course of the short spell most ships spent in Bermuda on joining or leaving the station.

The Navy's latest frigate, *Leander*, first of her class, now came on station under Lance Bell-Davies. I flew to Barbados to join her in early May. She had a Wasp helicopter embarked, the successor to the old Dragonfly that had done trials in the 6th Frigate Squadron, and an undoubted asset to the command. *Leander*'s dual cabin set-up allowed for a captain or commodore (like myself) 'riding' the ship to consign its commanding officer to a small sleeping cabin, next door to a bunk-fitted and larger day cabin which shared a bathroom. This seemed to have superficial advantages compared with the inconvenience that my presence caused to the commanding officers of all the other ships on the station, but Lance and I decided that the advantages were theoretical only (a conclusion required for the 'first of class' trials he was undertaking). I was against the design concept, feeling strongly that, in normal circumstances, the captain of a destroyer or frigate squadron should always command his own ship and undergo the same strains and stresses as the other commanding officers. No one except the Commodore West Indies routinely displaced commanding officers in small ships and, despite this, there was never any shortage of ships wanting to come to the West Indies!

I used *Leander*'s helicopter from off Grenada to go to the Leeward Coast, where the Police Training Camp was situated, and inspect the police force under training with their excellent English commissioner present. After a short visit to Grenada, *Leander* took me to Trinidad, where *Devonshire* now was, having formed a plot in my own mind which, with David Williams's assent, was put into effect. I had totally failed to obtain helicopters (much needed in British Guiana) from the Chiefs of Staff, but here was *Devonshire* with a suitable aircraft embarked and under my command. I therefore detached her Wessex helicopter to Anderson's Field, Georgetown, for three months with the necessary spares, informing the Chiefs of Staff that I had done so. The situation in Georgetown was certainly bad enough to warrant this, and my conscience was quite clear. As a result, the First Sea Lord became so anxious to get the anti-submarine helicopter back into *Devonshire* that he came over on to my side, supporting the supply of either Army or RAF helicopters to the British Guiana Garrison. Sure enough, these arrived just as the *Devonshire* helicopter spares were running out, and an operation on a shoe-string became, to my amazement, a major effort, with a horde of RAF engineers, aircrew and others established at the airfield to support a flight of Whirlwinds, later joined by some Army Scouts. It all helped the garrison commander no end.

That was well in the future when I flew from Trinidad to Georgetown, partly to welcome the naval helicopter, partly to join in the discussions that still went on nightly between the governor, now Sir Richard Luyt, the garrison commander and Peter Owen about the internal security situation. It was an anxious time, and Dick Luyt wanted to declare an immediate state of emergency on our advice. A lawyer reliable enough to draft the emergency regulations had to be found. Fortunately, Sunny Ramphal, a Guianese lawyer of some eminence, was home on holiday from the Caribbean Court of Appeal and readily agreed, when approached by the governor, to undertake the drafting. This went on all night. At 7 a.m. the next morning, as the emergency regulations were published, six ringleaders of the troubles were arrested by the police, embarked in *Devonshire*'s helicopter and whisked up to the Mazuruni Jail, way up-country, before anybody knew what was happening. It was a classic exercise in surprise, and a great joy to see the helicopter made use of so early. The effect was to quieten everything down, and after a couple of days talking to Robin King and the others and getting to know the new governor, I flew back to Bermuda once more.

It was a wonderful time for sailing and swimming. Mousse came out briefly, and we all thoroughly enjoyed ourselves, although there was never a shortage of incidents on the station. A new resident naval officer, John Brisker, had arrived, and showed himself to be a tremendous enthusiast. The new office block was ready and looking splendid. I established myself on the top floor and, at Brisker's initiative, decided to seek Admiralty approval to recommission the base as HMS *Malabar*, its old title. The berthing area was tidy, the married quarters ready, and all in all I felt that the place was respectable again. The liaison with Admiral Kirn at Key West and Admiral Daniels of Coastguard District 7 was continuing well and the Bahamas were very satisfied with the cooperation they were receiving, so that was one worry less. However, much had still to be done to obtain approval for decent communications in Belize, in Nassau and, indeed, in Bermuda itself. This was rather up my street, and various projects were proposed.

In mid-May I flew to Jamaica, joined *Tartar*, and made a visit to the Cayman Islands, which now had an admirable British administrator in John Cumber, who had just joined. We sailed then for Cartagena in Colombia and arrived there on 22 May for a few days' visit, during which I had great plans to fly up to Bogotá, particularly to buy a long-wanted emerald ring for Elizabeth. It was a fascinating old city, well fortified by the Spaniards. I managed to give one lunch party, and then received news of trouble in British Guiana which required my presence. This not only ruined my trip to Bogotá, but also the next plan, which was to take *Tartar* up the Orinoco about as far as it is navigable, to Ciudad Bolívar – this would have been great fun and a SNOWI 'first'. However, duty called, so we sped off for Trinidad, meeting *Devonshire* there. Before flying down to Georgetown, I sailed *Tartar* for Barbados (later rejoining her there to resume the planned cruise).

Martinique came next, and *Tartar* brought me in to Fort-de-France on a lovely morning. The overwhelming impression was of prosperity, tidiness and general well-being compared with the British Islands in the Caribbean, except, perhaps, Barbados. The senior French naval officer in Martinique was away in Paris, but his wife, not put out, gave a lunch party in our honour. So, full of French culture and civilisation with a strong Creole tang, we set sail for the Iles des Saintes, north of Dominica and just south of Guadeloupe. We anchored off the beach, and were greeted by the mayor, an enormous black man, who seemed to have more energy in his body than everybody else in the islands put together. On our way north for a day at Guadeloupe, we steamed past HMS *Diamond Rock*. This tall, conical, rocky islet was once commissioned as a frigate in the Royal Navy, and withstood all French efforts to take it. By tradition, it is piped by any HM ship to pass it. We moved to St Kitts, where *Tartar* anchored smartly among fishing boats just where Hood's ships had once replaced the French. Henry Howard, the administrator, introduced us to a Maltese lady called Mary Pomeroy, ex-wife of a British naval officer. She lived in Nevis, in the manager's house of the plantation once owned by the Nisbet family, whose daughter Nelson married. With a couple of others, including Christopher Codrington, the supply officer of *Tartar* (whose family had run a slave stud on nearby Barbuda in the distant past), I spent the weekend as her guest.

The time passed all too quickly, and we sailed north to St Thomas in the US Virgin Islands (once the Danish West Indies, and now a notable tourist resort famous for casinos and ardent Americans). There, I left *Tartar* to go south as hurricane guardship and shifted my Broad Pendant to *Whirlwind*, with Jerome Benson in command. I took her east to Road Town in Tortola in the British Virgin Islands. The modest Government House had just been refurbished because Princess Margaret was expected shortly. The view over the small bay and a fabulous tropical garden was very special. After the usual discussion about internal security and reinforcement plans and a very pleasant quiet time, *Whirlwind* sailed with me to Antigua, where we arrived in the middle of June. There was a new administrator, whom I had met in British Guiana earlier, David Rose, an extremely intelligent and pleasant Guyanese who had once been their superintendent of the CID. The visit was made more memorable because he took me to stay my last night at Clarence House, built for the future King William IV when commanding a ship in the West Indies. I walked down after breakfast to the very jetty that Nelson had so often used. As the boat took me out to my ship lying off English Harbour, I remembered how he had dealt with the dockyard commissioner of his day, displacing his flag and flirting with his wife!

From Antigua I flew to Nassau, to confirm that the Police Air Wing had been established and that the RAF Shackletons could therefore be released. They had done well and enjoyed themselves, leaving a huge, painted squadron badge decorating a local swimming pool. I had a run down the Out Islands in a police aircraft piloted by an ex-Fleet Air Arm pilot who seemed to like flying low, which gave an excellent view of that extraordinary string of coral-girt islets stretching some 500 miles between Grand Bahama and the larger island of Great Inagua, famous for its lake and flamingos.

From Nassau we returned to Bermuda again, at last, to find the family in great heart, everybody waiting for the arrival of the Tall Ships on their way from Lisbon to New York for the World Fair. I boarded the German naval training ship *Gorch Fock* outside the reef (successor to the ship I had visited at Flensburg as a cadet), entered harbour in her and admired their drill. I went on board several others later, including *Esmeralda* from Chile and *Dewaruti* from Indonesia, where the atmosphere was somewhat more relaxed. Bermuda did its utmost to entertain them, and we were involved in the parties.

Although every two or three months I would visit British Guiana and British Honduras by air, it was time now to take a ship into Georgetown again and return hospitality, so I joined *Tartar* at Trinidad in the middle of July. As hurricane guardship earlier in the season, she had rendered assistance to the population of Tobago, which was struck severely despite being reckoned to be south of the hurricane belt. So I went there first for a brief visit and saw some of the damage myself, particularly to the coconut plantations. The ship anchored off Scarborough, and I was looked after very kindly by the owners of a large plantation, now in ruins. From Tobago we sailed to Georgetown, crossed the bar at the entrance to the Demerara River at the right state of tide and secured alongside in the city. Dick Luyt was therefore able to return my call and I could give him lunch on board. I stayed with them, as usual, at Government House. Matters became pretty uncomfortable while I was there, and it seemed possible that we should have to call for an extra battalion to reinforce. However, I discussed this with the governor, Robin King, and the commissioner of police, and we decided that nothing needed to be done just at the moment. I therefore arranged to sail for Paramaribo, and notified the Chiefs of Staff accordingly.

On the last evening, having moved out of Government House, I went with Gerald Roberts to dinner with some extremely nice people who looked after the Colonial Development Corporation project known as BG Timbers and, after a good party, returned back on board at around 11.30 p.m. About an hour later, Gerald Roberts walked into my cabin with an immediate signal from the Chiefs of Staff, telling me that I was to stay in British Guiana. I felt that this was all wrong. The governor, the garrison commander and everybody else knew I was going and that I was satisfied with the situation on the ground. After a good deal of thought, therefore, I sent a signal back to London, referring to theirs and reporting that I intended to sail nevertheless, because the situation was under control, everybody was expecting us to go, and it would have a disquietening effect if the ship remained. I asked for the order to be reconsidered, and said that I would wait hull down off the Guianese coast the next day until I had confirmation from the Chiefs that I could continue with my programme. I spent a distinctly uncomfortable night and morning until the signal came saying that I could go.

The follow-up to this was a message some days later from the CDS himself, 'Dickie' Mountbatten, saying that he had returned from visiting his cousin, the

Queen of Sweden, and learnt to his 'surprise and concern' that I had virtually refused to obey an order from the Chiefs of Staff. I sent the best answer I could. Some years later, when I was VCNS, General Fitzpatrick, who was Director of Military Operations at the time of this incident, mentioned the affair to me. I remarked that I had long wondered why the Chiefs of Staff had wanted me to stay. 'You, as force commander, had their authority to call for reinforcements,' was his reply. I answered, 'I delegated that to the garrison commander on leaving.' 'But you didn't tell us.' Of course not,' I said, 'I could hardly be expected to leave without having delegated authority in that way.' 'Well,' he said, 'your mistake was not to tell us so.' This is an interesting insight into a difference in service attitudes: the Navy, I feel sure, would have trusted me to do the necessary delegation, and my training was not such as to cause me to cross every 't' and dot every 'i' in carrying out my job. I still fail to understand why they did not ask me directly instead of ordering a change in my programme.

On then we went to Paramaribo, up the Surinam River. Then it was back to Trinidad for a meeting with Rear-Admiral Tyree, the American commanding their South Atlantic area, and a transfer from *Tartar* to *Rothesay*, then commanded by Rodney Agar. Some time earlier, *Tartar*, on one of the Bahamas Patrols, had intercepted a Cuban party in a Boston whaler which had been run ashore on one of the islands while trying to make an escape. Robert Stapledon, the governor, had kindly decided that the Navy should keep the Boston whaler as a prize. As *Tartar* was about to leave the station, I had ordered the whaler transferred to *Rothesay*, and decided that its ultimate fate should be as the staff water-skiing boat in Bermuda.

I had been warned that in September Admiral Sir Roy Talbot, C.-in-C. South Atlantic Station, was to visit my command on his way, via the Panama Canal, to cruise round South America. His squadron consisted of *Tiger*, *Lynx* and, I think, *Plymouth*. Under the rules, these ships could come under my command while on my station should a need arise to use them. So I sailed in *Rothesay* from Trinidad to meet them in Admiralty Bay at Bequia, a wonderful harbour for the occasion. My call on the admiral was arranged for 9 a.m. in *Tiger*, and I determined that I would go there by Boston whaler, covering the distance in about three minutes as opposed to the twelve that a frigate's standard motorboat would have required. I could see all the telescopes from *Tiger* trained on *Rothesay* when no boat came alongside to take me, and they assumed that I would be adrift. However, all went according to plan. I left *Rothesay* at 8.57 a.m. and was alongside and going up the ladder to salute the admiral at 9 a.m. precisely, feeling distinctly smug. By now, nearly every sailor in *Rothesay* who wanted to could water-ski, and I did some water-skiing in the bay, which was great fun.

I suggested to Roy Talbot that no sooner were he and his ships through the Panama Canal than there could well be trouble in the Falkland Islands. Should I perhaps go down to Rio in a ship, in order to be closer in case that happened? This suggestion was treated with the levity it deserved. Strangely enough, however, when they were near Lima, trouble did occur in the Falkland Islands. *Lynx*, commanded by Peter Austin, which, being diesel-engined, had longer legs than the other frigates, had to race to Port Stanley as guardship, rather spoiling Peter's South American cruise.

Admiral Talbot's squadron duly sailed, and I took *Rothesay* north via St Vincent to Barbados, from where I flew back to Bermuda with Peter Boys-Stones, who had some time before relieved Faulkner as flag lieutenant and staff operations officer. The Commanders-in-Chief's Committee (UK) had decided to pay my command a visit and I was to accompany them on tour. They were the single-service administrative commanders of my units – the soldiers in British Honduras and British Guiana came under General Darling, now C.-in-C. Southern Command; the ships came under Admiral Madden, still C.-in-C. Western Fleet, and the aircraft, such as I had from time to time, were the responsibility of Air Chief Marshal Cross, who was also providing the aircraft for the tour. These were a Comet and, because the airfield in British Honduras would not then take a Comet, a Hastings. This was very convenient, as they kindly allowed Elizabeth to fly with the Hastings when they were in the Comet, and vice versa. The great men arrived in Bermuda in early October, where we helped to look after them. By then *Rothesay* had come up and the Boston whaler did its stuff, much to Admiral Madden's satisfaction, since he, having been Flag Officer Malta, was expert on water-skis. We had the boat at our dock at the house for the occasion, which proved to be its finest hour. (It had been so thoroughly used in *Rothesay* that we had trouble thereafter with the outboard motor, a large Evinrude beyond our resources to replace.)

The tour took us to Jamaica, with a side trip by Hastings to British Honduras, then on to Trinidad (where Admiral Madden left to return to Northwood), and so to British Guiana. Susan came down independently and joined Elizabeth there. I had a lovely two days in Grenada with them both on that most beautiful of islands, seeing over the route planned for the next royal visit, and then sailed in *Decoy*, with John Stevens in command, for Barbados. Here, we were to embark a battalion of the Worcestershire Regiment for jungle training planned by my new Royal Marine staff officer, Hugh Orpen. He had found a site for their camp on the windward coast of Dominica – jungly enough, in all conscience. With *Decoy* alongside at Bridgetown, I visited the troops at the airport, where they were given tea after their flight, and talked to some of them. When I said to one group, 'You won't be here long, we will be moving you on board in about two hours' time,' one of them turned round and said to me, 'That's not like Germany, Sir.' 'You're not in Germany now, as you will soon discover.' They dossed down somehow in *Decoy*, and we made a night passage to land them at dawn, weather permitting (as it did), on the windward coast. What very nearly did not permit was the administrator, Alec Lovelace, a very good hand, who lost his political nerve for some reason at the last moment. I received a signal from Hugh Orpen saying that we were no longer to carry out the exercise. Since I could do nothing else with the troops, I turned a blind eye to this, put them ashore as planned, and went to see Alec Lovelace myself, to find that his misgivings had, in my opinion, been rather amplified in the process of transmission to me. He was, very fortunately, quite happy with the outcome.

After a day or so staying in Alec Lovelace's house, I went to see the Worcesters in their camp, where they seemed to be having a high old time, although, unfortunately, one soldier was badly hurt through doing rather too exciting things swinging Tarzan-style by creeper across a mountain river. It was raining pretty hard, as is usual for Dominica, and I well remember coming back fairly late to Government House to find buckets all over the floor to catch water leaking through the roof, including some in my room. I also found the main reception room littered with recumbent sailors who had had too much to drink and been picked up by a kind Administrator in his own car and brought to Government House to sleep it off. I stepped through them quietly and turned in. They were all gone by morning.

Elizabeth and Susan, meanwhile, were staying with the Grahams at St Vincent, and we next met up at St Lucia, where the Bryans looked after us beautifully, laying on a yacht trip to Pigeon Island. From St Lucia the family went to Guadeloupe, and I took *Decoy* to St Barthélemy (known as St Barts), the smallest French island in the Caribbean. It had once been a Swedish colony, the only one in the West Indies. It remains in French hands, whereas the Danes sold their possessions to become the American Virgin Islands. The capital, Gustavia, was a copybook little colonial town in a lovely semi-circular bay, in which *Decoy* anchored. We moved to Antigua in time to be there when *Britannia* brought the Duke of Edinburgh (to whom I had already paid my respects at Nassau) to the English Harbour Dockyard. This was a tremendous affair, with locals outnumbering tourists for once and the Mountbatten Standard much in evidence on the barge. In that lovely setting, and with the relaxed West Indies atmosphere, steel bands and dances, it was an occasion we all remember, but I felt that my remaining time in the islands was getting very short indeed.

Elizabeth and Susan returned to Bermuda. I left *Decoy* with orders to meet me at Belize, and flew via Nassau and Miami to Mexico City, where there was to be a meeting, chaired by John Rennie, an Under-Secretary from the Foreign and Commonwealth Office, of the ambassadors, high commissioners and governors in the Caribbean area which I was to attend as their roving military adviser. I was placed at the bottom of the table. The affairs of the Caribbean area were discussed for the benefit of the Foreign Office coordinator and I remember principally the difference in attitude between the three categories of distinguished officials who were present – if you had not known them you could still have discerned who was an ambassador, who a high commissioner and who a governor. The most memorable remark was made by Ralph Grey in connection with financial aid becoming available from the Labour government in which Barbara Castle was Minister for Overseas Development. Ralph said, 'The Honourable Lady hopes to change the face of the world, but with the funds at her disposal all she can do is to put a light cosmetic touch on some part of it. And,' he continued, 'I can think of no more deserving place in this area than the country I have just left.'

When the conference ended, I flew south with Peter Stallard (who gave me a kind of safe conduct, since we landed in Guatemala City airport at the foot of a beautifully symmetrical volcano). On the way I saw Popocatepetl and

Chimborazo, their snow-capped summits gleaming in a cloudless sky. Peter and I then drove to Belize for my farewell visit and came on board *Decoy* for lunch, as did Gratton, the garrison commander, and his wife. The British Honduras Garrison gave me a beautifully-carved wooden sailfish, their badge, as a farewell present. We then sailed for Key West, and finally to Nassau, to say goodbye to those who had been so kind to us. My relief, Hubert Dannreuther (whom I knew quite well), had been appointed and so it was back to Bermuda, where 'Jack' Robinson, as Lord Martonmere, was now Governor, to prepare to turn over and depart. I knew now that I was to be promoted to Rear-Admiral in January, so apparently all was forgiven and the CDS had kindly protected me. A good friend, Bill O'Brien, was Naval Secretary, and he wrote to say that the First Sea Lord intended to send me as Assistant Chief of Defence Staff (Signals). This was a new job that had just been instituted, the late Signal Officer-in-Chief, General Whistler, having taken it on until my appointment came into effect. I was quite appalled by this prospect, and wrote to ask if I could not go back to the Navy, having been engaged in joint jobs for the last two-and-a-half years. I asked, in particular, whether there was a chance of my becoming Flag Officer Sea Training, which would throw me right in at the deep end and bring me wholly up to date with the latest in ships, weapons and tactics. I even began to consider refusing the appointment to seek work outside the Service, and hinted as much to Bill. He took the hint, and wrote back to say that I would be extremely foolish not to take the appointment. He told me (though he said he should not have done) that the First Sea Lord had another appointment in mind for me after my time as ACDS(S) was over. This clinched it, and Bill had saved me from doing something really stupid, knowing, as he did, that I hardly knew the First Sea Lord, since I had met him only once since he was a commander of a cruiser in the war, and then to demur with him, as Naval Secretary, at my appointment to Latimer. So I piped down and realised how lucky I was.

Mousse and Father gave us a tremendous welcome, and we decided almost at once to have central heating installed as soon as we went back to 'South Cottage'. I was now a captain again (the commodore rank having gone with the job), and was slightly put out to find that, nevertheless, my uniform grant only covered the expense of changing stripes from commodore to rear-admiral, which cost much less than changing from captain!

Although I had seen far too little of the family while in the West Indies, life had been very kind. We had had a lovely house in Bermuda, which they had all enjoyed, Tamara had found an interesting job there, and a lively social life with visiting ships, and Tom had, like me, endured a colonial education and survived. Susan had thoroughly enjoyed her job in Washington and was sad to leave it, but I did feel much happier that she and her mother had seen something of the islands and my friends there. From the professional point of view, it had been a marvellous experience: a good deal of sea time in a variety of small ships, extensive exposure to politico-military affairs and, above all, an independence in command which allowed a full measure of responsibility, fun and sight-seeing. I did not look forward to the change ahead.

CHAPTER SIX

Flag Officer and
Board Member

1965–71

It was a happy return to England. Elizabeth's parents and mine were still all pretty fit. Susan decided to get a job in London for a time, and Tamara, after a period working, to study architecture at the Bartlett School at London University. We decided, after some investigation, to send Tom to Yardley Court. I think Elizabeth thought it was a bit austere, but remembering Western Province Preparatory School, I was quite certain that Tom would find it a great deal easier in many ways than Saltus had been. We duly installed central heating in 'South Cottage' and settled comfortably back into our own home for a change. I was promoted rear-admiral on 7 January, and my appointment as the first ACDS(S) was due on 1 March, so, after a round of debriefing at the MoD and at various headquarters on the Caribbean situation, I had time at home.

It was strange to be going back to signals as a flag officer. Long ago, in China, when I had discussed specialisation with Father and decided to stay on general service for the time being, one traditionally gave up one's specialist identity on promotion to commander; later, it became captain. I was one of the first to do a signals job in that exalted rank, and the first in the Royal Navy to be expected to do a specialist job, however joint, as a flag officer. The prospect did not appeal; the reality turned out to be quite different.

I decided to make a brief courtesy call on General Whistler in Storey's Gate. He was charged with preparations for the Whitehall central signals set up. As I found my way into the building and entered the outer office, which had Micky Whistler's room to its left as you came in, I was frankly inspected by a short girl with pretty hair on the left of the door, who may well have been lying in wait. She turned out to be Micky Whistler's cousin, and the life and soul of the outer office. She became secretary to my deputy, Air Cdre. Foden, but was later to be mine. Micky was extremely friendly and welcoming, rather *dégagé* and, I think, quite pleased to be turning over. Tony McCrum (who had relieved me in Norway) was planning the move and Arthur Barrow (who had been on my Long Signals Course in *Mercury*) was now, as a retired officer, secretary of the Defence Signals Board. I learned that my offices were to be on the south side of the MoD Main Building and on the first floor – all the best offices are entered via the north door and found on the sixth floor!

After a short further spell of leave, I joined and took over. The job had been established by the Chiefs of Staff under the influence of Mountbatten, and was one of his more sensible innovations. Foden, my deputy, was a great help, much as I dislike deputies in principle, and had the two merits of being an electronic engineer and indefatigable. I was now responsible directly to 'Dickie', as Chairman of the Chiefs of Staffs' Committee, for those elements of signals in all three services which they either saw fit to confide to my care or which I felt I could make a strong enough case for taking over.

The Defence Signal Board of which I became chairman was, in effect, the old British Joint Communications Electronics Board under a new name. It dealt mainly with signals policy, and that was how I felt it ought to be left. The three services were represented by the Signal Officer-in-Chief to the Army, the Director-General of Signals Air for the RAF (both of these being general officers) and a mere captain (in the usual way) for the Navy. It also included the head of the Government Signals Planning Office (an old 'staffy' of Mountbatten's called Michael Hodges, a retired captain, RN, who worked in the Cabinet Office), the head of the cryptographic empire (who was another ex-naval captain, Fred Stannard) and a representative of the communications intelligence-gathering community. Arthur Barrow was the secretary of this gang, and the standing committees inherited from the British Joint Communications Electronics Board, some 16 of them, still carried on.

In taking the chair of this party, I was supposed to distil and, if necessary, reinforce policies acceptable to the Chiefs of Staff in a central kind of way and, hopefully, to improve the signals efficiency of defence as a whole. Much, however, fell outside my orbit: ship-to-ship communication, tactical communications in the field for the Army, and ground-to-air and air-to-air communications for the RAF. Quite rightly, matters vital to the operational efficiency of the individual services were left to them. This produced no particular difficulty – there were plenty of other things to do.

The central staff was small and, apart from Arthur Barrow's department and the secretaries, I organised it around three assistant directors: one for Operations, who was a soldier; one for Plans, who was a sailor, and one for Technical, who was an airman. There were also some valuable 'back-room' boys' – retired officers dealing with publications, frequency allocation and the like. The plans director was Gerald Sampson (who had been cadet captain of my last term at Dartmouth), the operations director was Tom Foster (whose daughter subsequently became the secretary to Arthur Foden, my deputy, so that Penny Whistler came over and took me on) and an expert Group Captain took on technical matters.

At an early meeting, I managed to get the board to agree that we should abolish every standing committee of the old BJCEB. I had served on one of these, the Equipment Committee, long ago, when I was in the Radio Equipment Department of the Admiralty, and remembered well how one went from meeting to meeting, taking out, at the eleventh hour, the minutes of the last session, which almost invariably served as the agenda for the next, and achieving almost nothing except continuity of debate. It was agreed that these committees should be replaced by working parties charged with specific purposes, each of which would be chaired by one of my 'central' assistant directors. Arthur Barrow and I watched to make sure that these working parties were not set up needlessly, nor kept going a moment longer than necessary.

All this was strictly Whitehall 'war', spiced, however, by countless calls on various functionaries and dignitaries to whom I owed some kind of responsibility. These included all the Chiefs of Staff and the deputy CDS, Logistics and Personnel, Air Marshal Sir Walter Pretty. There was another ACDS, an airman called Don Evans who was responsible centrally for operations, but, knowing 'Dickie' Mountbatten, I felt that this would not be the end of it. Sure enough, before long, we had an ACDS for Operational Requirements, another airman, 'Nebby' Wheeler, who came to see me to ask what I thought his job would be (a question I found difficult to answer) and a head of Defence Sales, Raymond Brown (one of the founder members of Racal Ltd), who, when he called, received a dissertation on how to do his job, which was extremely rash on my part and of which he has never ceased to remind me. Finally, an ACDS (Policy) was appointed, who was no more than the chairman of the directors of plans in another hat and one rank up.

I was fortunate in having been chairman of the directors of plans because I had a pretty thorough idea of how the Chiefs of Staffs' Committee, with everything over which they presided, was intended to operate and of how the checks and balances with the civil service and with ministers were meant to work under the old rules inherited from Maurice Hankey and the Committee of Imperial Defence. I determined that the Defence Signals Board should operate as a microcosm of the Chiefs of Staff, with the same kind of responsibilities, individual and collective, within its scope and with the same checks and balances. At that time, this concept stood us in good stead.

The Whitehall machinery is important, which is why I have dwelt on it so much, but nothing in it automatically generates efficiency or modernisation in the performance of the armed forces of the Crown, in whose aid it is all established. I felt it necessary to get into the field, particularly into Germany, in order to learn and to try to enhance my own credibility with my colleagues in the other services. At that time, Peter, poor soul, was Director of Plans, suffering under two of the most difficult officers in the Navy: Peter Hill-Norton as the ACNS (who was now involved in planning, which was not so in my time) and John Frewen, VCNS. Both were meticulous, very clever and ambitious. The battle over the large aircraft carrier was being re-fought and being lost. Peter, as the plans director, had to produce all the papers to rehearse again the arguments that had won last time in the 'Strategy for the Sixties', when I had been in his position with a different management. He seemed to have to carry on his shoulders almost any and every reverse which occurred in the debate. We had lunch together once a week, usually in the basement of a pub called 'The Lord Nelson' at the Trafalgar Square end of The Strand, but there was very little I could produce that he had not already thought of, and almost nothing that was helpful.

In the event, Mountbatten, knowing, I think, what was going to transpire and doing a Pontius Pilate act, was overseas when the Chiefs of Staff took the final paper and decided that CVA01 (the new, large aircraft carrier) should be cancelled and that the fixed-winged aircraft carrier force as a whole should not be replaced. The First Sea Lord and the minister for the Navy, Mayhew, resigned, Mayhew unfortunately not making his reasons as clear as the Navy would have liked. There was much irony in the resignation, at considerable personal sacrifice, of Admiral Luce, the first submarine officer to have been CNS, over such an issue but he did not hesitate. Varyl Begg, who had been Peter's captain in *Triumph*, the Cadet Training Ship, long ago, had been VCNS when I was director of plans, and whom I had met when he was Unified C.-in-C. Far East, was named as the new First Sea Lord.

About this time, 'Dickie', who was nearing the end of his tour of duty, held an inter-service paper exercise called UNISON at the RAF College at Cranwell which I, and many others, were called on to attend. I do not remember the burden of the exercise, which was a Commonwealth one and therefore probably added little to military knowledge because of security restrictions.

I had recently heard that Peter was not going to be promoted to rear-admiral, owing to the carrier débâcle and an indifferent report from John Frewen. Varyl let me take him aside at UNISON. 'I would like to speak to you about Peter.' He said, 'Why?' 'About his promotion.' He said, 'What?', and took me for a walk round the grounds. At the end of it he said, 'I'll sort that out.' This he did, averting a tremendous injustice. One of Peter's great qualities is the intensity of his commitment to any cause in which he believes. In the MoD, the ability to compromise and find ways round or through a difference of opinion is often essential. Peter, temperamentally, is not a compromiser – more credit to him for that. The injustice, which Varyl Begg was quick to sense, lay in setting aside Peter's brilliant service at sea and ashore, his dedication and his integrity, in the wake of the disappointment for the whole Navy for which he held far less than full responsibility. As his subsequent record shows – as a respected flag officer and one of the most successful Chiefs of Staff to a NATO admiral there has ever been, not to mention the great services he has rendered after his retirement from the Navy – Begg's decision was absolutely right.

After UNISON, I was able to go briefly to Germany and spend some time with RAF Germany and I British Corps, which was commanded by Sir John Mogg at the time. C.-in-C. British Army of the Rhine, on whom I called, was General Sir John Hackett, who, I think, tried to blind me with science during our talk, mentioning brains and computers with a fluency from which I shrank. The corps chief signal officer was Charles Page, a most able and impressive officer in the Royal Signals, who took charge of me and showed me all that I ought to have seen in the time available. I saw, for example, a brigade headquarters operating in the field, and was taken round by Dick Ward, its divisional commander, who had been on the CDS's briefing staff in the Planning days. In the course of this, the C.-in-C. Allied Forces Central Europe (a German) appeared, and it took me back a long way to see him wearing a belt on his uniform with '*Gott mit Uns*' on the buckle, such as I had seen *ad nauseam* in Berlin in 1939. I came back feeling slightly more 'khaki', and settled down for a time to work in Whitehall. Having seen much of the light-blue fraternity in AFNORTH days, however, I was struck by Northern Army Group's lack of the close Army–Air Force cooperation at joint command centre level achieved in Norway and Denmark. I felt that, given a clearly-defined Army support role on which to focus, the RAF would have done better, but they had other strike commitments which tended to predominate.

There were some obvious rationalisation projects available, to which the Defence Signal Board gave a green light. The idea was that the RAF should run nearly all the fixed communications world-wide, the Army should run nearly all the relay stations ashore, and the Navy would depend on both where its needs could best be met by the other services. It would continue to run broadcasts to ships and submarines itself. This scheme progressed apace, and eventually came to a slightly limited form of fruition. A Defence Communications Network run by the RAF was set up, and Arthur Foden, my erstwhile deputy, was made its first commander. I went to their inaugural briefing, followed by a party at which everybody wore 'spider' ties (the hallmark of the old RAF fixed-service network). Progress in the Army taking over the fixed relays, including the RAF ones, was less certain, and it was not completed in my time.

As well as national responsibilities, I had certain international ones under the various treaties and pacts to which the UK then belonged. Most important of these was NATO, and at this time the US Secretary of State for Defense, Mr McNamara, had decided it was necessary to make an attack on the bureaucracy in that alliance and try to cut through to some sensible decisions. Three working groups were therefore set up by the NATO Council: one to deal with strategy, predominantly its nuclear element, with MacNamara in the chair; another to deal with intelligence, with John Waterfield, a British Foreign Office official, in the chair; and a third to deal with communications, which underpinned the other two, with a retired Dutch general and politician called Den Toom in the chair. I represented the UK on the last of these three. This meant trips over to Paris, on a couple of which Elizabeth came too. One outcome of these particular meetings was the setting up of a NATO ad hoc, high-level Communications Working Group, on which I represented the UK. The chairman was Dick Coleridge, the Executive Secretary of NATO, a nice, well-connected chap, a peer of the realm, whose qualification for dealing with signals was that he had once been social flag lieutenant to the C.-in-C. Mediterranean Fleet. I think he was probably all the better a chairman for that and we made sensible recommendations, I am sure, to various authorities who eventually found themselves unable, for the most part, to finance them. Nevertheless, in the course of these meetings, I met and worked with a distinguished US general of engineers called Starbird, who was later to be a real help.

Back in London, Arthur Foden had been relieved by an amiable brigadier, David Gribbin, whose expertise was, unfortunately for me, rather less technical. Eric Cole, the Signal Officer-in-Chief, had also now been relieved by Peter Bradley, a pleasantly extrovert major-general. It was made perfectly clear to me, as I anticipated, when I called on Field Marshal Sir Richard Hull, the new CDS, that he was personally determined to be rid of Micky Hodges at the earliest possible moment. Unfair though this may seem, Micky, a congenital gadfly, had only himself to blame. It took all of six months to have him replaced by John Lakin from the Foreign Office, assisted by Walter Wells (who had been on my Long Course). I think Hull realised that the rest of the more important business of the defence signals staff would go on regardless, and he made no comment on our performance.

'Dickie' Mountbatten gave a farewell party at Broadlands to which I went, and I renewed my acquaintance with David Milford Haven, his nephew (who had also been on my Long Course, and who, sadly, was to die very early). It was a good party, but I agreed with those who felt that the course of defence would proceed more easily from now on; not only more easily, but also more constructively. My feeling was that 'Dickie', with his wide experience, his connections, his butterfly approach, very often generated more heat than steam. He gave stimulus to an organisation which may well have been momentarily salutory, but I felt that the restless brilliance did not emanate from any inner happiness or peace and so lacked stability, even conviction (more Prince Rupert than Prince Eugen, I suppose, and more courtier than statesman). Nevertheless, he was ever kind and considerate to me and I owe him much. The new regime was both more predictable and less entertaining.

In August 1965 there was to be a communications officers' conference at the South-East Asia Treaty Organisation HQ in Bangkok, at which I had to represent the UK. I took advantage of this commitment to pay a visit to the Far East where what was then known as 'confrontation' with Indonesia was in full swing. It had designs on the newly created Malaysia and a fair number of our troops were deployed, with interesting communications problems along the border with Kalimantan, as Indonesian Borneo is called. So I flew out early to Singapore and then up to Jesselton in North Borneo, where I had last been in *Alert*. I visited the new cable terminus just in time to see a message from Singapore. Almost the first transmission, it concerned Lee Kuan Yew's return in tears from his visit to Kuala Lumpur to try to achieve some kind of union of Singapore with Malaysia. Tunku Abdul Rahman, the Malaysian prime minister, would have none of it.

From Jesselton, I flew close past Mt Kinabalu, with its wonderful, rocky multiple summit, over Sandakan to Tawau, where we had a small force and the first operational hovercraft squadron. I had a good trip in one of the hovercraft up the river, skating neatly over the half-sunken logs and debris that encumbered it. In theory, hovercraft were an excellent means of river and amphibious transport for supplies and troops; in practice, it was no good sending troops tactically because the noise of the engine could be heard for miles. There were no particular communications problems, but it was an excellent jaunt to a part of the world I might not otherwise have seen. From there, I flew to Brunei, went to visit some of our troops in the field – including the Guards' Independent Parachute Company on the coast – covering a good deal of ground by helicopter. Unfortunately, I was not able to go to Sibu, where a number of naval amphibious helicopters had been disembarked and were doing yeoman service in the charge of a young commander called 'Tank' Sherman, who made a name for himself in the course of the operation.

I then flew to Kuching, which was a great deal easier than going there in *Alert*, and spent some time in the 3rd Division of Sarawak, where operations were in pretty regular progress. I flew out to see a couple of the jungle forts which had been built as strong points, from which the frontier could be better controlled, and visited relay stations on mountaintops through which tactical communications were established and maintained. The Gurkhas looked after me, as did the SAS, whose commander in the field, Lieutenant-Colonel Farrar-Hockley, has since made a name for himself. He certainly gave me a very entertaining and thorough briefing. It was a great way of shaking the dust of the MoD off one's feet and I came back feeling I knew a good deal more about land force tactical communications, although they were not strictly my responsibility. James Pertwee was then the director of naval operations under General George Lea, who had arrived quite recently. The director of military operations was General Peter Hunt (later to be a friend and colleague in the MoD), and I stayed overnight with him at Labuan.

I then went back via Singapore to see Air Chief Marshal Sir John Grandy (who had relieved Begg) and Sir Frank Twiss, the Fleet Commander, and up to Bangkok for the SEATO meeting. As a meeting, it was like most of the others: a big agenda, a few things to discuss, a few decisions that had probably been mostly cleared in advance, and an opportunity to meet people. The excitement lay in the expedition that they laid on for us into the war area by the Mekong River. We flew to Korat and Ubon, two American bases in Thailand, in an American cargo aircraft with the rear door open throughout. This gave a very interesting view of the runway on take-off and landing, not to mention the countryside between. From Korat, some of us went on to Pleiku in Vietnam, which was a main communications station for the American Forces in that country. I remember a great array of forward scatter antennae (developments of the early ones we had had in Norway in 1957), but more importantly I was able to see and operate a satellite terminal made by the Hughes Aircraft Company which was connected to the USA through one of the first two satellites ever placed in synchronous orbit. It was rather like operating a primitive gun mounting. One sat on a seat, with a couple of handwheels to twiddle. When one succeeded in aligning the antenna's dish in the right direction for the satellite, one could pick up the telephone and enjoy a very clear conversation with a similar terminal on the west coast of continental America. It was a convincing demonstration of the usefulness of such a satellite system and a great encouragement to me, since a major project during my time as ACDS(S) was to be directly connected with this novel type of communication. I then travelled back to Bangkok for a night, and next to my London desk.

Before I joined the MoD, a distinguished physicist, Hermann Bondi, had been directed to write a report for the British government on the military uses of space. This report came first to a body known as the Official Committee on Technology, which was chaired (when he could spare the time) by Solly Zuckerman, chief scientific adviser to the government. To the chagrin of the RAF, which regarded space as light-blue territory, I, as ACDS(S), was the Chiefs' of Staff representative on this august body and I attended with some regularity. The Bondi Report considered the pros and cons of an investment in space by Britain and recommended that we should certainly invest in space communications, possibly in space reconnaissance, but ignore the rest. It cost a million dollars in those days even to get to the starting post in terms of boosters and their instrumentation. A whole army of vested interests rose up in protest, and I used to find the meetings most interesting. All the mandarins were there: the permanent secretary to the Treasury, one from the Ministry of Aviation and Technology, another from the Foreign Office, and so on. When Solly could not preside over the whole meeting, Roger Allen, a civil servant from Cabinet Office, would take the chair until the great man arrived and take it on again as soon as the great man hurried off (rather like the white rabbit in *Alice in Wonderland*) to his next appointment.

Acceptance of the Bondi Report would mean that certain projects, such as Blue Streak and other rockets, would be cancelled and I well remember Sir Richard Way, who represented the Ministry of Technology, proposing, in the presence of Hermann, that it would be a good idea to spread the costs of Blue Streak launches over a longer period, so that they could be accommodated within the likely budget. Hermann's response was instant: 'Yes,' he said, 'I think that's a very good plan indeed, assuming that the object of the plan is to make an obsolescent rocket more obsolete.' That was the end of the 'plan'.

As I recollect it, the report was basically agreed and approved by the government as well as by the Chiefs of Staff, who had a word on it on my recommendation. It then fell to me to see what could be done under the authority to enter into satellite communications. In my view, and that of the Defence Signal Board, it was high time we did, and this launched me on a fascinating exercise which took the best part of nine months to achieve a satisfactory outcome. They were uncharted seas for all of us. First, the Chiefs of Staff had to approve the operational requirement, and before they could do that, they had to understand what it would do for them and have some inkling at least of what it would cost. The Ministry of Aviation and Technology was deeply interested and wanted to get their oar in everywhere. I sat firmly in the driving seat with the help of Gerald Sampson, an excellent civil servant called Donald Forbes, and a first-rate RAF wing commander, Padfield, who was good on the technical side in particular.

We felt that the British defence system at that time required a communications satellite in synchronous orbit over the Indian Ocean at about 75° east to establish absolutely firm communications between Whitehall and our forces in the Near, Middle and Far East. There was no such military satellite in existence at the time, the Americans relying on a system of drifting multiple satellites known as the Interim Defence

Communications Satellite Programme (IDCSP). We took some interest in this, but its lack of power and continuity meant it failed to meet the needs that we envisaged of communicating rapidly with small antennae, such as could be used tactically ashore and afloat. The test satellite over the Pacific through which I had communicated from Pleiku was a very inconsiderable object in comparison with what we had in mind as something that the Chiefs of Staff could reasonably be asked to approve.

Early on, therefore (this must have been late 1965), and armed with an agreed joint staff target, I went to the USA to see which way we should go. We were entirely reliant on them for a booster to put a satellite in orbit and there was no way a suitable satellite could have been manufactured in the UK within the kind of timescale we had in mind if, as I felt we should, we were to catch the tide that was flowing our way from the Bondi Report. On my first visit I went to the Ford-Philco factory at Palo Alto, California, where the IDCSP satellites were being built in an almost conventional production line. Ford-Philco clearly could do what we wanted, had plenty of space-qualified components at their disposal and an excellent quality control system, supervised partly by the Department of Defense and partly by the US Air Force, to whom we could subcontract the production of our 'bird'. As regards the booster, there was a choice of several and I had a memorable visit to the Martin Aircraft Works at Denver, Colorado, to discuss the pros and cons of the Titan 3C, which had a multiple-load capability. I remember, at the end of a tremendous demonstration of this system, asking, 'Where, if my government wished to buy a first-class ticket on the launcher, as opposed, say, to a second-class one, would you put our particular satellite?' The answer did not inspire great confidence, and in the event our recommendation was to launch using the Thor Delta B, a rocket dedicated to a single payload which had a very high record for reliability.

Back we came with all this information to set about preparing the operational requirement, which had to go through a special committee, thence through another committee, and eventually to the Chiefs of Staff. Sir William Cook, who was the Deputy Chief Scientific Adviser (Projects), was on our side, as was his assistant, Harry Pout, and thanks to a good paper prepared by my people, I had a remarkably easy passage. So far so good. Next it was necessary to get a costed project agreed and approved. This meant another trip to the USA, in particular to negotiate a Memorandum of Understanding: something built and launched there at our expense to meet our needs should be capable of doing certain things in any foreseeable set of circumstances. Although we were ahead of the Americans in our concept, there was no doubt that they would not be far behind and would soon overtake us, and I therefore felt that an agreement on inter-operability between our satellite and anything they put up was important to both sides. Because we had had to accept a limitation on satellite power as part of the agreement with the Americans to put us in space at all, this was agreed on a telegraph channel basis.

On arrival in the USA, I found that they would expect to exercise command and control over our satellite at all times. Since this would allow them to move it somewhere where we might not wish it to go or, indeed, to switch if off if they wished, I felt that I could not expect the Chiefs of Staff to approve such a limitation. 'Ham' Ridler, with whom I stayed, and our embassy and mission as a whole, were nothing but helpful, but the obstacle still stood. My opposite number in the negotiations was an American lawyer called Dave Alfrey, backed up by people from all three US services, but particularly by a delightful rear-admiral called Boyle. In what seemed an impasse, I went to my old acquaintance 'Bud' Starbird, who was head of the Defense Communications Systems of the US forces, for advice. He said, 'Why don't you talk to the presidential special adviser on communications, General O'Connell, who works in the White House?' I said, 'Will he see me?', and he said, 'Yes, I'll make sure he does.' O'Connell very kindly asked me to lunch, which I remember well, eating in the White House Mess with Vice-President Hubert Humphrey and various other dignitaries around. After a glass of Coca-Cola, I explained the impasse. Jim O'Connell didn't say much. He understood the problem, and commented, 'You talk about command and control of a satellite over the Indian Ocean – from where is this going to be exercised?' 'I suppose from Mahe in the Seychelles, where you have one of your space stations,' I replied. 'Who owns the Seychelles,' he asked. 'It's a British Colony.' 'Well,' he said, 'What are you worried about?' The penny dropped, I ceased to worry so much, and with Donald Forbes's help I set about drafting a Memorandum of Understanding for a final meeting with the Americans. We worked all that afternoon, putting off the meeting until about 9 p.m. At midnight everything was agreed except command and control being given to us. The Americans asked if they could caucus, and I said yes. I did not mention the Seychelles or their ownership. After about half an hour, Dave Alfrey came back, conceded command and control, and we had an agreement. By then Gerald Sampson had coined a name for our satellite system: it was to be called Skynet, and on return to the UK we got Skynet approved, money was made available and orders were placed and running in record time. Harry Pout described it as a *tour de force*.

Mercifully, the launch of Skynet 1 was a success, but the Delta B on which we placed so much reliance failed on the second launch. The management of the system on the ground was quite properly given to the RAF, and the money came off the RAF budget (which gave me a little quiet and naughty satisfaction, since I felt that, in the long term, this system would be of more value to ships at sea than to anybody else). The ship terminals were being produced by Hawker-Siddeley Dynamics, and I had the great pleasure, later on, of unveiling the first 'Scot' terminal in their factory.

Towards the end of my time, the Defence Signal Board felt that it would be sensible to strengthen our important links with the Australians on signals matters. I therefore went to see the defence signals people in Melbourne and Canberra, which was invaluable professionally. There followed a brief visit to Hong Kong to see the signals set-up there, including Stonecutters Island, where I had done my Annual Musketry Course as a midshipman, and which seemed to be the only part of the colony to have hardly changed.

For us, 1966 was a very happy year, with Susan's marriage to John Sykes on 30 April, Tamara, a lovely bridesmaid, safely back from an expedition to Turkey and all set to be an architect, and Tom enjoying Yardley Court (at least I think so). Elizabeth's father was at the wedding, which was a splendid effort. Father, crippled by his back, could not make it, but Mousse was there with a great turn-out on a glorious day, in a marquee at 'South Cottage' on grass that John had helped me lay not long before. My work in the MoD had meanwhile been made much easier by renting a flat in Compton Road in Canonbury, where Elizabeth, Tamara and I lived, and whence I could catch a 172 bus to the office every day. It was the first time that family responsibilities had allowed Elizabeth to come up and join me in London and made life so much nicer for us both. I was awarded the CB in the Queen's Birthday Honours in 1966. Liz brought Tamara and Tom to the investiture, where I was delighted to see John Cumber (ex-Cayman Islands) in the CMG 'pen'.

All in all, the signals job that I had feared so much had turned out to be a challenge and a delight. With Arthur Barrow as secretary of the Defence Signals Board, Penny Whistler as my own secretary and Gerald and the others all on side, it was really a splendid team effort. Arthur Foden was selected as my relief, and to cap it all, I was told that my next appointment was to be at sea, as Flag Officer, Second-in-Command, Far East Fleet, with Bill O'Brien as my Fleet Commander. It was the best job the Navy had to offer and I looked forward to it with as much trepidation as you would expect, but with considerable satisfaction. Arthur took over from me in February 1967. As there were two or three months to spare before I had to go east, Elizabeth and I decided to make the most of it, and went on holiday to Portugal. It was a wonderful change and relaxation, which we both thoroughly enjoyed.

Once back, I sorted out my whites and went to see John Bush, who was then VCNS, to be briefed before going east. He told me exactly what was expected of me in his usual, direct way, and said, 'When you come back you are going to be Vice-Chief of the Naval Staff.' I said, 'Nonsense,' to which he rejoined, 'Oh yes, who else is there?', and with that ringing in my ears, off I went. Last of all, I went to see Denis Healey, the Secretary of State. 'What are you going to do, Edward?' 'Second-in-Command, Far East Fleet,' I said, 'at sea.' 'That's no place for an intellectual,' said Healey. 'That from you, Secretary of State,' was all I could think of to reply. He then became serious. 'Tell me, Edward, because I do want to know, does your house in Singapore have a swimming pool or not?' I was able to reply that I was unaccompanied, and had no house in Singapore, let alone a swimming pool. He wished me luck, and off I went, marvelling at the ramifications of the political mind.

At the end of March 1967 I flew to Singapore, and spent a quiet night staying at Beaulieu House with Dennis and Paddy Mason, he being Chief of Staff. In full whites, sword and medals, I boarded *Victorious* at 9 a.m. next morning, 1 April. Since the flag of Charles Mills (whom I was to relieve) was still flying in *Victorious*, mine was hoisted, at my special request, at sea in HMS *Kent* (the immediate successor of the *Kent* that Father had commanded in China and which had worn his flag when he was Flag Officer Reserve Fleet). Charles Mills

I knew pretty well; he was also a signal officer, a vice-admiral and about to go as C.-in-C. Plymouth. The captain of *Victorious* was Ian Mackintosh, a submariner whom I also knew slightly, and so, as usual, as I went round inspecting the large guard on the quarter deck I felt that I was among friends. It was, however, a lonely moment, and I sat in the enormous cabin aft below the quarter deck in the afternoon, when everybody had disappeared, taking stock. There was no point in making myself very comfortable because *Victorious* was on her way home and my real flagship initially was to be *Hermes*, which was on her way out. Suddenly, the officer of the watch came down and said that there was a Captain Morton and a Commander Franklin alongside. They wondered if I would like to go water-skiing. This was delightful: they were two signal officers, a little younger than me, whom I knew well. They had a good, fast boat, and off we went down the Singapore Strait for an hour or two's exercise. It got rid of the cobwebs and did no end of good.

The next couple of days were full of calls and return calls: on Bill O'Brien, the Fleet Commander; on General Sir Michael Carver, the Unified C.-in-C. at Singapore; on Nigel Poett, the general; on Rochford Hughes, the airman, and so on. These calls were then returned, guards and bands were the order of the day, and everybody was kept busy. The next thing was for the Fleet staff to call on me and tell me what the Fleet Commander expected of his second-in-command. I knew most of them, and perhaps the most important one from my point of view was the Fleet operations officer. He turned out to be Jerome Benson, who had commanded *Whirlwind* with me in the West Indies. Singapore was full of senior officers of all three services – not to mention the senior people in the dockyard – although we no longer had a Flag Officer Malayan Area, as in the days of *Alert* (also now scrapped). The O'Briens lived in Nelson House in the naval base; the old Admiralty House (near Phoenix Park, the joint headquarters), with the former bandstand which *Alert* had converted into an aviary for Lady Lambe, had long since been disposed of.

It was with a sense of relief that I stood on the bridge of *Victorious* as Ian Mackintosh took her to sea down the Singapore Strait on 4 April on our way to take part in a two-carrier exercise with *Hermes* before the rendezvous at Aden. 'Never in Singapore' was really my motto during this particular command. The independence of being a seagoing officer was rather naturally subjected to all sorts of extraneous pressures and influences, mostly social, when one was at the main command base. I did, however, have a small flat there in part of *Terror*, the naval base establishment, which was useful from time to time.

Two-carrier exercises took place when an aircraft carrier came out from home to relieve the one on station, and they were usually planned by the flag officer aircraft carriers, now Derek Empson. On this occasion he did not appear, and we ran it. Basically, it involved strikes by the strike squadrons of each ship on the other, with the fighter squadrons and the airborne early warning aircraft of both ships acting in a defensive role. There was a good deal of healthy rivalry. Both ships had their escorts and RFAs, and there were submarines involved, if you could get hold of them. This exercise was uneventful, as I remember it; we anchored off Aden eventually, and my flag was transferred, bag and baggage, to *Hermes*. I flew over, to be greeted by the captain, Terry Lewin, whom I knew of old in the MoD, and whose commander, John Fieldhouse, was a submarine officer.

Charles Mills had left me a 'nasty' which preoccupied me a good deal on passage. As Flag Officer, Second-in-Command, Far East Fleet, I had a small seagoing staff, notably a staff officer operations, a staff torpedo and anti-submarine officer, a staff communications officer (who was also flag lieutenant), a secretary, and an assistant secretary. There were also staff ratings, mostly communications branch, a coxswain, who drove the barge and the car by turns, and cooks and stewards who were Hong Kong Chinese. Of them all, the staff officer operations was a key post, and therein lay my problem. A new one had only arrived recently, and Charles Mills told me he thought him quite unsuitable for his job. However, he went on to say that he had done nothing about it as he thought he had better leave it to me. I liked the staff officer operations on sight, he was obviously an intelligent and charming person, but did not seem to have a particular instinct for detail and tended to live for the moment rather than the future. I eventually made up my mind, sent for him and said that I was asking for him to be relieved. He was extremely upset. All I really found to say was that I had seen his report from Charles Mills, that it was not a satisfactory one, and that I thought that Charles should know whether or not he was suited to this particular job. I therefore judged it best that he should be relieved and given a new start somewhere else, rather than risk receiving a second successive unsatisfactory report from a flag officer. So that was that. He left, Robin Hogg, staff torpedo and anti-submarine officer, took over operations, combining this with his other job, and I was promised a good successor staff officer operations when they could find one.

I now settled down to get to know *Hermes* and the other warships and RFAs of the force under my command. There were also calls to make in Aden. Michael Le Fanu was now Unified C.-in-C. Middle East; John Martin, whom I had relieved as SNOWI, was Flag Officer Aden, and Andrew Humphrey, an air vice-marshal, was the air commander. There were also a number of generals around, led by Philip Tower, who had been on the same Joint Services Staff Course as myself at Latimer. The high commissioner was Sir Humphrey Trevelyan, a most courtly, courteous and acute gentleman. *Hermes*'s air group had a great deal of flying to do, and this went on apace in the exercise areas off Aden. These activities continued on passage to Singapore, where the Fleet commander, Bill O'Brien, an ex-captain of *Hermes*, had a good look at his old ship. We then moved back to Aden with frigates and RFAs in support, and were flying off there when war broke out between the Israelis and Egypt on 6 June 1967.

In the wake of the resounding Egyptian defeat, Britain was accused of sending naval carrier aircraft to cover an Israeli bombing attack on Cairo. These were alleged to have come from *Hermes* off Aden. Accordingly, on my return to Singapore on 22 June, I was asked to give a press conference to dispel the accusations. They had already been denied by the prime minister,

Mr Wilson, and by Denis Healey, but as is the way of the press these days, this had not satisfied them. So I held a press conference in Singapore, made the logs and so forth of *Hermes*'s air group available for inspection if required, and made the necessary denials. In the course of them, I had to acknowledge that air-to-air refuelling did put Cairo within range of our Buccaneers from the Aden exercise areas, but the logs showed that no one was in the air for long enough to have allowed such a sortie to have taken place. I thought it was a good press conference – I am not certain that everybody agreed. (As someone said, it was held to show that we hadn't, but proved that we could have!)

In July we sailed to Hong Kong, and it was nice to be back there again. *Hermes* anchored off the China Fleet Club, and I was able to see the authorities ashore and visit the ships in harbour. We suddenly received a call for help from the Hong Kong police. Dissidents of some kind had taken over the National Bank of China building, and in order to regain control as efficiently as practicable, the police asked if our helicopters could deposit some of their officers on the roof of the skyscraper while others made an entry at its bottom. This was achieved with great success, and much enjoyed by the air crew.

Hermes's current spell on the station was drawing to an end and we had a splendid cruise to Western Australia planned for her before she set out for home. This coincided comfortably with the school holidays and Elizabeth, Tamara and Tom were flying out to Singapore to join the cruise. Captain Fisher of the RFA *Retainer* had very kindly agreed to take Elizabeth and Tamara as 'indulgence' passengers, and Tom was to come with me in *Hermes*. So back to Singapore we went, and the family foregathered. Elizabeth arrived first and Ged Mansfield who was Commodore Amphibious Forces, normally shore-based and therefore entitled to a house in Singapore, had very kindly lent it to us until his wife came out. Tamara then arrived and I took some leave. We mounted an expedition by car up the east coast of Malaya that I knew so well from *Alert* days, and it was a lovely holiday.

When we came back to Singapore, I hoisted my flag in *Bulwark*, with Arthur Power in command, for an amphibious exercise off that same east coast, employing 3 Commando Brigade and the local tactical Air Force, commanded by Brian Eaton, a nice Australian air vice-marshal. The amphibious effort was interesting. I spent much of it in a helicopter since I was only witnessing it, the joint conducting authority being Brian Eaton and Ian Gourlay (ex-Yardley Court), who commanded 3 Commando Brigade. I must say that at times I was almost more concerned for the turtles than I was for the marines. However, all went well, and I learned a good deal about the system then in force for controlling brigade-level assaults by helicopter, backed by the amphibious landing craft also carried by the commando ships. (The experience was to be of great value to me later on, when a similar effort was envisaged as a rescue operation in Aden after independence should our people there be threatened.) My old friend from the West Indies, Gerald Roberts, was second-in-command of one of the commandos involved, *Bulwark* did well, the weather was kind, nobody was hurt and altogether it was a satisfactory performance.

Back in Singapore, Elizabeth, Tamara and I were able to use my little flat in

Terror (which Elizabeth was not entitled to occupy on her own – for a pretty obscure reason, we thought). Tom arrived, and it was then time for the girls to embark in *Retainer* and set off south. I shall never forget the sight of Tom dressed to come out by helicopter to *Hermes* with me: all you could see under the 'bone dome' was an enormous smile, and had his head been a little smaller, you wouldn't even have seen that. Once safely on board, he was made very welcome by the Chinese staff and everybody else, was shown his way to the canteen and settled pretty happily, brave little chap that he was, into the totally unfamiliar surroundings of the admiral's cabin aft. *Minerva* came with us as escort and to assist the helicopters in looking after things when *Hermes*'s aircraft were flying in case anybody ditched. We also took three RFAs: an oiler, *Retainer* and *Reliant*, which at that time had the then commodore of the RFA in charge.

It was now August, and we enjoyed good weather – rather less windy than required for flying – and a quiet passage through the Sunda Strait, passing Krakatoa towards sunset, with wisps of smoke coming from the smaller island spawned by the old volcano. At Cocos, *Hermes* spent two-and-a-half days in flying practice and the RFAs pressed on towards their destinations, which were Geraldton and Albany in Western Australia. The flying was somewhat inhibited by a heavy swell, but I think Terry and his ship got a good deal done. At Fremantle, Terry brought the ship alongside beautifully, as well as picking up a ditched Sea King on passage. The jetty was thronged with welcoming crowds holding up posters such as 'Welcome to the Royal Navy' and 'Is there anyone from Wigan?' Tom starred on local television. The mayor, Sir Frederick Sanson, a great character, gave us lunch and a splendid box with a badge of the city on it in exchange for the ship's crest. An old shipmate from *Middleton* long ago, the Berryman who had been the gunnery control officer as a sub-lieutenant RNVR, had settled inland from Perth and was most hospitable when we went to see him and his family. We thought Perth, on the Swan River, the most beautiful modern city imaginable. As well as touring it and its beaches and having lunch at Government House, we went for a wine-tasting jaunt up the Swan Valley, where Tom distinguished himself by spitting out quicker and further than anybody else. It was useful, however, as, following the example of my predecessors, who had included such 'switched on' people as Peter Hill-Norton and Michael Le Fanu, I stocked my cellar entirely with Australian wines, which were very acceptable for the mass of entertaining that I had to do.

While at Perth, my new staff officer operations, Commander Dick Fitch, arrived and soon got himself into the swing of things, even though at times I sensed Robin Hogg was a little reluctant to give up his responsibilities. No one could have worked harder or done better in the role, and his qualities were to be greatly needed in the months ahead. Jonathan Findlay, Flag Lieutenant, was also pretty good, but the Secretary, although a devoted worker, seemed unable to exert his personality sufficiently to keep the office properly organised and the work up to date. This was worrying, as very important matters, notably the confidential reports on officers, had to be dealt with accurately and punctually, and I was also convening authority for courts martial, with warrants from the Australian as well as UK authorities.

The programme for *Hermes* after leaving Fremantle was to turn over the duties of station aircraft carrier to *Eagle* in mid-Indian Ocean, and then return to the UK round the Cape. I saw very little point in spending the best part of three weeks in mid-ocean, and determined instead to fly to Mauritius, where there was an important naval wireless station on which the Fleet depended very greatly; to Kenya, to see the Kenyan Navy and also the maintenance base at Kilindini, near Mombasa; to Aden, to discuss plans for the evacuation of Aden, for which we now had a date; to Bahrain, to see the Senior Naval Officer Gulf and find out what use his facilities could be to the Aden covering force which I was going to command, and eventually to Gan, to join *Eagle* there. I would take the flag lieutenant and the staff officer operations with me, the rest would travel in the ships, keep the paperwork up to date and make certain that baggage and office gear were properly transferred to *Eagle*. I had also decided to go to Exmouth Gulf, where there was an important American wireless station on which the submarines of the British Far East Fleet depended for their communications when submerged.

By great good luck, one of the visitors to *Hermes* in Fremantle was Charlie Court, then the minister for development for Western Australia, and a tremendous enthusiast. When he heard I was going to Exmouth Gulf, he said, 'That's not good enough, now you're here you must see a great deal more of our north-west.' I think he hoped that I could help persuade British business or the government to invest money and resources up there. In any case, it was too good an invitation to be refused. So when the family part of the visit to Western Australia, which we all enjoyed very much, came to an end, I drove Elizabeth, Tamara and Tom to *Reliant* in Geraldton and, as soon as *Hermes* left Fremantle with her other RFAs bound westwards, I flew up to Learmonth, the airport for Exmouth Gulf. (This turned out to be the same airport where I had landed in the Lancastrian coming home from the war in 1946 and it was in much the same condition as it had been then.) After the official visit to the wireless station, where the US Navy made us most welcome, Charlie Court's people took charge. A bush pilot and light aircraft were placed at our disposal and we had a marvellous run round the outback.

We then flew in comparative luxury from Perth to Mauritius. Our two days in the island revolved round the wireless station, and we found a civilisation with a strong French flavour. In the prime minister's absence, I called on his deputy, Mr Ringadoo, and also on the governor, who lived in a beautiful French-style château. I was able to tell the ship's company of *Mauritius* something of what was in store for them with the evacuation of Aden impending, and of the great importance the Fleet attached to their efforts. Our next flight was a short hop across the Mozambique Channel to Nairobi, where the defence adviser took charge of me. I went to see the Kenyan Navy at Kilindini (a place I remembered well from Father's account of his time in the Eastern Fleet after the Japanese had rendered Ceylon untenable). We then flew north to Aden, and I stayed with Pru and Michael Le Fanu. There was a good deal to discuss: Aden was to be given independence at the end of

November and was in a far from quiet state, with an unstable political situation and a thoroughly doubtful future. Plans had to be made to draw down the strength of the garrison in an orderly way, and to focus British power in a maritime force at the end, so that the last troops, headquarters and aircraft could be withdrawn from shore and an ambassador established with some security for himself and for the important BP oil refinery in Little Aden.

Mike Le Fanu had a splendid High Commissioner, an excellent staff and, generally speaking, good service commanders. The commissioner of police was my old friend from British Guiana, Peter Owen. He was far from happy. I wondered what was the matter, went to have a drink with him, sat on his verandah (with the lights out for security reasons) and talked for an hour or two. No one was safe in Aden. He was perhaps less safe than most, and had been under fire, in one way or another, for rather a long time. He was naturally a bit 'twitchy'. More than that, he saw his job as a colonial police officer as being to turn over a viable police force to the new government in Aden, knowing as well as anyone that some of the ablest of his policemen were among the most disaffected Adenese around. The Army, on the other hand, regarded Owen's job as maintaining law and order by the civil power, under British rules, to the bitter end. They were not in any way interested in what happened to the police force after the flag had come down, and their chief concern was that they and their families should be properly looked after. 'The trouble, Edward,' said Peter, 'is that there are too many generals here, it was much easier in British Guiana.' But the trouble was far more deep-rooted than that. He was relieved early, when I was not around.

After Aden, we went up to Bahrain to see Tom Fanshawe (who was in charge in the Gulf under the Unified C.-in-C. Middle East) and his tidy establishment, *Jufair*. I also called on his US Navy colleague – always a useful thing to do. Before joining *Eagle*, I then flew to Singapore to report on my discussions to the Fleet Commander and to the Commander-in-Chief, and to give a presentation to him and the joint staff on how I thought the Fleet could play its part in supporting Aden up to the evacuation and afterwards. It seemed straightforward enough to me, but after I had finished, Michael Carver said, 'You make it sound too easy, Edward,' to which I could only reply, 'It will be all right if the resources I think we need can be made available.'

In the interval before my return to Singapore, Tamara had taken Tom back to England and Yardley Court, and had to prepare for her university term. Liz had taken off by train for Thailand, and penetrated as far as Chiang Mai, but she came back so that we could be together briefly before she returned home. I then flew to join *Eagle*, commanded by Ernle Pope, a good friend, at Gan. It was now nearly the end of September, and I took passage in *Eagle* and learned something about her *en route* to Aden, where I transferred my flag to *Fearless*, commanded by Mark Kerr. Classified as an Assault Ship, she was kitted up with a Supporting Arms Coordination Centre and the kind of operations room intended for use in amphibious or joint sea-land-air operations. Other ships were beginning to assemble: *Eagle*, a number of frigates and destroyers and *Albion*, now commanded by Godfrey Place, with a commando embarked. *Bulwark*, with another commando, was on the way, as was *Intrepid*, commanded by Tony Troup. We were gathering to make a show of force and to make certain that the planned departure from Aden was not held up through any fault on the part of the Fleet. There was a host of RFAs, as well as every LSL (Landing Ship Logistic) in commission.

All seemed well set, and I had had satisfactory conferences ashore when, on the morning of 6 November, I was woken around 5.50 a.m. by Jonathan Findlay, my flag lieutenant, who came in and said, 'I have bad news for you, Sir.' He handed me a telegram from Elizabeth with the shattering news that Tamara had been killed in the railway disaster at Hither Green the evening before. Poor Jonathan left, saying, 'I would have given anything not to have had to bring this to you, Sir.' After a while I sent a signal asking the Commander-in-Chief, Michael Le Fanu, if I could see him for urgent personal reasons that morning. He saw me at about 9 a.m., and I told him what had happened. I recommended that Godfrey Place was perfectly capable of taking charge of the force in the circumstances then prevailing, and requested compassionate leave to go to England for a spell and help Elizabeth. There was not the slightest difficulty about this, and Andrew Humphrey, the air commander, happened to be flying to the Gulf in his personal aircraft that afternoon and took me with him. A kinder or more sensitive companion I could not have had. From Bahrain, I took the first flight to England and arrived at 'South Cottage' on the morning of 8 November, just as Elizabeth was discussing the order of service for the memorial service for our daughter with David Bentley, the rector. She and Peter, who was a tower of strength, had been to see Tom at Yardley Court to tell him the dreadful news, and Peter came with me the next day to the cremation. The memorial service was held on 10 November in our little church at Headley, and the ashes were interred there. Later, Elizabeth and I went to Godden Green, where they also were inconsolable, and on the Sunday night I flew back to my job. What Elizabeth then endured I can only imagine, and it was only thanks to John Williams, the young doctor from the *Alert*, who was at Lewisham General Hospital at the time of the disaster, that she was spared the awful ordeal of identification of a dear child who had, we were told, been killed instantly.

Back in Aden there was much to do, and I was kept busy, for which I was very grateful. By then I had an assistant staff logistics officer, a staff gunnery officer and an assistant signal officer added to my complement in order to cope with the very great amount of detailed work that was now necessary. There must have been 15 RFAs under command, as well as the largest operational group of warships mustered by the Royal Navy since the Korean War. With a destroyer and four frigates, we badly needed some submarine time, and eventually one joined us on detachment. To keep people's hands in, I took the White Ensign ships to sea from time to time. A large contingent of the international press were hanging around Aden waiting for something to happen, so, with the Commander-in-Chief's approval, I arranged a press day at sea, gave *London* the tactical command, and instructed her captain to carry out the equivalent of marching manoeuvres with the ships and make as spectacular a show as possible. I took off in *Eagle*'s Wasp and took photographs.

Barge picnics with the Martins provided pleasant interludes. There were regular meetings with the Commander-in-Chief, the general and his Chief of Staff, an excellent officer called Charles Dunbar, as well as with Andrew Humphrey, the air commander, and Freddie Sowrey, his Chief of Staff. I would go to these by helicopter, my usual pilot being Tim Donkin, who had travelled out with Elizabeth to Singapore in July. I made a point of visiting all the units ashore, particularly the Royal Marine Commandos, and had an interesting day in Crater with the Argyll and Sutherland Highlanders, under the command of a character whom I had known before at the MoD and who came to be known to the public as 'Mad Mitch'. Most of his company commanders seemed to be twice his height, and maybe his small stature had something to do with his reputation. In any case, I think they kept a very good look-out for me, conspicuous in white uniform, wandering around with them in the least settled part of Aden at that time. I did form a very clear impression of the amount of sniping that went on and the difficulties with which our troops had to contend in operating within the rules of engagement that were imposed upon them.

Gradually, our time drew to a close, and we organised (more by way of amusing everybody than anything else) a review for the High Commissioner. It was a lovely day, the ships were well dressed in two lines, three in some cases, and Humphrey Trevelyan, on the upper bridge of a small minesweeper with the Commander-in-Chief and myself, passed the Fleet in review, everybody manning and cheering ship as he went by. He was, I think, greatly touched. On 27 November 1967, at the instigation of Michael Le Fanu, I gave a birthday dinner party for him in *Eagle*, with an enormous birthday cake produced by my Chinese chef. It was a very happy occasion. The next time I saw him was when I and the other Service Commanders went with the Commander-in-Chief to see the High Commissioner off on his aircraft for England. The days of the British flag in Aden now really were numbered.

Two days later, Michael Le Fanu departed, and Philip Tower became the Commander British Forces. Gradually, we embarked the last commandos, flew out the last units that were going home, and Philip Tower came on board *Intrepid*, to which I had now transferred. I then became Commander British Forces for the last few hours. At midnight on 30 November we weighed and sailed, and Aden became independent as soon as we cleared the three-mile limit. We left behind a skeleton high commission staff to look after the ambassador, Sir Robin Hooper, who was about to arrive, and also quite a sizeable number of British citizens. My orders were to keep a sufficient force within easy reach of Aden to intervene effectively should there be the kind of revolution that would endanger British subjects or the refinery. To do this, I kept an aircraft carrier (to which I transferred my flag from *Intrepid*), *Albion* (shortly to be relieved by *Bulwark* with a fresh commando embarked), three destroyers or frigates and the necessary RFAs, store ship, an oiler and an ammunition ship. The plan was simple: first, to use fixed-wing aircraft for reconnaissance and as a deterrent if trouble were signalled from the Embassy, then to secure the embarkation points by landing marines by helicopter, and finally, to embark everybody the same way or, if conditions allowed, by boat. In addition, the destroyers or frigates would stand inshore, ready to intervene with bombardment should that be necessary to effect the evacuation safely. There was a good deal of coordination required, and I used to exercise it all once a week, using the three RFAs, suitably disposed geographically, as the three planned evacuation points. It was easy to put everyone through their paces in this way, and most importantly, to exercise the communications. Since the aircraft carrier had to be free to operate as necessary for fixed-wing flying, I transferred to the commando ship for this purpose. I found the arrangements worked pretty well, and that I was in better touch with the air side generally than I could have been in the assault ship.

So there we were, stuck in the western Indian Ocean – indefinitely, it seemed at the time. *Hermes* came to relieve *Eagle*, and I transferred my flag again. Doug Parker, her new captain, had gone sick, and the commander, John Fieldhouse, was in acting command. I already knew him well from Lewin's time, and obtained approval for him to retain command. To give people a change at Christmas, I sent a couple of the RFAs to the Seychelles, another ship or two to Mombasa, but kept the main nucleus of the force together at sea, and planned to take them up to relax at Khor El Kuwai, a deserted and capacious stretch of water just inside the Straits of Hormuz which had been recommended to me by some expert on the Gulf. The staff arranged a pretty good range of activities, barbecues and so forth to take place ashore, and since it had to be organised to allow a quick return to readiness, an operation order was issued. This I gave the nickname 'Sandy Shaw', after the barefoot girl who sang 'Puppet on a String' at about that time. Unfortunately, there was a small Soviet squadron in the Arabian Sea, and people at home felt that we should stay not too far away from them in case something strange was brewing, so we never got to our sandy shore at all.

I spent my last Christmas at sea in *Hermes*, and very good it was. They had a particularly fine padre, we had a festival of lessons and carols in the hangar, and at Holy Communion on the quarterdeck on Christmas Eve there must have been well over 100 officers and men. *Hermes*, as always, was a very happy ship. Time in an aircraft carrier (and I had had plenty of that this year) is not particularly restful, even for the admiral. With everybody else busy day and night when flying is on, I had a guilty conscience sitting in my cabin aft, and would usually go up to the compass platform or to my bridge in order to witness the flying, often going into flying control to hear the kind of comments that were being made and to learn something more about this extraordinary business of landing very heavy, vastly expensive aircraft on a small deck, mostly done by young men of 22 or 23. Even if one stayed aft, the noise of the aircraft coming down on the deck above your head banished all thought of sleep. After Christmas, I shifted flag to *Bulwark*, partly to see something more of her, and also for a bit of a stand-easy, though they were active enough, too. However, the commando had been embarked quite a considerable time, and I wanted to find out how all that was going: how long it was sensible for this to continue for one particular set of marines. They also needed to stretch their legs whenever possible and I took her into Masirah, where there was nothing much except a large airfield on an island with beaches and hills – ideal for running about. While there, I took the opportunity to fly down to Salalah. Both of these stations were in those days commanded by squadron leaders, each very happy in his job and entirely up to it. (Before the end, I think they all became group captains; this upgrading of posts is often sadly the case and seldom necessary, but applies not only to the RAF.)

Having read Thesiger's book *Arabian Sands*, I arranged to fly across the Empty Quarter to Dubai by helicopter, a Wessex 5, escorted by a second similar aircraft in case of trouble. There must have been an operational justification for this fascinating excursion over the rolling sands, but I cannot now recall it. The consul-general in Mucat was married to the sister of Peter Russell, my secretary, so a call there was a must, and this we did from the ship off-shore, going in by helicopter in the early morning. We spent a whole day there, wandering round this spectacular, ancient Arab city, and among other things, being briefed on the plans for the Sultan's armed forces in the future. Then it was back to *Hermes* and a long tele-conference with the MoD. First the VCNS, now Peter Hill-Norton, tried to persuade me that I no longer needed an aircraft carrier to do the job off Aden. I was adamant that nothing else would serve to produce the kind of deterrent that was necessary to conduct a bloodless evacuation, and I prevailed. The CDS understood, but the Navy, the naval air groups in particular, were beginning to feel the strain.

Eagle was now well on her way back, and as soon as she joined and I had both carriers in company, Derek Empson, the flag officer aircraft carriers, flew out to conduct his own two-carrier exercise this time, and to inspect one or other of the ships. I therefore agreed with the Fleet commander that Ged Mansfield, the commodore amphibious forces, based in Singapore (who had had rather a dull ride since his ships had spent so much time off Aden), should come out and relieve me in command of the Aden force for the next spell of covering the ex-colony. The staff and I then transferred to *Fife*, commanded by Peter Lachlan, and played a supporting role in Derek Empson's exercise. I was able to board *Dreadnought*, the first British nuclear submarine, which was in company, and spend a night in her. (I am ashamed to say this is the only night I have ever spent submerged.)

At the end of January 1968, it was decided that the ambassador was settled and happy in Aden, and the covering force was withdrawn; the Fleet was able to go about more congenial business. Part of my job was to inspect the larger ships of the Fleet, other than the aircraft carriers, and also the ships of the various captains of the destroyer or frigate squadrons. By now I had already inspected *Bulwark*, and doing so was a considerable chore, not only for the staff but for me personally, since in the course of it I was bound to visit more or less every compartment they showed me – and more particularly, some that they did not. It also involved a great deal of detailed technical work for the staff.

After Aden, there was a backlog of inspections, which we gradually dealt with. They included an Australian frigate, *Yarra*, which did manfully, and impressed me with its enthusiasm, but also (and I do not mean to be discourteous) with its rather old-fashioned approach. I realised that they were doing extremely well a great many things that we were trying to do well towards the end of the war. They had missed out on the technical changes that had taken place, partly because they had started their own officer specialist training and ceased to send as many people as before to the UK. Instead, they were sending officers to the USA for training, but my impression of US naval operations rooms (or CICs, as they still called them) was that, as in the Pacific in 1945, they were nothing like as efficient as ours.

Nevertheless, it was evident to me and my staff that our own operations rooms were still not functioning properly. For example, I would ask a question of some perfectly competent officer, who would feel that he had to send for the specialist (or sub-specialist, as they were now called) in that particular discipline in order to answer my question fully or at all: for instance, I might ask the navigating officer what was happening on the anti-submarine plot, and he would say, 'Just a moment Sir, I'll get hold of the torpedo and anti-submarine officer.' Added to this, it seemed to me that we had far more intelligent ratings than we used to have, and that they were very often underused, underexploited perhaps, and therefore bored and not as interested as they ought to have been. This was particularly evident in the frigates. In the destroyers I knew best (as I had my flag in all of them from time to time), *Fife*, *Glamorgan* and *Devonshire*, the very complicated and semi-computerised air defence systems tended to be operated in quite different ways depending, it seemed to me, on the approach of the commanding officer of each to the advice he was being given.

No system is perfect, and I formed the conclusion that there was something wrong in the way that we were training our officers. This feeling also derived from two particular prejudices of my own. One was inherited from Father, who felt that specialisation was merely a necessary evil, and the other from my own particular signals specialisation, where time and again I had tried to get electronic warfare properly integrated into the operations room and found this almost impossible because it was regarded as a 'black art' on the part of the signalmen, and no part of the 'hard kill' gunnery, torpedo and anti-submarine systems. In general, it seemed to me that the ships which the Fleet Commander had placed under my operational command were well officered and well manned, and I kept these other thoughts to myself until towards the end of my time.

I now had a short spell in Singapore, wrote my reports on the Aden operation and then transferred the flag to *Devonshire*, commanded by Richard Emden, a senior captain, for a Fleet visit to Sydney. I took *Triumph*, the Fleet repair ship, for the jaunt, a number of frigates and destroyers, and a submarine. We carried out quite extensive exercises with the Australians before anchoring in Botany Bay to prepare for our ceremonial entry into Sydney harbour. This went well, and we passed under the bridge, up round Cockatoo Island and then back to our berths, so giving anyone interested a chance to have a look at us. I had not seen the Opera House before. It was now about two-thirds complete, and a great addition to the harbour view, I thought. Calls, dinners, cocktail parties and so forth went on, but the object of the visit was a run ashore for the sailors in something like the conditions which they most enjoy.

The ships dispersed to various port visits, and I detached in *Euryalus*, commanded by James Pertwee, for Wellington, to pay my first visit to New Zealand. The head of the New Zealand Navy at the time was Laurence Carr, a signal officer. The naval base commander was Ted Thorne, whom I had taught on his signals Long Course at *Mercury*, so I arrived among friends. The approach to Wellington (known as 'Wet and Windy', but reasonably kind to us on the day), was lovely. After a spell there, *Euryalus* was due to sail north to Auckland. Although I did not get to South Island, I was given a flight in a light aircraft to have a look at some of it, and happily fell in with Ted Thorne's suggestion that while the ship sailed north I should go overland, visiting their wireless transmitter station on the way. This was self-consciously naval: a collection of buildings up at Waioru, proudly claiming to sport the highest anchor in the world as part of their equipment.

After flying back to Singapore, I decided to break away and show a few others the delights of the islands off the east coast of Malaysia, so I hoisted my flag in *Defender* (sister of *Decoy* of Caribbean days), and took her and two other frigates up to Bangkok. By now, Jonathan Findlay's time was up, and his relief was a large, young officer called Chris Cobley, who turned out to be a bit of an expert on tape recorders. This was important, because in the long hours when I was by myself in my cabin I often listened to music of one sort or another, there being very little routine paperwork connected with the job, though there were gluts of it from time to time.

I made it my practice to expend my entertainment allowance to the full. In the bigger ships, I used to have dinner parties at sea for a fairly large, mixed bag of officers – ship and staff – not involved in duty that particular evening. I enjoyed these very much, and learned a great deal in the course of them. I well remember one young officer in *Eagle* saying to me after dinner, 'Sir, where have you been all your time in the Navy? The Fleet Air Arm never seems to have heard of you?' I suppose I replied that I had been around. Certainly it was a very good way of getting to know a cross-section of naval officers and hear their views, and the object of the evenings was to be as informal and cheerful as possible.

The visit to Bangkok was made all the pleasanter for me because the naval attaché, John Sayer (a cousin of Elizabeth) and his wife are delightful people. He had hit it off very well with his High Commissioner, and helped me to re-establish relations with the Royal Thai Navy, last met in 1953. Thanks largely to Sayer, they were about to buy a frigate from Yarrow, so they were naturally very interested in the ships I had brought in. John and Molly took me on some lovely expeditions and helped me with some good shopping. It all made a welcome change from the Indian Ocean off Aden.

On the return voyage to Singapore, I stopped at Pulau Redang, bringing the squadron to anchor in a large bay I knew on the eastern coast for swimming and a barbecue. This was well away from the village, and was,

I think, enjoyed. Certainly, as far as I was concerned, it was lovely to be snorkelling over those reefs again, and I found a couple of good cowries. At about this time I paid a visit to the American Naval Base in Subic Bay. This was a farewell call, as I had previously been there for exercises and had met the admiral, Fill Gilkeson, whom I liked enormously. In many ways, he had a dreadful job: Subic was not only a maintenance base, but also an important recreation port for the ships of the US Pacific Fleet. A little up-country, at Olongopo, there was a typical Filipino 'city of vice'. There was not much Fill could do about it, nor about the problems that the sailors brought back on board with them. Our own men were more restrained and much less involved, if at all, in the drugs scene, but our ships did not visit more often than was necessary to make use of the excellent US exercise facilities.

At the end of May I hoisted my flag in *Intrepid* once more, embarked my official car, a Humber, and also a small hovercraft to be demonstrated to the Maritime Self-Defence Force, and set sail for Japan. This official visit by the Flag Officer Second-in-Command Far East Fleet coincided with a flying visit by Rochford Hughes, the Air Commander, and his family. Tony Troup was an excellent flag captain, and ran a very good ship. The cabin arrangements in *Intrepid* allowed for a land force commander and a naval commander, so there was ample room for us both. We were met at Yokusuka by John Robathan, a naval aviator and the attaché, whom I had not known before. He and Anna, his wife, helped to make a great success of the programme which had been arranged around the Queen's Birthday. The ambassador was a splendid character, Sir John Pilcher, who spoke fluent Japanese. I had read a book or two before coming to Tokyo this time, including one splendid tome entitled *Five Gentlemen of Japan*, which did something to dispel my rather settled prejudices dating from China and the war. The commander of the Japanese Maritime Self-Defence Force was Admiral Samejima, who received me with great courtesy and returned my call, dealing happily with the usual ceremonial. To my surprise, Pilcher was extremely reluctant to accept the suggestion that the Royal Marine Band should play at his garden party on the Queen's Birthday and beat the retreat at the end of it, for which a suitable flagpole was already available in the garden. He was really anxious lest it should be considered a militarist affair. When, after all, he agreed to give it a go, it turned out to be a lovely evening and the Royals did well. At the end of it, Pilcher came up to me, thrilled to bits, to say that it had been a wonderful affair and that the French ambassadress had been in tears! I felt no higher compliment could have been paid, so that was good. I found it strange to be in the Embassy compound again and to see it cheerful and busy compared with the autumn of 1945, when Admiral Collins and John Robertson were holding the fort there. The drive from Yokusuka to Tokyo showed no sign of war and there was really nothing to recognise at all except the waters of the bay.

The car had been landed, and my brave coxswain drove me around the Tokyo area as necessary. The Robathans took us to Lake Chusenji and Nikko in lovely weather, far different from the winter of 1945. When *Intrepid* was due to sail through the Inland Sea and then north to the Sea of

Japan and the naval base at Maizuru, I sent the car with the coxswain to Kyoto and determined to do the journey myself overland, combining it with a trip to Kyoto with the Robathans and the Hughes family. We saw a great many of the interesting and beautiful temples and gardens. I then drove Robathan through mountainous and attractive country, and there, in Maizuru, was *Intrepid* waiting for us. The local admiral was an ardent Zen Buddhist, and he talked at length about his faith and the exercises in which he indulged in order to further it. My call on him was enlivened by a traditional Japanese tea ceremony, the girls, although dressed in national costume, being the Japanese equivalent of Wrens.

The main object of the visit to Maizuru was to demonstrate the hovercraft, in the hope of helping its sales, and I took the admiral and some of his staff on a three-hour jaunt across the bay and back. The weather was quite appalling and not altogether without risk to the craft. The danger is of broaching-to, particularly if there is a following wind. The craft starts to slew, and its airscrew tends to push it over. It was a safe ride as it turned out, but an extremely uncomfortable one. However, I believe that they were impressed by the seaworthiness the hovercraft displayed. Personally, I was very happy to get back to the ship.

We paused briefly at Hong Kong on the way south, and once back in Singapore, I again transferred the flag to *Albion* for exercises and for her sea and harbour inspections. Martin Ollivant was then in command, having taken over from Godfrey Place, and I remember being pleased with the ship's showing. The staff and I were due for a spell of harder work after the relaxation of the visit to Japan, and *Albion*'s inspection provided it. This over, I shifted to *Fife*, commanded by Peter Lachlan, for a farewell visit to Hong Kong. While I was in her, in July, I was promoted to vice-admiral. As usual, everybody enjoyed Hong Kong. The staff decided to give me a run ashore, and recruited two Hong Kong policemen to see fair play – one white and one Chinese. So we went round some of the sleazier parts of the mainland in good company, had an excellent dinner, and returned safely to the ship. There were all sorts of calls, and I was able to do some entertaining.

I was told that I was to relieve Hill-Norton as VCNS towards the end of the year. Michael Le Fanu had taken over as First Sea Lord from Varyl Begg. I looked forward to serving him again, although I never felt that I was one of his cronies, our personalities being so very different. It was time to write my haul-down report to give the Fleet commander my opinion of his Fleet and any part of its constitution or activities that occurred to me. I wrote also a separate letter, which Bill copied to the C.-in-C. Western Fleet, who was then John Bush. In this, I expressed my disquiet about the overspecialisation, as I saw it, of the seaman officer, and recommended that there should be a radical overhaul of the specialist system with a view to producing people who were tactically or warfare qualified rather than primarily trained in gunnery, signals, torpedoes and antisubmarine, navigation or other special disciplines. I said that I felt that officers nowadays knew more and more about less and less, and that, in the missile age that was approaching, there was no time for the kind of deliberations that too often went on in our operations rooms. I also said my piece about the manifest advantage of exploiting the more intelligent and potentially self-confident ratings that we now had in the service. These letters were finished on passage to Singapore in *Fife*. I then paid my farewell calls, Tony Griffin came to relieve me with the usual ceremonies, and I flew back to England on 18 August, giving me the tail end of the summer holidays with Tom at home.

The sense of loss of Tamara was acute at home, and everyone was very brave. I was thankful to be back. All was otherwise pretty well at Godden Green, although Father's back was a constant source of pain to him, and rendered him virtually immobile. Mousse was still able to get about, however. She would go up to London on Wednesdays, play her bridge, and generally do her very best to carry on enjoying life. Lionel Sturdee was still fit, and on hearing that I was to be appointed to the Admiralty Board, he very sweetly sent me a Navy List of 1801 that had belonged to his father. He lived in Winchester, and Tom was set to go to Winchester College, which seemed to have many advantages, although I should have preferred a rather less academic place for him.

The holidays over, Elizabeth and I decided to go abroad somewhere where she could catch up on all the sunshine that I had enjoyed and she had missed. We chose Cyprus, and saw almost the whole island at a beautiful time of the year. We returned having put in an offer for a holiday home in Lapithos. Next we had to find somewhere to live during my job as VCNS, and thanks to Elizabeth we settled on a flat, 14B The Oval, which suited us extremely well.

It was an interesting time to take over as VCNS: the whole fabric of the surface Fleet had been shattered by the Labour government's decision not to replace the large aircraft carriers, and many in Whitehall and in parliament were determined that never again should the Navy compete with the RAF by flying fixed-wing aircraft at sea. Those of us with sea experience, however, knew that, through no fault of theirs, the RAF could not always be where we needed them when we wanted them, so there was no substitute for some aircraft organic to the Fleet to provide a standing presence and fixed patrols, and to meet the initial brunt of any surprise attack.

In the first shock of the decision, Varyl Begg and John Bush, determined to bite on the bullet, had instituted a Future Fleet Working Party to shape a Fleet without aircraft carriers. This had reported that carrier-type ships were required if the Fleet was to operate globally, but had been overruled by Begg. All that was allowed was an 'escort cruiser', whose operational requirement was being processed when I joined. This was reaching the point at which a sketch design was being made, and Hill-Norton (who had relieved John Bush and was now to relieve Carver in the Far East) told me that whatever happened, I should not try to get it through politicians or the Chiefs of Staff at a cost of more than £22,000,000. It was to operate a number of anti-submarine helicopters, with their 'dunking sonars', on which the anti-submarine defence of the Fleet had come greatly to depend.

Hill-Norton had established an ACNS for air matters, and reorganised the whole staff on functional lines. These provided for a Directorate of Naval Warfare. My proposals from sea for a reorganisation of the seaman sub-specialist branches had been well received by both Fleet commanders, and were now the business of this new directorate. From my point of view, I therefore joined at a particularly fortunate time to carry my own proposals through, subject to the rest of the Admiralty Board agreeing, and this became one of the major aims of my time in office. Michael Le Fanu went along with it in general, but feeling that so much had already happened to shake the Navy, believed that the change should be evolutionary rather than revolutionary. Nevertheless, he supported the various steps that had to be taken, which, in effect, did produce a revolution.

Sub-specialist courses were replaced by a Principal Warfare Officer's Course in the space of something like four years. To achieve this, I thought it necessary to have a submarine officer as the Director of Naval Warfare, and had selected first Lance Bell-Davies, who was succeeded in due course by John Fieldhouse. It became their job to investigate with the schools what elements of special expertise should be included in the course syllabus, and to phase in the PWO Course, adjusting ships' complements and ratings' training and responsibilities to match. As a first step along the road in practice, two ships, *Jupiter* and *Achilles*, both Leander Class frigates, were detailed off as PWO trial ships. They were beginning their trials when I eventually took over the Fleet.

This project, and the through-deck cruiser, with its flat top, clearly able to take the Harrier-type aircraft that were just coming into service with the RAF, were among my principal concerns as VCNS. There were many others. Despite the support of Frank Twiss, the Second Sea Lord, I failed to persuade the board to have the new Type 22 frigate designed with economy of manpower as an overriding requirement. However, with the help of Sir William Cook, the deputy chief scientific adviser (projects), I succeeded in negotiating an agreement with the French to put the Exocet missile into the surface Fleet. I was able to make less progress with the requirement for a submarine-launched missile, Ondine, but at least succeeded in keeping it in the programme. As well as the French missile, which occasioned some difficulty with the controller, I was also able to override his preference and procure a working, US-made, lightweight anti-submarine torpedo. At a crucial meeting, I was offered the choice and made it. 'Edward,' said Michael Pollock, 'You've chosen the wrong one,' but he did not appeal against me to the board, for which I was grateful.

All these Whitehall battles loomed large, but perhaps I should explain the duties and responsibilities of the VCNS, which were paralleled by the vice-chiefs of the other two services. I was a member of the Admiralty Board, the other members being the under-secretary of state for the Navy, David Owen; First Sea Lord, Michael Le Fanu; Controller, Horace Law; Second Sea Lord, Frank Twiss; Chief of Fleet Support, 'Atty' Turner; Chief Scientific Adviser, Basil Lythall, and the Permanent Under-Secretary of State, Royal Navy, who was Sydney Redman. Pollock later relieved Law, and Andrew Lewis relieved Twiss. The job of deputy chief of the naval staff had been abolished, and his duties absorbed by VCNS. We would meet once a month, on a Thursday, and were collectively responsible for the naval component of the defence system. The VCNS was responsible for operations and superintendence of the whole of the naval staff, which included policy, plans, ship and weapon requirements and operations. The Commandant-General Royal Marines and Director of Naval Intelligence also reported to me. C.-in-C. Western Fleet, now Bill O'Brien, was directly responsible to me, as was the Commander Eastern Fleet on single-service matters, although for operations he reported to his Unified Commander-in-Chief. The First Sea Lord was CNS, so I reported direct to him in all these matters. He was Naval Member of the Chiefs of Staffs Committee, and there was also a Vice-Chiefs of Staffs Committee which handled certain business for the chiefs at their direction, the convention being that the vice-chiefs' decisions were then as authoritative as those of the chiefs themselves – the Chiefs of Staff never revised any decision that the vice-chiefs had already taken. The chiefs usually met once a week, the vice-chiefs less often.

I joined to find that a multitude of people on the naval staff found their minister, David Owen, extremely difficult to deal with. However, Michael Le Fanu, with his usual flair, had realised that we had with us a potentially very good minister indeed, and the word went out that however difficult or rude he might seem, our job was to help him all we could. David responded to this, and I never found him anything but reasonable, though the argument might have to go on for a long time, and you sometimes found that he was right, not you.

I had not been in my job long before it became painfully apparent that our brilliant chief, Michael Le Fanu, was not at all well. Nothing was said, and no name was put to the illness, but from time to time it became necessary for him to have a massive blood transfusion, after which he would return, firing on all cylinders. Later, you would notice him begin to fade, to lose interest and energy, and then the next transfusion would have to take place. Much has been written about him at his best, and then there was no one better. His instinct for what really mattered, his gift with people, his unique turn of phrase and the personal qualities that made him a born leader were renowned throughout the Navy, and indeed beyond. He was clearly cut out to be an exceptional CDS, and the luck of timing had lined him up for that post at the end of his three years as First Sea Lord. But with all the other problems which faced him, now he also had to battle with his illness, which was clearly leukaemia.

It had started quite suddenly when he returned from a visit to the Far East Fleet, where, off Pulau Tioman, he had visited something like 16 ships in two days, addressing the ships' companies, giving of his all in the visits and returning to Whitehall exhausted. As time went on, his health deteriorated, and I talked privately to James Watt, the medical director-general, about my master. I learned little more than I could see with my own eyes. Gradually, I had to attend the Chiefs of Staffs Committee Meetings in his place and do the odd other chore on his behalf. 'Sam' Elworthy, Marshal of the RAF, was the CDS, and I endeavoured to stand in for Michael.

The VCNS job involved very little travelling, although early on I went to a seapower symposium at the US Naval War College at Newport, Rhode Island. They really wanted John Frewen, who had made a great success with NATO when he had been C.-in-C. Channel; he was now simply C.-in-C. Portsmouth, the Channel command having been shifted to Northwood, so he and I went together. I thoroughly enjoyed his company and the whole affair. It was marked particularly for me by meeting the American admiral in charge at Rhode Island, Dick Colbert, and his English wife, who became great friends of Elizabeth and myself. The place was thronged with NATO and other foreign naval officers, so we made some useful contacts as well. Mostly, I just 'flew the desk' in Whitehall.

Around the middle of my time in office, there was a general election, which Labour lost. Peter Carrington came as the Secretary of State for Defence, and I remember briefing him on his taking over the job. It was one of Mike's bad days; I was sitting on his left at the table, but he asked me to speak. The new Navy minister was Peter Kirk, a nice man, but like so many Tory ministers, inclined to accept what you said as being the whole answer – which indeed it was meant to be. It often lacked the political dimension, however, and he was therefore nothing like as effective as David Owen had been.

Earlier that very month, Denis Healey had approved the construction of a through-deck cruiser at a cost of £42,250,000, and I now faced going through the whole thing again in order to convince Lord Carrington that the Navy needed such an expensive 'toy' to carry helicopters around. One still could not mention the Sea Harrier, for the Chiefs of Staff would, in a majority, have ruled against it and the ship, too. Eventually, approval was given, and it was only then that I realised that almost no one in the naval staff or at Ship Department, Bath, had ever believed that we would get it through. By the time the first ship was launched, I had left the Admiralty, so I bore no responsibility for naming her *Invincible* (not, I think, a good choice: it reminded me of the first choice of name for our second nuclear submarine, *Inflexible*; from my desk at Plans I intervened to change it, with the approval of VCNS, to *Valiant*).

The vice-chiefs had no representational function – we really were the 'desk wallahs', and I found that one of the great advantages of the job lay in getting to know the workings of the MoD fairly well and becoming acquainted with those civil servants who carried weight within the ministry. I represented the Navy on the Permanent Under-Secretary of State's Committee for Headquarters Reorganisation, which was never very far from anybody's minds (a legacy, I suppose, from 'Dickie'), so I knew Sir James Dunnett and the other permanent under-secretaries. I also represented the MoD on the Shipping Defence Advisory Committee, and met a good many important people in that industry as a result. That it was a grind cannot be denied but, as John Bush said to me once, 'You will find it much easier being VCNS than being director of plans,' and he was quite right.

However, I did meet interesting people. I fielded an American rear-admiral, 'Bud' Zumwalt, on his way from commanding the Riverine Force in Vietnam to be Chief of Naval Operations over the heads of countless older contenders. He was shyer than I expected, and enjoyed our lunch and talk; finding that his wife was a Russian from Shanghai helped the atmosphere. I also met Ralph Cousins, back from commanding the US carriers 'on the line' off Vietnam, and a very distinguished naval aviator indeed. He was to be Vice-Chief of Naval Operations to 'Bud' eventually, and to try to keep the US Navy on the rails amid a turmoil of 'reform'.

I also had two rather different experiences of television exposure. The first was at 15 minutes' notice, to rebut a long newspaper article by, I think, Geoffrey Williams alleging, wholly inaccurately, a vulnerability on the part of our Polaris submarines. This was easily done in a makeshift studio in the MoD basement. It came across well, except that I noticed a twitching of my left thumb of which I had been wholly unconscious at the time. I made a mental note for the future – if you can't keep your hands still, keep them out of sight! For the second appearance, I had all too much notice. It was to give the Trafalgar Night address at the Royal Naval College, Greenwich, in 1969. I spent considerable effort on the speech, borrowing some good phrases from Arthur Bryant and others, and learning much of it by heart. It went well, and I have used many versions of it since. The broadcast showed the cameras to be far more interested in the baron of beef than the speaker, which was convenient!

Also in 1969, I was summoned to give a disquisition on Soviet Fleet capability at a SACLANT symposium at Norfolk, Virginia, not long after 'Bud' had become CNO. It went encouragingly well, being acclaimed by the doyen of the Permanent Representatives, the Belgian Ambassador, as the best presentation he had heard in NATO: high praise indeed, and full marks to the naval staff.

I was always conscious of the immense privilege of being a Member of the Board of Admiralty. Le Fanu instituted a series of informal, short weekend visits at which the board could thrash out various problems and visit a naval establishment at the same time. We went to Yeovilton, the Naval Air Command HQ, *Mercury* and Greenwich, among others. It was Michael's way of working, and often good value. Formal meetings were held in the Board Room in the old Admiralty building, from the rest of which we had been mostly displaced by the Civil Service Department. The board would assemble in the little room on the left of the main entrance (in which Nelson's body had lain before the funeral procession to St Paul's). We would then file upstairs to the Board Room, which is festooned with carving by Grinling Gibbons, redolent of the Navy's history and equipped with a wind direction indicator, which often showed the wind as coming from France. The large table had a semicircle cut from one end – one board member, long ago, had been so ample as to require this. The minister would sit facing the fireplace and wind indicator, the First Sea Lord on his right, the permanent under-secretary on his left. I, as VCNS, sat on the First Sea Lord's right, at one end with the Second Sea Lord, controller, and CFS on my right in that order facing the minister and the chief scientist across from me with AUS(NS), our secretary. The atmosphere was conducive to state affairs, and our deliberations for the most part reflected this.

One day a face from the past suddenly appeared. I was asked to sit with the future cabinet secretary, John Hunt (then head of the Civil Service Department) on an interview board for candidates to succeed Fred Stannard as head of the Communications Electronics Security Department. Among them was Arthur Foden, ex ACDS(S), and I was delighted to be able to help him secure the post. I was not required to sit on naval promotion boards unless I wished to, VCNS being generally thought too busy. However, I regarded this as important, and I knew a great many of the eligible officers from sea, so I did so and saw the necessary confidential reports accordingly. It was, I am sure, worthwhile.

Eventually, the writing was plain on the wall, and Le Fanu realised that he could not hope to discharge the duties of CDS. He announced his retirement as First Sea Lord, and Hill-Norton was appointed. The letters and signals he sent out were infused as much with optimism as regret. The board charged me with organising a suitable surprise send-off. I arranged this in one of our Cutlass Class fast training boats on the Thames, having first made sure that Pru Le Fanu, stricken by polio since girlhood, could be managed down the ladders, and so on. All embarked safely, and Michael was in great form. Though cold, we cruised down river and secured alongside a barge off Greenwich for a good supper. In the course of this, we were boarded by the customs men to check that our drink was all 'duty paid'. It was, and they left quietly. The whole exercise was, I believe, a success. Certainly, Le Fanu was very nice about it.

Michael's departure was him at his best: he refused to have ceremonial guards and such frills, and staff and friends all mustered on the steps of the MoD outside the North Door. Down he came, escorted by me as his No. 2, threw his bowler hat into the waiting crowd, laughed, jumped into his car and was driven away. When Hill-Norton was appointed CDS and Michael Pollock chosen to relieve him, Michael wrote me a private letter, as he put it, 'To someone who ought to have been First Sea Lord but will be,' which was very generous of him. He died about a year later of a massive heart attack. His system could no longer stand the blood transfusions it had had to endure. With the Admiralty Board, I attended his memorial service in the Abbey in December. The First Sea Lord read the lesson, and the address was well given by Humphrey Trevelyan.

On his return as First Sea Lord, Hill-Norton promptly removed Leslie Townsend, my secretary, whom I had inherited from him and who had been a tower of strength through my time as VCNS. I asked Peter White for a name, and thanks to the kindness of Pat Bailey, whom he was then serving, secured Ken Wilcockson, a delightful, calm and considerate person who made an admirable interface between me in my less tolerant moments and people who wanted to see me.

An interesting episode worth a mention took place after Hill-Norton had become First Sea Lord. I was happily in bed at The Oval when the telephone rang. It was the duty commander to say that *Ark Royal*, under Lygo's command, had been in collision with a Soviet destroyer, but as far as was known, there were no casualties. I asked a question or two about the circumstances, and decided that matters were in hand and that I would not go in unless the duty minister became excited. However, I rang about a hour later to learn the score, to hear that First Sea Lord was in the operations room. Since he lived so close I felt only a little guilty, and did no more. Peter Hill-Norton did not refer to my absence the next day, and indeed, the whole incident had been well handled on the spot and by Fleet HQ. (In retrospect, I believe I was lazy and overcontemptuous of Soviet incompetence.)

Father and Mousse celebrated their Golden Wedding anniversary at Godden Green on 23 February 1969, and it was a wonderful day, with all of us there except our Tamara. Peter, who was then Chief of Staff at Fleet HQ, Northwood, was soon to be promoted to vice-admiral and go to Malta as the Chief of the Allied Staff to the C.-in-C. Allied Forces Mediterranean, an Italian admiral called Roselli Lorenzini. I was glad for this reason, too, to be home in England.

In summer 1969 I was rung up at the office and told that my mother was in St George's Hospital. Mousse had tried to dodge across Piccadilly, as usual, forgetting that she was getting older, and had to recoil from a taxi, which fortunately stopped instead of hitting her. In doing so, she fell and hurt her ankle. I found her in hospital, very shaken, but was able to take her home. Soon after she had to accept giving up driving, and this hit her independence hard. Father, in constant pain from his back and having retreated from society because he no longer felt comfortable except with good old friends, was no longer cheerful company. A slow and sad decline set in for both of them, but not before Mousse had been able to go to Malta and see Peter and his family there.

I was created a Knight Commander of the Bath on 1 January 1971, and received the accolade from the Queen herself. It was a great occasion, and a recognition of Elizabeth, too. Sadly, her father, that dear old gentleman Lionel Sturdee, died in Winchester on 19 December, just before this, but we think he heard the news. His loss was greatly felt. He had been a tower of strength, not least after Tamara's death, but had long been poorly, though he bore ill-health and bereavement with typical fortitude and humour.

By now I knew I was to relieve Bill O'Brien as C.-in-C. Western Fleet. My final injunction to Terry Lewin, who took over my chair, was to keep the Harrier in his sights come what may – I felt it was in safe hands, but I hoped there would be no 'crunch' for a while. Because of the reshuffle induced by poor Michael's illness, the timings were wrong, and I had a splendid spell of leave ahead, but the Chiefs of Staff had other ideas. A problem had arisen with the Royal United Services Institution which, faced with a large increase in rent for its premises in Whitehall, could no longer make both ends meet. They had appealed to the Chiefs for support. I was commissioned to report on the subject, given a small room in the old War Office next to someone studying court martial reform, and a share in his secretary. It was a far cry from having the services of some 200 of the cleverest officers in the Navy. I formed the view that the independence of thought and action of the RUSI were vital and subsidy by government would be inconsistent with this. They seemed to agree. I then realised that the Royal Institute of International Affairs at Chatham House in St James's Square owned their freehold. It seemed to me that the national interest could best be served by a single Royal Institute of International Affairs and Defence Studies, and that the way there lay in co-locating the RUSI and RIIA at Chatham House. Humphrey Trevelyan, head of the RIIA, agreed, and General Sir Napier Crookenden of the RUSI agreed, uncertainly, to give it a whirl with his council. I was, not for the first time, quite convinced by my own idea, and submitted a paper to the Chiefs accordingly. Naturally, the RUSI Council wanted nothing to do with 'those lefties' in St James's Square, nor did the RIIA people much relish 'those Blimps' in Whitehall – reactions which I thought proved my case. I was thanked for my paper, but the chiefs were let off the hook on which I had tried to impale them: the Heath government decided to reduce the RUSI's rent, and that institution gratefully accepted the government subsidy.

We now relinquished the flat at The Oval which had stood us in such good stead. Since we had bought the derelict village house in Lapithos we had been to Cyprus for most of our holidays. The spell of leave between the MoD and going to Fleet HQ was ideal, as we were able to get to Cyprus and see the work in progress. Eventually, in late July, we decided the only way to have it completed was to cohabit with the builders, and moved in. The result was that by August 1971, after many vicissitudes (including the marriage of our builder's daughter, whose house took priority over ours), it was finished. Now that it could serve as a holiday base, we decided to let 'South Cottage'. It seemed important to make Admiralty House at Northwood our home, since only then could we both perform the full social task that the job entailed.

CHAPTER SEVEN

Fleet Command

1971–4

In September 1971, I duly relieved my old chief, Admiral Sir William O'Brien, as C.-in-C. Western Fleet, C.-in-C. Eastern Atlantic and Allied C.-in-C. Channel at Fleet HQ at Northwood. Bill had suggested that we might wear full dress for the ceremony – guard, band, and so forth – but I had demurred as I had thought this was overdoing it, particularly in NATO's eyes. The naval full dress, even as modified by Mountbatten, was rather more elaborate than our allies (particularly the Americans, I thought) would have found suitable. So ceremonies were conducted in sword and medals, and they went well.

Bill, most unfortunately, had no further appointment (which I considered then, and consider now, a rank injustice). He would have made an admirable Second Sea Lord, but I believe he was not as highly regarded by Le Fanu and Hill-Norton, and Andrew Lewis, who relieved Frank Twiss as Second Sea Lord, was a fellow gunnery officer and a great personal friend of Le Fanu. Horace Law, on relief by Pollock, both gunnery officers, had been sent to relieve Frewen at Portsmouth, so there was no job available for Bill. On the subject of the full dress, he told me much later that he had never had occasion to wear his, and hoped that his relief by me might have furnished one. If I had been a little less pompous about the international image, it would have done no harm at all to have worn it, and now I wish we had.

Since the subject of gunnery officers seems to have encroached into this narrative, I would remark only that this admirable fraternity enjoyed, and indeed often earned, a predominance in the higher ranks of the Navy over many years. This tends to come to be self-perpetuating, since able and ambitious young officers would naturally elect for gunnery when they could. The changes in the Navy I was fostering make this a matter of historical interest only.

My flag was hoisted in *Resolution* for the day (namesake of Elizabeth's father's last command). I inherited Bill's delightful flag lieutenant, Simon Merriman, and as Bill and Rita drove off to retirement, Simon was in tears. This was an indication that we were taking over from a splendid and well-loved couple. In addition to a Fleet in good heart, they left us an Admiralty House in excellent order, with a first-rate staff led by Chief Petty Officer Jerry Lewis. For a time, I inherited as secretary Paddy Vincent (who had been a paymaster midshipman under Peter White long ago in *Duke of York*), until Ken Wilcockson could turn over the problems of the vice-chief's office and rejoin me.

The headquarters at Northwood consisted of a national element, administrative as well as operational, for the British Fleet above ground and an international one for NATO operational responsibilities, both Channel and Eastern Atlantic, in what was cheerfully called 'The Tunnel'. Ian Jamieson of my term was Chief of Staff on the national side, and Jan Klaver, a Royal Netherlands Navy rear-admiral was Chief of Staff for NATO. Both were bright and efficient, but their personalities were totally different: Ian was cheerful and calm, Jan was curt and aggressive, given the chance. There was an Air Commander Eastern Atlantic and Channel, who also commanded 18 Group RAF of Strike Command. He had inherited the resources and tasks of the old Coastal Command RAF, and had, supposedly, first call on those Buccaneer and Phantom Squadrons of Strike Command which replaced Fleet Air Arm squadrons previously borne on carriers. He was a very pleasant man called Bobby Craven (who was relieved by Tony Heward, followed by Douglas Lowe).

They had a rather difficult assignment in some ways, being directly responsible to me in the NATO chain of command, but responsible to their own British Commander-in-Chief in the national one. The latter, however, was Andrew Humphrey, a very dedicated light-blue officer, and an extremely efficient and likeable person. I had never forgotten his kindness to me in the Aden days, as well as our work together. He was one of my first calls, and we hit it off pretty well. He had been the Director of Joint Plans RAF after Derek Stapleton, and so had sat round the same table as myself for a short while in the early 1960s.

Since Bill had been in charge, I felt confident that the Fleet could look after itself for a while without my particular attention, and that my priorities must rest with NATO and, as always, with making contact with our principal support and ally, the United States. It was therefore very fortunate that I joined in time for the annual Military Committee Tour, which this year was to take in the USA and Canada. Elizabeth and I flew to Brussels, joined the tour there at the end of September, and went round with them to Washington, Norfolk and Ottawa in particular, but also with a side trip, from which the wives were excluded, to Nellis AFB at Nevada. Here we saw the new F111 aircraft with, among other things, an interesting ejection arrangement which sent the whole cockpit up into the air. There was then a jaunt to Las Vegas.

The chief merit of the tour, which ended in Ottawa, was in meeting the American and Canadian senior officers and one's colleagues on the Military Committee in congenial circumstances. The secretary-general of NATO, Josef Luns, had recently instituted a practice of a monthly lunch party for the major NATO commanders, SACEUR, myself and SACLANT (or in SACLANT's absence, his representative in Europe, then a Dutch admiral, Eddy Van Rees, whom I had taught on his Signals Long Course at *Mercury* in 1947), the Chairman of the Military Committee, General Johannes Steinhoff of the German Air Force, and the Assistant Secretary-General for Policy. Bill had been to the first of these, and had told me how useful he thought they would be. I later had reason to agree, particularly because General Goodpaster, the Supreme Allied Commander Europe, was not the easiest person to get to know. As C.-in-C. US Forces Europe, a principal influence in national as well as NATO councils, the incumbent of the post first filled by Eisenhower, his was an influence to reckon with. His reserve, engendered in part by his awesome responsibilities and the political problems he had to face, concealed a rare nature that I came greatly to like and admire.

While everything went on as usual at headquarters, and as soon as I felt we had settled into Admiralty House after the Military Committee tour, I decided that I must get some sea time and spend a few nights afloat. In October, therefore, I joined *Euryalus*, commanded by Eckersley-Maslin, in the Firth of Clyde, where she and another frigate were acting as target ships for the submarine 'Perishers' Course. This is the period in which First Lieutenants of submarines qualify, or not, for command. It is a very renowned and hardworking affair; those submariners who fail it are relegated (as they see it) to general service, where many then do well.

I spent a full day in the submarine. The 'Teacher' was Grenier, whom I found very impressive in the way he handled the officers on the course, and I learned a good deal. The weather was foul, and transfers from ship to submarine and back required a good deal of agility on my part – indeed, when the time came to leave and fly south from Prestwick, I was very nearly unable to get ashore. At Prestwick we had a small naval air station with a helicopter squadron, commanded by Jack Carter, so I had a look round them before flying south to Northolt. VIP movement at this time was in the hands of an RAF squadron dedicated to the task. It was equipped not only with Comets, but also with HS125 executive jet aircraft, and helicopters. It made one's travelling so much safer and more comfortable, and, as this record will show, as time went on I was to make very full use of this resource.

Back at Northwood, while programmes were being formulated for the next few weeks and months, I entered on my daily routine while at headquarters. This began with reading the important signals at breakfast, followed by a walk, usually with the flag lieutenant, to the headquarters building about ten minutes away, where I would go up into my office in the National above-ground block until it was time to go down for the staff briefing. This occurred in the Tunnel, and after it I would talk to Jan Klaver, or anybody else on the NATO staff, in my tunnel office, and also received NATO callers.

The briefing was national. NATO briefings only took place in the course of NATO exercises, because only then, short of a NATO alert, were forces assigned to my operational command from foreign navies. An exception was the Standing Naval Force, Atlantic, a mix of destroyers and frigates assigned to SACLANT, when they were in my area. I found that my national briefings spent too much time discussing the programmes of various frigates, and I decided to change this. I remarked at an early one that I thought there were too many ex-frigate commanding officers about and insufficient attention was being paid to the programmes and activities of the nuclear submarine force.

(By this I meant our Fleet submarines, not the ballistic missile submarines, which were controlled from a special office, under a separate 'hat' I wore as Commander Task Force 345.) As a result, my future operational briefings opened with those submarines, followed by the aircraft carriers, the amphibious ships, cruisers and then the frigates. I felt that such minor details helped to focus people's priorities where the source of our naval strength increasingly lay. There was also a daily intelligence briefing to a restricted number of people, and the whole performance took perhaps an hour out of the day.

I would receive an average of six calls each day, mainly from flag and senior officers, commanding officers on taking up and relinquishing their commands, officers joining or leaving my staffs and visiting VIPs – military or political. Whenever possible, callers plus wives came to lunch at Admiralty House. From time to time, assisted by the staff, I would hold a bigger 'stag' lunch there for ships' junior officers detailed off for this by their commanding officer. There was, of course, a certain amount of paperwork, but nothing to compare with that endured at the MoD, though there was a particularly busy time in the office when the Fleet half-yearly recommendations for promotion to commander and captain had to be co-ordinated. Promotion meetings were held with the subordinate flag officers before I submitted my consolidated lists with candidates in an order of priority for consideration and decision by the Admiralty Board. I tried to see the VCNS at least once a month and, whenever he wished it, the First Sea Lord. As a Commander-in-Chief, I was a member of the Promotion Committee for officers of flag rank which the First Sea Lord held twice a year.

The last ships of the Far East Fleet were now on their way home, as that Fleet was being closed down and its headquarters disbanded. The final occupant of Admiralty House, Singapore, from the Royal Navy was Tony Troup, and the last Commander British Forces was Brigadier Peter Benson, husband of Jack's daughter, Betty (a strange coincidence mirroring my Aden title, though his responsibilities were wholly different and far less clear-cut). The ships transferred operational command and control to me as they left the old Far East Station. On 1 November, the Far East Fleet was formally abolished and my title changed to that of C.-in-C. Fleet, dropping the 'Western' part of it.

Every operational ship in the Royal Navy was now under my command. To handle them I had five subordinate flag officers: two Flag Officers Flotilla (Power, ex-*Bulwark* and Williams, of Yardley Court and *Devonshire*), a Flag Officer Carriers and Amphibious Ships (Treacher), Flag Officer Sea Training at Portland (Mansfield) and Flag Officer Submarines at Gosport (Roxburgh). In addition, the flag officers at Gibraltar, Devonport, Chatham and Rosyth reported to me in their NATO capacities, as all were subordinate commanders of the C.-in-C. Eastern Atlantic Area or Channel. Flag Officer Spithead reported to me for his operational responsibilities for ships of the Fleet and their support. I was the administrative authority for Flag Officer Malta, and of the ships assigned to the Commander British Forces Caribbean Area, who himself reported direct to the CDS. Commodore Hong Kong and his ships also came under my authority in many respects. The shore-based flag officers in the UK had certain administrative responsibilities to C.-in-C. Naval Home Command at Portsmouth, and those overseas, including Commodore Hong Kong, to the MoD. The admirals at the old Home Ports, Devonport, Portsmouth, Chatham and Rosyth, also had a direct responsibility, related mainly to dockyards, stores and such like, with a political connotation, to the Admiralty Board in the person of the Chief of Fleet Support. Although this sounds complicated, everything was, at heart, in aid of ships of the Fleet and there was very little room, as far as I could discern, for any conflict of interest, providing 'party politics' did not intervene.

While negotiations were going ahead for my calls on the other nations of the Channel Command, Belgium and the Netherlands, Tom's half-term came up at Winchester, and we managed to get hold of a Comet and visit Norway, the most important flank of the Eastern Atlantic Area, and one which depended heavily on British ships, marines and aircraft for early support in war. We went for about a week, I had a brief audience of the King, and it was interesting to visit the AFNORTH HQ again and see the tunnel in the rock complete. Some of my old staff, notably 'Happy' Eldjarn, the Norwegian radio engineer, were still hard at it. The Allied Commander-in-Chief, now General Sir Walter Walker, invited us to a dinner in his home at Holmenkollen, conspicuously well presented by his Gurkha orderlies. We then flew north to Bodo to spend the night, missing our stop at Harstad owning to bad weather, but enjoying magnificent views of the snow-covered mountains *en route*.

It was interesting to meet the Task Force Commander North Norway, who was almost as legendary as his predecessor of the 1950s. His name was Zeiner Gundersen, and he was reputed to have covered every mile of the frontier between Norway and Finland on foot – probably, knowing him, in winter. I met his service commanders and visited the Joint Headquarters in its own rock. We liked him and his wife very much, and they have been friends ever since. When the time came to go in the morning, I found the Norwegians busy trying to clear snow and ice away from the Comet. Zeiner was already there, so I left the car and talked to him, neither realising how long it would take nor prepared to show that I was getting cold. (I hope my hardiness was duly appreciated.) Eventually, we took off after a memorable visit, arriving back at Northolt on 10 November.

A week later we took a Comet to Gibraltar to spend two nights with Rodney and Miquette Sturdee, before going on to Malta in the morning. Here we stayed at the Villa Guardamangia with Peter. John Templeton-Cotill, Flag Officer Malta, occupied the Villa Portelli, not a stone's throw from Fort St Angelo, where Elizabeth's parents had been in the 1930s and where she had spent some of her holidays from West Heath. Templeton-Cotill gave a dinner party for us with a large number of Maltese present, including Lorrie Sant, a 'strong man' of the Labour Party, and was hoping to arrange for me to see Dom Mintoff, the prime minister, with whom he got on rather well. This was uncertain, as Dom was forever difficult and, not unreasonably, was trying to shed the British yoke while retaining as many of its advantages as he could. The next day, we heard that he would see me on some beach or other on Saturday morning. Since we planned to spend as much of the weekend as we could with Peter and his family and I had NATO calls to make, Peter being the Chief of the Allied staff, I asked Templeton-Cotill to explain this to the prime minister, who, surprisingly, saw the point and agreed to come in to the Auberge d'Auvergne, where his office was, on Saturday morning especially to see me.

We spent the Friday working: a call on Admiral Lorenzini, a Good Conduct Medal to present to a Sergeant of Marines, a visit to the M'Tarfa hospital (much helped by Elizabeth) and a general look round at what was left of the naval and air facilities in Malta, including the Maritime Headquarters at Lascaris. Eventually, on the Saturday morning, fairly early, I saw the premier, and had a very pleasant and amiable interview with him (although at one point I clearly touched on a sensitive issue, because I saw the blood starting to mount in his cheeks; however, it subsided). We then had a lovely time with Peter and his family, a picnic, with swimming and a visit to the Verdala Palace. Before leaving, I held a press conference, at which, among other things, I was asked whether Malta remained an essential strategic base for the British Fleet. To this I said, 'No,' and explained that we were, as ever, committed to the Mediterranean, but in support now of NATO, and that we had developed facilities, both at sea and elsewhere, which rendered Malta as a base more a convenience – and a very good one – than an essential. I also referred to the pleasure which all our ships and their companies took in visiting Malta and in the welcome they always received from the Maltese people.

I returned to Northwood to find that my remarks had caused a furore. In fact, Mintoff demanded that they be withdrawn because, he said, they belittled Malta's strategic importance. He also registered a formal diplomatic protest. This was promptly rejected by the Foreign Office, who responded that the admiral had replied accurately and correctly to the question he had been asked. That was the end of the matter, but I'm afraid it didn't help Templeton-Cotill much, and I felt myself to be *persona non grata* in Malta for a while.

Next it was time to go to The Hague to visit the Royal Netherlands Navy, having been invited by their Chief of Naval Staff, Admiral Maas, one of the members of the Channel Committee supervising C.-in-C. Channel. The British ambassador kindly gave us dinner in the lovely old embassy, and the next day we were honoured by being received by Queen Juliana at the Soestdijk Palace outside the city, accompanied by Johnny Maas, and spent a pleasant half an hour with her. That evening, the minister of defence, De Koster, gave a dinner party for us in Amsterdam, and the following day, while Elizabeth did some touring, Johnny Maas took me by helicopter over the polders and the newly-reclaimed land. I saw something of the Netherlands Navy, went on board one of their submarines, *Svaardvis*, and generally had a full and interesting tour of an efficient outfit.

On the following day, we called on the C.-in-C. Allied Forces Central Europe at Brunssum, a German general called Bennecke, who had us to stay at his schloss, complete with drawbridge and, upstairs, one of the more sloping and rickety-floored rooms that we have slept in. It was also pretty chilly. However, he and his wife were most kind (although I found the bows and heel-clicks a little too reminiscent of the past). Fred Rosier, an old colleague from Planning days, was the deputy Commander-in-Chief as an air chief marshal and in his usual great form, so we had an enjoyable visit.

The complications of that headquarters and its subordinate headquarters appalled me; AFNORTH was simple by comparison. There still seemed to be no effective joint arrangements at the appropriate levels for the Air Forces and the Armies to get together, and across the Army group boundaries, liaison seemed to be tenuous in the extreme. Americans, British and Germans all seemed to go their own ways; Dutch and Belgian troops were not deployed forward except for exercises. However, I am sure it was a good move for the Allied C.-in-C. Channel to make that kind of call and Andy Goodpaster had readily agreed that I should do so. The next day, in Bonn, I called briefly on the German Chief of Naval Staff and on Admiral Zimmerman, their chief of defence (therefore a member of the Military Committee). It was all extremely cordial. There followed a week in Northwood, mainly occupied with the final meetings on the half-yearly promotions as well as routine national and NATO business. On 6 December we flew to Brussels for a Military Committee Meeting, where we were well looked after by the Van Reeses, he being by common consent C.-in-C. Channel's representative in Brussels as well as SaclantRepEur. He was clearly enjoying himself and on top of his job, and I felt that I had a friend at court.

I had earlier been to Faslane, to give the Trafalgar Night speech and to join at sea a Polaris submarine on return from patrol for a 'hot' debriefing (the full one being carried out at Northwood). This is something which, as CTF 345, it was my business to encourage very senior officers and selected ministers to do, in both their interests and those of the submarine officers and men whose dedication and scrupulous care in their vital duty is fostered by such attention. I returned with my confidence in their performance and capability as strong as ever. Nevertheless, I formed the opinion that Fleet and patrol submarines, particularly the former, would do well to have working-up arrangements more formal than those customarily co-ordinated by Flag Officer Submarines and his staff. They did not share this view, but after a protracted study by the Fleet Engineer Officer and Captain of the Fleet, I became convinced change was needed. Accordingly, a captain 3rd Submarine Squadron was established at Faslane with responsibility to Flag Officer Submarines similar to that of Flag Officer Sea Training to me. He soon became accepted and effective.

It had been a busy time – and a considerable test of memory for facts and faces – since I had taken over only three months earlier. I had managed to visit Portland with Elizabeth, where we spent the night with Ged Mansfield and I went to sea for a day. I was a little unhappy that the 'sea day' I witnessed allowed a laxity of station-keeping and lack of alacrity in manoeuvre that I found surprising, and told Mansfield as much. Those particular skills were becoming outdated tactically, but still served the purpose of developing a 'seaman's eye'. People were wary of the cost of their ships and equipment, and striking the right balance between audacity and prudence – between tradition and trusteeship – was eminently a matter on which flag officers had a duty to give a lead.

Tom's Christmas holidays were about to start, and we were bound for Cyprus, where the Commander-in-Chief at the time was Air Marshal Sir Derek Hodgkinson, who had been on the directing staff at the Joint Services Staff College at Latimer during my course and was an old contract bridge mate. It was time to get away and allow all the retinue a proper Christmas, too. Thanks to the headquarters in the island, where there was a resident naval officer, Bob Greenshields (whom I knew from *Vengeance* days), I was able to keep in touch. I made this an official visit, in the course of which I called on the president, Archbishop Makarios and the vice-president, Mr Kuchuk, accompanied by Robin Edmunds, the new high commissioner. It meant taking uniform, but it also meant a free and comfortable trip. I was most interested to meet Makarios, who was courteous in an oily way, but impassive and opaque. He knew, I am sure, that my Uncle Jack had been commissioner of police when he had been deported to the Seychelles, but was far too polite to mention this (and I certainly was not going to raise it). I explained how I had been involved in the Cyprus Patrol and how pleasant it was now that ships could come and visit the island and enjoy its people's hospitality, and so on. I think the visit was reasonably successful, and I was also pleased, when I met Kuchuk, to see Mr Denktash there with him. The Turkish visit was the more relaxed and informal. I am afraid we were missed at Godden Green, but we went there pretty regularly, kept in close touch, and we were back for the New Year.

I now had a new Chief of Staff, Ernle Pope, my flag captain in *Eagle*, having relieved Ian Jamieson on 2 November. I decided to make another visit to the Mediterranean, including Naples and Rome, in the early part of the year. The C.-in-C. Allied Forces Mediterranean had now moved from Malta to Naples, leaving Peter behind to sort out the old headquarters, having been given responsibility for this direct from the Military Committee itself. This was necessary because the Italians were much more anxious to move everybody to Naples than to make suitable accommodation and arrangements for non-Italians there. Peter dug his toes in, obtained the necessary authority, and refused to let the move go ahead until the proper arrangements were completed. Roselli Lorenzini had been relieved by an Admiral Pighini, and I felt a visit from me might help.

January 1972 was spent mainly at the headquarters. Alan Trewby (who had been my term engineer officer as a cadet at Dartmouth) came to call, having taken over as Chief of Fleet Support from Turner, and so, later, did Colin Dunlop (who was now Flag Officer Medway and had been Father's secretary until he retired). To lunch on the same day came Ian Gourlay, now Commandant-General Royal Marines (who had been at Yardley Court with us). It was, as you can imagine, great fun that so many old friends were still around.

On 3 February we flew to Naples and I went on immediately to Catania, joined *Tenby* of the Dartmouth Training Squadron and took passage in her to *Antrim*, commanded by David Loram, transferring at sea for a formal visit to Rome. *Scarborough*, leader of the squadron, was with us, and we berthed in Civitavecchia, with Graham (who was captain of the squadron at the time) making an awful hash of his alongside. Before I could make him a signal, he reported on board, saluted and said, 'Sir, it was all my fault,' so I said, 'I'm glad to hear that,' and that was all that had to be done.

The Italians, as ever, were delightful and I stayed ashore with Elizabeth at the Hassler Hotel, at the top of the Spanish Steps, in great comfort. The usual exchange of cocktail and dinner parties occurred in the three days that we were there, and after my own entertainment in *Antrim*, the Fleet Royal Marine Band, which had embarked for the occasion, 'Beat the Retreat' alongside the ship. Cabin accommodation in this type of destroyer is excellent for entertaining: one can manage 12 people round the dining table, and there is a splendid area of deck just forward of the cabin for drinks before and after. The weather was kind to us for the time of year, and I called on General Viglione, the Chief of Defence Staff, as well as on Gino de Giorgi, head of the Navy, who spoke excellent English.

Antrim moved from Civitavecchia to Naples on 10 February, where I called on Admiral Rivero, the Allied C.-in-C. Southern Europe. He had a resplendent array of buildings as a headquarters and far more officers on his staff than anyone would wish to have to control. As usual in NATO, all 'the regionals' had to be represented, and the staff comprised Greeks, Turks and Italians, as well as an infilling of Americans and a stiffening of British, including his chief signal officer, who came from the Weapons Electrical Branch and seemed to be doing extremely well. Rivero himself was a little man, hailing from Puerto Rico, with a reputation of being a tiger of great intelligence.

I was given a briefing, which concentrated on the kind of naval exercises in which ships of the Fleet took part, and on the Naval On-call Force Mediterranean (an international body called up from time to time, to which we assigned a ship or two; it was the nearest equivalent in the Mediterranean to the Standing Naval Force Atlantic). On the initiative of my NATO Chief of Staff at Northwood, Jan Klaver, we were set on obtaining approval for a parallel Standing Naval Force Channel for mine countermeasures purposes, and negotiations were already under way. As a result, all this was of some interest, and I was thankful I did not have Rivero's problems with nationalities, such as, for instance, having to maintain a balance between Greek and Turk and yet keep them a little at arm's length, one from the other. I met Pighini and his skeleton staff, and heard nothing but good of Peter.

I had a full programme ahead and, as we were planning to go to Cyprus for Easter, Liz went early, towards the end of February, and I flew to Brussels to make my long-delayed official call on Andy Goodpaster, Supreme Allied Commander Europe at SHAPE, and to attend SHAPEX, his annual conference at which many senior political and military personages congregated. I had a classic SHAPE briefing, the kind for which Spaak, when he was secretary-general, used to put on dark glasses, but was able myself to take a rather more professional interest, having worked in one of the major subordinate headquarters long ago and visited all three quite recently. I was helped a good deal by Rupert Wainwright, a British rear-admiral who was senior naval officer on the SHAPE staff and a very intelligent person, with whom I stayed. He was able to put a gloss on what I saw and heard that I found useful. I suspect we then had one of Joe Luns's lunches, which were hosted alternately either by himself in Brussels, or by Andy or myself at our headquarters or in some suitable venue. (For example, I once took a ship as close to Brussels as I could get for the lunch.)

I then flew via Northwood to Puerto Rico to join *Ark Royal* and a squadron on detachment for exercise and weapon training in that part of the world. This included the Standing Naval Force Atlantic, with John Fieldhouse in command. There was one worrying moment in a US destroyer, whose captain oscillated so freely between his combat information centre and bridge that he nearly hit a consort before my eyes. Eventually, after a day at Tortola, where it was nice to visit Road Town again, I went to SACLANT's headquarters at Norfolk, Virginia, to call on Admiral Duncan. His previous job had been head of personnel, US Navy, but we had met and Liz and I had come to like him and his wife during the Military Committee visit. His Chief of Staff on the national side (Duncan wore two hats, being C.-in-C. US Atlantic Fleet as well as SACLANT) was Dick Colbert, my friend from Newport, Rhode Island, so that made the visit doubly pleasant. I stayed with the deputy SACLANT, a British admiral and aviator called Compston, and underwent the usual briefings, including an interesting one on the nuclear side of life and another from Commander Submarine Forces Atlantic, whose relationship with my Commander Submarine Forces Eastern Atlantic had to be very carefully nurtured. Indeed, the Commander Submarine Forces Atlantic representative at Northwood was always a specially-selected US Navy submarine officer, who was indispensable in orchestrating our patrols.

Back at Northwood, we were visited by the C.-in-C. Royal Netherlands Navy, Johnny Maas, and his wife, Barbara. Liz being away, Susan came to act as my hostess and did extremely well. We had a large dining room at Admiralty House which could seat 20 or more comfortably. In the ordinary course, Elizabeth and I would sit opposite each other in the middle of the table, and found it easier to control things that way. The Fleet Royal Marine Band provided a string quartet, and it was great fun choosing the music (often Russian) for them. All in all, it made quite an occasion. Susan and everybody else seemed to enjoy this particular evening.

A couple of days later, I flew to Cyprus to join the family and had a lovely ten days there. We came back home, and on 11 April I flew for a quick visit to the Far East, stopping briefly at Singapore, including a look at what had been our Naval Base and was now a private dockyard. Admiralty House was unoccupied, and I was rather sorry to see that the last naval incumbent had left his footprints and initials in some new concrete round the edge of the swimming pool. The boards with the names of naval commanders-in-chief and the Fleet commanders were still up in the house, and I think the expectation was that the names of the commanders of the Singapore Navy would subsequently be added to them. Our funny little house by Sembawang village still stood.

Then on to Hong Kong, where I stayed with the commodore, Roger Wykes-Sneyd, and his family and visited some of the minesweepers which formed the Hong Kong Patrol Force. An exercise was laid on by Roger for me to see the procedure adopted in maintaining immigration control over the waters of Hong Kong. Sure enough we found a motor-junk in the wrong place and the 'illegal immigrant' on board was arrested in my presence. She turned out to be the younger and extremely pretty daughter of the commodore himself, known commonly as 'Maggot', so her 'arrest' had to be suitably celebrated. The set-up at Hong Kong was tidy but, as bigger ships visited all too seldom, I fear time lay fairly heavily on the commodore's hands. This was the first visit on which I noticed that the May Road flat in which Father and Mousse had been so happy long ago had been demolished for development, although the commodore's flat in Bowen Road where I stayed still retained its view of the harbour – just. The basin of the dockyard had been filled in, the contractor with the lowest tender having made millions by charging to dump rubbish in it, and a skyscraper had been built in which the naval and other British military offices were concentrated. This place was where my naval career had really begun, and it had changed more, I think, than any other I had known well over the past 35 years.

Shortly after returning to Northwood, Peter came to stay on his way to report to the NATO Military Committee in Brussels that he was now satisfied that the remaining people from Allied Forces Mediterranean in Malta could go to Naples to rejoin their commander (now styled Commander Naval Forces Southern Europe). General Tom Pearson, the new C.-in-C. Allied Forces Northern Europe, came to call and be briefed, and then it was off to Brussels for an official visit to the Belgian Navy, run by Commodore Lurquin. I called on the Air Force general, Crekillie, who was their Chief of Defence Staff.

I had the honour of lunch with King Baudouin, who showed himself knowledgeable about NATO affairs and seemed to get on well with his military. Lurquin was quite an operator, well in favour of the Standing Naval Force Channel, and had somehow or other managed to obtain money to build a nice little naval base at Zeebrugge. He had also obtained approval for three frigates, and intended to call them by Flemish names, all of them, convinced that when his successor wanted three more and would call them by French names, he would be halfway to getting approval!

After the visit to Belgium, we went up to Rosyth to stay with Flag Officer Scotland and Northern Ireland, David Dunbar-Nasmith of Peter's term, who had relieved me in *Alert*, and also to see Peter White, who was now the admiral in charge of the dockyard there and in his usual tremendous form. I walked round *Valiant* in refit – hard work, but interesting in the stringency of the techniques required.

Our next call was on the French Naval Commander Atlantic in Brest, but before flying there I paid a quick visit to Northern Ireland, where one of the Royal Marine Commandos was, as usual, operating. This was my first flight into Aldergrove, and my first experience of the precautions involved.

I found the commando in good heart, and having an HS 125 at my disposal, returned later the same day. The lost and dismal aspect of parts of Belfast struck me greatly.

As flagship for Brest I chose *Albion*, commanded by Jimmy Jungius. The Fleet Royal Marine Band was embarked, and we were able to do things in style, which is just as well because the French set high standards in such matters. We were neither of us prepared to meet such a delightful person as Admiral Daille. He spoke good English, and we stayed ashore with him and thoroughly enjoyed not only the formal occasions, but also the little excursion on which he took us to a favourite island. I paid a visit to the École Navale, where '*Honneur et Patrie*' was emblazoned everywhere, and was impressed by the enthusiasm and smartness of the cadets I saw. Unfortunately, in the middle of the visit, I had to rush off to Brussels for one of Luns's lunches, and at the end of it, when *Albion* sailed, we went up to Paris to call on the head of the French Navy.

We flew back then for a spell at headquarters. There had been changes in the higher ranks in the Fleet: Ray Lygo had taken over as Flag Officer Carriers and Amphibious Ships from Treacher, and there was a certain amount of work to catch up. We were asked to the Royal Naval College at Dartmouth for the 'Glorious 1st June', where I spoke at dinner and we spent the night. Since the weather was now reasonably settled, I decided to risk a visit to the Inshore Survey Squadron based at Great Yarmouth, commanded by Tony Merriman (a godson of Elizabeth's father). These little craft could be guaranteed to make me seasick in any sort of sea and they very nearly did. However, I spent the whole day with them, and managed to do reasonable justice to the excellent lunch that was laid on in Merriman's own vessel. They showed me not only their survey work, but also the extraordinary Heath Robinson tactic used to determine the depth of a wreck – two of the craft slung a wire between them and towed it over the wreckage, trailing it at a recorded depth until it snagged – very practical, if a little time-consuming.

Soon after my return, we made a long-planned trip with the air commander, now Tony Heward, and his wife to the Faroes and Iceland. It was fun to do this together as a 'maritime command' in the proper sense, and we flew in an Andover provided by Tony. The airstrip on the Faroes was on one island, the town and the harbour on another. Finding the airstrip depended on being able to see a particular waterfall; this was achieved in rather cloudy weather and down we came quite comfortably, to be greeted by the Danish naval captain in charge, embarked in his ship *Vedderen*, and taken to Thorshaven, the capital. The islands are the site of a NATO early-warning radar station, the importance of which I remembered from my days in AFNORTH, though I had never seen it before. We also had some pleasant sightseeing on the windswept islands which we destroyers used for shelter and refuelling during the war before the technique of refuelling at sea had been developed.

From there, we flew to Iceland, site of the important US Navy Air Base at Keflavik, from which early-warning aircraft, and in particular anti-submarine patrol aircraft, operate in the eastern Atlantic area. We had a good briefing at the base, and I was particularly impressed with the amount of information they managed to obtain from the technical debrief of the P3C aircraft on their return from patrol. Tony was responsible for the Nimrods which were our equivalent, having replaced the Shackletons, which now attempted to maintain some kind of early-warning patrol with the radar sets removed from the Navy's Gannets. Like me, I think, he found this briefing something of an eye-opener. After all the wartime weeks off Reykjavik, it was rewarding to be ashore in that pretty town for the first time.

The day after our return to Northwood, I flew to Naples, as did Andy Goodpaster, for Admiral Rivero's change of command ceremony. Peter, now there, met us at the airport, and I stayed with them in a nice flat they had found, right above the harbour. The ceremony was an eye-opener: we all sat in rows of chairs facing the grand headquarters buildings, and after the usual honour guard ceremonies, listened to Admiral Rivero's speech. This, with its translation, seemed to be interminable. Then came the tear-jerking command, 'Haul down my flag,' down it came, and that was the end of it. The new Commander-in-Chief was my friend Dick Colbert, and no better choice could have been made. In ability, temperament and style, he was ideal for an international command containing so many politico-military complexities. Married to so energetic and extrovert an English lady, he was extremely pro-British, and this too was to be a help to the Fleet's efforts to maintain a presence in the Mediterranean, including the deployment of amphibious forces backed by aircraft carriers, for which joint exercises with the US 6th Fleet were invaluable. Peter seemed to get on extremely well with his admiral, Pighini, and I was very glad that I had made the effort to go.

Back again at Northwood, preparations went ahead for the next expedition. One of the problems one faced on these visits was that presents were given and received, and I had no allowance to cover this kind of thing. I had a suitable plaque for 'Fleet' and one, if more appropriate, for 'Channel Command' which cost me nothing, but something personal had to appear as well. My custom was to give half a round of Stilton cheese bought from a shop in Jermyn Street. My petty officer cook was adept at cutting them in half across the middle horizontally, and I would get one of the Northwood shipwrights to make a box for each half so that they looked grander. I mention this because our next visit was to Portugal, and the ambassador there, David Muirhead with whom we stayed, was particularly fond of Stilton. Where better to find port to go with it than Lisbon?

I was to use *Fearless*, with Simon Cassels in command, as my flagship for the visit, and Elizabeth and I flew to Lisbon in order to be comfortably ensconced in the embassy on the eve of her arrival. This worked well, we remained 'unofficial' until the ship came in, and had a wonderful view from our bedroom as she made her approach up the Tagus. We then went down to see her enter harbour, passing the Belem Tower and the fine monument to the Navigators at the harbour entrance. As soon as she was comfortably alongside, I nipped on board in plain clothes, changed into uniform, and was ready to make and receive my calls.

The head of the Portuguese Navy was Admiral Vasconcelos, whose son, now a captain, had been on one of the NATO Signal Courses I had taught at *Mercury* long before. He was friendliness itself, and the whole visit was a success, including a visit to COMIBERLANT, who had recently been established in a NATO headquarters nearby. The establishment of an IBERLANT area at all was something that the Royal Navy had resisted, since it interposed another command between Commander GIBLANT at Gibraltar and the rest of the eastern Atlantic area. It was done entirely for political reasons, at American insistence, and the incumbent commander, who doubled as head of the US Military Aid Assistance Group to Portugal, was, of course, American – and not, I found, impressive. Fortunately, he had a British commodore as Chief of Staff. It was a very happy contact with the Portuguese Navy, and my closest, except on one occasion later when, at sea with the Standing Naval Force Atlantic, I decided to 'ride' the Portuguese vessel of the party and was forced by bad weather to spend the night on board. I remember it for a slightly hair-raising experience of transfer by jackstay, and also for the remarkable collection of what appeared to be extremely racy novels in the captain's cabin, kindly put at my disposal. They are loyal allies, and not to be underestimated at sea.

The NATO maritime exercise schedule for each year included a major autumn exercise in the northern part of the eastern Atlantic area and a substantial summer exercise in the south-western approaches. This year, I embarked in early July to spend that time at sea. My practice on such occasions was to visit as many ships during the exercise as time allowed, always by helicopter, being winched down and up again, and spending perhaps an hour in each ship. It was hard work and if the weather was foggy or otherwise uncomfortable, it was not without its hazards – I nearly lost one of the staff who came with me on one occasion when his feet caught momentarily in the guard rails of a ship while he was firmly attached to the helicopter winch-line. The most enlivening ascent and descent, which relied entirely on the skill of the helicopter crew, was with a nuclear submarine. There is a cliff-edge effect from the fin and the downdraught of the helicopter rotor-blades which makes a rapid entry and exit imperative.

In this exercise, ROYAL KNIGHT, I embarked in *Ark Royal* as my base (under the command of John Roberts, but in his last weeks), and spent four days at sea, coming ashore to Plymouth, where Elizabeth joined me, and at the end of the exercise 'wash-up' hosted a reception in *Tiger*. David Williams had just been relieved as Flag Officer Second Flotilla, by Jock Miller, a very junior promotion, for whom, at Michael Le Fanu's instigation, we had dipped down the seniority list of captains. The flotilla shore office was in Devonport Dockyard, and I paid them a short visit, finding Miller nervous but apparently confident, having inherited a very good staff. Rae McKaig, the admiral at Plymouth, was about to be relieved by Arthur Power, who had just come in from sea, and was going as our military representative in Brussels to relieve General David Fraser later in the year. On take-off back to Northolt from the grass airstrip at Plymouth, we saw people duck as we approached the hedge at the end of the field. We were fairly conscious ourselves of it being a hairy moment, but all was well.

Two days after we got back to Northwood, Elizabeth, Tom and I flew to Turnhouse in Scotland, had lunch with Martin Lucey, the new FOSNI, and then fulfilled a long-standing promise I had made to Peter Stallard (ex-British Honduras and now Lieutenant-Governor of the Isle of Man), that I would bring a squadron to visit him. We flew ahead, stayed at Government House with our friends, and the ships entered port next morning. Because of the lack of room in the harbour at Douglas, particularly at the height of the tourist season, I kept the squadron pretty small, but had *Abdiel*, the minelayer and depot ship for the Clyde-based mine countermeasures squadron, as my flagship. She brought a couple of her brood and an RNR minesweeper with her. Part of the Fleet band was embarked, so we were able to receive His Excellency on board with due ceremony, as well as the Deemster and various other functionaries, and give a substantial cocktail party in the mine-deck, cleared of mines for the occasion. The weather was kind, and on the whole it all went well.

This very pleasant interlude ended on 24 July, when we flew back to Northwood, and almost immediately Elizabeth and Tom went to Cyprus as the summer holidays began. I was due to join her on 5 August, and Peter and his family were due back in England from Naples on 31 July. On my last visit to Godden Green before departing, Mousse was extremely weak and in bed, with her excellent nurse a little anxious about her. She had, I think, only one real interest left in life, which was to be certain that Peter was back so that if she were no longer there, he would be able to help look after Father. As I remember it, when I last saw her she had just rung up Peter, and heard his voice. I kissed her goodbye and set off for Cyprus. Before I left the country, I heard that she had fallen into some kind of coma, and I made special arrangements to be kept in touch in Cyprus through the American wireless receiving station on the plain below Lapithos. We received one or two messages saying that she was still in a coma, which was extremely unusual since there was no medical reason such as kidney trouble why she should be.

On 15 August 1972, I heard that she had died. She was a very strong-minded woman, and I am quite certain that she felt that she had lived enough and literally turned her face to the wall, remaining in coma through will-power until her peaceful end. Thanks to the RAF, I was able to fly home immediately and join Peter for the funeral, which Father felt unable to attend, and all the other things that had to be done. Father said little. I think he felt stunned, having always expected with good reason that he would be the first to go. I flew back to Cyprus and rejoined the family.

The next visit planned was to the Turkish Navy, and a small squadron, led by *Antrim*, was organised to be there with me. Accordingly, on 22 August Elizabeth and I flew from Cyprus to Izmir, where she stayed with the British resident naval officer at the NATO headquarters and I took a helicopter out to *Antrim* offshore, piloting it much of the way, it being comfortably stabilised. On our passage up the Sea of Marmara, the wardroom very kindly dined me and, of course, I had to make a speech. *Antrim* was affiliated to the Royal Irish Rangers, and there were a couple of pipers on board, which enlivened the proceedings. I was presented by the commander with a cummerbund, special to *Antrim*, which was black on one side for use in naval uniform, and a dark Irish Ranger green on the other. In the course of my speech I was able to explain how gratified I was with all this since I had been 'conceived in Constantinople and born in Ireland' – perfectly true, but I doubt they believed me for a moment.

The C.-in-C. Turkish Mediterranean Fleet was Admiral Bulent Ulusu, who had been on the Allied Forces Mediterranean staff with Peter, for whom he had formed a great regard. We were therefore in very good hands, and the visit was an undoubted success. As part of the show, we flew to Ankara so that I could lay a wreath on the memorial to Ataturk. The flight back in the hands of the Turkish Air Force was exciting, since there was a violent thunderstorm at Istanbul and we were struck by lightning during our descent. Safely down, I went forward to say thank you to our pilots, and peered into the flight deck. I have never seen a place so littered with half-smoked cigarettes in my life. Still, all was well, *Antrim, Danae* and a consort whose name I forget were due to depart, and we flew back from Istanbul to Northwood as the big autumn NATO exercise, which was largely under my operational control, was soon to start.

The Autumn Maritime Exercises in the eastern Atlantic area followed a fairly conventional pattern. The European maritime units would deploy, and the Striking Fleet Atlantic, commanded by Don Engen at this time, would come into the area and operate to cover an amphibious landing by the British and Netherlands Marines somewhere on the coast of Northern Norway.

The autumn 1972 exercise, STRONG EXPRESS, was distinguished by the participation of the Allied Command Europe Mobile Force. This was a multinational brigade designed to be deployable anywhere in Allied Command Europe at a moment's notice to demonstrate Allied solidarity in a tangible manner at any particularly threatened part of the command boundary. This exercise also coincided with the Military Committee tour, which was of the Northern Region this year. We all met in Denmark first, and then went north. I visited 848 Squadron at Bardufoss, watched the marines' sea- and airborne assault and the operations of the ACE Mobile Force as 'orange', opposing the local Norwegian forces and those landed. It was fairly chaotic, and I earned the thanks of Peter Snow of ITV by giving him and a television crew a lift in my helicopter at a crucial moment to film more of the action. Many of the ACE mobile force had never been to North Norway before, but appeared cheerfully to exert themselves, even if they occasionally lost their way among the mountains. I think SACLANT, who was in overall charge with SACEUR, rated it pretty good training; I certainly found it energetic, and it had plenty of cover from Soviet ships and aircraft. At the end of it, I took General Goodpaster and General Pearson by Nimrod to Rosyth for the hot 'wash-up'.

In between this kind of set-piece activity, I would take such opportunities as I could make to visit ships. For example, I saw something of the

Hydrographic Squadron: *Hecate*, when I was in the West Indies before the SACLANT call, and *Hydra* in British waters. I was particularly interested in the two principal warfare officer trials ships, and went on board both of them in the course of exercises to see how the operations rooms were working. They were well chosen, in that their commanding officers were completely different personalities, *Jupiter*'s Ronnie Laughton being brash and extrovert, and De Courcey-Ireland in *Achilles* being a rather intellectual and quiet character. Both seemed to find that the system worked well, and their ratings blossomed under the increased responsibility. This was the source of some satisfaction to me.

I also had the honour of having the Prince of Wales in the Fleet, and had seen him off from Brize Norton when he joined us in November 1971. I remember he was anxious that his baggage was too extensive, and I was able to reassure him. His first ship was *Norfolk*, under Bill Cook, an admirable, wise and calm captain whom I had known on my staff before. I visited the ship before HRH joined, but not while he was there. He was then appointed to *Minerva*, a frigate, and I went on board her by jackstay during one trip to the West Indies to see how he was getting on. His captain was John Garnier, who much later became Flag Officer Royal Yachts. When he brought the ship alongside to transfer me back to the flagship, it was not done well. Since he made no comment, I said, 'I am sure you would like to do that again,' which he did, and did it properly. Much, much later, at a Royal Navy Club dinner when I was chairman, the Prince of Wales in his speech remembered this and remarked that I had told his captain to go round again, to which I said, 'Not quite in those words, Sir.' Later, HRH was transferred to *Jupiter*, commanded then by John Gunning, and I think that the contrast in styles was probably good in both instances.

I am not a great believer in addressing ships' companies unless they happen to be one's own: it is the captain's job to talk to them from time to time. In my ship visits, unless the captain of the ship specifically wished me to make an address for a special reason, I preferred to talk with the sailors rather than at them, and would go round talking to anyone who did not get out of the way fast enough. It was also of value to go into the senior rates' messes, where one was made welcome and heard much that was relevant to my job as well as to theirs. There was usually some kind of tactical activity going on, so I would visit the operations room to see how it was performing, and probably go down into one or other of the machinery spaces.

The working rig I wore was very convenient for this, as it was for the winching up and down from the helicopter or the swing across on the jackstay, either of which was inevitably part of the visiting process. The 'woolly-pully', as we called it, had been introduced about the time I joined the Fleet, and I welcomed it with open arms. Strangely, the C.-in-C. Naval Home Command at that time did not like it worn ashore, but his successor soon adopted it. It is a practical rig, which could look smart, and should do so. I was successful in pioneering the introduction of barathea for officers' uniforms, replacing the traditional doeskin, which, with the advent of air-conditioning and, ashore, central heating, had become too heavy as well as expensive. Sadly, however, I was unsuccessful in my representation to replace the men's nylon overalls on account of a fire risk. An Inter-Service Clothing Committee turned this down. With hindsight, I now much regret not reacting more strongly, but I was assured that they were flameproof.

One of my occasional duties was to sit as a member of the UK Commanders-in-Chief's Committee. This met at Wilton, where there was a small staff consisting, as far as the Navy was concerned, of one sailor and one marine. My two colleagues were the C.-in-C. UK Land Forces and the C.-in-C. Strike Command, one of us in turn being chairman for a year. Andrew Humphrey, C.-in-C. Strike Command, I knew, C.-in-C. Land Forces I didn't, but I called on General Eugster at Wilton, spent the night with him, and saw something of the staff and had a first meeting there. The committee was charged with reinforcement planning, mostly by air, of a station such as the Caribbean, and with evacuation planning should the military be asked at any time to help, the preferred method of evacuation being by civil air lift, if the situation allowed.

My predecessors as C.-in-C. Western Fleet had felt that they perhaps had better things to do than serve as chairman of this particular committee, but I decided that I would be delighted to take my turn in 1973. The faces fell a bit when I said this, but I was perfectly entitled to do so. The attraction was the chairman's tour in the course of his year, in which he was provided with a Comet, could take his wife and some of the committee staff, and choose, within reason, where to go. This seemed too good a chance to miss.

In October 1972 I visited *Bulwark*, in great heart under Lance Bell-Davis, and then took *Fife* (commanded by George Kitchin of Peter's term, who had worked for me in Plans) to Wilhelmshaven to see the Baltic Approaches Command and their headquarters. For the first time, I received a presentation by German naval officers with an unaccustomed lightness of touch and sense of humour. I remarked on this to their admiral, who replied that they were consciously emulating the British Navy, so I congratulated him. We had a cocktail party and dinner in *Fife*, which concluded the visit on the right note.

At the end of the month I flew to Norfolk, Virginia, for Charlie Duncan's change of command ceremony. This was held with a great deal of pomp and circumstance, as indeed it should be, on the deck of a large American aircraft carrier and Charlie made a speech. It was a brave speech and an astonishing one. The US Navy at the time was being properly put through the mill by 'Bud' Zumwalt and, particularly on the personnel side, changes were being made with which I happened to know many people disagreed. Charlie Duncan spoke out, and made his position extremely clear for a serving officer. I think it went well, it was probably water off a duck's back as far as 'Bud' was concerned, but I have always held it greatly to Charlie's credit. At about that time, 'Bud' was congratulating himself on having appointed the first woman admiral in the US Navy. Somebody once asked me what I thought of him; I said, 'Half hero and half mountebank,' and I feel it was not a bad description. He certainly needed to knock heads together, and he was good at doing that, but he often went overboard because, I think, of his personal predilection for doing something dramatic.

Some time earlier, I had asked for approval to make an official visit to the Republic of South Africa, in particular to thank all the people in the Cape who had been kind to the officers and ships' companies of the Far East Fleet whose ships came home that way. Carrington was Defence Secretary, and approval was given for the visit to take place in 1972. So Elizabeth and I, with a carefully-selected staff (because this was the most popular trip ever), set off on 21 November, making a stop in Cyprus because the VIP Comets did not fly at night. This was one of their great advantages: in the interests of economy of air crew every night was spent on the ground, and the passengers had a good night's rest as well. We had dinner in Cyprus with the Commander-in-Chief, at the lovely Air House at Episkopi, and then went on the next day, flying what was called the 'Cento route', a key part of air reinforcement planning since it overflew the territory of the other Cento allies, Turkey, Iran and Pakistan. We had a wonderful view of Ararat, Lake Van and the mountains round it, and eventually came down to spend the next night at Mombasa. We stayed with the Deputy High Commissioner at Nyali Beach; Tony Duff of my term was the High Commissioner at the time and kindly came to the coast to see us. I had time to pay a call on the Kenyan Navy to see their new base near Kilindini, and also to visit the civilian firm that did much to help keep ships going on the Beira Patrol, maintained to assist enforcement of sanctions against Rhodesia. This Fleet chore, mainly for the aircraft carriers until the basing of a Shackleton flight in Madagascar released the task to frigates and destroyers, was to continue throughout my spell in command, remaining a constant factor in the programming of ships.

Then it was on to Capetown, which I had not seen since I was a small boy at Western Province. We were greeted by 'Flam' Johnson, the head of the South African Navy, and stayed with Oz Cecil, the senior British naval liaison officer in South Africa. Now a commodore, he had been a lively sub-lieutenant in *Duke of York*, and our parents were good friends. The next day brought us to Simonstown, remembered well from long ago. It had changed extraordinarily little and still had the aspect of a small town at the end of the railway. Apart from something known locally as the 'Simonstown Hilton', the view as we approached was much as it had ever been. The 'Hilton' is, in fact, a large building in the dockyard in which refits of the Daphne Class submarines bought from the French are carried out and has a big synchrolift at its entrance. Otherwise, things seemed just as they were when Peter and I used to fish for mossbunker off the jetty at Bull's Nose, where *Wallflower* lay alongside. Admiralty House at Simonstown is a lovely place, but it was not available for 'Flam' because Bierman, his predecessor, the Chief of Defence, still insisted on occupying it. We went round the dockyard in some detail, and met many of the officers and men of the South African Naval Defence Force, including a good many French wives. (Those who had gone to France to collect the French submarines had collected other things as well.) Since the main object of my visit was to say thank you, Os had arranged the necessary entertainments, and I was able to meet countless kind people who had looked after our men on their way home from the Far East Fleet. I had *Euryalus* in Simonstown as flagship, and I used her to return hospitality to the best of my ability. Formalities over, Oz and Annette Cecil drove us out to the Cape of Good Hope, round Cape Point, which is now a National Park. It brought back many memories of happy days there in the 1930s. Eventually, we reached the 'Boulders' by Miller's Point, and saw the house in which the Ashmores had lived in the 1930s and the Sturdees some seven years before, when Elizabeth was a baby. The beach itself, like the rest of Simonstown, had changed remarkably little and it was fun to see it all again and swim there. It was interesting, but not exactly fun, to revisit the Western Province Preparatory School at Claremont, where Peter and I had first gone away from home as weekly boarders. I came back, I suppose, rather grand, but when I entered what used to be, and still is, the new boys' dormitory, my heart sank into my boots. The old headmasters were now long gone, but the son of one of them was still there, and the school seemed in good heart.

Fortunately, we did have time to see Dick and Betty Luyt. Dick was last governor and first governor-general of Guyana. He was now the vice-chancellor of Cape Town University and a man whose opinion on the situation in the Republic of South Africa I valued higher than most. He was in good form, but depressed about the political situation. He jealously preserved the independence of his university, and in particular his right to choose the subjects taught and who should teach them. On other matters he had to trim his sails to the prevailing wind from Pretoria. He contemplated resignation, but not unless there was absolutely no other way of making his feelings known. He had an ally in the vice-chancellor of the Witwatersrand University, but the situation was bad. Not long before we saw them, Dick had been to Oxford to try to deter the council that is responsible for administering the Rhodes Scholarships from excluding South African citizens. While he was there, and before their decision was taken, he was told that the police had invaded the campus of his university. He flew home at once, and told me that on arrival at Daniel Malan Airport, he was greeted by a host of his students and carried shoulder-high off the tarmac. He went to the university and, he said, 'What could I do but tell them to stop demonstrating and get back to work? They greeted me like a deliverer, and I told them to toe the line.' There was nothing else to be done, but I believe his protests at what had happened did render the campus of the university a good deal more immune from interference by the police.

After a couple of days we flew north to Pretoria. The British ambassador, Peter Snelling, took charge of us, we stayed at the embassy in great comfort, and we thoroughly enjoyed meeting him and his wife. He took us to the Voortrekker Memorial, high on its hill overlooking Johannesburg and part of the Rand. I called on 'Boosey' Bierman, chief of defence, an admiral, who was very pleasant, and also on P.W. Botha, the minister of defence at that time. My meeting with Botha was interesting, perhaps mainly in retrospect. He was quiet-spoken, and seemed to me to be a quintessential Afrikaner; yet in his time as prime minister and president of his country, I believe he did more to initiate reform than any of his predecessors. Again I said my piece about thanks for their help. I said that I had seen and admired their maritime headquarters at Silvermine, of which they are immensely proud, and that I understood as well as anybody else the importance of the sea routes round the Cape. Certainly, I was prepared to agree that we should hate to see control of them in unfriendly hands. Further than that I could not go, nor did I think that any formal link between NATO and the RSA made military, let alone political sense. They were talking about some kind of cross-Atlantic agreement with Argentina, which seemed quite sensible to me, but I pointed out that that would be entirely their own affair. The fact that they were still prepared to accommodate our nuclear submarines at the Simonstown Naval Base for a visit was important, and I am sure that I left relations no less friendly than when I arrived.

We departed in our luxury Comet on 28 November, and for the journey back I had made a departure from the recommended schedule. I wanted to return to Mauritius in order to see the naval wireless station and other facilities, and to show Elizabeth the island. From there, the usual route was to stop over in Bahrain, where I had been more times than I can remember. Instead, I arranged that we should stage at the Seychelles where an international airport had just been opened at Mahe. Unfortunately, we arrived in Mauritius shortly before a cyclone was due to strike. As a result, sighteeing was curtailed. I did my stuff with the naval establishment there and made the necessary calls, and then the pilot said it was high time to take the Comet away, lest the approaching cyclone should damage or even capsize it. So we took off early for the Seychelles, landing in Mahe in torrential rain. Next morning, I had a little business to do. I called on the available minister (the prime minister, Jimmy Mancham, was away), but another was there waiting in the Ministerial Office, which reminded me somewhat of British Honduras in the old days. While we were talking, somebody else, also a minister, came in, then yet another minister. They were very friendly, spoke good English, and gave me an attractive book on the Seychelles, with a picture of a very pretty Seychelloise clutching a coco de mer nut on the cover.

'Work' now done, Sir Bruce Greatbatch, the governor, took Elizabeth and me on an unforgettable tour of the main island. It was a gorgeous day, very clear after the rain, and we travelled in a 1½ ton truck, standing up in the back with Bruce near the driver's cab. Bruce knew the route backwards, so whenever we came to a place where a good photograph could be taken or he wanted to tell us something, he would hammer on the top of the cab. The driver would stop, Bruce would spin us a yarn and we would take our photographs, and we thoroughly enjoyed ourselves. It was a fabulous drive.

The time sadly came for us to go, and as the Comet took off we had a wonderful view of the coral reefs fringing the island and of the nearer outlying islands. After a fuelling stop at Bahrain, we alighted finally at Akrotiri in Cyprus. Here Liz detached to go to our house at Lapithos and I came back to headquarters for the three weeks that were left before the

Christmas holidays. Again Christmas in Lapithos was a wonderful change and relaxation, and the weather was kind.

We came back to work at the beginning of the year, and on 5 January 1973 Simon Merriman left us. We were very sad to see him go, he had been a splendid flag lieutenant with a great sense of humour, but I liked the look of his successor, John Lippiett, who was, naturally enough, a bit intense when he joined. The next excitement was a change of command ceremony at Portsmouth for the Standing Naval Force Atlantic, and afterwards, many of us had a NATO lunch in *Victory*, hosted by the Commander-in-Chief, now Andrew Lewis. The next Navy minister, Anthony Buck, came to call during the month, and later there was another of Luns's lunches in Brussels. After this, we went north to exercise VIKING SHIELD in Oslo. This was a command post exercise run by C.-in-C. Allied Forces Northern Europe, Tom Pearson. We always enjoy our visits there, and on this occasion had the honour of dining with the King at the Commander-in-Chief's house. The next excursion was to Gibraltar, from 9 to 15 February. There were a number of ships there during the spring exercises, the equivalent of the old combined Fleet exercises, when Home and Mediterranean ships met, as in my *Vengeance* time. I took the opportunity to visit many of them.

A very big event on 17 February was Elizabeth launching HMS *Sovereign*, a Fleet nuclear-powered submarine, at Vickers, Barrow. This honour was granted by the Controller on behalf of the Admiralty Board. Some ten days or so earlier, she had visited the Vickers office at Millbank, where she met Lord Robens, the chairman, and his wife, both very special people, chiefly so that she could choose a present. Lady Robens made absolutely sure that she had a good one and Elizabeth made absolutely sure that *Sovereign* had a good launch. We liked her first commanding officer, Laybourne, and what we saw of the other officers and the whole occasion was as happy as it was memorable.

Soon afterwards, I attended the 'DASO' of *Repulse* on completion of her refit: this is the firing of a Polaris missile by each crew on the eastern Atlantic test range, extending from off Cape Kennedy to Ascension Island. The spectacle is best observed from the escort ship, but I boarded the submarine for the test and was rewarded by feeling the kick as the missile left her. The main object was to witness the intensely-detailed briefings and drill and to satisfy myself about the dedication and quality of the people, USN and RN, involved. I then visited Commodore Amphibious Forces in *Intrepid* off Puerto Rico, and heard Gus Halliday give a first-rate exposé to a largely American audience, who were rightly impressed.

With the agreement of the staff, I had decided that the UK Commanders'-in-Chief Chairman's tour should be split into two parts, covering Africa first, then the West Indies. There were good reasons for both, since evacuation and reinforcement plans affected both areas. In particular, I had a personal reason for going to Ethiopia, because it seemed to me that trouble might be brewing there for the future. This was a surprise to the staff, but I stuck to my guns. Accordingly, with Elizabeth, and in a Comet loaded up with some of the staff, we set off. Our first stop was Rome, where we stayed with

O'Brien, a Canadian admiral commanding the NATO Defence College, at which I gave a lecture as C.-in-C. Channel on maritime affairs in general. The next day we set off for Gibraltar, and we spent the night at The Convent with the Beggs. While there, I heard that I was to relieve Michael Pollock as First Sea Lord in March 1974. The next day's journey included a refuelling stop in the Gambia at Bathurst, *en route* for Nigeria.

We arrived at Lagos that evening, to stay with the high commissioner in the new residence (the kind of modern architectural horror, quite unsuited to the climate, that the Property Services Agency seems to like to inflict on people). The next day I paid a formal visit to the Nigerian Navy at the nearby naval base, being accompanied by a splendid character called Admiral Wey, a close associate of General Gowon, then the president, and clearly very much in charge of everything within sight or out of it. The guard was pretty smart, and I had a chance to talk to some of the British ratings and others helping their Navy and to see their plans for an expanded naval base. We departed by boat, partly, I am sure, to avoid having to go through the crowd of prostitutes which customarily hangs round the gate of the naval barracks. The senior officers, Wey, the captain of the base and the captain of the Training College all carried walking sticks, and as a memento of the visit I was given a terrifying one, carved to represent some kind of mythical sea monster, mostly snake in appearance. (It has one advantage: Elizabeth refuses to borrow it.)

From Lagos we flew across Africa, over the Sahel to Addis. The approach to Addis was spectacular, set as it is within a circle of mountains. We stayed at a smart hotel (I suppose it was a Hilton or similar), right in the middle of the city, overlooking a wide, open area and the market beyond, where later we did some good shopping. I liked the ambassador, Willie Morris, on sight, and there was plenty of work to do in the preparation and coordination of the various plans which the committee I was representing might have to put into effect. On 26 March we left, flying over Abyssinia; it was plain to see why it had been given its name, with great gorges and clefts everywhere cutting into the brown countryside. We refuelled at Masirah, and had a lovely walk along the beach before arriving for the night at Muscat. The consul-general now was Donald Hawley, and he and his wife looked after us admirably, making it a very pleasant visit. Things had moved fast since the old Sultan had been deposed, although a flag still flew above the prison immediately opposite the consulate-general. I saw the naval base, which had been much developed, and the bazaar where I had once bought Elizabeth a 'Mogadishu Star'. We had some brief discussions with officers attached to the Sultan's armed forces, and then flew on to our familiar airport at Akrotiri. I had taken my shorthand typist, Sally, with us on the trip, so had been able to dictate all I wanted to say by way of a report and vet the reports of the staff in the aeroplane.

Tom was due on holiday very soon, and Liz left the aircraft in Cyprus. Jack Carter took her up to Lapithos to get everything ready for the Easter holidays. I then called at Brussels for one of Joe Luns's working lunches on 29 March.

Back at Northwood, a shock awaited me. The intelligence people said that there was too much Palestine Liberation Organisation activity in Cyprus for them to recommend that we should go there on holiday at this time. Jack Carter went up to tell Elizabeth and take her down to stay with him at Episkopi. We made a quick switch: Elizabeth flew to Athens, booked into a hotel there, and had it all ready when Tom and I arrived in the very early morning of 6 April. We hired a car and spent 15 days touring in the beautiful spring weather. On our return to Athens, Admiral Margaritis, the head of the Navy, took us out to dinner, including some plate-smashing, and arranged a guide and car for visits to the Parthenon and Sounion.

Trouble in the UK fishing industry came to a head on 1 May, when Iceland declared a 50 mile exclusive fishing zone encroaching widely on international waters. Although at the time Britain recognised only a 3 mile limit, 12 miles was tacitly accepted. Outside this, we regarded our right to fish as unassailable, and the Navy, supported by 18 Group RAF, was ordered to provide any necessary protection. Patrols were therefore established, and the ships and aircraft involved were placed under Flag Officer Scotland and Northern Ireland's operational control. The 'Cod War' as it came to be called, developed nastily, with thin-skinned frigates and destroyers having to hold off well-handled and robust Icelandic cutters, often interposing themselves between the cutters and their prey. This 'campaign' continued until November 1973, when an agreement was reached and patrols reverted to normal. It was a testing time, especially for the young commanding officers. I privately welcomed this: the flotillas needed the challenge, I thought, since their normal operations lack the stress attached to carrier flying and submarine work. They did well, and we were all proud of them.

A NATO event of May 1973 was the commissioning of the Standing Naval Force Channel, consisting of three mine countermeasures vessels: one British, one Belgian and one Dutch. The first commanding officer was to be a Belgian, Van Begin. The Belgian chief of defence, General Crekillie, came to Northwood with him on 4 May. Then we flew to Brussels for SHAPEX, Andy Goodpaster's annual study period, and on conclusion of that, at 4 p.m. on 11 May, Prince Albert of Liège came for our commissioning ceremony.

Channel Command could now hold up its head as being on terms with the Atlantic Command with its Standing Naval Force, and one up on the Mediterranean, which only had an 'on-call' force. The effect was perhaps more psychological than military, but it was of real benefit to the command and to the small member nations. Certainly, it has proved an enduring success. Jan Klaver, whose brainchild it had been initially, has every reason to be proud. He was shortly to be relieved by another Dutch admiral, Pierre Besnard, and about this time Tony Heward had been appointed air member for personnel on being relieved by Duggie Lowe, who was to see me out. So we had a busy time at Northwood, the First Sea Lord came to dinner, other people as well, and speeches were in order. Ken Wilcockson never failed to produce well thought-out suggestions for these.

The second half of the committee's tour was now due, and on 23 May off we set to the Azores to refuel the Comet, and to take a good look at a pretty little island village and, incidentally, an important maritime patrol aircraft base. Next stop was Puerto Rico, where I had the opportunity of going to sea in *Devonshire*. The ship was in good form, and making excellent use of the admirable facilities that the Americans allowed us to exploit. We then went to Nassau, which seemed to me to have changed little. As well as the Wilton staff and John Lippiett, we were now joined by the Commander British Forces Caribbean, then Cameron Rusby, who had come down from Bermuda to meet us and accompany me round his command area.

Belize was our next stop, and a busy programme had been laid on for me there by the garrison commander, including a visit to the training area at Mountain Pine Ridge and a look at the new and expanded facilities on Stanley Field; I felt the garrison deployment should be adjusted to aid its protection. I then flew down to Stan Creek, and over towards the Guatemalan border, which we probably infringed by mistake, to have a look at the sites of some of our observation posts. The governor was Richard Posnett, with whom we had acquired merit by bringing his wife's cello out in the Comet. I called on the premier, George Price, who was now living up at Belmopan, the new capital which had been built after Hurricane Hattie, not only because of the damage the hurricane had caused, but also because status in Belize was geared so much to the site of a house in the old city: people living on the riverfront considered themselves 'higher-class' than those who lived elsewhere. Over the years, with much in-breeding, Belizean society had become stratified. By moving to a new site away from the river, effort was being made to break all this down. Only the more energetic and go-ahead inhabitants moved, but they were the people best qualified to help their country progress. We had a picnic expedition out to Sargeant's Cay, then it was time to leave Belize – I felt sure, sadly, for the last time. It was a place which, never having had to endure the climate for longer than a few days, I liked very much, and the people are still genuinely unspoilt.

The next stop was another old haunt, Grand Cayman Island, where we were looked after by the governor, Roy Crookes, and his wife in their house on that wonderful seven-mile beach, now rather built up. There was no time to go to Little Cayman or Cayman Brac, and on we went to St Lucia, where the British government representative in the West Indies now had his base. It is a sensible choice, because St Lucia is quite one of the nicest of the islands, and in history, being to windward, the most important. We landed at the international airport at the southern end, and flew in a light aircraft to the airstrip at Castries, to stay with the Lairds in a lovely house just outside the town, but not so well situated as the house that the administrator enjoyed when I first knew the place. This is now the residence of the governor-general, a St Lucian. I called on him, and we attended an investiture resulting from the New Year's Honours. The premier, John Compton, and his wife remembered me. At the time *Fox*, flying my flag, and *Fawn*, two hydrographic survey ships, were in harbour. I visited them, as well as discussing the relevant plans with Laird and Rusby. We noticed great changes in St Lucia, brought by the opening of the international airport and the development of several large hotels.

Then we flew north to Bermuda, to take a good look at our old haunts there. The Rusbys put us up in the 'The Cottage' by the dockyard, the lovely house that we had had, 'Enfield', having been lost to the commodore but saved for the services by moving the Army staff officer up from Nassau to live there. I was delighted with the appearance of *Malabar*. We had a party in the grounds of the ratings' canteen and club (which had been the officers' club until I changed that long ago), and everybody seemed in very good heart. We looked round the new married quarters in Prince Albert Terrace, also a product of my scheme, and were pleased to find them appreciated. After a refuelling stop at Gander and a night in a hotel there, we arrived back in England and at Northwood just in time to receive our French friend, Admiral Daille, from Brest.

When he left, I went to Chatham and joined *Fife*, now with David Halifax in command, for an official visit to Sweden in company with *Arethusa*, under Captain Skinner, of the 7th Frigate Squadron, and two other frigates. Elizabeth flew to Stockholm on 13 June, to be there to greet us. The ship made a good entry, and berthed well near the palace. The first to call was a pretty Swedish girl with a bunch of flowers, who was presented as the 'Summer Queen' of Stockholm, so with all the press in attendance, I accepted these, gave her a kiss and we had our photographs taken. She was thereafter suitably looked after by John Lippiett. This was an auspicious beginning, and I set out on my own calls – on Benkt Lundvall, the head of the Swedish Navy, on the Crown Prince (since King Gustav was not well enough to receive people), on the C.-in-C. Royal Swedish Fleet, and so forth. I had the C.-in-C. Fleet's Royal Marine Band embarked, of course, and *Fife* had worked up a first-rate guard for the return calls. Benkt came first, and then the Crown Prince appeared, to be greeted by a Royal Guard. He knew his ceremonial, and did it all very well indeed. We paraded the Queen's Colour from the Fleet, a rare occurrence. After all the ceremony in *Fife*, he took off some of his splendid gear, and we went on board *Arethusa* so that Skinner could show him round a frigate. Not only were the Millards, our ambassador and his ex-Wren wife, great hosts when we were ashore, but we also had an excellent naval attaché there in Symonds-Taylor, and he and his wife looked after us when we had any time off, taking us in their boat on the fjord. The visit passed all too quickly, and Elizabeth and I flew back together to Northwood. We were there in time to entertain the head of the Turkish Navy, Admiral Kayacan, who was visiting the First Sea Lord, and then set off for Annapolis, for another of the seapower symposia that used to occur from time to time.

We returned to Northwood at the end of the month and had a spell there, including giving our annual garden party, which turned out to be in pouring rain – a pity, because our civilian gardener had the garden looking lovely. However, there was just room for people indoors. Everyone seemed to come, and it was a successful operation for entertaining the locals, rather than staff and service people. Tom was learning to fly a light aircraft at that time on an RAF scholarship from Winchester, working from an airfield at Fairfield. We went down there one Saturday to allow me to inspect the Combined Cadet Force of the Gordon Boys' School nearby, and then saw Tom land after his first solo flight, making us very proud after the trepidation subsided.

Meanwhile, preparations were going ahead rapidly for a major event of my time in command: a display by the British Fleet and the RAF associated with it in front of as many of NATO who could be persuaded to attend. I gave it the nickname 'Sally Forth'. We had approval from the MoD and the Foreign Office. Lord Carrington had agreed to host the affair from the political point of view, and I invited Andrew Humphrey, C.-in-C. Strike Command, to be there at my side as my guest afloat throughout. I feared fog, but 24 July dawned clear, and we could not have been luckier with our weather. Everybody who was coming, including nearly all the NATO ambassadors, led by the Secretary-General and the major NATO commanders on this side of the ocean, assembled in Edinburgh the night before, and embarked in *Fife*, *Devonshire* and *Kent* in the morning. We then had a demonstration of British maritime power: a steam-past by the destroyers and frigates, minesweepers showing off their paces, *Ark Royal* steaming close by at speed, and a nuclear submarine on the surface doing the same. Roddy Macdonald, who was in command of *Bristol*, my flagship, gave me kittens at one stage when he took station ahead of the line of destroyers and frigates. I though he had misjudged it, and in fact he nearly did, cutting it very fine for a ship so new with relatively untried engines. It gave me an uncomfortable moment – I hope neither of us showed any sign of how we were feeling. After our steam-past, Andrew and I transferred by jackstay to *Fife*. We had arranged chairs on the hangar-deck aft, where the great men, our guests, with Carrington in the middle, Luns on his right hand, sat and watched the proceedings, including fly-pasts by aircraft from Strike Command, as well as others. There was a demonstration by an RAF Harrier, and a great deal of activity by helicopters. An irritating Soviet trawler was looked after by the RAF launch *Seal* with an interpreter embarked – a detail which tickled Joe Luns.

The administrative arrangements had been the responsibility of Flag Officer Scotland and Northern Ireland, helped by my staff, and before the Sea Day, after which everybody flew straight home to Brussels, there was a dinner, hosted by Peter Carrington, secretary of state for defence, in the Great Hall at Edinburgh Castle, which was also a tremendous success. I was thankful that the Sea Day went without incident and was such a triumph. We had a good press. There was a press conference afterwards in *Bristol*, given by Peter Carrington, who had transferred by jackstay, and no one can do that kind of thing better than he. The signals that we received from the Secretary of State for Defence, First Sea Lord and formally from the Admiralty Board could not have been better. It was a thoroughly well executed joint Royal Navy–RAF operation, and it did both services great good in NATO.

Towards the end of July, out of a clear, blue sky, I was asked by David Malim, Managing Director of Marconi Space and Defence Systems, to unveil the first 'Scot' terminal, the small, stabilised satellite terminal for ships to be used with Skynet. It was nice to be remembered for that after six years had elapsed. By now, my appointment as First Sea Lord from March 1974 had been announced publicly, and my days at the Fleet and as a major NATO commander and a member of the Military Committee were numbered. Some time earlier, Peter had accepted the job of Master of the Royal Household, and had taken up his duties in March 1973. Before he retired, the First Sea Lord had offered him promotion to admiral and the appointment of British Military Representative in Brussels, which would have given him another two years' service. However, Peter felt he had given his word to the Queen, and there could be no going back on that, nor do I think would he have wished to do so. He was to serve 13 years as master, and gave inestimable personal service to Her Majesty, being honoured with the KCVO on his retirement.

A project at the Northwood HQ which took much of my time and interest involved the use of modern data-processing equipment to centralise command and control of the Fleet in the headquarters, so saving, allegedly, people, space and expense at the subordinate headquarters such as Plymouth and Pitreavie. It was a complicated and expensive business, overseen by an excellent captain called Lambert, and subcontracted to Computer Sciences International. It would not be ready in my time, nor for some years thereafter, but required very careful planning.

Every year there was a command post exercise throughout NATO, known as WINTEX, to test the emergency procedures for bringing NATO forces into a state of alert, fuelled, armed and deployed, and exercising the kind of control that national military and political leaders would wish to have as the theoretical situation approached war and earmarked units became assigned to their international commanders. In the course of these and other exercises I had found that the number of differing manual plots in the headquarters, each with its different security clearance and application, was too complicated and dispersed. I therefore had installed what I called my 'gadget room', in which I sat, more or less by myself, with a collection of telephones, including one to the president of the United States, and with coloured television screens in front of me. I could manoeuvre, or have someone sit with me to manoeuvre, cameras to scan the different plots while I talked to the people who were running them to find out what it was they portended. I found it a most helpful interim expedient.

The programming of the ships of the Fleet had a major effect on morale and efficiency, and it was the duty of the operations staff, in conjunction with flag and commanding officers afloat, to try to arrive at an optimum mix for each ship of visits, home leave and exercises. The programme had to take account of factors determined by the MoD, namely refits, fixed Fleet commitments, such as provision of ships for the Beira Patrol, for Commander Caribbean Area, for the Standing Naval Forces Atlantic and Channel, and the On-call Force Mediterranean, for royal escort, and so on. It was also desirable to keep a frigate at short notice in UK waters against a sudden emergency. Flexibility, especially in the destroyer and frigate force, was therefore hard to achieve. Nevertheless, I felt it of great importance to maximise time in company when I could. By dint of careful long-term planning, we were able to arrange for a sizeable deployment to the East and Australia by a balanced group, including a Fleet submarine. No aircraft carrier could be spared, nor would deployment of one outside the NATO area have been welcome to SACLANT or conducive to flying efficiency. Later, in my successor's time, and particularly when the Beira Patrol ceased in June 1975, such group deployments became for some years a regular and welcome feature of Fleet activity.

Between May and November 1973, these problems were aggravated by the need already mentioned to provide destroyers and frigates for the protection of our fishing Fleet from arrest by the Icelandic Coastguard. The technique of 'riding off' the Icelandic Coastguard cutters involved some risk, and required nerve. Naturally, some commanding officers enjoyed it more than others. A good press helped, and the men's sporting instincts were aroused. Nevertheless, it was not a popular duty. The staff officer with a special responsibility to me for matters of morale and discipline, transcending the normal concern of everyone in authority with such fundamentals, was the Captain of the Fleet. His difficult job required supreme tact and discretion, and the Commander-in-Chief relied on him greatly. The selection of the right personality among the senior captains was most carefully made, and recent command experience at sea was a necessary qualification if respect was to be engendered in ships' companies. Unhappily for us both, the appointers sent me one delightful but unsuitable officer who was quickly found another appointment more suited to his talents. In 'Roddy' Macdonald, Hugh Janion and Tom Baird, I was admirably served, and all were deservedly to rise high in their profession.

In comparison with the other major NATO headquarters, Northwood was modest in size, but it was clearly going to need a great deal of money spent on it to effect centralisation of operational control. Unless carefully controlled itself, it would expand, and indeed, there was pressure, and for good reason, for Flag Officer Submarines to move from HMS *Dolphin* at Gosport to join the Fleet HQ. I felt strongly that my staff, who were not able to travel in the same way as I, lost something of the feel of ships and the sea by being incarcerated in Middlesex. Before we went further down this road, therefore, I obtained the agreement of Horace Law, then C.-in-C. Naval Home Command, to approach the MoD with a project to move Fleet HQ to Portsmouth, rather than shifting Flag Officer Submarines to Northwood. I felt this would help everyone retain touch with the seagoing forces under command a great deal better, and it seemed to me that there was already the nucleus of a protected headquarters in Portsdown Hill, carried over from the war. A report was accordingly submitted for study by the naval staff.

Times were hard, and clearly, the move of a headquarters like mine to Portsmouth (incidentally, further away from High Wycombe and Andrew Humphrey's Strike Command HQ) was not going to find an easy passage, and I think the RAF also felt that it would make us and 18 Group more dark-blue than ever. The project foundered early in the Labour government's 1974 Defence Review, partly through lack of funds and partly because my successor was even more reluctant to move further from the RAF Headquarters. In the event, Flag Officer Submarines had to move to Northwood.

I still regret that this initiative failed, and often wonder if it would have succeeded if attempted three or four years earlier. I remember as a commanding officer how far from everything that then concerned me Northwood seemed to be, helpful though people always were. I am sure Flag Officer Submarines is able to keep in touch with his forces, but otherwise, only the Commander-in-Chief and the Captain of the Fleet easily find time to visit afloat. The subordinate flag officers, particularly those at sea, of course keep in far better touch, and the harm is not done so much to the Fleet itself as to the devoted staff at headquarters who try to organise and administer ships they so seldom see. Additional benefits would undoubtedly have accrued through the two Commanders-in-Chief, Naval Home Command and Fleet, being in close touch, especially at staff level, where economies could also have resulted. But none of this was to be, and as First Sea Lord I had to accept the inevitable with the best grace I could muster.

However, that moment was still to come, and meanwhile, in September 1973 at Northwood, we had an extremely pleasant visit from Admiral Lundvall of Sweden. Also, who should turn up with the new US defence attaché but Fill Gilkeson of Subic days! Among other visitors was the C.-in-C. Imperial Iranian Navy, Attaie. He spent a good deal of his time commuting to the USA in contract negotiations – undertaken in person, for obvious reasons – to acquire some highly sophisticated Spruance Class destroyers for his Fleet. I considered these were beyond the Iranian capacity to maintain properly, but they never had the chance to prove me right or wrong.

After a good deal of preliminary organisation, we held the first ever Greynvile Term Reunion at Admiralty House on 14 September. Twenty of the 22 survivors of our term total of 32 were able to come, the exceptions being Duff, high commissioner in Nairobi, and Stewart Moore, having trouble with the climate on his farm in Queensland. Poe, our first term officer, was also present, and in good form; Kennedy was already dead. Everybody enjoyed themselves, the retinue and the band did their stuff, and those we could not accommodate in the house were put up for a pittance in the staff officers' mess. The cost per head, I think, was something like £5. A photograph was taken, of course, and everybody was given a copy in a folder with, on the other side, a photograph of us on our first day at Dartmouth. Having a pretty good crib myself, I was able to recognise about half of my term-mates, but half had to be identified by a process of elimination. We all agreed that we must repeat the process one day, and since he was not there, Duff was unanimously detailed off to organise it.

Two days later we set off for our last Military Committee Tour, which, this year, was of the Southern Region. We called first at Naples, where Dick Colbert, my friend from Newport, Rhode Island, was now the Commander-in-Chief, and so would accompany the Military Committee and the major

NATO commanders on the tour. He was in reasonable form, though pale, and obviously a round peg in a round hole. After a day in Rome, we flew to Venice and had a demonstration there by the Italian Army, with Leopard tanks careering round the place, while the wives did some sightseeing.

The Italian visit over, we went on to Athens, where our host was General Angelis, the Chief of Defence of the Greek armed forces. A dignified person, stern, good-looking and, I think, feared, he was complemented by General Korkas, the Greek military representative to NATO, who was short and lively and spoke excellent English. When the 'Colonels' fell, Angelis, poor man, was locked up in prison, and many years later committed suicide there. Now, however, he was in his element, and we attended excellent presentations and official functions. We all enjoyed a splendid conducted tour of the Acropolis, and then moved on to Thessaloniki in the north. Here, the ladies saw what sights there were, and we flew by helicopter to the Bulgarian frontier, to have the defences of the Rupel Pass through the hills explained to us. This was an interesting trip over a beautiful stretch of country I would never otherwise have seen.

Turkey, and 'Sami' Sancar, then took over, and we spent a couple of days in Istanbul with the most wonderful conducted tour. In the afternoon, in a high wind, there was a demonstration of a divisional strength landing by parachute outside Istanbul. Ambulances scurried to and fro across the field after the drop, picking up the injured. However, the Turkish high command did not turn a hair – quite rightly, in the circumstances. Luckily, Peter Hill-Norton, president of the Military Committee for this tour, was more tactful than he can sometimes be. We next flew to Izmir, and boarded a fleet of helicopters, most impressively ranged on the military side of the airfield, to fly to Ephesus. The place had blossomed with Turkish soldiers and police in their distinctive white helmets, looking like snowballs, so our safety was well assured. It was a lovely day, and we walked on through the ruins of the great city before a slap-up lunch at Kusadasi and the return to Izmir for the flight home. On the way, we stopped in Rome to drop off the Italian representatives and Dick Colbert. It had been a good, if rather exhausting, tour. It gave an excellent idea of the enormous spaces and variation of terrain in the Southern Region, and some grasp of the capacity of the land/air defence arrangements. We could not visit Cyprus since that country is firmly no part of NATO, although the British sovereign base areas were then an important element in the strength of the Cento Alliance.

Back at Northwood, with time running out fast, we were called on by the Dutch minister of defence, Vredeling (whose edict that soldiers need no longer salute their officers had caused our friend, General Van Rijn, to resign), by Ian Gilmour, the new minister of state for defence, and, very happily, by Admiral Gladstone and Commodore Ted Thorne (to whom I had taught signals long ago at *Mercury*), to say goodbye on behalf of the Australian and New Zealand defence staffs in London respectively.

At the end of October we went to Naples again, to visit Dick Colbert and to see Pighini and Peter's relief, Mike Fell, a naval aviator. It was the last such trip and Caroline Coates, my Wren personal assistant, came too. We were glad that it was a good one for her. We stayed with the Colberts at the 'Villa Nike'. Dick was far from well – indeed, in the grip of the disease that was to kill him soon after Christmas. We were their last house guests, and the bravery of them both was a marvel. Dick knew he must surrender the command he was so proud of, and was upset at the choice of successor – a man as different from himself as chalk from cheese. When, a month later, he flew back to the USA to be met by 'Bud' Zumwalt at Andrews AFB, he dressed in uniform and walked from the plane to salute the Chief of Naval Operations. Weeks later, he died.

In early November I seized an opportunity to get among the ships at sea again, and flew to the West Indies, where there was quite a nice little group exercising in the San Juan exercise areas. I spent a couple of nights with them in the Tortola-Virgin-Gorda area, and gave a dinner party for the commanding officers present. After returning to Northwood, Ralph Cousins, now SACLANT, called, and then it was to Brussels for my last lunch with Luns and my final appearance at the Military Committee as Allied C.-in-C. Channel.

Whether meeting in Chiefs of Staffs session, or with the defence ministers present, I had always enjoyed my attendances at NATO Headquarters, not least because of the personality of the secretary-general, who had become a personal friend. Joe Luns was a Dutchman, who had been foreign minister for his own country for some considerable time, and ran both the Military Committee and the NATO Council, which I also sometimes attended, entirely to his own satisfaction, not necessarily always to that of everybody else. He was a brilliant linguist, and once pulled the leg of the Canadian and French ambassadors by addressing the former in French (one of the official NATO languages) and the latter, to his fury, in English. I remember when the American Defense Secretary, Melvin Laird, who had been an exceedingly good NATO man, was being lunched out, Joseph stood up to make a farewell speech. After the first two or three minutes, Mel Laird looked up at him and said, 'Spare me the commercial, Dr Luns,' to which Joseph, quick as a flash, replied, 'It's now or never, Mr Laird,' and everybody dissolved in laughter. Joe had served in the Dutch Navy during the war, so he had a soft spot for things naval. He was delighted that the Standing Naval Force Channel had been created, and never failed to speak highly of the Royal Navy and its showing in SALLY FORTH. He was less sympathetic to some of the other Allies. At some point, the Americans decided to reveal to NATO more of the extent of their satellite reconnaissance than had so far been disclosed to anyone but the British. I sat alongside Joe during the presentation, which was given, very well, by an American general and his team. At the end of it, Joseph thanked them and remarked, 'As Napoleon said, "*Il ne faut jamais sous-estimer votre ennemi.*"' He then turned to me and said in a quiet aside, 'I'm sorry Edward, of course Napoleon said nothing of the sort, but I thought it sounded better coming from him than from me.' These two examples give some idea of this remarkable man, and the private lunches with him, Andy Goodpaster and Johannes Steinhof were worth a guinea a minute.

Field Marshal Sir Michael Carver, who had taken over from Hill-Norton as CDS, came to see us on 22 November at Northwood, and that evening we were asked to a dinner given by the Admiralty Board at the Royal Naval College, Greenwich, to mark the centenary of the college. This was attended by HM the Queen, and Peter Carrington, Secretary of State for Defence, replied to her speech – brilliantly as usual.

On 8 December we heard by signal from the captain of *Endurance* in Port Stanley that the Patent of Baronetcy of Elizabeth's grandfather (which she had suggested to the governor of the Falkland Islands when he came to call earlier in the year would best be kept in the Falkland Islands) had been presented formally. I have a photograph of the occasion which took place on what is celebrated in the islands as 'Battle Day', beside the War Memorial. The presentation was well done with proper military ceremony, and was very well received in the islands.

I paid my last visit to Scotland and to a Polaris submarine returning off patrol at the end of November. December was spent mainly at Northwood, dealing with the various farewells. The senior rates' mess at HMS *Warrior*, as the headquarters was called, very kindly dined us both out in style, and on 13 December the officers dined me out formally, when various speeches were made, Duggie Lowe speaking kindly about me, and I having to reply, in a rather more light-hearted vein I hope.

On 17 December, the subordinate flag officers dined me out in *Fife* in Portsmouth, and on the 19th I had an audience with HM the Queen in Buckingham Palace on relinquishing my appointment. Peter was there to meet me and show me in, and the Queen said something about how nice it was to see the two brothers together. It was an interesting and rather peculiar British convention that whereas the Allied Commander-in-Chief was received by the head of state in the other two countries of the Channel Command on taking up his appointment, in his own country he was only seen on surrendering it.

Meanwhile, we had some time ago taken possession of 'South Cottage' when our tenants left and between 8 and 10 December much of our furniture and gear had been moved down and we had been able to get there to help settle it in. So all was set when Terry Lewin arrived to relieve me on 20 December, with the usual ceremonies now repeated in his honour. My flag was hauled down that evening. Ernle Pope found a clean flag that had flown at my headquarters, and presented it to me quietly before I left, with a suitably inscribed card.

I felt I was handing over an efficient command and Fleet to Terry, and I could not have wished for a nicer person to take it on. He also inherited John Lippiett, to whom we were sorry to say goodbye, as we were to the whole retinue, who, despite changes, had remained loyal and hardworking throughout. Terry was to use Admiralty House as a mess rather than a full-time home and I fear that the atmosphere changed somewhat. Elizabeth's entente with the wives, and not least the NATO wives, had been of enormous help in running a happy international outfit.

Christmas was spent at 'South Cottage' for the first time for over three years, and on 28 December off we went to Cyprus. I was awarded the Grand Cross of the Order of the Bath on 1 January 1974, but sadly, after a short while on Cyprus, I received a telegram saying that Father was becoming very weak and I should come home. This I did, and I last saw him on the afternoon of 10 January. He was in bed, breathing quite easily, but with his eyes shut. I spoke to him, but received no reply, and told him then what a wonderful Father he had been to Peter and me. I think he smiled. The nurses expected no change, and I left after about an hour and drove down to 'South Cottage'. When I arrived I received a telephone call from Patricia, who had popped in to visit Father for a short while after me, to say that the nurses had since rung up to say that he had died.

Peter and I did the necessary, the cremation was arranged at Beckenham, and we spent some time going through his papers, which he took pride in keeping in excellent order, retaining those we felt should be retained and destroying those we thought he would wish to have destroyed. We had a memorial service at St Lawrence's, and Father's ashes were deposited, unmarked, in the little corner of the church next to those of Mousse. It was the end of an era. As time moves on, I realise more and more how much I owe to the two of them.

CHAPTER EIGHT

First Sea Lord

1974–7

My operational command responsibilities were now at an end, meaning I would never fly my flag at sea again. As First Sea Lord, one was simply senior professional member of the Admiralty Board, and if one embarked, no flag was flown unless there was a quorum of the board present (three members, I think), when the Board Flag, three anchors on a red ground, which replaced the flag of the Lord High Admiral of England, could be flown. The Queen alone could now fly the flag of the Lord High Admiral when at sea, a change dating from the unification of the MoD in 1964.

I knew the MoD well from past experience, even in its new form, and the job of being the chief of naval staff did not worry me in prospect. However, the position carried with it many representational duties, and also the honour of being the first and principal naval ADC to the Queen. The Chiefs of Staff were, in a sense, among the great officers of state. They were invited to all kinds of state occasions, including the State Opening of Parliament, the Remembrance Service at the Cenotaph, duties concerned with state visits by visiting dignitaries, and so forth. In these, one represented one's service as an individual and, collectively, the military establishment under the Crown. It was one's duty also to visit abroad representing the Royal Navy, and to be the host, as one of the Admiralty Board, of visits by one's foreign equivalents to this country. There would therefore be a heavy programme, in which, happily, Elizabeth would be involved throughout, and less happily, a number of speeches would have to be made. We both looked forward to it with confidence.

Ken Wilcockson was an admirable secretary, and Dick Fitch (who had been my staff officer operations in the Far East Fleet) had already joined to be my naval assistant. I would inherit June Light (whom I knew from my days as VCNS) as personal assistant, and we knew she would also do a splendid job helping Elizabeth on her side of affairs. When Tom started up at King's College, where he was to study law, he would be able to stay with us in the Mall House flat, and Susan was happily married and raising her family. We would keep 'South Cottage' to ourselves at the weekends, and there was No. 4 at Lapithos waiting for us for the holidays. Peter had a grace and favour house at St James's Palace, and was very busy in his job, but I was sure we should see something of each other in the years ahead.

Accordingly, I was content and interested on 1 March 1974, when

I relieved Michael Pollock on the very day when the Wilson Labour government took office having won the general election. Michael had been promoted Admiral of the Fleet on leaving his post, and was in good form. We had the usual short turnover, in which he told me how bad things had been and wished me luck with a Labour government and a new secretary of state, Roy Mason having been appointed.

Among the anxieties he voiced, he had one in particular. He felt that the secret programme known as Chevaline, vital for the improvement of the Polaris missile force, was in a thoroughly bad way. He had tried to have its management improved but had got nowhere, and he urged me to put it at the top of my priority list. It was a complex and expensive programme, but we learned early that the Socialist government was prepared to go ahead with it, having accepted the arguments that had convinced its predecessor. I therefore expressed my anxieties to Michael Cary, the Principal Under-Secretary of State, and Hermann Bondi, an old friend, who was the Chief Scientific Adviser. His deputy for nuclear matters, who was in charge of the Chevaline project, was neither a businessman nor an industrialist. He had no proper staff to supervise the hundreds of small contracts that had been let in connection with the project, in addition to the work being done at the Atomic Weapons Research Establishment, Aldermaston.

Inefficient management apart, the Navy was deeply unhappy, notably the Submarine Officer, David Scott (an old Yardley Courtier), who was charged with naval supervision of the project. Flag Officer Submarines, John Roxburgh, said frankly that on present form, he would refuse to order submarines to sea with the system. I decided to take my stand on safety and explained to Michael Cary and Hermann Bondi that unless the project was transferred to the management of the Admiralty Board in the person of the Controller, I did not believe that the board could ever be satisfied that the system would be safe to go to sea in a submarine. This, as it was meant to, put the cat among the pigeons.

We had a meeting with Roy Mason, the Secretary of State, who ruled that the project should be transferred to Admiralty Board control, but agreed that a senior member of the scientific service should join the project team. They chose Ted East, who, though senior to David Scott, agreed to serve under him and through constant soothing by David, became a satisfactory team member. I strengthened the team in the eyes of serving submariners by bringing in an active and much younger submarine officer than David, Peter Herbert, who was made a Commodore and, virtually, chief of staff to the project.

The detailed management problem was corrected by engaging the British Aircraft Corporation as prime contractor – after fairly extensive negotiations in view of the mess they would be expected to manage. This rapidly staunched the drain on funds, although a considerable overspend had become inevitable. The Controller of the Navy took charge of the whole issue, and the Navy was allowed greater input into the safety problems and all the other practical matters involved in integrating Chevaline with current weapon systems in submarines.

In the course of all this, extensive discussions were held, at my level also, with American experts on the Polaris system, and at one stage I went over to see Admiral Rickover himself. At that time we were also considering what would be necessary to improve the propulsion systems of our nuclear submarines and some of our engineers had rather ambitious ideas. After seeing 'Rick', I was less enthusiastic, told the Controller so, and, I believe, had some influence on changing his plans in this respect. I took 'Rick' a present of a box made of oak from *Victory*. He seemed to be pleased. I think we hit it off pretty well, as a matter of fact, but he promptly asked if he could have it carbondated, to which I replied, 'Of course,' although I thought it a silly request, since it was bound to be less than 200 years old. I ought to have seen the joke.

It was about a year before I felt comfortable in my mind over this supremely important matter, but meanwhile, many other things were going on. We had to brief the new ministers, including the new parliamentary under-secretary of state for the Royal Navy, Frank Judd, a sensitive, energetic and intelligent man with a great social conscience. The Chiefs of Staff, led by Michael Carver, first of all gave a collective defence briefing for the secretary of state and all his ministers. There was also a restricted briefing for the prime minister, foreign secretary and secretary of state for defence on such matters as the strategic nuclear retaliatory capability, in which the Navy had to lead.

Next came a dark-blue briefing by the Admiralty Board, in a good deal of detail, by individual board members, for Mr Judd, while Tony Griffin, the controller, also had to give a specific briefing to Dr Gilbert, the minister of state for defence procurement. John Treacher was my vice-chief, later to be relieved by Lygo, whom I selected, as I did Peter White to relieve Alan Trewby as Chief of Fleet Support when the time was due. David Williams took over from Derek Empson as Second Sea Lord, and Derek went as C.-in-C. Naval Home Command at Portsmouth, replacing Andrew Lewis.

Much of the authority and influence of the First Sea Lord over his service resides in the selection of senior officers for the higher levels of responsibility, as well as in deciding on the appointment of all captains and flag officers. A 'flag plot' was maintained for me by the naval secretary, a delightful rear-admiral whom I had known before called John Forbes, and he also advised on the jigsaw of the captains' appointments. I would see many of these officers on their appointment, and all of them on their retirement. I remembered how upset Father had been when his time came to retire from the service and he had to ask to see the First Sea Lord, John Cunningham at the time, to be thanked. I resolved never to put anybody else in that position.

As First Sea Lord, I took no part in promotions of captain rank and below. Promotions on the flag list and to flag rank were controlled by a committee, of which I was chairman, consisting of the Second Sea Lord, the two Commanders-in-Chief, Fleet and Naval Home Command, flag officer Naval Air Command, the Chief Naval Engineer Officer and the head of the Supply and Secretariat Branch. Promotions in the medical branch, including the dentists, and in the Royal Marines were endorsed by me on the advice of the Medical Director-General and the Commandant-General

Hong Kong naval base, 1967.

Aden; the flag is in HMS *Fearless* with HMS *Intrepid* and HMS *Albion* in the background.

Visiting the Crater, Aden, with Lt-Col. Mitchell of the Argyll & Sutherland Highlanders.

An unusually happy event during the Aden evacuation: a birthday party on board HMS *Eagle* on 27 November 1967 for the last British High Commissioner, Sir Humphrey Trevelyan. On his right is General Tower and on my left is Sir Michael Le Fanu, the C.-in-C. Middle East.

A joint fly-past off Aden seen from HMS *Hermes*, whose Sea Vixens and Buccaneers lead the formation.

Last Christmas at sea, HMS *Hermes*, 1967.

Promotion at sea.

Admiralty House, Northwood. The figurehead from HMS *Challenger* was later removed to an appropriate location, the Oceanographical Institute.

The 'gadget room' at Northwood under trial.

HMS *Fearless* entering Lisbon, 1972.

HMS *Bulwark*, October 1972. Visiting the Senior Rates Mess with her captain, Lance Bell-Davies.

CINCFLEET visiting survey ships at Castries, St Lucia, in the West Indies in the summer of 1973, flag in HMS *Fox*.

Northwood revisited as First Sea Lord. On my right are Admiral Lewin CINCFLEET and his NATO Chief of Staff Rear Admiral Besnard, and on my left Air Marshal Lowe, the Air Commander, and Rear Admiral Roberts, the Fleet Chief of Staff.

HMS *Sovereign*, the first visitor after the commissioning of the nuclear-powered submarine, with Commander Laybourne and Admiral Raikes, Flag Officer Submarines.

Visiting Monterey as guests of the US Navy, in October 1974.

Chief of Defence Staff, carrying Vice Admiral L.H. Ashmore's sword.

Presenting the Queen's Sword at Dartmouth, April 1977.

Goodbye to all that.

'Britannia's Bulwark' – the Naval component. The Silver Jubilee Review of the Fleet (Admiral Sir Henry Leach) by Her Majesty the Queen, 1977.

British warships in line ahead, *c.* 1935.

Royal Marines, tendered through the Second Sea Lord. I did not therefore have the same authority over promotions as over very senior appointments, and was wont to speak last on them. Nevertheless, it is obvious that the nature of an appointment, if successful, qualified or, if not, disqualified an officer in the lists. With the reduced size of the Navy and a tendency, in my view, to a bloated flag list, mine was a difficult as well as a responsible task. Some jobs clearly groomed people for stardom; some seemed not to.

I was anxious to avoid a bandwagon running through a succession of jobs, which might reduce incentive in a wider range of important senior appointments. I was, in fact, the first Fleet Commander-in-Chief to have been made First Sea Lord for a very long time. This was because the 'royal road' had led through the unified headquarters at Singapore and Aden. These no longer existed, and I did not reckon it to be in the interests of the Navy for the Fleet Commander-in-Chief to count on becoming First Sea Lord next, nor for the Fleet to have anybody but one of the best as its Commander-in-Chief. The difficulty was that there were practically no jobs to play with. However, I did eventually send Lewin to the Naval Home Command – much, I think, to his dismay though he was very good about it and said nothing at the time. This short-toured Empson, but I thought it a price worth paying. Treacher was sent to the Fleet, where, at a difficult time for the aircraft carrier force, I thought it good to have a naval aviator. Kirsty, his wife, went to Northwood with him, and Admiralty House started to play its full role again instead of being a 'mess'.

In no time at all, the government had informed the Chiefs of Staff, through Roy Mason, that there was to be a root and branch review of defence expenditure and of the roles of the three services. I thought to myself, 'Off we go again.' Chevaline excluded, the whole cost of the strategic deterrent continued to be borne on the Navy vote, and I was thankful that *Invincible* was building and another ship of her class had been laid down. The issue of the Sea Harrier had not been solved by my predecessor, but I had hopes that the new chief of the air staff, Andrew Humphrey, might be helpful, if not actively so. Just as fundamental an issue was the need, in the foreseeable future, to replace the Sea King, to restore an organic, airborne early-warning capability and – perhaps more important still – to maintain an appreciable building progamme for Fleet nuclear-propelled submarines. Numbers of frigates and destroyers, maids of all work of the Fleet, were essential if our accustomed range of peacetime tasks was to continue to be carried out, and the replacement of the wooden-hulled Ton Class mine countermeasures vessels was soon to become inescapable.

In the Defence Review as a whole, it was important, first and foremost, to obtain a feel for the government's commitment to NATO, since it was NATO, and in particular the three major NATO commanders, whose strategy determined force requirements. Member nations could then argue among themselves and decide the share that each should take of each slice – land, sea or air – of the total. Once this was established, it was necessary for each government, allowing for the flexibility that the NATO system of 'earmarking for assignment' allowed, to assess commitments out of the

NATO area or not covered in other respects by the NATO umbrella – national commitments which had, somehow or other, to be met. All this having been done, the national services argued among themselves, ultimately at Chief of Staff level, in those relatively marginal areas where there was a choice as to how commitments might be met by one or other service activity.

In the 1974 review, the Chiefs then produced and costed a self-styled 'critical level' of forces which we agreed was necessary to meet irreducible commitments across the board. In the course of time, this was agreed by Roy Mason (who was, I thought, an excellent secretary of state for defence) and then by cabinet, so that a White Paper could be produced for parliament. As can be imagined, all this took a tremendous amount of effort on the part of the staff. I told VCNS that I would handle it myself, although his input was always welcome, and this I did through a small committee consisting of the assistant chief of naval staff policy, Peter Berger, assistant under-secretary naval staff, Alastair Jaffray, and the director of plans, William Staveley. Other members of the naval staff or the Second Sea Lord's or Chief of Fleet Support's side were called in as required.

The Navy came out of it without having lost a major weapon system, but with a decision on the Sea King replacement deferred, and with no decision on the Sea Harrier having been taken. However, we had obtained approval to build one Fleet submarine every 15 months, and to obtain for them the Sub-Harpoon, a version of the American ship- and submarine-launched surface-to-surface missile modified and improved to suit our requirements. The Royal Marines and the amphibious forces also survived. At one time this had appeared to some rather doubtful, and had led Ian Gourlay, the Commandant-General Royal Marines, to make a personal appeal to me, which he did extremely well. As a result, I undertook to support the marines through thick and thin, providing he accepted as their main role the support of Allied Forces Northern Europe, and this he did. He also developed a close relationship with the Dutch Marine Corps, and these two factors, I think, turned the tide.

We had moved in to the Mall House flat on joining and found it suited us extremely well. We had a far smaller staff than at Northwood but entirely adequate since much of our entertainment was of the government variety, and less had to be carried out in our own residence. We went to 'South Cottage' for weekends and to Cyprus for holidays, or at least that was what we planned. The flat was in a building known as Archway Block North, the whole of which used to be the residence of the First Sea Lord, the First Lord living in Admiralty House, just off Whitehall. The rest of Archway Block North was now offices, except for one or two flats occupied by civil servants. Admiralty House was used for official entertainment, although parts of it were available as flats for the secretary of state for defence and another minister.

I aimed to be in the office at 8.50 a.m. each day, which gave Ken Wilcockson, Dick Fitch and the staff time to sort out papers and signals before I arrived. I tried to have something like half an hour's walk first, either round St James's Park or perhaps in the direction of the City and back through Embankment Gardens, and very pleasant these walks were, especially if, as often happened, I met somebody I knew. I had an official car, and a delightful civilian driver called Ron Stirling, who would take me to the country on Friday evening, and bring me back on the Monday morning. I would leave the office late unless there was an entertainment of some sort, but never so late as when I was Director of Plans, nor even when I was VCNS; very rarely, if ever, did I need to bring work home, which was just as well because the security classification was often high.

In the ordinary course, therefore, we were well looked after domestically, as indeed we should have been, and all one's energies and resources could be committed to the job. This concerned not only the subjects I have already mentioned, but every military or politico-military conundrum with which the government felt it was faced, which would, of course, then be referred to the Chiefs of Staffs Committee for a recommendation. We would meet once a week on a Tuesday, and there would be briefing papers and a briefing session beforehand. At the end of each meeting, I would call the relevant members of the naval staff into my office to tell them what had happened, what I thought about it, and what, if anything, they now had to do. Later, the minutes would come out, and I would have to check carefully to make certain that neither I nor anybody else had been misled. As well as the formal meetings of the Chiefs, we would have periodic informal ones, known as a COSI (Chiefs of Staff Informal), with only CDS and the three chiefs present, plus, perhaps, someone to take notes. These were valuable, and it was also of extreme value to be located in the same building as one's colleagues. I could walk along the sixth floor and, always by appointment, visit Andrew or Peter Hunt, the soldier, or Michael Carver, the CDS, to discuss something man-to-man, and obtain, one hoped, an agreed line.

A continuing task of immense importance was to secure approval to buy the Sea Harrier for the Royal Navy. This meant an agreement of some kind with the Chief of the Air Staff, since, although Peter Hunt saw the need, Michael Carver seemed to regard the issue as the Navy wanting a new toy. He had been reluctant enough to continue to support the strategic nuclear retaliatory capability and Chevaline. The case I put to the Chiefs for the Harrier was that it was not the RAF's fault but the Navy's that we were unable to say when and where we wanted the RAF in time for them to deploy before the threat materialised. We therefore needed something organic to the Fleet to improve our 'on-site' reconnaissance, take out shadowers and take on the unexpected attack. Given this capability, we would also then have a capability for extended but limited strike.

Andrew saw the point, and I had no difficulty in agreeing with him that the manning of these aircraft, as far as aircrew was concerned, should be divided between officers of the RAF and the Royal Navy. I knew, of course, that no RAF officer could be content to make a career of flying Sea Harriers, and that to prosper he must transfer to shore-based aircraft, whereas Royal Navy aviators would progress up the Harrier command chain and, sooner or later, would dominate these squadrons. However, Andrew was intent that the Navy's purchase of vertical and short take-off and landing aircraft should be directed towards the development of an advanced Harrier, rather than the GR1 already flying with the RAF in Germany, suitably modified. He talked gaily of plenum chamber burning as a means of boosting performance but I was told that this was years away, if ever likely to be achieved. I knew, too, that unless we obtained aircraft as quickly and cheaply as they could be procured, we would be unlikely to get them at all. As a result, Andrew and I were unable to agree on the RAF supporting the Sea Harrier the Navy felt it wanted, although he did agree not to oppose it and loyally maintained his agreement despite all kinds of provocations – the last by Denis Healey in the Overseas Policy and Defence Committee itself, with the prime minister in the chair.

Before reaching that point, however, I had had to secure the agreement of the Chiefs of Staff and the secretary of state for defence. An important part in this was played by taking Roy Mason to the British Aircraft Corporation airfield at Dunsfold for a Harrier demonstration. This was followed by a very careful briefing, given by Peter Berger and a naval airman. We had rehearsed it well, it came across as I hoped it would, and the aircraft's performance was spectacular. I sat next to Roy Mason at lunch, and he turned to me and said, 'Edward, I don't think you are going to get the Harrier as soon as you expect,' so I took what comfort I could from that.

In the end, thanks to Andrew's forbearance, Peter Hunt's support and, I think, the fall-out from the Dunsfold visit, the Chiefs of Staff were able to agree a paper recommending that the Harrier should be bought for the Royal Navy. Once the Chiefs of Staff had agreed something, the Chief of Defence Staff became their spokesman, and Michael Carver, however much he might in his heart disagree with something, would, if acting as the Chiefs' advocate, speak clearly and well in support of the agreed position. This he did at the Overseas Policy and Defence Committee on the subject of the Harrier. Andrew Humphrey declined to respond to Healey's intervention, I was asked if I wanted to say anything, and was able to say, 'No, the Chief of Defence Staff has said it all.' Mason spoke in favour, we received approval, and I came back to my office walking on air. I found that Dick Fitch and Ken Wilcockson had laid on a bottle of champagne in anticipation, which I would never have dared to do. I came in and said, 'We've got it,' and then we all had a glass or two.

Two major problems were now left for the surface Fleet: the Sea King replacement, and the provision of airborne early warning. This the RAF had taken over, using the Shackleton equipped with radar fitted in the Naval 849 Squadron of Skyraiders and Gannets since 1951. As a result, we were more naked at sea than we had been for nearly a quarter of a century. I knew that suitable radar could be bought and mounted on a helicopter, and would give a major improvement in long-range and low-level air warning. However, the RAF were restive after the Harrier decision, and it was no good, in my judgement, going for such a radar without having previously obtained approval for the aircraft on which to fit it. In a small way, but an important one, it was analogous to the problem we had had with the through-deck cruiser. The Sea King was the core of our surface anti-submarine warfare capability; with the submarine force, it was our major contribution to SACLANT, and vital to the containment of the Soviet threat. I did not feel I could approve any approach which might jeopardise its replacement and therefore told the staff that the AEW Radar must wait.

Its lack was to be sorely felt in the Falklands campaign, but the fact that their forces knew the Sea Dart's envelope profile, as we had exported it to the Argentine Navy, helped to save the day. They knew the efficiency of that weapon, and therefore flew beneath the envelope by day, and the Argentine bombs did not always fuse. At night, when they could not come in below the envelope in safety and to enter it was to invite destruction, they stayed on the ground. Thus we were able to keep our small force of Harriers nearly 100 per cent operational by day. Thereafter, the case for the Sea King AEW Radar was made, and by then Sea King replacement had been approved in principle.

The maintenance of numbers and quality in the destroyer and frigate force was a continual struggle for the naval staff. To provide the numbers in the programme required two or three building starts a year, and prices increased annually. The Leanders were an excellent design, and various types of modification were made to them. The Type 21 Amazon Class frigate was designed commercially at the initiative of the board's predecessor, seemed to give good value for money, and was a fine-looking ship. The next design, the Type 22, turned out to be large and expensive. We kept it in the programme, but I was somewhat doubtful as to whether the capability we could expect from it would justify its cost. However, during one of my visits to sea, I met Jim Eberle in *Ark Royal*. He was then Flag Officer Carriers and Amphibious Forces, a job I had sent him to, having heard much of his reputation for ability, and being determined to try him out in the Fleet curtailed his time as Flag Officer Sea Training. Eberle told me of a development in American ships that seemed of the highest importance. Back in the office, I discovered that, true to their usual practice, the Americans had told us of this 18 months before, but neither the director responsible nor the VCNS had recognised its significance. I judged it to be a system that eminently justified proceeding with a second batch of Type 22 frigates, and told Ray Lygo to give it every priority. No one could drive a programme through better, and he was quick to recognise yet another application of computer power and passive sensors, fundamental to future tactics.

There were, of course, many preoccupations and cares on the shoulders of the Second Sea Lord, who is responsible for the personnel of the Navy. Recruitment of officers, particularly technical officers, and retention of experienced ratings were probably at the heart of his problems. Pay and conditions in the Navy are very different from those of the other two services, and yet we had to labour under an inter-service system which suited us badly.

Apart from the odd deployment to Northern Ireland, in which the commandos played their part, the other services enjoyed the company of their wives and families almost everywhere they went. When they were in Germany, for example, where a great many of them served, or indeed in Cyprus, they enjoyed local overseas allowances to bring their standards of living up to a level which was often the source of much argument with the Treasury. There was no 'sea-room' in Germany, and the average sailor, seeing a non-commissioned officer come back from there with a Mercedes and a caravan, wondered what he was missing. It was to be some time before the sailor, who in many cases had not been provided with a married quarter and had to buy his own house, was able to realise what a good investment the Navy, through perhaps a too old-fashioned attitude to the welfare of families, had more or less compelled him to make. In the early and mid-1970s, therefore, we had to divert money that we could ill afford, from things that would give the Russians pause, to improving living conditions ashore, not only in terms of married quarters and amenities, but also in the shore training establishments and barracks, many of which dated from before the First World War.

These matters carried considerable political overtones, so they were often discussed at the Admiralty Board with our minister in the chair. The old Board Room was familiar to me now, but I do remember, at my first meeting as First Sea Lord, being asked by Mr Judd to speak, and saying, after Le Fanu's example, that I would like, please, to speak last. This practice continued. The last word was usually less important than it sounds, although I remember once exploding effectively after a debate on the rationalisation of libraries and historical sections in the MoD, 'At least leave us our history.' (The Naval Historical Branch still survives, albeit co-located.) Rather, it allowed me, before the minister as chairman did so, to sum up the professional consensus with candour and emphasis.

Another political hot potato, at a time when union power was in the ascendant, lay in the dockyards, which were Peter White's responsibility. The government had introduced a chief executive, dockyards – a civilian – some time earlier, but results did not meet expectations. The cheerful humanity of the admiral superintendent, who would wander round his dockyard with his labrador, talking to anybody, had been removed by the various reorganisations which had begun in 1958. The general manager was clever and expert in the material aspects of life, but lacked the common touch. Friction between the Navy and the dockyard civilian management was frequent, and motivation of the workforce difficult to maintain. This was a situation in which ministers, particularly Socialist ministers, felt that they could well be expert. Peter White, who as well as the dockyards had to look after the whole stores and ammunition supply systems of the Navy, the Royal Fleet Auxiliary and so on, had quite a job on his hands.

The problems of Tony Griffin, the Controller, were just as manifold, and were compounded by the fact that the Ship Department at Bath sat on a different hill from the Weapons Department, so that the two branches of his controllerate which most needed to be integrated were separated by geography as well as by a host of traditions or bad habits. When I visited Bath, it seemed to me that the Ship Department went on reasonably happily in its old ways, but that I had never seen so many bright, intelligent and – because underemployed – unhappy weapons electrical officers anywhere as in the

Weapons Department. We started to change this when Tony left voluntarily to become the first chairman of British Shipbuilders and Dick Clayton took over. I told Tony, whose motives, as ever, were of the highest, that I thought he needed his head examined for wanting that job, but he thought it the best way in which he could serve both his country and the Navy. Unfortunately, political and industrial circumstances were to be much against him.

The other members of the Admiralty Board in my time included the deputy under-secretary of state, Derek Stevens, who was our main link with the civil service and accounting officer for the Navy Department, and Basil Lythall, the Chief Scientist, Royal Navy, who, as integration proceeded, had other responsibilities as a deputy chief scientific adviser to Bondi. Basil had a particular expertise in underwater and anti-submarine matters, and was a good and cheerful colleague. It was open to the secretary of state to take the chair at the Admiralty Board rather than the Navy minister if he wished, and from time to time one of the more senior civil servants would attend our meetings. I would also sometimes take the chair at a committee of the Admiralty Board which consisted chiefly of the naval members, when we would discuss what line on professional matters we might wish to take in a wider forum. I would also, once every three or four months, attend VCNS's meeting with the directors of the naval staff, to learn what I ought to hear from the horses' mouths. I also heard a good deal from my callers, and a certain amount from my personal staff, the naval assistant and secretary.

A strong VCNS – and in Treacher, and later Lygo, I had two – was, it seemed to me, essential. It allowed me, as CNS, to be much more 'purple' in my dealings with my colleagues on the Chiefs of Staffs Committee. I might, and often did, have to agree a line that was not necessarily the line recommended by the naval staff. I would come back and debrief, say what had been decided, and then it would be for the VCNS to make sure that the staff understood, toed the line, and got on with it.

I have dealt in broad outline with the Whitehall scene because, as far as the Navy was concerned, professionally the buck stopped with me, and the Navy's case and its contribution in the defence case had to be represented by me, with my Chiefs of Staff colleagues, to the government through the Whitehall machine. The job of the First Sea Lord, needless to say, did not end there. It was also my business, as the incumbent, to represent the Royal Navy on visits to my opposite numbers abroad and by entertaining my opposite numbers at home. The programme of a visiting chief of naval staff was my responsibility, and Elizabeth and I had to play some part in it. As we were also involved in state occasions, I had a good deal less control over my diary than I had enjoyed as a Commander-in-Chief. The programme of visits abroad and reciprocal visits by chiefs of naval staff to this country was carefully worked out by my office in conjunction with the Foreign and Commonwealth Office, so that no one should feel overlooked nor anyone else overdone.

Half a Stilton would no longer do as a present. My predecessors, for years, had given something called an 'Armada' dish: a silver plate which, as time went on and inflation progressed, became successively smaller with each First Sea Lord. Even so, each plate, engraved, cost something over £50, which was as much as the Treasury were prepared to concede could be afforded. I found a substitute, which I, at least, was satisfied with, in a small desk blotter such as Father had given Mousse years ago. Made of silver, this could be bought for about £30, suitably engraved on the top. More than once I handed one to one of my opposite numbers, whose desk was piled high with papers, and was able to say, 'I hope you will find this pretty useful now,' and they would appreciate the joke.

Except as a member of the Channel Committee, which met rarely, I now had no direct link with NATO, my responsibilities being national. However, Michael Carver, CDS, who was our representative on the NATO Military Committee and so on, did not much enjoy the Nuclear Planning Group which derived from those committees set up by Mr McNamara long ago, so on occasion I attended it on his behalf. It was always nice to get into the NATO forum again, where Hill-Norton had succeeded Steinhof as chairman of the Military Committee.

At the beginning of April, Elizabeth went to Cyprus, and I followed as soon as I could for a fortnight's very happy holiday in our house. Little did we know how long it would be before we lived there again. The day after returning to the office, we went to dinner with the C.-in-C. US Naval Forces Europe, Worth Bagley. We had known his predecessor, Bush Bringle, well, and it was a matter of importance to the Royal Navy that the Americans still saw fit to keep a four-star officer in London in a strictly national capacity. The 6th Fleet – while earmarked for assignment to the Allied C.-in-C. Southern Europe, and its commander, Dick Colbert's relief, Stansfield Turner – came under Bagley in ordinary peacetime organisation. For senior members of the naval staff, he was a very important line through to the naval side of the Pentagon. The pressures were on to reduce the status of the job to three stars, and this was entirely understandable, since there was little work for him to do, but knowing the American emphasis on rank, it was obviously my job to try to dissuade them from doing this. In the course of time, however, the pressure prevailed, and Bagley was relieved by Moorer, a vice-admiral who had the distinction of being the young brother of Tom Moorer, a very distinguished and successful chairman of the Joint Chiefs during most of my time as C.-in-C. Channel. We enjoyed our dinner at the admiral's pleasant flat above the US Navy Headquarters in Grosvenor Square.

The morning after a dinner at the Guildhall in honour of the Queen of Denmark, I paid a visit to Culdrose by helicopter, taking the whole day to see the mass of new building that was going on there at vast expense. Everything was in order, though I did criticise what appeared to be penthouse flats for visiting VIPs in the officers' quarters, built, I think, by an enterprising architect at an expense that I personally would not have approved. Dinner parties of one kind or another happened often during our time in the Mall House flat, and sometimes the hospitality was returned there. The small staff, which included a leading Wren especially to look after Elizabeth, a valet for me, a chief petty officer steward and a cook, could not have been better. It was unusual for us to have more than two or three quiet evenings during the week.

On 14 May we left for Mons, because it was time for Andy Goodpaster's annual SHAPEX, to which national Chiefs of Staff were invited. With my links with NATO so fresh, I was very anxious to go. We were kindly given lunch by General Sir John Mogg, the deputy to Andy, in his extremely comfortable château. I had met him before when, as ACDS(S), I had visited the 1st British Corps. He was then the corps commander, and had come with his wife to dinner with Charles Page to meet me. He was a Greenjacket, genial, shrewd and a very nice man altogether. His job was derived from the one which Field Marshal Montgomery had occupied when the American supreme commander was first appointed to NATO and the British were given a particular responsibility for training. This had long since been rather eroded, and I think John Mogg found time for plenty of contemplation. Admiral Rawbone, who had relieved Rupert Wainright at SHAPE, gave a dinner party for us to meet the British naval officers of the headquarters, and altogether we had a very enjoyable time before flying home to Thorney Island, where Ron met us and took us straight to 'South Cottage'.

Later in the month I visited *Collingwood*, where our weapons electrical people are trained and was impressed. It is an enormous establishment, but appeared to me to be well run and smart at the time I went there. Although it was strictly the Second Sea Lord's business, I was preoccupied with the position of the weapons electrical engineer officer in the Navy in the wake of modern weapon developments. His responsibilities and those of the seaman officer were on converging courses, and it was important to be sure that they were not collision courses but that both had fulfilling and complementary careers. At the beginning of June I visited *Ganges* (or Shotley, as it is known), our original boys' training establishment, and the only one until *St Vincent* was founded in the 1930s with Father as the first First Lieutenant. The boy entry at 15½–16 was coming to an end. The hutted facilities and the tall mast were reminiscent of the old Navy and although the place was already half empty, everyone was in good heart.

I visited the Joint Services Staff College (now known as the Joint Services Defence College) at Latimer around this time, to find Freddie Sowrey, whom I had known in Aden, in charge. They had great plans for expansion, which I found rather difficult to take, since much had already been done. In fact, I had other plans for the place, but was keeping them to myself, since it was not strictly my responsibility. By the time these became public, Freddie had been relieved by David Loram, who had been my flag captain so often in *Antrim*. He was to provide redoubtable opposition to what I wanted to do: move the Joint Services Defence College to Greenwich, to save money and to concentrate the Defence Establishment; in addition, I feared for the future of Greenwich, on which the City University and others had cast longing eyes, unless we could increase the tasks it undertook for defence. The activities of the Naval Staff College, the War College and the Nuclear Engineers Course did not fill the place, which, however historic, was costly to keep going. A joint service presence was just what the doctor ordered, and it semed to me that our costings showed great advantage. David Williams, the Second Sea Lord, was far from convinced about this, and there was a good deal of opposition from the other service Chiefs of Staff. This issue was to run and run.

On 3 July, Elizabeth and I went to Greenwich for a very happy occasion, a government dinner in honour of the Queen's Birthday, and the next night I dined with the Armourers and Braziers, and made a speech, most of which Ken Wilcockson had written for me, thank goodness. He and Dick were very handy at roughing something out since I seldom had time to write much myself. A couple of weeks before this, the Chiefs of Staff, in full fig, had marched behind the cortege of the Duke of Gloucester's funeral from Victoria Barracks, Windsor, to St George's Chapel. Elizabeth was able to join me for the service, and we had a good view of the royal family as they came out of the choir at the end, followed by 'Dickie' Mountbatten and others. I had only met the Duke of Gloucester once, being presented to him by 'Dickie' at Immingham Dock during the war, when he had visited our destroyer squadron and come on board *Jupiter* – what a long time ago it all seemed.

On 11 July, Elizabeth's submarine, *Sovereign*, commissioned for the first time and we both flew down to Devonport for the occasion. I tried to make about one visit to the Navy a week if I could, and the week after *Sovereign*'s do, I went to Faslane to see the Polaris force, the 3rd Submarine Squadron and the training facilities that we had set up as a result of my initiative at Northwood. There followed the usual dinner of the three service staff courses together at Greenwich, which the Chiefs of Staff tried to attend, and the Royal Tournament on Saturday 27 July, where I took the salute surrounded by grandchildren and godchildren. The day before had seen the Annual Signal Officers' Reunion at *Mercury*, which I have never missed when in England, and which was attended, as it invariably was, by 'Dickie' Mountbatten. Though getting noticeably older, he was in good form and he certainly did the branch no end of good by his loyalty in this respect.

July 1974 saw more serious and troubling developments. A coup in Cyprus displaced Makarios with Nicos Sampson, a notorious terrorist and EOKA thug. Makarios escaped by the skin of his teeth to the Sovereign Base Areas, and was flown out by the British. We, with Turkey and Greece, were guarantors of the 1960 Constitution against external aggression. Since 1963, under the auspices of Makarios, the 1960 Constitution had been in many respects ignored. The British, I think, had regarded this as an internal matter, rightly or wrongly, and in 1967, under the threat of what seemed to be a possible Turkish invasion to rescue the Turkish Cypriots from the persecution they were enduring, Norman Costar, then the high commissioner, had advised the British to evacuate from the northern part of the island. In the event, no invasion had materialised, and Norman had come in for intense local criticism for scaremongering. Be that as it may, most of the Turkish Cypriots had to remove themselves from their villages and, for example, in Lapithos, which was now a hard-core EOKA village, no Turkish Cypriot was left: all had taken refuge in the Turkish enclave round Nicosia. Their houses were shuttered and empty, and they no longer dared visit the fields which they had managed to cultivate between 1963 and 1967. Those living in Kyrenia could only visit the Nicosia Turkish enclave and return in the safety of a United Nations convoy.

Now a murderous adherent of EOKA and Enosis held the power in Cyprus. The 'Colonels', chauvinists to a man, ruled Greece. The situation of the Turkish Cypriot community was perilous in the extreme. All vestige of constitutional rule had been abrogated, the UN forces were neither of a size nor sufficiently equipped to deal with what might occur and the British had a brigade or so in the island, plus a number of expensive aircraft and facilities that badly needed looking after. Predominant in the Chiefs of Staffs' minds, when they considered what military measures could be taken by us in this situation, was the fact that Cyprus was host to innumerable British citizens, including a great many dependents of the forces there, many not living in cantonments but scattered all over the island. While no British citizen had ever been murdered by a Turkish Cypriot, we could not forget the numerous political murders of our men and their women by Greek (or possibly Greek Cypriot) people. In any move to support the Turkish Cypriot population, we would have to reckon with Greek knives. Not for the first time in history, a British garrison was hamstrung by its dependents in a transition from a peaceful to an emergency situation as unexpected as it was sudden.

The Turkish prime minister, Ecevit, and his foreign minister, came to London, invoked the Treaty of Guarantee, and saw Harold Wilson and Callaghan. The next morning, I heard the prime minister say, 'They are going to invade.' On 20 July they did so, using forces assembled at Mersin and landing on the north coast, both east and, notably, west of Kyrenia, about four miles from our house. Accompanying the invasion, there were some terror tactics. The destroyers of the Turkish Navy shelled the coast in one or two places, and a few bombs were dropped, including three on our village (one only 150 yards from our house, which, as we learned later, blew out the windows).

Sampson appealed to Greece for help. Britain kept quiet and, to the best of my knowledge, Admiral Arapakis refused to order the Greek Fleet to sail. (I believe this to be true, and it is remarkable that his head is still on his shoulders.) With Turkey only 40 miles away, disposing the largest army in NATO, the outcome in military terms was a foregone conclusion. There were some skirmishes with the Greek Cypriot National Guard on the coast, particularly around the camp at Lambousa, and two or three casualties among the British residents. *Hermes* and some other ships in the Mediterranean were deployed to mount an evacuation of the north coast as early as practicable. Meanwhile, the Turks left the new main road over the mountains of Kyrena from the north to Nicosia open and unmolested and Greek Cypriots poured along it. All the people in our village that could, including those from the house next door, fled. Their animals and their old people, they abandoned. When resistance failed to crumble as quickly as expected, the Turks put in more troops and pushed further over the mountains into the Mezaoria; they then stopped. Nicos Sampson was displaced, and in due course negotiations were held in Geneva, called by Jim Callaghan with Turkish and Greek representatives, but to little effect. The naval evacuation by our ships was well conducted and successful. When next back in Cyprus, I heard countless stories about it and about the sense of humour and cheerful efficiency of the officers and men involved.

After summer holidays in the South of France, came our first official foreign trip in my new position. It was, rightly, a call on the Chief of Naval Operations in the United States. Jim Holloway, whom I had not met before, turned out to be perfectly delightful and very intelligent, an aviator with a charming wife. They became friends, and have remained so. I felt that if he was Bud Zumwalt's choice, Bud had done much to redeem some of the damage and disturbance he had caused his service. The RAF took us to Andrews AFB, and thereafter for our internal flights we were assigned a splendidly-equipped US Air Force VIP aircraft with an assiduous and hospitable crew. All ceremony in Washington had to be conducted in whites, and included a visit to Arlington Cemetery where I laid a wreath. Then there was an opportunity to get to know Jim and meet some of his admirals, as well as to see some of our people who enjoyed a privileged position in the Navy building. Lance Bell-Davies, as a Rear-Admiral, had relieved David Scott as head of the British Navy Defence Staff in Washington. As a good submariner and the son of a naval aviator who had won the Victoria Cross, he was very well equipped for his job and was greatly liked and respected. He and his wife, Joan, accompanied us on our trip. I had with me Dick Fitch, a US Navy captain as a personal liaison officer, and June Light came too for the ride.

First, we went north-west to Seattle. I was taken to the Boeing works to hear about the Boeing hydrofoil, which was being produced for the Italian Navy among others but which I did not find likely to have much application in the Royal Navy. We also visited the enormous US Navy yard at Bremerton, part of which was being developed to accommodate the Trident submarines. I was flown over it by helicopter, and noticed the battleship *Missouri* lying alongside. I mentioned to Admiral Zech, the very pleasant commander of the 13th Naval District, that the last time I had seen that deck was when I stood on it at the surrender of Japan and how interesting it was to see her again. He very kindly ensured that I was sent, suitably mounted, a piece of *Missouri*'s deck with his compliments, so that has been added to our other timber souvenirs: a part of the mast of *Victory* which belonged to Elizabeth's grandfather, and a piece of timber from *Mikasa*, Togo's flagship at Tshushima, which I was to acquire later on board her in Japan.

We also visited the Naval Torpedo Station, which was of considerable interest since Lance and I were given a pretty comprehensive, technical briefing on the pros and cons of the Mark 48 torpedo. This was at that time the standard American deep-running, submarine-to-submarine and submarine-to-surface ship torpedo, for which we had no equivalent. It was a question of buying this or developing our own and, contrary to the view I had taken on the lightweight anti-submarine torpedo some four or five years earlier, I felt that the Mark 48 was too complicated, too expensive and, above all, too noisy for us. However, that was a problem for the VCNS and the Controller, rather than for me. As always, I was struck by the sheer scale of things in the USA. This dockyard alone (and I knew there were half a dozen others round the country) was far larger than all of ours put together. Similarly, the air stations or airfields that one passed were crammed with more aeroplanes on each than there were in the whole of the RAF. (This may be an exaggeration, but it was my impression.) It is just as well not only that they are on our side but that they are, certainly in the Navy, so very well disposed towards us.

We then went down to the Naval Postgraduate School at Monterey, looked after by Admiral Linders, and had a good walk round. It was extremely interesting and, particularly in certain aspects of anti-submarine warfare, it would have been most valuable to have sent some of our officers there, notably weapons electrical officers. The difficulty was that it would take a great bite out of their careers. Also, it was very expensive. After Monterey, we went to San Diego, another enormous base, to be looked after by our friends the Gilkesons. They lived on Coronado Island, in a lovely house, and were in great form. The tour of the installation was a bit perfunctory, but by this time we could take an American base more or less for granted. San Diego is the main operating base of the US Pacific Fleet (except for submarines, which go to Seattle) this side of Pearl Harbor. It is festooned with air stations, and I met one or two of our Fleet Air Arm officers there, flying the F14, the most advanced American naval aircraft then available, and thoroughly enjoying and profiting from the experience. Our final leg took us back to Norfolk, Virginia, to stay with Ralph Cousins, SACLANT, and his wife, Mary. The deputy SACLANT now was Ged Mansfield, another old friend, and it was a fitting and happy place to conclude our tour. We were bid a fond farewell from our American aircrew, and the RAF took us most comfortably back home.

There was plenty of work to catch up on. I visited the Admiralty Weapons Department at Bath the following week, and then a week later flew to Plymouth, spent the night with Arthur Power and, with Elizabeth, visited the Royal Naval Engineering College at Manadon fairly thoroughly the next day. This was an important visit for me. I already knew Dartmouth well, and with the current state of affairs in the Defence Review and the general contraction of shore facilities, one never knew when one might not have to call for a paper on closures or amalgamations. It was better to have trodden the ground first should one have to consider any such thing. For the same reason, I visited a good many other shore training establishments in the course of time.

At the end of October, we had an official visit by my Italian opposite number, De Giorgi, which involved dinner with the Italian ambassador, a return dinner by the Admiralty Board, and so on. His programme would send him to see other parts of the Navy rather than sitting in London, but it was my job to make certain that it was properly arranged and he saw what he wanted to, or what I thought he would want to. A little later, in November, I went down to Yeovilton, the Fleet Air Arm station where their museum is, for the

Taranto Night dinner, at which I had to speak. It was interesting there to meet 'Pegleg' Lamb, whom I had last seen writhing on the deck of *Implacable* during the operations against Truk after a 'pecking' aircraft had almost severed his leg. He was in great heart, and the museum was most impressive. I had known Peter Austin, Flag Officer Naval Air Command, since Alverstoke days, and at my request I was given a demonstration of a new fire-extinguishing material called AFFF or 'Light Water', which had just been introduced into the Fleet Air Arm only. It was almost instantly effective. I made certain that, though costly, its wider introduction into the Navy was investigated. On Remembrance Day, for the first time I had the privilege of laying the Royal Navy's wreath on the Cenotaph. The evening before, we had attended the British Legion Festival of Remembrance at the Royal Albert Hall, in a box near the Royal Box, and thoroughly enjoyed it.

In early December, accompanied by Elizabeth, I made an official visit to the Federal German Navy. We were in for four-and-a-half very cold days. The visit began at Bonn, where I was met by Admiral Kuhnle, my opposite number, and an enormous guard, after which I called on Zimmerman, the chief of defence, whom I knew, and spent some time being given briefings and so forth by the Navy. They had clear ambitions (which I think the Americans, on the whole, supported) to expand into the Eastern Atlantic Command. I tried not to appear to discourage this, though I did express the view that a great deal more had still to be done to safeguard the Baltic approaches. We then went north to the Baltic, where Paul Hartwig, Commander-in-Chief of the Fleet, took over. He showed me various interesting things, and gave me a good briefing at his headquarters. I went on board one of their smallest submarines (about 300 tons), and was very impressed, as I expected to be. There did not seem to be the same emphasis as in the Danish Navy on coastal forces, partly, I think, because of the size of the Federal German Naval Air Arm. I was astonished how many of the German senior officers whom I met had had their homes in East Prussia, Dresden or elsewhere on the wrong side of the Iron Curtain before the war, and felt sorry for them, although they appeared philosophical about this. I came home reasonably reassured, my dominant impression being of the hold that Bonn had over the whole Federal German Navy, not excepting the Fleet Commander.

I had, with some slight misgiving, approved the broadcasting of a naval soap opera, *HMS Hero*, the script of which had been written by my assistant secretary, Ian Mackintosh. I was invited to Alexandra Palace to meet the cast, and was piped on board the set somewhat hilariously. I watched an episode being produced, and found it interesting. It had a long run, and was a considerable success (although many of us had to grit our teeth during some of it). Later – and this was Ray Lygo's brainchild – a BBC programme was devoted to *Ark Royal*. It was introduced by Rod Stewart singing 'Sailing'. This was also a great success in public relations terms, and indeed, in terms of the morale of the Navy.

Os Cecil, our friend from South Africa, was now Flag Officer Malta, and early in February we flew out for a couple of days to see them and to test the water with Mintoff. I was able to see a group of ships on their way out to the Far East under the command of the Flag Officer Second Flotilla, now John Fieldhouse. I watched them enter Grand Harbour and berth, and when Fieldhouse came to call at the 'Villa Portelli', I said, 'I want to ask you one thing about entering harbour. Do they think they did it well?', to which he said, 'No Sir, and it's early days in the deployment,' so I left it at that, remembering how ships used to go in and out of Sliema Creek and, indeed, Grand Harbour 10 or 15 years earlier.

I realised how much our officers had lost in terms of practical sea time with ships in close company. Developments in tactics and weapons systems no longer required ships to operate as they had done and, moreover, their numbers had become so small and their costs so high that this was probably just as well in the interests of damage limitation. Nevertheless, the reputation of the Royal Navy requires a standard of berthing and manoeuvre second to none, and I was always anxious to impress this on people in the right position in the chain of command.

The Defence Review was safely behind us, and we wondered what next shock the government would produce for the Chiefs to digest. Meanwhile HRH Princess Anne had graciously consented to a suggestion from the Admiralty Board that she should become Chief Commandant of the Women's Royal Naval Service and in March there was a great party at St James's Palace to present Wren officers past and present to her. A year later she was to come to a WRNS officers' reunion there, where Elizabeth met a host of friends. This did much for pride and morale in a very important branch in which the service as a whole takes great pride.

In April, our friends the Holloways returned our visit and we arranged a programme which I hope showed the Chief of Naval Operations everything he wanted to see. They were certainly most appreciative. As well as the official dinner given by the Admiralty Board at Admiralty House, we were able to have them to lunch at the flat, and on another day to take them out to the theatre. They were followed by the Cousins, SACLANT, on their way to SHAPEX, which took place in May this year. We went over to Brussels in lovely weather and stayed at the 'Villa Du Lac', this time with the McKaigs. Andy was in good form, as were Joe Luns and the others, and it was pleasant, as usual, to be in the NATO atmosphere. After that, we had the official visit of the Stevensons from Australia. I remember this in particular because we were able to take them to Glyndebourne, she being very musical. Summer was the preferred time for visiting the UK, and no sooner had the Australians gone than the Indian Chief of Naval Staff and his wife, Admiral and Mrs Kohli, arrived for their programme, which followed the usual lines and which we also enjoyed.

Among visits that we made at this time was one to Rosyth, where I had to do something to help a film being made of the submarine service which involved me peering through a periscope on board *Swiftsure* for the service's 75th anniversary. I was pleased to be involved in this since both Father and Elizabeth's father had been submariners in their time. I then paid a fairly routine visit to the Royal Marines and the Navy in Northern Ireland, which included a trip with the Loch Foyle Patrol, quite a busy part of the border security patrols. We also went to Pangbourne College, a source of good officer material for the Navy, and I was impressed by the practical work in particular.

In June, it was our turn to go away, first to Sweden, where Bengt Lundvall had shown great initiative and organised a maritime symposium in Stockholm for members of both NATO and the Warsaw Pact. We took Derek Stevens (now deputy under-secretary of state Royal Navy) and William Staveley (who needed a break after having been director of plans throughout the Defence Review) and their wives with us. Jimmy Holloway was there, a Russian delegation led by one of Gorshkov's vice-chiefs, the heads of both the West German and East German Navies, and many others. It was really a remarkable turn-out in response to the Swedish invitation.

The theme was that the sea joins nations, rather than separating them. Much of the discussion turned on matters like cooperation in survey, navigation, pollution control, ice-breaking, and so forth. We broke down into four syndicates, and I was put in charge of one of these, including a quite amiable Soviet rear-admiral and the new Dutch CNS Veldkamp, among others. Carl Gustaf, now King of Sweden, attended and had lunch with us, and I admired the way in which the very protocol-conscious Swedes organised things, being pleased that Holloway, the Russian and I were treated on an equal basis from that point of view. The ladies had a good programme, and there were all manner of festivities. In addition, we had a day at sea, and were subjected to a wire-guided torpedo attack by Swedish coastal forces, which was most impressive. They ran the torpedoes shallow so that you could see exactly how many would have hit you if you had stayed afloat long enough.

There was a tremendous banquet to end with, speeches and all the rest of it, and then we moved down to Gothenberg to see the launch of a supertanker, which I fear was simply on her way to be laid up in some fjord somewhere. A great final party was given by the Mayor of Gothenberg in the City Hall. This was a glittering occasion, flashing with gold braid, candles and the odd tiara – quite a Congress of Vienna affair. Gothenberg has a long history of excellent relations with Britain, and particularly maritime Britain, and it was all great fun, and a well-deserved personal triumph for both Bengt and Karen Lundvall.

No sooner were we back in England for the Trooping of the Colour than we had to set off for Annapolis for another symposium given by the Americans, mainly for the navies of the Western Hemisphere, including the South Americans. This was conducted entirely in English, so I did not practice my Russian as I had a fortnight before, but it was interesting and well conducted, and I had to deliver a talk on the Law of the Sea. (As a result of the subsequent publication, I was later made an honorary life member of the US Naval Institute, and so receive a copy of their monthly *Proceedings*.) The staff, notably Captain Richard Hill, had done most of the work, but I had given it a rather novel and more open slant.

The Cecils, who maintained a small flat on Gozo in a village called Zebbug, had very kindly suggested lending it to us for the summer holidays, and we were delighted at the prospect. It had a low-power wireless set installed, so I would not be out of touch. I therefore decided to go to Cyprus at the end of July, and on to Malta from there by one of the RAF Nimrods which often flew between the two islands. Everyone was warned that I was coming, including Sancar, who, as Chief of Staff of the armed forces, was really the uncrowned king of Turkey, and who knew we had (or used to have) a house on the island. We had been told that the fairly reassuring situation that Elizabeth had found on a visit in November no longer existed, and that the house had been ransacked. I wondered what I would now find.

'Tank' Sherman, the resident naval officer at Episkopi, drove me up to Nicosia, where I called on the High Commissioner, a rather nervous, bearded little man called Stephen Olver, and then went over to the north, with the defence attaché joining my party, to call on the Turkish general. I offered to pay for the petrol since it was a private visit, but the colonel said to me, 'No not at all, we should never find the general's headquarters unless we were being allowed to take you there, I'll put it down to "Intelligence".' The general was courteous and friendly, and suggested I might like to see my house, to which, of course, I said yes. 'Tank' and I had booked a bungalow at the Mare Monte Hotel near Lambousa, which was more or less open.

In the afternoon we went up to No. 4 with the Turkish general's ADC. The little house looked fine from the outside, the 'Freedom Fighters' billeted there were apparent and polite, camped out in the house next door. To my astonishment I found No. 4 fully furnished. I went back to the general and thanked him for all that had been done, but asked him please to remove the furniture that was not ours. I explained that we still hoped to recover, or replace, our own in the course of time. He agreed to see that it was removed. 'Tank' and I made our way back to Episkopi, I spent the night with them and took off for Malta the next day. I left feeling more comfortable about No. 4, and that it was full marks all round for effort for the Turkish authorities, but it was important that I had taken the particular line I had over the furniture. Many 'ancient Brits' in North Cyprus were in terror of leaving their houses lest these should be looted and vandalised, not so much by the military as by various hangers-on, so it would never have done for us to be beneficiaries of Turkish generosity.

The looting had, in part, arisen as a result of the Geneva negotiations. The foreign secretary, Jim Callaghan, had secured agreement from the Greek side that the Turkish Cypriot refugees clustered in our sovereign base areas could go north but, as part of the agreement, they had to leave all their belongings behind. As a result, they arrived in the north with nothing but what they could carry, and were allocated houses by lottery by the Turkish Cypriot authorities. They then had to find something to put in them, since, as Greek property, most of them had been thoroughly ransacked. The less honest elements, naturally enough, organised raids on houses that had not yet been looted, mainly foreign houses, in order to supply this demand.

The refugees who came to Lapithos were mostly from the Paphos area, and have since turned out to be extremely kind and good neighbours, but we were unable to return to the village yet. The police force hardly existed, and the conditions were not right for leaving a property untenanted for any length of time. I was reasonably sure that No. 4 could be left with confidence, although 'Tank' had said, 'I am afraid, Sir, that you'll never live there again.' This was unsettling, as he was in no sense a defeatist officer – far from it.

Soon after our return to England, we were due to make the First Sea Lord's official visit to the Italian Navy, and this began on 1 September. We had a lovely four days, full of Italian warmth and hospitality, and became genuinely fond of our host, Gino De Giorgi, a deceptively quiet little man who was in the process of doing great things for his Navy. The Italian naval attaché, Mottolese, and his wife Miranda, who were friends from London, came out to help escort us, and the British naval attaché in Rome, Captain George, and his wife were among our party throughout. The first day was mostly taken up with wreath-laying at the Piazza Venezia, signing the President's book, and calls on De Giorgi and Baldini, the C.-in-C. Fleet, while Elizabeth tried (with her usual success) to avoid spending too much money in Rome. I have never known anyone who could spend so long choosing a postcard without giving the least offence to her escort.

From Rome we transferred on the Wednesday to La Spezia, to be greeted by the C.-in-C. North Tyrrhenian Sea Naval District, who turned out to be Admiral Oriana, an old friend from the West Indies. He had brought his ship, *Impavido*, into Bermuda while we were there, and the entertainment we laid on for him included snorkelling among our rocks off 'Enfield'. With true Italian dash, he had determined to swim through a tunnel under one of them, and came up somewhat damaged. However, this made a pleasant link between us all.

The visit was of interest professionally, since I was given a trip on the Boeing *Sparviero* hydrofoil, with its computer-controlled foils, an in-service version of what we had seen at Seattle. There is always a body of opinion in favour of coastal forces for the Royal Navy, and a study was in progress at the time, so this visit was relevant. (I am afraid that my recollections of weather in home waters through the years of war and since tend to set me rather against such devices.) The afternoon was, if possible, even more interesting. I went to the naval airfield at Luni and had an excursion in one of their specially-fitted helicopters full of the kind of electronic warfare kit that we now have in the Royal Navy, but which was then just a twinkle in our eye. It was made by a firm called Elektronika, and I was most impressed.

The next morning, Oriana took me to Livorno, to the Naval Academy for the usual guard of honour, followed by an enjoyable tour and lunch. As had the French, the Italians gave me a cadet's dirk as a present, and I began to hope I might have a collection of dirks large enough to provide one for all my male grandchildren, perhaps to open envelopes with. Then we went to Pisa, and with Elizabeth and the rest of the party, I enjoyed a wonderful flight by helicopter to Venice, passing over the mountains and along the edge of the Lagoon and the Lido, then over St Marks, to touch down on the mainland side of the city. Here, Admiral Bruni was waiting for us and we had a memorable trip in his barge along the canals to arrive at the Danieli Hotel for the evening. The next day Gino joined us for our 'fun' day (as if we needed one after the treatment we had been given).

On the way home to England, our RAF aircraft called at Gibraltar. The governor and Commander-in-Chief was now John Grandy, whom I knew well from Germany, Singapore and London, and we stayed at the Convent. It was a short visit, and I remember talking to Grandy about his successor. He was anxious that it should be a five-star officer, and that I should do it, although it was the Army's turn. My own view was, and remained, that a four-star officer was perfectly adequate if the right chap could be found. Although John didn't know it, there was a certain amount of discussion among the Chiefs of Staff at this time, not only about the Gibraltar job, but also about that of C.-in-C. Allied Forces Northern Europe, which was also held by a British officer. The Norwegians wanted Peter Whiteley, who had been Chief of Staff there and was now Commandant-General Royal Marines, having replaced Ian Gourlay. The Army were reluctant to surrender this job to a marine. However, Michael Carver agreed a compromise, which was that if a soldier were to go to Norway, Whiteley could go to Gibraltar, and vice versa. In the event, Whiteley went to Norway, where he was a great success, and Bill Jackson, a very distinguished soldier, made his mark in the Gibraltar job after Grandy. In my opinion, the fact that both were four-star officers made not the slightest difference.

We now welcomed the head of the Japanese Maritime Self-Defence Force, Admiral Samejima, and his wife, who were accommodated at the Dorchester. He had the usual programme – Northwood, Portsmouth and *Victory* – and our part in it was as usual, too: an Admiralty Board dinner on the first evening, and eventually a theatre evening, with supper at 'The Ivy' afterwards, just before they left. Elizabeth, very cleverly, took Mrs Samejima to Wisley, which I am sure she enjoyed, and this contributed to a really successful visit. Next, Elizabeth managed to get down to Southampton to have lunch in her *Sovereign*. Shortly after this we were visited by Thanabalasingham, head of the Royal Malaysian Navy, followed by the head of the South Korean Navy; both invited return visits from us.

We just had time to attend the annual Battle of Britain Service in Westminster Abbey before I was due to leave for the Far East. This time I was flying commercial, and Elizabeth could not come too: the trip would cover New Zealand, Australia and Indonesia, and would have been wildly expensive. This was very sad, and detracted from the impact as well as the enjoyment of the visits, which, as always, were pretty hard work.

On arrival at Wellington with Dick Fitch, I received a great welcome from Ted and Fay Thorne, with whom I stayed. Ted had been head of his service for a little while now, having relieved Laurie Carr who was now immersed in politics. He was disappointed, I think, at missing out on becoming the chief of their defence staff. I called on the present incumbent, a soldier, whom I liked. The main business was to visit the Royal New Zealand Naval Base, and I was walked round HMNZS *Philomel* and thought about *Blackpool* (now scrapped), which had operated from here after being transferred from the Royal Navy until she was returned in 1971. There was not time to go to sea, and that evening I flew to Sydney for the Australian visit.

The next morning I went on board HMAS *Perth*, which had just returned from working-up with the Americans off San Diego in California. They produced a smart guard and an interesting ship, and I had the impression that their tails were well up. The captain told me they had had a good report on the work-up (although I have a hunch that this is part of the American stock in trade to encourage the continuance of what is, for the Australians, a pretty expensive affair). With American weapons systems predominant, however, this is inescapable, and the days when people were sent to *Mercury* and our other establishments to be taught their business are now virtually over. Both Royal Navies are accordingly somewhat the losers. Flag Officer Eastern Australia and his wife looked after Dick Fitch and myself well, and then it was time to fly to Canberra, where David and Myra Stevenson greeted us, and I stayed with the High Commissioner.

The minister of defence made a good impression, but the defence establishment was clearly pretty dominated by the parliamentary under-secretary, Arthur Tangye, who had been there so long he was practically an institution. A reassessment of strategy in progress made sense to me, although I had doubts that enough resources would be kept in the inhospitable forward areas to guarantee it working. We visited Parliament House, and were given a good conducted tour of their impressive war memorial. They had asked me what I would like to do by way of an expedition, and I had opted for a dive on the Great Barrier Reef, so this was arranged. Then it was back to Sydney for a farewell day with the Stevensons, sailing in their yacht in the harbour, before taking the flight north. There was a weekend to fit in, as the official Indonesian naval programme started on the Monday, and I had asked to spend it in Bali. This also gave me an opportunity to have my white uniform washed and set up properly.

I was already the guest of the Indonesian Navy for this weekend, and Admiral Subjakto had arranged that we should be properly looked after. We stayed at the Sanur Beach Hotel, in a lovely position overlooking the Indian Ocean, and had a car at our disposal to see something of the island. Then it was time to fly to Java for the official part of the visit. In Jakarta we stayed with Sir John Ford, the ambassador, rather a complicated person, I thought, but very hospitable, and we particularly enjoyed the hospitality of his swimming pool. There was a full day of calls, guards, presentations and the like at Navy Headquarters in Jakarta, with Admiral Subjakto and his impressive deputy, Soegito (who succeeded him not very much later when Subjakto was appointed ambassador in London). I called, among others, on the foreign minister, Subandrio, who struck me as excessively clever and probably untrustworthy.

The highlight of the visit was a trip to Surabaya, the headquarters of the Indonesian Fleet, where we were looked after by Rudi Purwana, the Commander-in-Chief, who was a proper buccaneer of the Indonesian piratical type. We arrived in the morning by an Indonesian Air Force plane, after a spectacular flight which seemed to be mostly over semi-active or active volcanos, were met by Rudi, and moved straight off to see the dockyard and the odd ship. I do not know how much sea time the bigger ones did, or indeed were capable of doing, but they were all very proud of the development planned for their dockyard, and seemed to be great enthusiasts, if nervous of their Commander-in-Chief.

I arrived back in London on 12 October, and we went to the State Opening of Parliament on the 14th. In this, the Chiefs of Staff, among others, meet Her Majesty on arrival at the Peers' Entrance to parliament, and follow in procession upstairs to where she goes to robe in the House of Lords. Then again they follow in procession to the chamber of the House of Lords, where they wait around, looking at the judges, the bishops, peers (and perhaps most of all, at the jewels of the peeresses) until the Commons arrive. After The Queen's Speech is presented by the Lord Chancellor and read, they join the return procession, and eventually form part of the seeing-off party. The new SACLANT, Admiral 'Ike' Kidd, arrived on the Tuesday, and I had lunch at Grosvenor Square to meet him. He was a well-known ex-controller-equivalent of the US Navy, and quite a change from Ralph Cousins, his predecessor – as great a character but in a different mould. We took him and his wife to Covent Garden that evening, to see *Romeo and Juliet*, which they thoroughly enjoyed.

When they had gone on their way to SHAPE, I fulfilled a long-standing engagement and went north to Aberdeen and by helicopter to an oil-rig run by British Petroleum in the North Sea, 'Forties Alpha'. I was lucky with the weather, but I was glad to be making my visit at what should have been a peak period in the equinoctial gales – crews get bored at being visited only when the weather is bound to be good. The manager in charge of the rig was a retired naval officer, and he impressed on me the very rigorous discipline that was imposed on anything likely to cause a fire. The living conditions seemed to me tolerable, and the crew were cheerful and efficient (which they certainly should have been, considering the money they were earning).

The next week Elizabeth flew to America, and during her first week away I spent a good deal of time in the Portsmouth area, beginning with dinner in *Victory* on Trafalgar Night, and following up with the Trafalgar Night Dinner in *Excellent*. I then paid a visit to *Excellent* (now the Ship Fighting and Management School, rather than just the Gunnery School), going on to *Phoenix*, the Damage Control School. There was plenty to do in the office the following week, and one day the junior naval attachés had me to lunch. At the end of the week, Dick Fitch and I got our whites out again, and paid an official visit to the Venezuelan Navy. This had had considerable links with the Royal Navy, though not as strong as those of Colombia, but obviously turned mostly to the United States for advice and equipment. Nevertheless, Britain had been hoping for a frigate order from them, which was of some importance to us, and this had been long in the balance. In the event, it went to Italy, mainly owing to internal Venezuelan politics. The custom is for the appropriate 'commission' on equipment for the Venezuelan armed forces to go to the chief of the armed force concerned; in the case of the frigates, the head of the Navy had taken so enormous a 'commission' that it exceeded the bounds of what passes for propriety, and he was dismissed. The president himself then accepted a 'commission' from the Italians, which the British were not prepared to match, and a new chief of naval staff, Admiral Felix Mendoza Acosta, was appointed. He had an English wife, Patricia, and was to be my host for this visit.

The red carpet came out (naturally enough, in view of the circumstances), and Sir Roland Smith, who was the agent for more large British companies than one can number, also helped to entertain me in his large and beautiful *quinta* full of quite obviously valuable Old Masters. I had no idea what I was going to find and Caracas was an eye-opener, set, it seemed, in a volcanic crater, and humming with life and traffic to such a degree that it might have been in eruption. Apart from various briefings, I made a visit to the naval academy, and collected another dirk. The Venezuelans were smart and efficient, and there is, I think, something Teutonic about them compared to the otherwise Latinate South American nations – they are, or would like to be, the Prussia of their continent. However, the historic links with the Royal Navy (which I had read up before coming, including a life of Simón Bolívar, the Liberator) were much in evidence. His decisive victory at the Battle of Carabobo was commemorated in a large war memorial, to which I was taken ceremonially. The bas-relief round the plinth depicts the guns dragged into action by British sailors, whom Lord Cochrane had sent to help.

From Venezuela, I flew to Bermuda. Brian Straker, a signal officer whom I knew well and was now Senior Naval Officer West Indies, met me at Kinsey Field, and I stayed with them. SNOWI and his team were disappearing as a result of the Defence Review, which reduced our presence in the West Indies to a resident naval commander in Bermuda, another in the Bahamas to look after the Caribbean and the Atlantic Underwater Test and Evaluation centre set up in Andros, a garrison in Belize and the Army staff officer, Pine-Coffin's successor, now to be in Jamaica. As a result, 'Enfield' would revert to civilian occupation. It was all rather sad, but in my view absolutely justified by the change in our defence priorities, coupled with the political changes in the Caribbean. Brian was in good form, and apart from talking to his officers and sailors and taking a look at the *Malabar* base and the usual call on the Governor, my chief object was to visit the new Maritime Museum. This I did on 7 November, when I presented on behalf of the Admiralty Board various drawings and sketches of the first sailing warships to be constructed in Bermuda Dockyard. The museum is in the keep of the old dockyard, in an area which, ten years before, I had suggested to 'Shorty' Trimingham might be developed a casino. However, I am sure a museum is a much better idea, and they have great plans for its development and for the restoration of Commissioner's House which overlooks the keep. We caught the flight back to London so that I could be on duty at the Cenotaph on the Sunday.

Each year, one of the Chiefs of Staff takes the salute at the Jewish

Ex-Servicemen's Remembrance Day Parade in London, and this year it was my turn. I was carefully briefed by Edmund de Rothschild, who runs the organisation, and did my stuff on Horseguards Parade. It is not usual for naval officers to take long march-pasts, and I found this one quite trying, since the steady flow of people passing, at all of whom I tried to look, made me distinctly dizzy. From time to time I had to look skywards, which I hope was taken as a religious gesture, rather than the avoidance of *mal de mer* or the determined gaze of the marchers. Afterwards, we had a very good lunch at the Oriental Club with the de Rothschilds, which made recovery painless.

At this time I replaced Lewin with John Treacher as C.-in-C. Fleet, and Lewin then took over at Portsmouth from Empson. It was the Navy's turn to provide the VCDS, and there I sent Henry Leach. I had given these appointments a great deal of thought, of course – they were among the most important I had to make. I was certain that Lewin would be a better successor to me if he had had experience of the shore command as well as of the Fleet and NATO. I also felt that Treacher, a martinet, would be right for the Fleet after Lewin's rather more emollient approach (which was probably appropriate after me). Leach was a splendid, dedicated naval officer, whom I had seen as director of plans when I was VCNS, and found a bit rigid. I reckoned that the new job would be bound to broaden his horizons and, I hoped, bring out his sense of humour and certainly ensure that he was better known and appreciated outside the 'dark-blue' circle. Dull and frustrating though the job was likely to be, there was no longer any great, unified headquarters overseas in which to spend time broadening one's service horizons.

Before Christmas, we flew up to Rosyth, and stayed at Admiralty House so that I could take the passing-out parade at *Caledonia*, the Engine Room Artificers Training Establishment, which was commanded at the time by Tony Dring, who had been my engineer officer in *Alert*. This was yet another establishment whose future was uncertain, since it seemed prudent to consider amalgamating it with *Sultan*, a training establishment for mechanicians at Portsmouth, and I had to watch my footwork.

We enjoyed a family Christmas at South Cottage and some leave before returning for the Annual Board and Commander-in-Chief's Promotion Meeting, which I held in London this year, and to clear preparations for our next visit abroad, which was to be India. This was arranged so that we should be there on Republic Day, their national day, which is always celebrated by a great parade in New Delhi. The Comets, alas, were no more, the squadron having been a victim of the Defence Review and much regretted by all senior officers, so we went out in a VC10. This time I took Ken Wilcockson with me, to give him a run – so far, Dick Fitch been allotted all the excursions. We arrived comfortably in plain clothes, and were well met before going to the British High Commission, set in its own compound, where the High Commissioner, Sir Anthony Richardson, and his wife made us very welcome.

The programme began next day with a call on Admiral Kohli, my opposite number, and a general briefing at headquarters. The Indian Navy at that time had two major shore commands: one on the Malabar coast and one on the

Coromandel coast. My efforts to arrange for my visit to include the latter, where submarines and other ships supplied by the Soviet Union were based, mainly at Madras, had failed, though I was to go to Bombay. I called on the minister of defence, Bansi Lal, a strange man, who had been governor of Hariyana. He had made himself thoroughly unpopular with his birth control policies, so he had been transferred to defence. When I met him and asked him one or two questions about defence policy, he refused to answer. I therefore asked him to tell me something about birth control policy, which he did. He clearly felt that what he had been doing was all for the best, that the rise in the birth-rate had to be stopped, and those who did not like it must lump it. Whether he was an honest politician or just ambitious I do not know – he was certainly a ruthless one, and later, I believe, unsuccessful. Throughout the programme, I was treated as an honoured guest, and there was ample time allowed for sightseeing. We visited Bombay, where the admiral commanding Western Command was Cursetji, who was destined to relieve Kohli quite shortly. He is a Parsee, and a very intelligent person, I thought. Although I visited a ship or two, I best remember the dockyard, where they were planning to build broad-beamed Leanders, and had made some very thorough preparations accordingly. All seemed pretty good in theory to me, and it worked out quite well for them in practice.

We stayed comfortably in the hotel overlooking the 'Gateway to India', but could not escape noticing the slums and shanty-towns along our route, and were told something about the difficult problems these presented for the authorities – and indeed, for the people. Elizabeth went sightseeing while I was driven to the atomic energy research station near Bombay. I was shown round it by the director, including the room where special equipment was being used to handle radioactive isotopes. This was being done with great care and, I suppose, sophistication but the setting was rather a let-down, since a glance at the ceiling showed ill-supported cabling with the insulation drifting away from the wires. As well as Ken Wilcockson, I had the naval attaché with me, but none of us would have been able to recognise whether or not other things were going on there – for example, in the weapons field.

From Bombay, we flew to Pune for a presentation and lunch at the National Defence College. It was interesting to see the old hill station of the Raj flourishing, tidy and well cared-for. The house in which we had lunch had obviously been the British Staff College commandant's house, and although small by Maharaja standards, was substantial enough. The presentation was given impeccably, in best Sandhurst English, by a tall and imposing Sikh officer. I was in sword and medals for all this, and had to sit at the end of the hall, in a chair specially manufactured, they told me, for the King of Tonga, who had visited the college earlier. This was all very well, but he was a most enormous man, and it was difficult not to squirm in so large a seat, where even my sword, let alone my feet, could not touch the ground. Perched like this, in front of this formidable Sikh, I felt not a scrap like a First Sea Lord.

Then it was on to Delhi in an aircraft of the Indian Air Force, in bad weather. We flew high, I think in order to maintain our programme, and icing conditions were severe. Only when ice in lumps seemed to be falling off the wings did we come down lower, and the naval attaché, an aviator, found it more nerve-racking than most of us. However, we arrived safely and after a last night in Delhi, made a comfortable flight back to England. My own chief impression, underlining the vastness of the subcontinent, was of the varieties of people, culture and costume that had passed before us during the Republic Day Parade and the president's reception afterwards. I remember well, too, Indira Gandhi's hooded gaze and Bansi Lal's defence of compulsory sterilisation. The fact that the republic holds together as it does still seems to me extraordinary, and to owe more to the institutions and communications left by the British than to anything else.

In February 1976 we paid a quick visit to Gibraltar, to see part of the Fleet. I also visited the RAF at Brawdy, and a small installation near Milford Haven, where Douglas Baker, ex-*Ursa*, was the resident naval officer. My Canadian opposite number paid his official visit, there was a reception at the Soviet Embassy where I could practice a little Russian, a dinner with the Fleet Air Arm, and so on. March brought the Turkish chief of naval staff, Admiral Rifat, to visit us, and also a visit from General Méry, the French chief of defence, to see Michael Carver. We all joined in the usual Chiefs of Staff lunch, and I found him quite the most impressive foreign senior officer I had met for a long time. The main excitement of the month, however, was the completion of the purchase of a house for Tom, who moved in with great help from everybody, including Ron. We felt it was right to set him up on his own. He was not really able to engage in a full social life while living in the Mall House flat and, seeming not to involve himself in university clubs and so on, spent much time working or reading. Also in March, I visited *Mercury* and other training establishments, including the new-entry ones in the West Country, staying overnight at Admiralty House, Plymouth. I took the passing-out parade at *Sultan* for a mechanicians' qualifying course at the beginning of April, and was given a smart pen-stand that I use to this day. Brian Straker, the last Senior Naval Officer West Indies, sent me a haul-down report and called on me. It was a sad coincidence, perhaps, that the station should have closed down in the year marking the bicentennial of American Independence, the celebrations of which were soon to hit us.

On 1 April, 'Monty' was buried at St George's Chapel, Windsor. Peter Hill-Norton and Michael Carver were among the pall-bearers at the State Funeral, and Elizabeth and I attended. It was a good service, and I remembered how greatly the little man had impressed me during his visit to Russia. We went to the flat in Gozo that we had just rented, for a relaxing and sunny spell over Easter, and came back just in time for the State Visit of President Eanes of Portugal, a strange, unsmiling man who conducted himself with great dignity. The new chairman of the US Joint Chiefs of Staff, an Air Force general called George Brown, came to visit the UK Chiefs of Staff, and gave every evidence of being as good a replacement as one could hope for Tom Moorer, with much the same quiet sense of humour.

On 10 May we went by HS125 to Denmark, where our hosts were Sven and Lizzie Tostrup. Here we had a full and very delightful programme for three days. It was the last visit on which Dick Fitch was to accompany me, which was sad, but it turned out to be full of interest. The first day consisted mainly of calls and briefings, including a visit to the chief of defence, General Blixenkrone-Moller, signing the Queen's Book at the Amalienborg, and in the afternoon calling on the British ambassador, Ann Warburton. She had only just arrived, and was, I think, Britain's first woman ambassador anywhere. It was rather a happy chance that our visit should have come so soon, since she was well involved in the official parties, including the best one, dinner that evening at the Naval Club. I remembered this from AFNORTH days with Weilbach, and how much of the most interesting decor consisted of journal sketches by Danish midshipmen of the old days. Some of these hung on the walls, while others had been made into coverings for the occasional tables, and very handsome they were too. Sven gave me as a present a large and fearsome sword with a history. Apparently, after the defeat of the Danish Fleet at the Battle of Copenhagen in 1801, there was panic ashore that the British were going to land. Instead of this, Lord Nelson turned diplomat, and was cheered to the echo by the Danes for his chivalrous conduct of negotiations and care of the wounded and prisoners. However, in the panic, various pikes for which there were no shafts were beaten into sword-blades, and it was one of these, suitably mounted with a strong, protective brass hilt and pommel, that I was given. (I am afraid that Sven's silver desk blotter was rather puny by comparison.)

The next day, while Elizabeth had a wonderful sight-seeing tour, I spent mainly at sea in a new patrol boat of the Royal Danish Navy. We travelled from the Copenhagen Naval Base north through the Sound and round the top of Zealand to their Gunnery and Tactical School. The ship was impressive and fast, with a good operations room and, mercifully, the sea was calm. I was given an excellent briefing on their tactics, which made great use of electronic warfare and of the geographical environment in which they had to operate. They knew their islands at the eastern approaches to the Baltic better than anybody else, and made great use of land cover and sophisticated operational procedures to achieve surprise attack on any approaching hostile force. I was also briefed on their mining plans, which are important to NATO. On the way back, we stopped at a small church at Odden, where there was a very well-kept graveyard containing some bodies of Britons who had lost their lives during the war. The naval attaché had provided a poppy wreath for me to lay on the memorial. That evening, there was an excellent dinner for our Danish hosts at the British Embassy.

The next day, a helicopter took us up the Skagerrak to the northern tip of Jutland, and the naval base at Frederikshavn. Here, I visited the Naval Reserve Officers' College, and also their radio station which I had been unable to visit during my AFNORTH days. I had lunch and an interesting discussion at the college, and then it was back to Copenhagen and a private dinner with the Tostrups. He, I was interested to find, as well as being chief of their naval staff, was also a director of the East Asiatic Shipping Company, something that our rules – rightly – do not yet allow.

My schedule now became busy. Admiral Luther, head of the Federal German Navy, came to visit. We gave him and his wife lunch at the flat, and there was an Admiralty Board dinner in the evening before he set about his programme. The following day we had dinner with the Bagleys, to meet again the US secretary of the Navy, Middendorf. Then, in Westminster Hall on Wednesday 26 May, we were invited to witness the presentation of a copy of the Magna Carta to the Speaker of the US House of Representatives by the Speaker of the House of Commons to mark the bicentenary of the United States of America. Callaghan was now prime minister, and he made a good speech, as did the leader of the Opposition, a woman called Margaret Thatcher. The band of the Life Guards played, and the whole event was most impressive. I had only previously been in Westminster Hall for Lyings in State of the King, both George V and George VI, so this made a pleasant change.

Cento was meeting in London in ministerial session, and that evening we went to a dinner at 10 Downing Street in their honour. Tony Duff of my term was there, as he was then second permanent under-secretary of state at the Foreign Office. There was an interesting turn-out, including Henry Kissinger, Roy Mason and Anthony Crosland, the foreign secretary, and I was the duty Chief of Staff. We had already been to a lunch given by the Foreign Office to Cento and, in between, a reception given by the organisation's Turkish secretary-general, so it was quite a day. The following day was more relaxed, and we took the Luthers out to supper at 'The Ivy', as usual, after a theatre visit. On Friday we went to the church at Petersfield for the funeral of Admiral of the Fleet Sir Algernon Willis, who had been a friend and helper of Father's. I had known him in Russia and when he was C.-in-C. Portsmouth, interpreting for him on both occasions, and was glad to read the lesson at Lady Willis's request. After it was all over, she hung around outside the church door for far too long, I thought, with Algie waiting in his coffin to one side. I felt, punctilious officer that he was, that he would not have approved at all.

Dick and Kathleen Fitch had now left us, and Ben Bathurst joined. Bathurst I had known before as the senior pilot of the helicopter squadron in *Eagle*, where he had caught my eye as a very intelligent and likeable officer. Dick Fitch I appointed to *Hermes*, which delighted him, to relieve Derek Reffell, whom I had also sent there early in his career. It was time for our visit to the Royal Swedish Navy, to which, knowing the Lundvalls as we did, we were looking forward very much. Sure enough, it turned out to be an 18 carat visit from start to finish. Bengt was determined to show me as much as he could in the four days available, and in addition, I was bringing a wedding present from the Admiralty Board to our honorary admiral, the King, who had just announced his engagement. On advice from the naval attaché I took him two pairs of binoculars ('his' and 'hers'), to take in the boat that he much enjoyed using in the waters round Stockholm, with a compass graticule fixed in his as an embellishment. He seemed delighted. I do think it was a practical present, and they were very good binoculars.

The British ambassador was Sam Falle, who had been a cadet with me in *Frobisher* in the summer of 1937, and had then distinguished himself by falling in love with a Danish girl, remaining faithful to her until they could marry after the war. Now, here she was with him in the British embassy in Stockholm. I hope they enjoyed our visit as much as we did.

I spent the next day at sea, witnessing attacks by submarines, aircraft and surface units, and having lunch on board *Visborg* with Admiral Kierkegaard. The weather was fine, and it was an impressive display of Swedish training and efficiency. I also saw something of the extensive tunnelling works that are part of the Swedish Navy's preparations for war, and learned a little, too, about the measures they take to ensure no one can navigate in their protected leads as well as they can themselves. I understood the tight measure of security that they impose over the approaches to their naval base, and indeed to their capital city, except for the conventional navigational channel, and therefore the furore that ensues when a submarine is thought to be intruding. We went back to Stockholm that night, and the next day I visited the Naval College for a briefing, accompanied, as usual, by our naval attaché and by Nils Rydstrom, the Swedish naval attaché in London and doyen of the London naval attachés.

Back in London, the head of the Bangladesh Navy, Admiral Khan, arrived. His visit was important, as they were thinking of buying a frigate from us as the core and centre of expertise for what must otherwise be a small-ship Navy. He made sense, and in due course achieved his ambition. We made a quick visit to Wimbledon, but it was now the beginning of July, and time to fly out to the United States, where the bicentennial celebration of independence was due to be marked, among other things, by the arrival of the Tall Ships in the Hudson River and the presence there of representative ships from all the USA's friends and allies. We flew via Washington to New York, where I had arranged *London* in the Hudson River to be used as my headquarters. It was a wonderful opportunity for us to entertain so many American friends and relations in a proper naval environment on a great occasion. After the president had passed the ships in review, we went to a large reception ashore, where we were introduced to Prince Rainier and Princess Grace of Monaco, with whom we sat and talked for a while, she proving quite as beautiful as her photographs. Then, as soon as we decently could, we went back to *London* to find that Joe Luns had already given up and begun, as I had invited him to, to treat her as his 'refuge', and was busy drinking and spinning yarns with her captain. We then went to Newport, Rhode Island, for a great reception, after which I had to go to Washington. We returned to England at the weekend. I had not realised it before (nor, fortunately, did anyone else at the time), but the choice of *London* for the occasion was hardly the happiest historically. It was in an earlier *London* that Admiral Graves flew his flag when he was defeated at the Battle of the Chesapeake by the French Fleet under De Grasse. As a result of this, our armies on the Continent could no longer be supplied from home, and this contributed greatly to the loss of the American Colonies.

I had a long-overdue day at sea and later went to Aberporth, where there is a guided-missile range across Cardigan Bay, for a demonstration of the impressive new Sea Wolf short-range missile, to be fitted in the Type 22 frigate. By now, Patrick Duffy had replaced Frank Judd as minister for the Navy and sadly we were to lose Roy Mason as Secretary of State for Defence. He was replaced by Fred Mulley, a very senior Socialist minister whom none of us really knew. Andrew Humphrey had been relieved by Neil Cameron as Chief of the Air Staff, and was due to take over from Michael Carver as CDS in October. Meanwhile, Peter Hunt had also gone, being succeeded by Roly Gibbs.

My three years in office would end in March 1977, but that there was still plenty to do became apparent not long after Mulley joined. The economic state of the country under the regime of Denis Healey as Chancellor of the Exchequer was not good, and yet another Defence Review appeared to be impending. Various costing exercises were set in train, and we got on with them. About this time, the NATO Military Committee, meeting in Brussels in Chiefs of Staff session, were informed that SACEUR, Andy Goodpaster, was being relieved, summarily, by General Alexander Haig, to them unknown, unheralded and unsung. To make matters worse, Andy, a friend to all and greatly trusted in Europe, was deeply hurt by what he felt was shabby treatment and scant reward for his service. As acting CDS, I took the chair of the Chiefs when Carver's furious telegram came through asking for our views. In the cooler London atmosphere, we decided to respond that we would, however reluctantly, accept whomever the Americans saw fit to send. Personally, I felt arguing would make no difference, and would generate far more heat than steam. In the event, the nomination was approved, and we British did our best to make Andy's farewell visit to England as great an honour to him as we could.

I had now obtained approval for Terry Lewin to relieve me. This had been approved by ministers, but had not been announced, when John Treacher got in touch with me from Fleet, to find out whether I intended to employ him again or not. I replied that while nothing was certain in this world, I did not at the time have a particular job in mind for him. John took the point at once and, having a young family, said that he would like to take retirement on completion of his current appointment. I was not happy about this, there were other jobs open to him apart from that of First Sea Lord, and I was reluctant to have someone accumulating all the valuable experience of command of the Fleet, as well as of the NATO responsibilities and interests that went with it, who was not set on remaining in the Navy as long as he was required. I therefore told him that he would be relieved early and I selected Leach, then vice-chief of defence staff, to take over from him. This then made David Williams, Second Sea Lord, the obvious person to relieve Terry in Naval Home Command in the early Spring of 1977, freeing him for the top job. I am afraid Treacher was somewhat upset, particularly because we were already planning well ahead for the Queen's Jubilee Year, 1977, when there was to be a major Review of the Fleet. The Admiralty Board had received excellent proposals from Treacher, only one of which I was unhappy about: that the ships in the review should embark their families, so that while they manned ship and cheered the Queen as she went by in the Royal Yacht, their families could be on deck behind them and see the whole show. As, in addition, Royal Fleet Auxiliaries were being arranged to take on board families who were naval or others with naval connections but who did not have husbands in the warships present, I became very old-fashioned, and set my face against this, getting rather lukewarm support from colleagues on the board except Peter White. Treacher, however, stuck to his guns, Lygo came round to his way of thinking, and I gave in promptly and, I hope, gracefully. I am sure that Treacher and Lygo were absolutely right.

So, with this settled and the flag plot established, we came back from Gozo at the beginning of September with me feeling that this was the last lap, and that in six months' time I should be looking for a job. Although I would welcome a reduction in tempo, at the age of 57, I would be very reluctant to have nothing to do, or simply to engage in charitable activities for the rest of my life. A friend called Joe Hooper, who was then the director of the Government Communications Headquarters at Cheltenham, said to me once, 'What would you like to do when you retire?' I replied, 'I would like to do something, and I suppose electronics is the only thing I know anything about that would be useful,' so Joe said, 'Would you like me to write to Plessey?' I said, 'No, I would rather you wrote to Racal.' This was because Dunsterville, who was a friend, spoke so highly of Racal, I had a few shares that had done well, and I liked what I heard about what sounded an unusual outfit.

Soon, it was Michael Carver's farewell reception. I was sorry to see him go in many respects, as I felt he had been an admirable CDS through all the perils of the 1974 Defence Review, and that we could ill do without him now. However, Andrew Humphrey was a dedicated, intelligent, if rather intense person, and I hoped that he would inherit the mantle well. Meanwhile Al Haig had conducted his first SHAPEX, SACEUR's annual study period, as a personal *tour de force*. Young, with scant command experience and no combat command outside Vietnam, fluent above all, he was on his mettle to impress. Perhaps he did; I liked both him and his wife; but here, surely, was a political general. However, he seemed to realise that his political masters were all the nations of the Alliance, not just his own. Time and effort would be needed to prove the reality of this and convince the Alliance accordingly. He was not to have it.

From time to time, the incumbent First Sea Lord holds what is known as 'Admirals' Day' in the MoD for retired officers. I had done this once, early in my time, and did it again on 21 October 1976 for the last time. This, I hoped, would also swell the coffers of the Royal Navy Club, which held its Trafalgar Night dinner that night, although I went to the Royal Naval Engineering College at Manadon, where I gave the speech and toast to 'the immortal memory'. I walked round the college the next morning, and saw much that was good. Bill Pillar, my engineer officer from *Alert*, was the captain at that time. I paid another visit to Culdrose, and had a splendid trip in a dual-controlled Gazelle with a strong-minded pilot who insisted that I took control and landed the machine as well as exercising me in a 'hover' manoeuvre.

The end of October saw us setting off for the Far East for visits to the Navies of Malaysia, Japan and Korea. First stop was Kuala Lumpur, to be greeted by Thanabalasingham, and then very kindly taken by the defence adviser to 'Carcossa', the large house of the high commissioner, where we were to stay. It was now Friday evening, and there had been quite a long preliminary discussion about what we were to do for the weekend. I was particularly anxious to take Elizabeth to see the islands off the east coast, but we experienced difficulty obtaining Malaysian consent for this as they felt that it was late in the season, the monsoon might be starting, and the coast not at its most accessible. However, I persisted. The weather turned out to be ideal. We had taken June Light, my personal assistant, with us for a treat, and on the Saturday morning flew to Kota Bahru, and then by helicopter to the frigate *Hang Tuah*, lying off the Perhentian Islands. Where *Alert* had had a large, teak quarterdeck before the days of helicopters at sea, *Hang Tuah* had a perfectly adequate helicopter landing spot, on which we put down. She was anchored much where I used to put *Alert*, off the smaller island. When we went ashore, we were greeted ceremonially by the head man, and signed his visitors' book, in which we found the name of my doctor in *Alert*, John Williams, who would regularly treat the sick on the islands during our visits. After a great welcome, we set off again in the ship's boat, and went to one of my favourite beaches, to swim and snorkel over the coral.

The captain of the ship, a Malaysian officer, Nick Peterson, entered into the spirit of everything, and that evening after dinner with the officers and a film, I had a short discussion with him and asked if we could go south to Pulau Redang early the next morning so that Elizabeth could see that as well. He agreed, and off we went. On approaching Redang, he wanted to anchor off; I persuaded him that it was perfectly safe to take the ship into the harbour, where I had been often in *Alert*, and showed him exactly where to drop the hook. This he did, and said in delight, 'I didn't know we could do that. Now I shall have something to show the midshipmen next time they are on board for training.' We had a wonderful picnic ashore, entertained by some rather piratical fishermen who came by at one stage. All good things come to an end, and at 3.30 p.m. our helicopter arrived, it was back to Kota Bahru, and then to Kuala Lumpur.

The next day was all calls and briefings, including a call on the minister of defence and the prime minister (which I hope helped Thana with the naval case I am sure he was trying to make), followed by a very relaxed supper in Thana's house, 'The Nest', our hostess being an ex-beauty queen of Malaysia. The final day was most interesting. I went to Port Klang, which I used to know as Port Swettenham, to see some of their fast patrol boats fitted with Exocet missiles, which they seemed to be running reasonably well. One of them then took me at speed to Lumut near Penang, which I remembered of old as a very pretty, unspoilt little place. It was now being turned into a major naval base, at vast expense. A helicopter appeared, and I flew over the works, which were certainly widespread, but had a long way to go to reach completion. We then flew on to Kuala Lumpur over the countryside, and I noticed how much of the rubber seemed to have been replaced by oil palm. That evening, the high commissioner gave a dinner for us. It had been a delightful visit, friendly and relaxed, and the trip to the islands was magical.

The next morning we set off for Japan, where we arrived in plain clothes to be met by my host, Admiral Nakamura, who commanded the Maritime Self-Defence Force (as the Japanese Navy is still known). Then we were whisked off to the British embassy, to stay with Sir Michael Wilford and his wife. Before coming, I had been given a careful brief from Rolls-Royce in the person of Denis Spotswood, a Marshal of the RAF now working with them, since they were most anxious to sign a contract with the Japanese for the construction of marine gas turbines in Japan. The brief made it plain just how far they wanted me to go. Later in the visit, I had quite a set-to with His Excellency about this, rather late in the evening after a dinner party, because he wanted me to be a much more aggressive salesman than I judged was right or than Rolls-Royce wished. I eventually said, 'Goodnight,' and left the room, as Ben Bathurst reminded me years later. However, we were made very welcome and prepared for the fray.

I decided that I would need to be very dignified with the Japanese, since formality in official matters was a national characteristic. The first evening, in uniform, we had a dinner at the Takanawa Hotel, which was extremely friendly, and I gathered how important it was to admire the appearance of the food as well as to appear to enjoy the taste. The next day, I arrived at the Defence Agency in sword and medals to face a tremendously extended honour guard ceremony, following the American pattern. I then called formally on Nakamura, had a briefing and discussion in his office with his staff, before going on to see the Chairman of the Joint Staff Council, who was my old friend, Samejima. After that, he took me in to see the minister of state for defence, and eventually, at 11 a.m., we set off by helicopter to an airfield nearby, where Elizabeth and her lady liaison officer awaited us, and boarded a small, amphibious aircraft, the US1, for Iwakuni in the Inland Sea. It was a very comfortable machine, and after lunch on board we were in good form when we alighted in the water off the island. I was glad to have Ben, an aviator, with me, as the performance of the aircraft was quite extraordinary. Owing to an advanced form of boundary layer control, the speed on landing could not have been more than 20–25 m.p.h. The ability of this aircraft also to take off in a short distance and fly low economically was regarded very highly by the Japanese in terms of anti-submarine reconnaissance. I certainly was extremely impressed.

The object of the trip was to visit the Japanese equivalent of the Royal Naval College, Dartmouth, at Etajima, and again ceremony was carried out with great precision, and one had to perform accordingly. The superintendent of the college was Vice-Admiral Katori, a short, tough man, and pretty dedicated, I should say. After seeing a physical training display, we were put up in comfortable rooms at the Etajima Club, and had a pleasant plain-clothes dinner with the admiral in the evening. We would be forgiven for having nightmares after the 'physical training display' – very largely an exhibition of Japanese martial arts, karate, kundo and swordplay with razor-sharp swords, one of which I was allowed to test the edge of very gingerly. It was done with tremendous verve and enthusiasm, and not a little noise, and was rather a frightening performance to a Westerner.

In the morning, we were woken up early by a bestial clamour. This went on for about 20 minutes, and I discovered later that part of the normal training schedule for the Japanese officer cadets is to shout at each other for 20 minutes each morning, in order to develop their powers of command. It was this noise we heard – 700 or 800 young Japanese bellowing to one another. The college itself was interesting. It was built mainly of red brick before the First World War. The Japanese had a very high regard for the Royal Navy, and were so determined to make the college resemble Dartmouth as much as possible that they imported bricks from Europe. After watching an enormous parade, I walked round the college for quite some time, finding it austere and forbidding. I also was taken to visit the nearby Naval Museum. This was a building with a grand staircase inside the entrance, at the top of which were three statues: in the centre was Admiral Togo, the victor of Tsushima, on his right was a statue of Lord Nelson, and on his left, believe it or not, John Paul Jones. As we had paused at the foot of the staircase, Admiral Katori, who was an aviator, turned to me and said, 'Do you realise, Admiral, that four-thirds of the officers in my entry to the Naval College died during the war?' I said, 'You mean three-quarters.' 'No,' he said, 'four-thirds.' 'Oh,' said I, 'seventy-five percent.' 'Yes, Admiral,' he replied.

The exhibits were quite extraordinary to me, and made a deep impression, for two-thirds of the museum was devoted to the kamikaze campaign. There were photographs of the pilots, their letters and poems, records of their thoughts, and so forth. The first team who were asked to volunteer for the initial attack stepped forward as one man, and this was photographed, too. I enquired about the officer in charge of this campaign, and was told that it was a certain admiral, so I asked, 'What happened to him, did he survive the war?' 'He committed seppuku,' was the reply, to which I commented, 'He could hardly do less.' I came away from Etajima convinced, as I had long suspected, that the fighting spirit of the Japanese was dormant, that they were cherishing their warlike traditions, in the Navy at least, and that given either the need or perhaps the opportunity, there would be a resurgent Japanese Fleet and naval aviation.

A helicopter took us to Kobe, where I called on the Sub-Area Headquarters and changed into a suit. We went on by car to the Miyako Hotel at Kyoto, where we were to spend the night. We spent most of the weekend sight-seeing in Kyoto, before returning to Tokyo by the Bullet Train, to a dinner hosted by Admiral Samejima, before returning to the embassy for the night. Monday was a busy day. First we went to the Imperial Palace, myself in full fig, to sign the Emperor's Book, and afterwards had time to look at his unique collection of bonsai trees. The palace grounds are extensive, but the buildings that we saw were modest enough and there was no great sign of life. I then took a helicopter to Yokosuka for my call on Admiral Kunishima, C.-in-C. Self-Defence Force. The admiral's barge took me to the base at Funakoshi for the honour guard, a briefing, an exchange of plaques and introductions to the staff. I then went on by barge to see one of their large helicopter-carrying destroyers, *Haruna*. Here, I was presented with an American-type baseball cap, peaked as for a Japanese admiral, and with four gold stars embroidered on its front. I wore it for the rest of the visit. *Haruna* was an impressive ship, American in style, as one would expect, and carried HSS2 large anti-submarine helicopters.

The next ceremonial call was on the admiral commanding the Yokasuma District, who later gave us lunch. I think it was here (perhaps it was at Kobe) where, with great seriousness, I was presented with a prayer suitable for admirals plus its English translation, and that Elizabeth showed herself to be a dab hand at writing Japanese characters with a brush. After lunch, we visited *Mikasa*, being shown round by a retired naval officer who knew everything there was to know about her, her great battle against the Russian Fleet in 1905, and their great naval hero, Togo. It was fascinating to see this old ship, built by Vickers at Barrow. Her battle scars had not been repaired and, in case you should miss them, the splinter holes were outlined in paint. She was lovingly looked after. I was grateful to be given a piece of her deck with a medallion of Admiral Togo in its centre, thus completing our collection of naval timber at 'South Cottage'. The ambassador kindly hosted a dinner that night in honour of the Japanese Self-Defence Force, and the next day it was time to go. Nakamura and our liaison officer came to the airport to see me off. I left at 8.30 p.m. for Seoul, and Elizabeth at 10.30 p.m. for Hong Kong, seen off by Mrs Nakamura. It had been a good and friendly visit, and I think that they relished the change of approach of a British naval officer compared, perhaps, with those of the US Navy – admirable as they are – of whom they see so much. I am in no doubt whatever that the utmost care is being taken to cherish and preserve the traditions of the Imperial Japanese Navy, and we would do the same in their place. Nevertheless, in the current peace-loving, war-hating atmosphere in Japan, it must take a very dedicated young lad to join something like the Navy. A little fanaticism on their part at a place like Etajima must therefore to be tolerated in that light.

Colin Little, the naval attaché in Tokyo, was also responsible for South Korea, so he came with me to Seoul. There was a defence attaché in South Korea, a soldier, and he came round with us. My host was Admiral Hwang Chong Yon, whom I had met briefly in London. Rear-Admiral Kim was my personal liaison officer for the visit, and a very nice chap, too (although I met more Admiral Kims in the course of two days than I imagined existed). I arrived in plain clothes, to be greeted, nevertheless, by an honour guard, but I changed quickly into uniform at the hotel, and went straight off to a national war memorial in the countryside to lay an enormous wreath and perform a ceremony which involved casting incense into a holy brazier before signing a visitor's book in front of an enormous guard and band.

They next took me to Panmunjom, the frontier post on the border between North and South Korea, manned by the UN, but with a very strong US Army backup. I had a briefing on the kind of incidents that occurred, and learned then, as throughout my visit, that there was still no love lost between North and South. In fact, 'my' Kim had family in the North, but resolutely refused to have any contact with them at all; the converse also applied. I called on the minister for defence, who was amiable, and after an afternoon briefing, had a good formal dinner with the Navy. The next day was a busy one. I flew first to the Naval Academy, where they were drawn up as for divisions in a rig clearly derived from the West Point cadet. I took the parade standing in the back of a jeep-type vehicle, holding on for grim death to a pole that was neatly placed in front of me, afterwards having to make a rousing speech from a rostrum to the serried ranks of very tough-looking young Koreans. They then marched past well. In the background there was a large, I suppose life-sized, model of the 'turtle-boat' invented by their sixteenth-century naval hero, Admiral Yi. Hwang gave me a book about him as part of my present, the rest of it being a delightful celadon-green vase, which is now a lamp in the study at home. I then saw something of their Fleet, mostly fast, missile-armed patrol boats, and took passage in one of them round the coast to a shipyard of which they were very proud. It had only been established for about three years, and was not only turning out fast patrol boats for export, but also building watertight doors and other bits and pieces for the US Navy itself. It was easy to foresee that one was on the threshold of a great boom in shipbuilding in South Korea.

I went back by air to Seoul, flying over the lovely landscape of a country known for good reason as 'The Land of Morning Calm'. I remembered the glimpses I had caught of it on my way home before the war in the *Tsingtao Maru*, and although it looks its best from the sea, it was interesting to have an aerial view of so much of it. It was now time to say goodbye, and Hwang came to see me off. To my surprise, I saw Concorde sitting on the tarmac at Seoul. Brian Trubshawe invited me to have a look at it and, once on board, I was offered a free trip back to the UK, as they were about to set off. I should love to have taken them up on this, but Elizabeth was in Hong Kong, and I was expected there, so, regretfully, I declined. The aircraft was on its proving flight and, apparently, behaving extremely well.

I thoroughly enjoyed the experience of the visit to Korea, and was very impressed by what I had seen of the people. There is no love lost between them and the Japanese, who were, among other things, Admiral Yi's redoubtable enemy. They seemed, under a difficult dictatorial regime, to be doing their utmost to make their country strong. The record of their troops in Vietnam, of course, was second to none. I felt glad to feel that they were on our side.

I arrived in Hong Kong that evening to be met by Garnons-Williams, the captain in charge, the commodore's post having been one of the reductions of the Defence Review. I found him in excellent form and Elizabeth, who had been staying with her cousin, Guy (then chairman of the Hong Kong and Shanghai Bank), and having a lovely time, came and joined me, and we spent the night at Bowen Road, the old commodore's residence. This was an all too short final visit to Hong Kong for me, but we were due in London for Remembrance Sunday in two days' time, where I was to lay the wreath on the Cenotaph for the Royal Navy for the last time.

The staffs of all three services and the central staff were busy trying to produce financial statements for the defence of the country which would meet the requirements of Mr Callaghan's government. Following so soon on the Defence Review, which had produced a critical level which we had defended successfully, it was now necessary to find what commitments could be given up so that something below that level could retain validity. As always, equipment programmes had a good deal of inertia or momentum attached to them, and the only way to make reasonable savings quickly was in personnel. Our new secretary of state, Fred Mulley, was a very different personality from his predecessor, who had disliked meetings and could only be brought round a table at rare intervals. Fred, I think, liked meetings, and his technique was to start off making wounding remarks, with the object, I suspect, of making everybody angry with him, and so more apt to be off guard. I hope we did not fall for this treatment too often. The minister of state for defence equipment, John Gilbert, was also quite sharp, and I had quite a tussle with him, although he was usually the Controller's man. There was a question of selling *Bulwark* to Chile: the head of defence sales, a good man from the motor industry, Ron Ellis, had negotiated what looked like a deal. But at our meeting with Gilbert, when he heard that the Navy still needed the ship, he changed sides, and the minister concurred.

Eventually, the new figures demanded were ready, and Fred was very carefully briefed on them by the Chiefs of Staff. We produced, as I remember, three options: the first represented what we thought was necessary to maintain the commitments that were laid upon us; the second, what we considered unsafe, but tolerable, and the third, what we considered quite unacceptable if our commitments were to be met without undue risk. When Fred, fully briefed, went to the cabinet meeting, Andrew Humphrey, Chief of Defence Staff, was in Brussels for a Military Committee, so when the Secretary of State returned from what seemed to me a very short cabinet, I was sent for, and went into his office. 'Well, Edward,' he said, 'I have agreed a figure,' and he mentioned, need I say it, the third option. I asked him to repeat this, and he did. Then I said, 'Secretary of State, I must reserve the position of the Chiefs of Staff.' 'Yes, Edward,' he said, 'I thought you'd say that.' I left his office, called the Chiefs together, and sent a telegram to Andrew in Brussels, telling him the news and of the action taken. We recommended that this was a situation in which the Chiefs of Staff must exercise their right to see the Prime Minister himself. Andrew accepted this, and came back. We had concocted a paper which we decided to slant towards the 'threat' assessment on which we had based our figures. Callaghan agreed to see us, and did so with Fred Mulley on 10 December. This somehow got to the press; I am pretty sure the MoD was not responsible, but the papers were full of it. We did not succeed in changing the cabinet's decision, but I hope we put a damper on any efforts that there might otherwise have been to cut defence still further. Somehow, the word got around that I was going to resign as First Sea Lord, though that had never been in my mind nor suggested to me by anyone. However, I doubt that the rumour did any harm. I did not believe that one Chief of Staff resigning would have done the slightest good; if all had gone, plus the secretary of state, then something would have had to happen, but we were nowhere near that situation.

The Prince of Wales's naval service was coming to an end, and he was giving up command of his minehunter and going back to public duties only. The Commander-in-Chief asked if I would like to see him to say goodbye. I said yes, so he came to see me, informally, in plain clothes in my office at the MoD on 16 December. We had a little chat. I thanked him for his service, and I told him that I thought, had circumstances been different, that he would have made a successful naval officer. He was worried because he had lost an anchor from *Bronington*, his ship, and wondered, so he said, whether he was going to have to pay for it. I remarked that I had not been in the least worried about his anchor, but had been anxious about the men who were diving in bad conditions during the night to try to get it back for him, lest they should exceed the normal risks that they would take for anybody else's anchor. I am not certain that that had occurred to him, and I think the point went home. I was sorry to see him leave the service because I thought that there was much that the Navy could still do for him. But it was fine to see him going in good heart, and he very kindly honoured us with a Christmas card. We also received a Christmas card saying 'Best wishes from Jim and Audrey Callaghan', which was nice, but did not cost as much as the money we wanted for the Navy.

Before Christmas leave started, I managed to get down to the Fleet again and visit Jim Eberle in *Hermes*. I had decided he was to relieve Peter White as chief of Fleet support. His general approach continued to be 'high, wide and handsome', and I thought a little of stores and dockyards would show whether he was able to master detail into the bargain. It was now time for some of the Honours List recommendations, which were my responsibility for the Navy, although the Second Sea Lord did much of the collating. There were, quite properly, rather fewer honours available now the services were smaller, and it was no longer possible to recommend someone for the award of the CB, then the KCB afterwards. There just were not enough to go round, and the CB was therefore reserved for people who were unlikely to be promoted to vice-admiral and so perhaps be eligible for a knighthood. There was also a long-standing convention that the Order of the Bath was reserved for seamen officers ('executive officers', as they used to be called) who commanded ships. The others would be eligible for the Order of the British Empire, which is a very important but less senior order of chivalry. Accordingly, when Peter White became eligible for a knighthood, he received the KBE from the Queen. This caused a great deal of upset in his branch, I understand, and Colin Dunlop, who had been Father's secretary, wrote an enraged letter to Peter saying 'how disgraceful'. I was happy to see Peter awarded the GBE in the New Years Honours 1977. There would never have been a GCB for him. Engineer officers were now receiving the

Order of the Bath, and in later years it has been awarded more widely than I chose to try to confine it.

I used to visit my revered old Commander-in-Chief, Lord Fraser of North Cape, once every year or so, as he appreciated a call by the First Sea Lord to keep him in touch. He lived in a small house in West Molesey, being affectionately cared for by Renee Duncan and her husband. He was surrounded by trophies of his wonderful career, and would sit and chat quite happily. His brain was first-rate, but locomotion was no longer his strong point. It was always a great pleasure to see him, now become a dear old man.

We spent Christmas leave in England, and had a lovely time. Retirement beckoned, but it was not to come quite yet.

CHAPTER NINE

Chief of Defence Staff

1977

The Queen was to celebrate her Siver Jubilee in 1977, and we aimed to fit in a couple of visits to Iran and Pakistan (where the head of the Navy was Hasan, whom I had taught, as I had his predecessor, on their Signals Long Course at *Mercury*) before the royal festivities started. I also faced a busy programme of farewells before turning over to Terry Lewin in March at the end of my three years.

Early in January, having just returned from a visit to AFNORTH, the chief of defence staff fell ill at home. I heard from Tony Heward, now the air member for personnel, that Agnes Humphrey had telephoned the top RAF doctor in the middle of the night. Andrew had been collected by ambulance and whisked into their hospital at Hawton. No one could tell me what was wrong with the poor chap. As senior member of the Chiefs of Staffs Committee in office, I took over as acting chief of defence staff, and daily asked the RAF how he was. I found I could get very little sense out of them, but formed the impression that he was not all that comfortable. I found I had so little to tell the secretary of state about Andrew that I eventually asked the vice-chief of the air staff (Neil Cameron having gone off on an overseas tour), to keep Mulley in touch himself. Since no one could tell me when he would return to duty, I became worried, and cancelled my tour to Pakistan. After a fortnight or so, it became apparent that his health was very bad indeed, though no one could or would say what was wrong. Tragically, on 25 January, Andrew died. An autopsy showed a malignant tumour at the base of the spine. This explained why all the blood transfusions he had been given did no good, and why, as I heard later, he had been in a coma for much of the time. Fortunately, he knew little about it, but poor Agnes was, of course, distraught. He was 56 years old, and they had no children.

The Chief of the Air Staff, Neil Cameron came back from his tour, and there was a good deal of doubt about the succession. I decided this was an excellent moment for me to get away and continue with the programme for our visit to Iran. Andrew Humphrey had been chief of the air staff for three years, and in the process had gone through the Air List like a knife through butter. Justified or not, he had removed a great many officers of air rank, and had promoted a number of younger men, so it was not easy for his service to sustain the shock of his loss. Elizabeth and I boarded an HS125, Roland Gibbs, Chief of the General Staff, took over as acting CDS, and we flew to

Tehran via Naples, where we had lunch with Roddy Macdonald. This was great fun, in a pleasant house he had found for himself overlooking the sea. We had tea in Ankara, where Admiral Rifat, head of the Turkish Navy, came out to the airport to see us, and then went on to Tehran in the evening.

Our Persian hosts were Vice-Admiral and Mrs Habibollahi. On our first day we saw a great deal of the sights of Tehran, with escorted tours of some of the palaces, which were very impressive though jazzy, after the Turkish style, with mirrors wall-to-wall. The ceremonial was extensive, and the guards large but well turned out. It was cold in the evenings, and I needed a greatcoat, but by day we had brilliant weather. We stayed in a comfortable hotel with a view of the mountains to the north, and saw little of the ordinary part of the capital. I called on the Shah with my host and Sir Anthony Parsons, our ambassador, and had a pleasant 40 minutes while Elizabeth saw the Empress Farah for about the same time. The Shah was cheerful, and I detected no sign of the disease that was to kill him a few years later. He was full of confidence about what he styled 'The White Revolution' and the support of his people. He expressed his feelings of friendship for my country, and described some of his plans for afforestation, for rehabilitation of villages in the countryside, and so forth. It was all very informal, although I had to back out of the room. The only hint of foreboding came from the very subdued behaviour of Habibollahi throughout the audience.

I had previously called on Azhari, the head of the defence forces, who was clearly more courtier than general, and not an impressive or endearing character. There was a great banquet in full fig that evening, for something like 150 people, at which Habibollahi and I had to make speeches. The next day, accompanied by our liaison officer, Admiral Kamyabipur, and Ken Wilcockson, we went to Bandar Abbas to see Admiral Azadi, the Fleet commander, and to visit their main naval base. There was quite a British community helping in the dockyard, although the ships were predominantly American in origin, and it was nice to meet them. They all seemed in very good heart. We had lunch in the Officers' Club, and then flew to Isfahan for our 'break'. (We had some difficulty in choosing between Isfahan, Tabriz or Persepolis, but are now sure we made the right choice.)

We stayed in a converted caravanserai hotel called the Shah Abbas, and had the most magnificent day of sightseeing in the mosques and round the souk of the old town, watching women making carpets, and all the other activities of the bazaar. They told us, as an example of the Shah's generosity to his people, that he had insisted on little stools being provided for the carpetmakers, who before this had had to work all day on their knees. Even so, the stools looked extremely uncomfortable. The great mosques were wonderful, and the rectangular area in their midst was, we were told, where the game of polo originated. We also visited one of the large Muslim teaching establishments.

Then it was back to Tehran, flying with the Iranian Air Force, and thence to Bandar Pahlevi on the Caspian, to see the Naval Training Command in the north. It was a pretty little place, with a comfortable rest house which, at my instigation, provided us with caviare for breakfast, reminding me of the restaurant car on the Trans-Siberian Railway. The main electronics training school that I visited was most impressive. Each individual student had a cubicle equipped with a tape recorder, a small word-processing machine, a slide projector and heaven knows what else beside. This allowed a form of programmed instruction of some 300 young men to be supervised by a couple of instructors. The students only came out of their cubicles when they wanted help, but otherwise worked their way through the recorded instructions. I had never seen anything like it before, and thought that some American firm of consultants must have had an extremely lucrative contract (some of the money for which, no doubt, 'rubbed off' along the way). The Iranians are not stupid, and I think the system was effective in inculcating theory.

The flights between the Caspian and Tehran were spectacular, traversing a great mountain range covered in snow, and round one particular peak, Mt Damarvand in the Alvorz range, we circled several times in order to take a good picture. The skiing season was still in full swing for the rich and powerful from Tehran, and we had a clear view of the slopes. A dinner party at the British embassy ended a memorable visit – my last as First Sea Lord – to a foreign navy, and one made delightful by the personalities of our host and his wife. We heard later, after the revolution (of which, at that time, neither I nor, I think, Anthony Parsons detected the slightest sign), they managed to get to the United States, where I hope they are happily settled.

We were back to England in time to attend the Navy's Faraday Lecture, and then to host the Yugoslav chief of naval staff for the usual visit. While I was away, there had been a great deal of newspaper speculation as to what was to happen among the Chiefs of Staff after Andrew's death. Almost as soon as I was back, Fred Mulley got hold of me and said that he would like me to take over as chief of defence staff until the RAF could regroup, a new chief of the air staff taking over from Neil Cameron, who would then relieve me as chief of defence staff at the end of August. It was, of course, the RAF's 'turn', and Andrew had only held the job for three months. However, I did not rate Neil as sufficiently experienced or strong, though he was undoubtedly the best airman available. Moreover, he had not been at all fit during part of his time as ACDS (Policy). I said to Mulley that I would rather take the job on for the full three years, and thought that this would be right. Fred told me, however, that he had consulted with all the ex-chiefs of defence staff, and their view had been that the RAF should take their turn; in addition, Mountbatten had said that he would be sorry to see Lewin lose his turn as CDS in due course. I did not feel I could decline to hold the fort as the ministers required of me, and therefore accepted Mulley's proposal.

I was promoted to Admiral of the Fleet and appointed CDS on 9 February 1977. Lygo, who had been promoted to admiral in January, took over as Acting First Sea Lord until Lewin could be relieved and take over from him. We therefore had to move out of the Mall House flat in time for Lewin to move in comfortably, and go to the flat occupied by the CDS in Kingston House near the Park, a very poor substitute. I sent my farewell signal to the Navy on the evening of 9 February, apologising for the fact that my unexpected appointment as CDS did not give me time to pay a final round of visits and say goodbye as I would have wished.

There was still much to do, and it was to be a glittering summer, with the Queen's Silver Jubilee, through which I felt singularly privileged to lead the armed forces of the Crown. Lewin took over as first and principal naval ADC, and at my farewell audience, Her Majesty was represented by Princess Margaret and the Duke of Gloucester, who were extremely kind. I was pleased to meet him for the first time. I could now wear Father's sword legally, the uniform regulations having changed from his day, when a chased scabbard was the entitlement of any flag officer – now it was only uniform for an Admiral of the Fleet. I had made some changes to the uniform regulations myself, which I am sure were right. One involved removing the requirement for every flag officer to have full dress on promotion. Most of them never wore it, so I altered the rules so that only full admirals, the naval secretary, the defence services secretary, and Flag Officer Royal Yachts need so to equip themselves. Some officers who already had the kit asked if they could continue to wear it, but I refused this suggestion. I also introduced barathea as a replacement for doeskin in officers' service dress and attempted, unsuccessfully, to obtain approval for Velcro to replace white ribbons for supporting the GCB collar when worn without the mantle.

February was a convenient time to change horses, the promotions, honours and major appointments all having been done. I decided that David Williams should relieve Lewin in Portsmouth, and agreed the name of his successor with Terry. When Terry joined, I told him that whatever he did, he was not to lose Lygo from the Navy, but I think he found this advice impracticable. On 11 February, Ken Wilcockson and Ben Bathurst came to say goodbye, and I was able to thank them both for all they had done. The principal staff officer to the CDS was a splendid brigadier called Roly Guy, and I inherited as ADC Larry Robertson, a very extrovert young Guards officer, who was a good deal better than I thought at first sight. Among other things, he had been a tower of strength to Agnes Humphrey after Andrew's death. Guy had quite a time with me, I am afraid, and at one stage was driven to say that I should not speak to him the way I did. He was quite right. He also spoke up for Larry Robertson when I was intolerant, and I was very grateful to him.

I had long since given up attempts to use a monocle on my left eye, and had now discovered that I was troubled with a cataract. This reduced the effectiveness of my right and better eye, but would not be ripe for operation for a year. It was no more than a mild irritant, and I ascribed its development so early in life either to my walk through Nagasaki, or to so many bright days at sea in the Pacific War, when I was constantly on the bridge and in a strong radar radiation field day and night. Later, medical opinion did not support this theory.

I do not remember any particularly tiresome issues before the Chiefs of Staff during this period, but one which caused me some trouble was a revived proposal to move the Joint Services Defence College from Latimer to Greenwich, to save money. I had been much in favour of this as First Sea Lord, but it ran up against difficulties with the other two services, partly because Greenwich was so 'naval', and partly because everyone rather enjoyed the 'country club' element of Latimer. However, the financial arguments seemed to be pretty conclusive at this time, and when the Chiefs of Staff failed to agree on the move from Latimer to Greenwich, I eventually persuaded them to agree that since there was no particular military aspect to the decision, it should rest with the Permanent Under-Secretary, and we should delegate it to him. This we did. In achieving this agreement, I had also used the argument that with the demise of the great overseas headquarters, there was all too little contact between the Navy and the two other services. There was no 'sea-room' in Germany. Therefore, the siting of the Joint Services Defence College in a naval environment had a great deal to commend it from the point of view of all three services. In the event, the Permanent Under-Secretary, Frank Cooper, decided in favour of the move, and the Chiefs of Staff had to accept it. I think it took less than three months after I had left the scene for them to hold another meeting, in which Terry Lewin conceded that Latimer should stay where it was. It appeals to my sense of humour that Latimer eventually moved to Greenwich, for the reasons which were originally mooted.

A major problem was the replacement of the Shackleton airborne early-warning force. The Americans had produced a version of the Boeing 707, the E3A, which they called the Airborne Warning and Control System (AWACS). They were very anxious that we should join them and buy this aircraft for use in the NATO area and were hoping that the French and the Germans would buy it too. Nobody at that time showed the slightest sign of doing so. It was a very expensive machine and was, in my judgement, more elaborate than was needed either for the air defence of the UK or for the air defence of the Fleet as replacement for the Shackletons. Our national need was for an aircraft that could operate at maximum effectiveness over the sea, since all the approaches to the UK were by that route.

Had we been able to muster support from the other Allies to buy the E3C, I am sure we should have done so, but they were all holding back and a cheaper alternative was mooted by the RAF, of re-equipping some of their Nimrod force with a special British-built radar to do the job. It would not have the sophisticated command capability of the AWACS, but none of us felt that was needed: we could not see ourselves adopting the tactic of exercising supreme command from an aircraft in a crisis, as the Americans did with 'Air Force 1'. So the airborne early-warning Nimrod with a Marconi radar was conceived, the Chiefs of Staff agreed it as the solution, convinced Fred Mulley, and it was ordered.

The doubts that we have since learned existed about its technical competence never surfaced at the time. Had they done so, I would have found it difficult to accept that British industry could not, in the five or six years available, emulate what the Americans had already done and demonstrated. In the event, as is now history, the programme went sadly awry, no one stopped it when it should have been stopped, and a great deal of money was wasted. I am still convinced that the decision was right at the time. I do not have enough inside knowledge to know whether, as some allege, the goalposts were moved by the MoD in the course of the development programme, the management of which was clearly defective.

As I had expected, I found the central military staff too big for the responsibility it had to discharge: coordinating service inputs and briefing me. Responsibility for expenditure of funds lay with the services, their allocation was the government's task, advised by the Chiefs of Staff Committee, the accounting officer, who was the Permanent Under-Secretary of State, and if appropriate, the Chief Scientific Adviser. Although I had a loyal and intelligent central staff, the briefers were necessarily either operating at second hand or flying by the seat of their pants. I would have much preferred to have been briefed by the same people as briefed their own Service Chief of Staff, who were experts in their fields. In my judgement, the centre was either too big or too small to last, and had I been allowed a full term (and I imagine Mulley, at least, knew this), I would have attempted to reform the MoD in the direction of a smaller central staff. This may well have been one of the reasons why I was not to stay on. I have very seldom, if ever, found the arguments advanced by the individual services in advocacy of their own role or need to be lightweight; on the contrary, they are always deserving of respect. Equally, given full debate, I have never found it impossible for the Chiefs of Staff to agree on a sensible solution, and not necessarily the lowest common denominator. We all knew that if we split, we were lost; whereas if we could agree, we were strong. Although it never came to that point, I had resolved that unless one of my colleagues was patently irresponsible, it would be better for the CDS to side with the minority, rather than let a majority view go through. I felt, and feel, that the CDS, alone and unsupported by his colleagues on the Chiefs of Staff Committee, is no more than a civil servant in uniform, incapable of exerting single-handed that influence on government which the national interest demands that the defence forces bring to bear in debate. Surrounding CDS with a large 'purple' staff, as has since happened, does not in my view change the situation at all. The net effect is to make life easier for ministers, which has never been part of my stock in trade. The problems of deterrence and defence are not simple, and are not susceptible to a quick fix. A principal safeguard in this business remains, I think, that the CDS, who must speak for all his colleagues, must have done a proper stint as a Chief of Staff of his own service first. Nothing else can so well develop a full sense of responsibility at so high a level. The Zumwalts and Haigs of this world, who lacked that experience, showed it. The analogy that command of a ship should precede command of a squadron or Fleet is exact.

The Service of Thanksgiving for Andrew was held in Westminster Abbey on 18 March. This was very well done, sad occasion that it was. Humphrey Trevelyan read the lesson and Sam Elworthy gave the address. I took no pleasure in having succeeded Andrew, who promised, had he lived, to be a great CDS.

At the end of the month, Liz and I went by HS125 to Naples, stopping off there to refuel and have lunch with Roddy Macdonald, who was still Chief of Staff to the Commander Naval Forces Southern Europe. We went on then to Akrotiri, and spent the night with the Commander British Forces Cyprus at Air House. The next morning we drove across the line with the defence adviser, Colin Huxley, and were together at Lapithos for the first time since the spring of 1974. Our house guard then was a retired Turkish sergeant brought over from the mainland, and the Turkish flag flew from the mast of Tom's mini-sail, lashed to the corner of our top verandah nearest the power cables! We were somewhat reassured and, of course, delighted to see our friends again.

We stayed that night with Donald Gordon, the high commissioner, having previously been given a briefing by the Chief of Staff to the UN force in Cyprus. The next day, I called on the commanding general, Quinn, an Irishman, inspected a guard of honour, and went round some of the UN forces, partly by helicopter. The RAF then flew me by helicopter to the Eastern Sovereign Base Area, where I was met by Air Vice-Marshal Austen Smith, and also Brigadier John Acland, Commander UK Land Forces Cyprus. I went on a tour of the area and formed the opinion that we had too many troops there, for their own good or ours – a view which nobody on the spot disputed at the time, although it was to be strongly repudiated some weeks later in London and the reductions I felt were tolerable were not made.

I visited 9 Signal Regiment, and talked particularly to some of the naval ratings there, who had an interesting job on hand. After lunch, I went by helicopter to Episkopi, to visit some of the soldiers in the Western SBA, followed afterwards by a briefing in the headquarters, including some words by Jeremy Smerdon, current Royal Naval liaison officer. After an interview with the British Forces Broadcasting System, I went to Air House, and thence, with the Austen Smiths, to dinner at Flagstaff House, hosted by the Aclands. It was known by then that, at my instigation, the Chiefs of Staffs had decided that the job of Commander British Forces in Cyprus should alternate between the Army and the RAF, a change that, once settled, was pretty readily accepted by the services concerned.

The next morning was spent in visiting the air base at Akrotiri, and also the Satellite Communications Station, working off Skynet, which I was specially pleased to see. The weather factor and land area available in Cyprus make it an excellent training area, both for troops and for squadrons of the RAF. It struck me that the establishment of people there on accompanied tours was far too big for the job that had to be done. As had happened in Singapore, and to a lesser extent in Aden, everybody over the years had done their best to make the place more comfortable and more fun to be in. When not working – and often they were working hard – they were living in the best holiday camp available to the forces of the Crown. No wonder they were liable to be overmanned. The bases nevertheless had an important function in supporting Cento and maintaining surveillance over the eastern Mediterranean, as well as being a stabilising influence on the island itself.

At 10 a.m., we flew by HS125 to Ankara for the Cento meeting in Chiefs of Staff session the next day. We stayed with the Balls, he being the UK permanent military deputy, an air vice-marshal's job, and after lunch, I talked with him and our ambassador, Sir Horace Philipps. At the meeting, Sancar represented Turkey, but Evren, the Chief of the General Staff, was also present. George Brown was there for the United States, Azhari for Iran, and a general from Pakistan, whose name I forget. We broke to go to the Ataturk Mausoleum, lay wreaths on his tomb and visit the museum, and then had a very good Turkish lunch before reconvening in the afternoon. The Sancars gave a dinner in the evening, after which we were quite ready to go back to the Balls' flat.

The next day, the Turks had organised a visit for us all to Ephesus, so we flew to Izmir, and then by helicopter to Selcuk. This time we not only went sightseeing round the ruins, but also visited the Selcuk Museum, with its extraordinary statuary, and the Church of St John. Afterwards we went to Kusadasi for lunch at the Kismet Hotel, hosted by the Evrens. We always enjoyed Ephesus and again it was a lovely day, and the place was cleared of tourists for our benefit. Larry Robertson took an eloquent picture of the four CENTO Chiefs of Staff (excluding Sancar, whose absence saved his dignity), sitting on a somewhat restored multiple loo of late Greek vintage. It had clearly been constructed as a social meeting place, presumably unisex. At 4 p.m., we boarded our HS125 again and flew to Rome where, during the refuelling stop, we talked to our Ambassador, Alan Campbell, at his house. Then we flew to Northolt, and late on Friday evening we arrived home at 'South Cottage'. It had been a thoroughly enjoyable expedition and had helped to keep the Cento flag flying pending a ministerial session in London, which I find a good deal less memorable.

The next week, just before Easter, I took Lord High Admiral's Divisions at the Royal Naval College Dartmouth, on behalf of the Queen, and presented the Sword of Honour and the Queen's Telescopes. Before lunch in the captain's house, I talked to some of the cadets, wrens and marines under training, and found them a lively lot. The atmosphere at the college seemed good, and the floors still smelled the same as they had when I was a cadet 44 years earlier. In my informal address, I related Frank Twiss's classic comment about the Japanese prisoner of war camp being 'not so bad after Dartmouth' and, I hope, made them realise their luck.

Easter leave ended on a Friday, and the next day we were off to Australia for the periodic meeting between the chiefs of defence staff of Australia, New Zealand and the United Kingdom. We went by VC10, accompanied by a fairly large staff, and reached Canberra on Sunday after refuelling at Perth. We were met by the high commissioner, Donald Tebbitt, and John Badcock, whom I had known before in the Royal Signals, and who was defence adviser and head of the British defence liaison staff. The Tebbitts gave a pleasant and relaxed dinner party that evening, although we were really quite pleased to turn in at the end of it. The next day, I talked to the Australian Joint Services Staff College in the morning, and in the afternoon met with the Australian Chiefs of Staff: Macdonald, the general, who was the CDS designate, Tony Synnott, head of the Navy, and Roland of the Air Force. Also present was Sir Arthur Tangye, the secretary of the Department of Defence, and still a power in the land, having been in his job for a long, long time. After a useful discussion on Pacific matters, I called on Denis Killen, the minister of defence, at Parliament House, which was in itself interesting to visit. The strategic concept, wanting a discernible threat, seemed sound and the kind of thing the UK chiefs would applaud. ANZAC expeditionary forces were out of the question, Vietnam having delivered the mortal blow. Then there was a reception by John Badcock in our honour, followed by dinner at his house. The British-Australian-New Zealand military discussions were held on the following day at the Department of Defence, and we had lunch at the Royal Military College at Duntroon, followed by a dinner hosted by General Macdonald. Peter Stanford, a naval signals officer and secretary to the Chiefs of Staff Committee, was with me, so I did not have the bother of making any kind of record myself.

We were next bound for Victoria, to stay with Sir Henry and Lady Winnaker in the fine, old Government House where Michael Ashmore had once been ADC to 'Jumbo' Delacombe. My visits here were to the Royal Australian Air Force Museum and Academy at Point Cook, and then to the Signal Division at Albert Park, where I had been before as ACDS(S). Not much had changed, and co-operation was as close as before. Liz was able to see her Sturdee relations, including the widow of the General, and there was rather a formal dinner party at Government House. We left the next morning for Perth, where we stayed with 'Digger' and Molly Kyle. I had known him before, when he had been Vice-Chief of the Air Staff and I was on the Chiefs of Staff Committee. The object of this visit was to have a look at Cockburn Sound, an extensive, sheltered harbour which I had seen before when *Hermes* was in Fremantle in 1967, but on which a good deal of words and money had since been spent. The idea was to make it into a main naval base in Western Australia. This was going quietly ahead, and indeed, geography was all in its favour. The trouble was that not many people in the Royal Australian Navy particularly wanted to move from Sydney, where many of them were well dug in, or even from Melbourne, to Western Australia. Moreover, the potential threat is from the north, and in our discussions on strategy it was not immediately obvious that there was a major Australian role for Cockburn Sound.

Our VC10 took off early the next day, as I wished to make a protracted stop at Diego Garcia in the Chagos Archipelago, an atoll on which we had a signal station, but which was being extensively developed by the US Navy as a forward operating base. The representative of the British Commissioner for the Indian Ocean Territory was the Royal Navy liaison officer. His predecessor had been to see me at Northwood some time ago, and I had formed the impression that things were not all that easy for him or for our small unaccompanied naval party there. They were delighted to see Elizabeth, and I found them in excellent heart, having just raised quite a sum of money from the Americans in a sponsored charity run round the atoll. I received a briefing from the officer in charge of the 'Sea Bees' (the United States Naval Construction Battalion, who had a shorter tour on the island and rather more logistic support from home than the Royal Navy party), and gained the impression of a busy and reasonably efficient team. They were clearing coral heads and reefs to make a proper channel into the lagoon and establish moorings where aircraft carriers and the like could berth in emergency. It was not the most frequently-visited of locations, and I am sure our appearance did good.

We then flew on to Seeb, to refuel and switch aircrew. I was met by the ambassador, Jim Treadwell, and the three Chiefs of Staff to the Sultan of Oman's Armed Forces. This was a useful meeting from the Chiefs' of Staff point of view, and well recorded by our secretary: clearly a great transformation was underway. Nine hours later, early on the Saturday morning, we were back in England at Brize Norton, and taken by car to Headley Down. On the way from Oman we had stopped at Bahrain, where I met the ambassador, Mr Giben, at the airport, and also Hugo Hollins, an old friend who, in retirement, was running ports and lights in the Gulf, and had a steam yacht, *Relume*, to help him do this. I had last seen him when I had stayed with him and his wife when he was Flag Officer Gibraltar, and felt that he exemplified British naval experience in action, in the tradition of James Cook and his successors.

Back in Whitehall, I reckoned that it would be a good idea to pay an official visit – the first one for a CDS – to the People's Republic of China. The Foreign Office had no objection, and arrangements were put in train. Having virtually started my career on the China Station, I thought it would be rather neat to visit China in early August, and so, more or less, end it there. There was one snag: the date depended on when the Central Committee of the Chinese Communist Party was to meet. It was not scheduled for August, but there was a danger that it might be brought forward, which it was, so that was a small ambition unfulfilled. (Neil Cameron went in my place some four or five months later, and gained a certain amount of notoriety as a result of some remarks he made about the Soviet Union. I was doing a bricklaying course at the time, and when asked what I thought of bricklaying, I said I found it easier laying bricks than dropping them – fortunately, I think this was only reported in the local Portsmouth paper.)

At some stage the government asked me to entertain and invite to a Chiefs of Staff Committee my opposite number from Romania. He was a singularly graceless and unpleasant fellow, and at one stage he had to be firmly snubbed as politely as possible. Fortunately, he did not enjoy the full range of a visitor's entertainment, having been invited, not by the Chiefs of Staff, but by the politicians, who were then lumbered with him.

A great event of 3 May was the launch of *Invincible*, to which the Admiralty Board very kindly asked us. HM the Queen performed it, and I felt it was the end of a long road, certainly as far as I was concerned, and, one hoped, the beginning of a new era. The ship looked, and is, very small, even compared with *Hermes*, but given her presence, the surface Fleet could consider itself viable in wide areas of the sea that would otherwise be denied to it by the air threat. The next day, the Chiefs of Staff, among other guests, were summoned to Westminster Hall for the presentation of addresses by both Houses of Parliament to Her Majesty congratulating her on her Jubilee. It marked the beginning of the festivities for the 25th year of the Queen's reign. Soon after, our old friend Zeiner Gundersen and his wife, Marit, arrived on an official visit, he now being the chairman of the NATO Military Committee in succession to Peter Hill-Norton. While he did his stuff with the MoD, Elizabeth took Marit to Windsor Castle, and in the evening we took them to see *La Traviata* at Covent Garden, and then to dinner at 'The Ivy'. It was a specially happy visit for us, and I hope for them, and it gave me an opportunity to give him a thorough briefing with the Chiefs of Staff present. Almost immediately, it was time for the annual descent on SHAPE for SHAPEX, and on this occasion SACEUR was again Al Haig, who, hopefully, was now settling in.

A whole team of us flew to SHAPEX from Northolt in two RAF Andovers, and Liz and I were put up by Harry Tuzo, deputy SACEUR, at his lovely French château, Saint Pierre. The exercise went on for two days, with a big reception by SACEUR on the evening of the first day, and consisted very largely of presentations organised by Tuzo and a guest speaker, also organised by him. It was amusing to see Al performing, still without a note, and talking fast and at length. It all sounded good, but conveyed little. We came back to England for rather less than 48 hours, and set off on the Sunday afternoon for Brussels for the Military Committee Meeting, followed by the Defence Planning Committee (the assembly of the NATO defence ministers, with their military advisers in attendance). For this visit, we stayed with an old friend, Tony Morton, at the Villa du Lac, in great comfort as usual. On the first evening, Zeiner Gundersen hosted a buffet supper for the men, which gave me a chance to meet old friends and new faces. Zeiner, still the typical Norwegian, straight up and down and quiet spoken, was in good form and, I think, enjoying himself. We attended the Military Committee on Monday, with a lunch hosted by the Belgian chief of defence (which went on for hours, as Belgian lunches do). The next day was the Defence Planning Committee, and Fred Mulley's first appearance at NATO. I thought he did well, and the Secretary-General seemed to get on with him. There was an elaborate buffet lunch, which gave me a chance to have a word with Joe Luns, and in the evening an enormous dinner at the Palais D'Egmont, hosted by Van den Boeynants, the Belgian minister for defence. The Defence Planning Committee continued the next morning, mostly discussing their communiqué (usually the most important part of any collective meeting for politicians). After this, we returned to London.

Al Haig set me a bit of a poser on this trip. His problem was that the Germans felt (rightly, I think) that in view of their contribution to NATO they were short of four star commands compared with some of the other nations, particularly, perhaps, the British. Al felt the political pressure was such that something had to be done about it, and he discussed as possibilities either giving a German the post of C.-in-C. Air Central Region (held by the RAF), or C.-in-C. Allied Forces Northern Europe (held by the Army, but at the moment occupied by Peter Whiteley ex-Commandant-General Royal Marines), or even the deputy SACEUR (which had been British since Monty first started the job). I felt that all these were pretty poor options, particularly the Norwegian one, which I did not think was realistic even to suggest; of course, Al then came up with his real proposal, which was to have a second deputy SACEUR, who would be a four-star German officer, and responsible for logistics in Allied Command Europe. This seemed to me to be quite a good solution if another German officer was inescapable (as, in my heart, I felt it was). I therefore said I would canvass the Chiefs of Staff about this and expected them to agree; in fact, I all but committed them.

When I put it to them, they did not like it, but they saw the arguments in the same light as I had. We stipulated that the British deputy SACEUR should continue to be responsible for training and operations under the supreme commander. This was agreed, so the Germans got their post. The trouble with senior German officers in NATO is that they have a direct line to Bonn much stronger than the line that any British equivalent feels he has to his own Ministry of Defence. It is, however, paralleled by the direct US 'national' line: Al Haig, as well as being SACEUR, was C.-in-C. US Forces Europe, and so had a dual responsibility. One can accept this for the Americans, who are the heart of the Alliance, but it is difficult to welcome it in the German case. However, it is a fact of life.

This year, I was asked for the first and only time to the Royal Academy Dinner, which is a great occasion, and much enjoyed it. We were then visited by the German chief of defence staff, who made an official descent on London, and were able to take him to a concert with suitable German music – Karajan conducting Beethoven. Soon after came the equivalent from Thailand, with no such musical accompaniment, and meanwhile, I was able to fit in a visit to RAF Strike Command and see their new headquarters. On Sunday, for a change, and at the request of an old friend, Tom Fanshawe (who was now a retired captain, and head of the Sea Cadet Corps), we went to the commissioning of Training Ship *Benbow*, the Mitcham and Morden Sea Cadet Unit. Tony Miers, who had been so kind to me in Cyprus, took a particularly interest in this unit, and made sure that I did everything properly. (He remains quite a tiger, though a cheerful one, even in retirement.) I thought their new headquarters represented a jolly good local effort, and all sorts of people came to their great day. There was a commissioning cake for Elizabeth to cut, and refreshments were provided by the Mayor of Merton. It made quite a change from NATO.

On 30 May we were invited to a splendid occasion: the Gala Performance at the Royal Opera House in honour of the Queen's Silver Jubilee. There were extracts from various operas, and performances of selected pieces of ballet, and I doubt if the Opera House had looked so beautiful for a very long time. I then flew to Northern Ireland, to spend a couple of days visiting our forces, where I was taken round by the general officer commanding, and briefed by him and the head of the Royal Ulster Constabulary. No sooner had I arrived and got in the car to go from Aldergrove than they put a flat plain-clothes cap on my head to make me look like a dog-robber, but for much of the tour I was in a Land-Rover, and almost more worried about the angle at which my bodyguard's rifle was pointing than by what might be lurking outside.

I was determined to visit South Armagh, and went to Crossmaglen and Newry, pitifully poor-looking places, and dangerous for Loyalists and the security forces. The troops, officers and men, were in good heart, but theirs was an unrewarding job, though excellent training in alertness and survival. This was well recognised, and the other ranks were often new and inexperienced, hence they benefited. For officers, particularly NCOs, repetitive tours are tiresome indeed. When I left Aldergrove, the station commander presented me with a picture, a montage really, of all the aircraft of the VIP Flight which I had used for so long and was soon to stop using. It had some biblical quotations underneath that I've looked up and were more or less appropriate. It was a very kind gesture, and much appreciated. (The picture has hung in my office at Racal for years now.)

Jubilee Day was 7 June, and after attending the Thanksgiving Service in St Paul's, I caught a flight to Canada for the Nuclear Planning Group of NATO in Ottawa. I had attended previously on Michael Carver's behalf, and the meeting consisted very largely of a briefing by the US Secretary for Defense on developments in the Allied nuclear arsenal, which is so predominantly American. It is of less interest to the British, who, being a nuclear power, know much of it already, but it is nevertheless an important NATO gathering and one at which one needs to show one's commitment to the nuclear element of deterrence. There were the usual junkets, and I was also taken on a visit to the Canadian parliament. This is interesting, because when you enter the Gallery, the Speaker 'recognises' you, and then the Members, if they feel so inclined, stand up and applaud.

I was home in time for the Jubilee Trooping the Colour by the Scots Guards in honour of Her Majesty on her Official Birthday, a spectacle we always enjoy. The Prime Minister and the government gave a reception for Her Majesty, to which we were invited, and it was a busy time for dinners of a more or less official variety. Now the various special occasions laid on the by the three services were approaching. I was in the happy position of not being responsible for any of them, while being asked with Elizabeth to all. For the first, I certainly had some part in the initial planning: the Review of the Fleet at Spithead by Her Majesty in the Royal Yacht. Peter had written to tell me that the Queen had invited me to stay in *Britannia* for the night before and the night after the review, and at dinner that night, 27 June, I sat between the Queen and the Prime Minister. The First Sea Lord was on the

Queen's left, and 'Dickie' Mountbatten on the prime minister's right. Peter was at the same table, and the Prince of Wales and Prince Edward were there as well. The Admiralty Board used *Birmingham* for their guests, and Elizabeth was invited to join them there. After dinner in *Britannia* the Royal Marines beat the retreat alongside the ship at South Railway Jetty, and we all came to watch.

Tuesday 28 June was the day of the review. There was a big lunch party in *Britannia* and I was again sitting at the Queen's table, between Audrey Callaghan and Pat Duffy, and thoroughly enjoyed the occasion. Joseph Luns was sitting on Her Majesty's left, and the prime minister on her right. Peter sat at the Prince of Wales's table, and Flag Officer Royal Yachts, Hugh Janion (whom I had appointed, and who had proved a great success), sat at Princess Anne's table. There was some wind, but the review was a great success. The Queen and Prince Philip were on the quarterdeck, with the First Sea Lord to answer all their questions. I had a happy time on the bridge with Peter as the yacht went through the Fleet. The Trinity House yacht *Patricia* led through the Fleet, *Birmingham* and *Engadine* following astern of *Britannia*. The ships manned and cheered ship handsomely, and one could see the families on board behind them – no trouble at all; indeed, I think the Queen was delighted to see them there.

Terry Lewin had told me that the Admiralty Board had decided, presumably with the approval of the secretary of state, that when the Fleet dispersed from the review the next day, it was to be treated as a salute to CDS and a farewell to me. Before this, however, there was a grand Fleet dinner in *Ark Royal*, hosted by Henry Leach, the Commander-in-Chief, at which I sat on Her Majesty's right. It was held in the decorated hangar, and went, I thought, extraordinarily well, although Henry, on this very special occasion for him, was not particularly relaxed. (Those of us who were present at the dinner were each given a plate in commemoration, and it is a very special thing to possess.) We came back to *Britannia* for the night, where I was again well looked after by the staff, all of whom seemed to count Peter as a friend.

Next day, at breakfast, rather ostentatiously reading the *Daily Telegraph*, I sat next to the prime minister, and Jim had said to me, 'You know, CDS, I think we ought to see more of each other,' so I said, 'Yes, Prime Minister.' 'Yes,' he said, 'I think it would be a good idea if you were to come and see me fairly regularly, once a month or so.' I said, 'And bring Fred?' 'Oh yes,' he said, 'bring Fred along too if you like,' so I said, 'Yes, Prime Minister.' Next time I had the Chiefs of Staff together in COSI, I recounted this episode, and said that I had no intention of adopting this practice, and it was my strong advice to my successor (Neil Cameron and Terry Lewin were sitting there) to avoid it also. I expressed the view that a CDS on his own was far too exposed, that he was only in a strong position when he had his colleagues with him, that he could not easily refuse if he was sent for, but should not in any way foster any such relationship as Jim had suggested. The outcome was bound to be that he would be 'shopped' over something or other. The prime minister was not only in the strongest position, but he was most probably much cleverer than any of us were likely to be. They all seemed to agree, but nevertheless there was an episode I remember, some four or five months after Neil had take over, when he had a discussion with the prime minister alone. Their two versions differed, and the prime minister's, of course, carried the day. Jim meant well, but I felt the suggestion carried more dangers for defence than possible advantages.

Wednesday 29 June 1977 was a proud day for us. The Queen disembarked about 10.30 a.m. I left with Terry Lewin soon afterwards, and drove to *Vernon*, where there was a helicopter waiting. Elizabeth and the family, Tom, Susan, John and their children, had already embarked in *Birmingham*, which had sailed for Spithead. Terry and I arrived on board by helicopter at 11.15a.m. By then, a number of the ships were underway and preparing to steam past after lunch. There was a buffet in the wardroom of *Birmingham*, with Captain Pat Symons as our host, and a very good lunch, too. It was a lovely day, and I was delighted that for this special occasion I should be in the successor to the ship in which I had served nearly all my midshipman's time. As an Admiral of the Fleet, I flew the Union Flag at sea, which does not often happen, and the steam-past was led by *Ark Royal*, *Hermes* and *Fearless*. The two flotillas of cruisers and destroyers then went by, followed by the submarine flotilla (with Winston Churchill MP, he told me later, in *Churchill*), and finally the fast training boats from Portland, which enjoyed a slap-up 'rush'-by. *Birmingham* was on the opposite course, and made a good alongside at South Railway Jetty at 5 p.m., when we landed, giving our thanks to Terry and the ship. The event was filmed, and we have a copy. The ships' companies cheered roundly. Having had a successful review by the Queen, they were all on their way to enjoy some summer leave. I received a memorable farewell signal from C.-in-C. Fleet, and felt that the Navy could not have given me a better send-off. I had been exceptionally honoured, and remembered with pride in how many of those ships my flag had flown.

That same week, there was a magnificent Three-Service Musical Pageant at Wembley, where again I sat next to Her Majesty. She thoroughly enjoyed the whole thing, as did the thousands of people there, who rose and cheered at the end. In early July I paid my visit to Latimer, where David Loram was now the commandant and a formidable opponent to my plans for the place. However, I enjoyed a good lunch there after talking to them, and had shortly to speak again at the Tri-Service Staff College Dinner at Greenwich, an annual event. I do not remember much of what I said on such occasions; I usually addressed the threat we all faced, the need for inter-service cooperation to meet it, and the importance, above all, of the deterrent. I would try to draw on my own experiences and prejudices to liven things up.

On 7 July, the Army did their stuff. There was a review of the 4th Division in Germany at Sennelager. Nigel Bagnell commanded the review, and the Chief of General Staff was in attendance on Her Majesty. It was magnificent to see the columns of Chieftain tanks roll by, dipping their guns in salute. Only later did I hear from one of the soldiers present how relieved everyone had been to see, on the given signal, that every vehicle started and moved off: it was a sign that the trouble they had been having with their propulsion was now more or less overcome.

On 12 July, the Admiralty Board and their wives dined us out in *Victory*. It was a happy occasion, and included the presentation to me of the shipbuilder's model of *Blackpool*. I asked David Williams to have some wall brackets made in the dockyard, and it later joined the 'display' at home (but is now representing the West Indies Squadron in Bermuda's Maritime Museum). A dinner at Charterhouse to say goodbye to Sam Elworthy on retiring to New Zealand followed next, and on Thursday I took the salute at the Royal Tournament, surrounded by the family. By now, Michael Beetham had been appointed as Chief of the Air Staff to succeed Neil, who was preparing to take over from me. The Beethams had nowhere obvious to live, and since we did not much enjoy Kingston House North, and 'South Cottage' beckoned, we moved out at the end of the week, and took up residence with Tom at Claylands Road. Longbone, my admirable petty officer valet, stayed on in London to help look after us. Tom, who had gained a good law degree but was struggling a bit at Knapp-Fishers, where he did his articles and assistant solicitorship, had written comprehensive orders for his house: Longbone said they were more detailed than any ship's standing orders he had ever seen and they kept him very much in order! There was room for Elizabeth to come up when she wanted to, as she did the next Tuesday, for dinner with the Carringtons in their private house. Then, on the Wednesday, there was a reception at Buckingham Palace for the Diplomatic Corps, and on 26 July a dinner to celebrate the Queen's Birthday, given by the Lord Mayor in the Guildhall.

Quite recently, Anthony Eden, Lord Avon, had died, and on coming back from that funeral, I suspect Callaghan thought it would be a good idea to have a young foreign secretary in his government. To everyone's astonishment, he appointed David Owen. As he and his wife were friends of ours, this gave us great pleasure. I remember when the Chiefs of Staff were assembled outside the Cabinet Room before one of the regular meetings and David came in, I was able to go up and say, 'Let me be one of the first to congratulate the new foreign secretary.' Later, he spoke to me about Rhodesia, in which he had become thoroughly embroiled, and took me out one day onto the balcony somewhere and said how much he needed support. I could not be much help. The Chiefs of Staff were quite rightly firmly opposed to any formal military involvement in this situation, and indeed, had been so for a long time.

Farewell dinners and other engagements were pressing on us rather hard at this time. I took a 'Beat the Retreat' at the Duke of York's Barracks one day, we went to a Buckingham Palace Garden Party another, and so on. However, on 29 July, there was the RAF Review at Finningly, beginning with a very good lunch, followed by a wonderful display of aircraft. The Chief of the Air Staff, still Neil Cameron (I think on his last day in the post), sat alongside the Queen, with the Duke of Edinburgh on his other side and

Fred Mulley alongside him. It was a hot afternoon, and the noise of the aircraft engines was strangely soporific. Most unfortunately, Fred dropped off, and all the cameras zoomed in on him. The press next day was most unkind, and Fred Mulley's sleepiness became a standing joke for some months. I was cross that no neighbour had jogged him at the time. I knew how upset he would be, and wrote on behalf of the Chiefs of Staff expressing our sympathy and support. He was very grateful, and sent a nice little note back. When I told the chiefs what I had done, the reaction was not unanimously enthusiastic, but naturally enough, they accepted it.

That evening, the Lundvalls came to stay with us, and soon after, since the leave periods for everybody were approaching, the Chiefs of Staff dined us out in Roly Gibbs's flat before they dispersed. We went to Colchester for the first time, for a tattoo, and then came the final formal engagement outside London, when I attended the Royal Marine Commandos' parade in honour of the Queen at Plymouth. This was a splendid affair, and very well done. Prince Edward and Prince Andrew were also present, taking a considerable interest, it seemed. Life then became very quiet, it being the time when I had hoped to be in China, until, in the middle of August, we had the Cento permanent military deputies' visit (which was nice for Elizabeth and myself, in view of our links with Turkey through the house in Cyprus).

Almost my final jaunt was a visit to the British Aircraft Corporation Military Division at Warton, where, after a protracted briefing, I was given a ride in the new Tornado strike aircraft. This was a great excitement, and the senior test pilot, Eagles, who was ex-Fleet Air Arm, took me first over the Irish Sea, where we went supersonic, and then, contour following, over the hills of Cumbria. I well remember the kick in the back when the afterburners were engaged and the wings swept back for the supersonic phase of the test flight, but I was most impressed by the steadiness of the aircraft as a weapon platform, flying over the Cumbrian hills. They had sent up a Jaguar with a photographer, to take photographs of this singular occasion (for me, anyway), and the photographer told me afterwards that his aircraft was bumping so badly that he found it extremely difficult to take photographs at all. The Tornado, on the other hand, rode the turbulence masterfully.

Before leaving, I received some delightful messages of good wishes, including a particularly charming letter from the chief of the general staff thanking me for all I had done for the Army. My farewell audience was with the Queen, presented by Peter, and I remember the brief conversation well. On my final morning there was a three-service guard paraded outside the North Door of the MoD, and the representatives of the Chiefs of Staff, the Permanent Under-Secretaries and the Chief Scientific Adviser were on the steps to shake hands and say goodbye. They had asked me before the ceremony whether they should play 'Auld Lang Syne' as my car drove off. I said, 'No, on no account. I should much prefer you to play 'Goodbye' from the *White Horse Inn*,' and so this did strike up, reminding me of when Peter and I were taken to it in the 1930s, the first musical comedy we ever saw. The head of the US Navy, Jimmy Holloway (in uniform, bless his heart), and Dabney stood with Elizabeth to the side while all this went on. In one of the photographs sent to us later, I detected half a familiar face peering out from behind a bearskin, and checking, found it was Penny Whistler no less, though I was too busy looking at soldiers to notice her there at the time. Afterwards, the Holloways came on for a celebration lunch at Tom's house, and that was that. The Personal Staff gave me as a farewell present a large scrapbook, which is now full of photographs, and has, on its last page, a letter from the secretary of state for defence, thanking me on behalf of the Queen for my services. It was 44 years almost to the day since I had joined Dartmouth as a naval cadet. I felt very conscious of my great good luck, and of the marvellous support of Elizabeth through so many years of change and separation, the last few of which, with our travels together, had at last put gilt on the gingerbread. Peter had years of responsible and distinguished service to Her Majesty still ahead of him, and I was lucky indeed, at the age of 57, to have a new interest opening up in industry with Racal, but that is another story.

Since opting for AFNORTH instead of AFMED in 1956, I had consciously set course for appointments with a three-service interest. In the event, I was fortunate in spending some 13 of the ensuing 21 years in responsibilities extending far beyond the Navy, and I include in them, of course, those involving membership of the Chiefs of Staffs Committee. But the Royal Navy was my nursery, and ships my home in impressionable years, as this canter through them has shown. The bluejacket, his fine qualities, his ability to surprise, confound or disgust his officer, his sense of humour, receives too little attention in these pages. The smart young men in *Birmingham* in 1977 would not have recognised themselves in those hardy lads manning her predecessor in 1938.

I felt that the Navy I was leaving had coped in a practical way with the changes in society and technology of so many crowded years. It still seemed to be possessed of a good spirit, and to maintain a sensible discipline. It enjoyed the respect of other navies for its professionalism, and retained a special place in the affections of the British people. Its role had changed substantially, but a maritime contribution to the security of the country and to deterrence remained indispensable.

If I have an anxiety, it is that in a peacetime service lacking romance, fighting spirit may flag in the absence of physical hardship and calls on mental and moral endurance. Love of the sea, comradeship, a sense of fun, a response to challenge must all be in some way imparted at as early an age as the nation allows the Navy to take its young. I have never been an advocate of sail training on entry, considering it a waste of valuable time. I am not so sure now; but doubt is one of the luxuries of retirement.

Index

Only the main text has been indexed. Headings are arranged in alphabetical word-by-word order; subheadings are arranged chronologically.